specialeffects

AN ORAL HISTORY

To Louis, Laurence, and Alexandre

specialeffects

AN ORAL HISTORY PASCAL PINTEAU

INTERVIEWS WITH 38 MASTERS SPANNING 100 YEARS

Translated from the French by Laurel Hirsch

Harry N. Abrams, Inc., Publishers

Special makeup by Pascal Pinteau

Preface

This book would not exist if, at seven years old, I hadn't been transfixed by a clip of *Jason and the Argonauts* that was shown on television. A gigantic bronze statue chased the sailors along a cliff, then grabbed their boat and broke it into pieces. Since these images could not be real, what magic could possibly have created them? Relentlessly I asked this question, seeking to discover the many facets of the world of special effects. Later on, I would have the privilege of becoming friends with Ray Harryhausen, the extraordinary magician of my childhood who was the creator of the bronze giant and so many other wondrous marvels. Through the course of my encounters, the desire to pay homage to the art of special effects and its most talented and captivating practitioners burned in me. It would be quite impossible to mention everyone and everything, but I hope that this journey behind the scenes of film, television, animation, makeup, and theme parks will lead to an appreciation of the astounding progress achieved in a century, often because of the passion of artists who remain largely unknown to the general public. My thanks to them for opening the doors to their imaginary worlds.

Pascal Pinteau

Contents

The Dawn of Special Effects

Semblances of Life

In 1879 the Altamira Cave was discovered near the village of Santillana del Mar in the Spanish province of Santander. With the beauty of the stone paintings and the striking depictions of the fauna that lived in the region some seventeen thousand years ago, it has been dubbed the "Sistine Chapel of Paleolithic Art." Drawn in iron oxide, magnesium oxide, and charcoal, the bison, deer, horses, and boar cavort on the stone. Primitive tools were brilliantly employed to create the illusion of life and to prepare the magic ritual before the hunt. Using the relief of the cave wall to accentuate the drawing, the anonymous artist produced what may be the first "special effect"—a galloping horse depicted with eight hooves instead of four. Even today, a visitor to Altamira is under the impression that the horse is running like some animated character projected onto a stone screen.

First Illusions

Special effects, illusions, and other imitations have existed since the dawn of humanity, marking the history of human culture and taking various forms to gratify an insatiable desire to attain the unreal. Traces of strange special effects can be found in ancient Egypt, where the faithful often asked the gods to resolve the problems of their daily lives. They would kneel before wooden idols, ask their questions, and await a sign. Their fervor was rewarded when an effigy of Anubis or Amon Ra would come to life and respond with a nod of the head or a few words. The overjoyed visitors could not have imagined that these articulated wooden statues were being animated from behind the scenes by temple attendants who also lent them their voices. The human-sized likenesses were manipulated simply by cords, whereas the stone and bronze statues, too heavy for such a method, were animated by counterweights filled with water from a neighboring river.

Over time, these mechanical effects were perfected. In 280 B.C., during a festival, King Ptolemy exhibited a statue of a man dressed in a gold-embroidered tunic. By an ingenious mechanism, the statue was made to rise from its seat and pour milk into a goblet without spilling a single drop. Much later, the great mathematician Heron of Alexandria created stunning animated fountains and numerous clepsydras (water clocks). Skillfully applying his knowledge of mechanics and hydraulics, he brought to life complex scenes through the use of steam. He placed braziers under large water-filled urns, the mouths of which had been fitted with valve pistons; as the pressure built, the pistons would rise, activating the pneumatic mechanisms, which would then return to their original positions. Coming to life, Heron's characters would continue to repeat their movements until the fire died out. In A.D. 50, the Roman emperor Claudius presented a spectacle on Lake Fucinus in which a silver triton was made to rise up from the water and then sound a trumpet to announce the start of the festivities. Technical mistakes were not tolerated, and if there were any malfunctions, the emperor would condemn the special effects designers to partake in the lethal circus games!

The Advent of Pyrotechnics

It was in China, probably around the second century A.D., that "black powder," a mixture of sulfur, saltpeter, and charcoal, was discovered. Initially, the explosive properties of this powder were used for artistic purposes. The Chinese presented their invention to the Romans, who employed it in their theatrical performances from the fourth century, but its use died out. During one of his famous travels, Marco Polo was impressed by this "art of fire" and brought it back to Europe, where it did not immediately meet with success. The black powder produced a bright light and a great bang, but no emotional response. Once again it fell into obscurity, until 1346 and its first military use, in the battle of Crécy. The explosive spectacle of the first bombardments inspired artists, and the idea of fireworks was born. New mixtures of powder were empirically devised, and little by little the elements that gave color to the shower of fiery light were identified. By the nineteenth century, the full palette of colors and pyrotechnical effects were finally complete, and they remain in use today.

Theater's First Magical Illusions

Dating back to ancient times, theaters in large cities have been replete with mechanical devices. Scenery changes were made in plain view: painted canvases were hoisted, and the wooden slats of the stage trapdoors would suddenly shoot up. In time, animated stage settings began to appear. A series of twisted rollers were used to imitate the movement of the waves. Model ships glided along tracks, giving the impression that they were sailing off to the horizon. Over the centuries, developments in mechanics led to inspired special effects. Large scenery canvases were mounted on two turning cylinders to create the impression that the actors were moving. And the illusions continued to evolve. One could be present at the battle lines, or in a volcanic eruption, or on the high seas in a storm. During the Renaissance, great artists improvised as stage directors; in Milan, even Leonardo da Vinci (1452–1519) devised a theater with a revolving stage and other animated stage works. Invited by François I in 1515, Leonardo moved into the manor house at Clos-Lucé, near the château d'Amboise; there, despite his declining health, he proved his creativity was still intact, dreaming up extravagant festivities. During one of these, Bengal lights illuminated a path while the silhouette of a lion emerged from the shadows. Thinking that a beast had escaped its cage, the guards quickly formed a phalanx in front of François I. The great cat came to a halt in front of the French king and burst into pieces, revealing its mechanics. Inside the automaton was a bouquet of fleurs-de-lis, an homage from Leonardo to his benefactor.

Near-Perfect Automatons

In 1737, following Leonardo's example, the Frenchman Jacques de Vaucanson transposed clockwork mechanisms to create the "Flute Player." The automaton played twelve different tunes with unnerving precision. Breath actually exited from the mouth of the figure, and its cardboard fingers, covered in leather, closed the holes of the flute. The humanoid, which measured about 70 inches (178 centimeters), was seated on a rock that was set on a pedestal. A box concealed the counterweight mechanism: a wooden cylinder 22 inches (56 centimeters) in diameter and nearly 33 inches (83 centimeters) long, which turned on its own axis. Fitted with barbs, it sent the pulsations to the fifteen levers that controlled the air delivery, the movement of the lips and tongue, and the articulation of the fingers through a device made of chains and wires. Nine bellows pushed air that was more or less compressed to three pipes attached to three small reservoirs located in the belly of the automaton, where they converged into a single pipe that led to the flute player's mouth. The amount of air that passed through the lips depended upon the changeable size of the opening. There was a movable tongue in the mouth cavity, which opened and closed the airway. Following this first prodigious

Eighteenth-century Japanese automaton with wooden mechanisms and a metal spring. This "walking" geisha offered the food on her platter while bowing her head.

These nineteenth-century Japanese marionettes were manipulated by strings to appear to walk, turn their heads, and swing their arms. Visible in the foreground is the wooden system that enabled the marionettes to glide across the entire stage.

chessboard through a slit in the chest, slide his own arm into its hollowed-out arm, grab one of the chessmen, and play his turn.

The Incredible Robert-Houdin

The magician, maker of automatons, and inventor Robert-Houdin (Jean-Eugène Robert, 1805–

Robert-Houdin
Photo courtesy of Maison de la Magie de Blois

feat, Vaucanson made a second musician and then a decoy duck of gilded copper that could drink, eat, quack, and digest. As its abdomen was transparent, the audience could follow the digestive process from the gullet all the way to the sphincter, which would eject a green blob! The three automatons were brought together for a traveling show that took them through France, Italy, and England. Although nothing remains of these marvels, a superb replica of the duck by Frédéric Vidoni is on display at the Museum of Automatons, Grenoble.

Among the other outstanding eighteenth- and nineteenth-century inventors of automatons must be noted Baron von

Kempelen, who in 1769 created the renowned "Chess Player" that held Catherine the Great of Russia in check. Paradoxically, although Kempelen made talking machines that were actually capable of articulating words, his most famous work was an illusion—a hollowed-out mannequin cleverly presented on a piece of furniture replete with useless mechanisms, behind which a Polish officer named Worouski, whose legs had been amputated, was hidden. After opening the doors of the chest and proving that nobody could be inside, Kempelen asked a player to move the first piece on the chessboard. Worouski would then hoist himself into the torso of the mannequin, examine the

1871) was also one of the great forebears in the world of special effects. Like Vaucanson, he was first interested in clock making, then constructed ingenious automatons before applying his expertise to magic. At the 1844 Paris Exposition, he presented a "writer-draftsman," which won the silver medal and was bought by the famous circus impresario Phineas Taylor Barnum. The

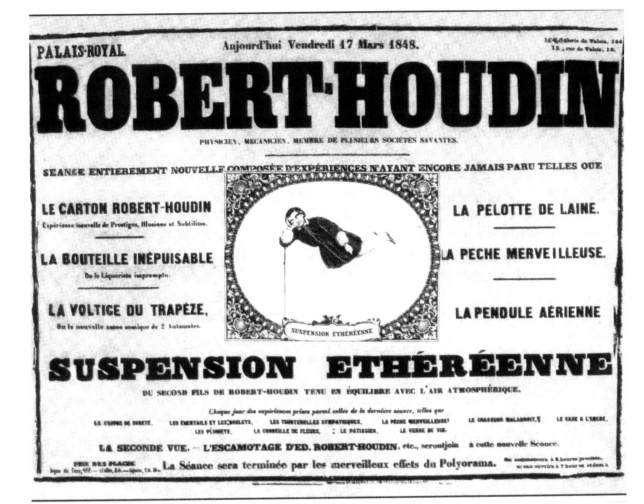

Poster advertising a March 17, 1848, Robert-Houdin performance featuring his famous "Ethereal Suspension"
Photo courtesy of Maison de la Magie de Blois

automaton was seated at a small table and held a pencil in its hand. If asked for a symbol of loyalty, it would draw a dog; of love, Cupid. Capable of making true mechanical wonders, Robert-Houdin also devised rigged automatons such as "Enigma the Singing Bust," which an assistant would activate by pulling the strings hidden in the sides of the mannequin.

In 1845, at his Théâtre des Soirées Fantastiques, Robert-

Houdin inaugurated a new golden age of magic. For his trick called the "Fantastic Orange Tree," he would borrow a handkerchief from a woman in the audience, roll it up into a ball, and place it next to an egg, a lemon, and an orange. He would then spirit away the handkerchief, egg, and lemon, making it appear that they had been merged into the remaining orange, which he would then pretend to squeeze. Another sleight

of hand, and voilà! The orange first became minuscule and then was reduced to powder, which he sprinkled into a vial of alcohol. An assistant then appeared with an orange tree that bore neither fruit nor flowers. Robert-Houdin would then pour the contents of the vial into a vase that had been placed on the top of the tree and set them alight. The branches would blossom in artificial flowers and quite real oranges, which were duly distributed throughout the dumbstruck audience. The single orange left on the tree then split open into quarters, revealing the borrowed handkerchief. Two butterflies emerged from it and flew off. Robert-Houdin then plucked the handkerchief and returned it to the woman, to the applause of the audience. The device that brought the orange tree to life was controlled by foot pedals. The oranges were stuck onto points hidden within the leaves that would appear on demand. The cloth flowers were concealed in small metal tubes and would emerge when deployed. The last orange was made of four pieces of metal mounted on hinges. As soon as it opened, two artificial butterflies guided by steel wires would glide to the ceiling, their wings activated by a small spring-loaded mechanism.

Following the "Fantastic Orange Tree," Robert-Houdin had a great success with his "Ethereal Suspension," a trick that is still performed today. In it, he pretended to have his son breathe ether fumes from a jar. While the son feigned sleep, Robert-Houdin would slide a crutch, the point of which was attached to the stage, under his son's right arm. He would then raise his son's legs and place the body in a horizontal position. When he let go, the body remained suspended in air, with no support other than the crutch. The amazed audience was unaware that the boy wore

The "Chess Player," in an April 1869 photograph by Robert-Houdin, was one of the magician's fake automatons.
Photo courtesy of Collection Christian Fechner

The "Singing Lesson," one of Robert-Houdin's most beautiful creations. This model, known as "du perron," is on display at the château in Blois.
Photo courtesy of Collection Christian Fechner

a metal corset and leggings that hugged his body under his clothes. Attached to the top of the crutch, this articulated support was fixed with a mechanism that allowed the boy's body to remain at a right angle.

Having become the living symbol of magic, Robert-Houdin performed it for royalty. In 1856, the French government sent him to Algeria to mitigate the influence of the marabouts and quell a brewing rebellion. Announcing that he would deprive one of these holy men of his strength, Robert-Houdin presented him with a small box placed on a mount, which the magician easily raised to prove that there was nothing holding it down. However, when the marabout tried with all his strength to lift it, he was unable to do so. The

metal box had been fixed to the mount through electromagnetism. Robert-Houdin made such an impression that he was honored by the marabouts, who from this point on were convinced of the "superiority of French magic." In addition to his magical devices and special effects, Robert-Houdin invented a carbon-filament light bulb in 1863, sixteen years before the American Thomas Edison. He also devised the protective pad, sensitive to electricity, that was worn by fencers, an innovation later adapted for use in automatic doors, odometers, and ophthalmic tools to study the inner eye. More than a century after his death, Robert-Houdin remains one of the most highly respected illusionists and magicians of all time.

The "Triple Mystery" pendulum made by Robert-Houdin reveals none of its mechanisms; nevertheless, its hands move and indicate the time with perfect precision.
Photo courtesy of Collection Christian Fechner

Dragons emerge from the facade of the wonderful Maison de la Magie in Blois as if saluting the statue of Robert-Houdin. A visit to the exhibitions and attractions is truly enthralling.
Photo courtesy of Maison de la Magie de Blois

LA BAIE DE NAPLES : Le jour.

LA BAIE DE NAPLES : Le crépuscule.

Three hand-colored photographs on glass plates that were rear-projected on a screen to create the decor of the dance pavilion at the 1900 Exposition Universelle in Paris. Through a cross-dissolve process, the three sequential images simulated the passage from day to night over the Bay of Naples.
Photos courtesy of the Laurence Botelle Collection

Technology in Service to the Theater

Beginning in the seventeenth century, the technology used in theaters continued to improve. Complicated stage effects, superb scenery, and sophisticated mechanics delighted an ever more demanding audience. On August 19, 1862, the Théâtre du Châtelet in Paris presented its first production: an extravaganza entitled *Rothomago*. With a seating capacity of twenty-five hundred and a stage measuring about 80 by 115 feet (24 by 35 meters), this was the largest theater in the capital. It drew a huge audience by presenting the most popular entertainments of the late nineteenth century: phantasmagorias such as the 1866 production of *Cinderella,* with its cast of 676, as well as military dramas. These productions provided the Châtelet with opportunities to use special effects and pyrotechnical devices that for a long time were unique to that theater. In addition, a new lighting system that employed gas lamps illuminated the large hall. The theater's great successes included adaptations of

GRAND THEATRE, LEEDS, Six Nights and One Matinee, COMMENCING MONDAY, SEPT. 24th.

A poster portraying action from Quo Vadis, *a theatrical spectacle presented in 1901, foreshadows gladiator films to come. Notable is the importance given to the use of special effects and forced perspective.*
Photo courtesy of the Laurence Botelle Collection

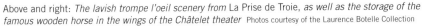

Above and right: *The lavish trompe l'oeil scenery from* La Prise de Troie, *as well as the storage of the famous wooden horse in the wings of the Châtelet theater* Photos courtesy of the Laurence Botelle Collection

two of Jules Verne's novels—
*Around the World in Eighty
Days* and *Michael Strogoff*—in
1876 and 1880. Public
demand for *Around the World*
was such that the show was

*One of the most spectacular battle scenes
from* Michael Strogoff, *an adaptation of the
Jules Verne novel during the glory days of
the Théâtre du Châtelet in Paris*
Photo courtesy of the Laurence Botelle Collection

revived twenty-five times
through 1940, with a total of
3,007 performances.

The First Projections

The art of projection first
appeared some three thousand
years ago in the Far East, with
the earliest performances of
shadow theater. Candles were
used to illuminate the back side
of a white cloth that had been
stretched in a large wooden
frame. The figures were flat
puppets with articulated limbs
that were manipulated by long
wooden sticks. When these cardboard figures were placed close
to the scrim, the audience seated
on the other side would see
distinctly silhouetted shadows;
when the figures were held at a
distance, the shadows became
vague and less precise. The first

true projection, however, was
not until much later, in 1671,
when an ingenious German
Jesuit, Father Athanasius Kircher
(1601–1680), perfected the
magic lantern, the precursor to
the slide projector. His apparatus
used a candle placed in a box
fitted with an opening and a con-
verging lens. When a plate of
painted glass was placed in front
of the lens, the magnified image
that appeared on a screen about
six to ten feet (two to three
meters) away seemed to come
from nowhere, and the audience
was thrilled.

Music hall magicians would
seize upon this invention. In
1795, an illusionist who called
himself Robertson frightened
audiences by making monsters
suddenly appear from the shadows. He added mechanisms to
the magic lantern that enabled

*The magician Robertson effected "the
appearance of images of the deceased" for
their relatives, in exchange for a tidy sum.
One of the more questionable uses of special effects.*
Photo courtesy of Collection Christian Fechner

several glass plates to be
illuminated in succession and
installed adjustable lenses that
produced a progressive, blurred
effect. He named his improved
lantern the Fantascope, because
he claimed that it revealed the
presence of phantoms! Not very
scrupulous, Robertson took
advantage of families in mourn-
ing, overcome with grief, and
supplemented his income by
projecting "spectral" portraits of
their dearly departed. As they
grew more popular, magic
lanterns lost their supernatural
aura and became indispensable
entertainment at family parties
during the nineteenth century.

The End of the Reign of the Still Image

Many inventors studied the phenomenon of "retinal persistence" (also known as persistence of vision) in an attempt to discover a method of producing moving images. It has been known for millennia that images registered by the human eye remain there for a certain very brief amount of time; for example, a flashlight quickly whirled in the dark will give the appearance of an incandescent circle. This slight imperfection in our vision inspired an English doctor named Paris to concoct a toy, the Thaumatrope, in 1826. The gadget was composed of a cardboard disk suspended between two strings. Rapid rotation of the disk caused the visual superimposition of two pictures, each printed on one of its faces. Thus, a cage and a bird became superimposed, creating the composite image of a captive animal. In 1834, the Englishman William George Horner invented the Zoetrope. In the middle of the apparatus was one cylinder, upon which was set a dozen small mirrors. A second large and hollow cylinder, which encased the first, had vertical slits cut into it. Ten drawings that showed the different stages of a motion were printed on a stationary band of paper placed inside the second cylinder, under the slits. By turning the cylinder and looking across the slits, one could see the successive reflections of the drawings on the turning mirrors and create an animated cycle.

Drawing Motion

Prior to the invention of film, Émile Reynaud, a Frenchman, was the first person to project animated works of fiction, which he did through the use of his Praxinoscope. Around 1888, Reynaud mounted painted images on plates of glass, which were then attached one after another on two flexible steel bands. The sequence came to life as it was reflected in a series of mirrors mounted on a rotating drum. Projection occurred when light passed through the device. The painted figures surrounded by black appeared as illuminated silhouettes superimposed on a static background that was projected independently by a magic lantern. Reynaud's *Pantomimes lumineuses* were composed of several hundred drawings. By making the front band turn retrograde and by repeating some of the movement both for comedic effect and to prolong the suspense, he was able to create a fifteen-minute show. The invention was such a

Émile Reynaud projects the animations of his optical theater for Auguste and Louis Lumière, the inventors of cinematography.
Photo courtesy of the Archives Grévin

The technicians had to perform tasks as exacting as they were precise to maneuver the scenery and special effects from the wings. Photo courtesy of the Laurence Botelle Collection

The Châtelet lighting console: a set of rheostats that controlled the intensity of light of three thousand electric lamps. A state-of-the-art device in 1900.
Photo courtesy of the Laurence Botelle Collection

This odd lantern projected the passing of the clouds over the downstage scenery so as to intensify the realism of the exterior scenes.
Photo courtesy of the Laurence Botelle Collection

to the Twenty-first Century

After a century of progress, scenic effects reached an impressive state of technical perfection, as demonstrated by this image from the Céline Dion show A New Day, produced by Franco Dragone and presented in Las Vegas starting in 2003. At the back of the 230-foot-wide (70-meter) stage, a video screen nearly 35 feet tall and 110 feet wide (10 by 33 meters) displays images composed of 5.3 million pixels.
Photo courtesy of Tomasz Rossa

The bride scene. In the background, electroluminescent diodes that constitute the surface of the giant video screen can be made out.
Photo courtesy of Tomasz Rossa

Left and above: Mechanical devices make it possible to suspend actors and dancers by cables so they can cross from one side of the stage to the other, as if they are flying.
Photos courtesy of Tomasz Rossa and George Bodnar

success that Reynaud gave more than ten thousand performances in eight years. But the dazzling advent of cinematography ruined him overnight. Overcome with bitterness, he threw most of the bands into the Seine River and died a pauper.

The Birth of Film

Inspired by the drive movement of the sewing machine and their profound knowledge of photographic techniques, brothers Auguste and Louis Lumière devised a single apparatus that combined the functions of a camera, a printer, and a projector. Their invention was the synthesis of technical principles that had emerged during the nineteenth century—animated images, the photographic recording of motion, and the drive mechanism to move the film, which was first employed by Edison's Kinetoscope. The Lumière brothers registered their patent for the Cinématographe on February 13, 1895, and the first cinematic showing for which viewers paid a fee— thus revolutionizing the entertainment world—took place on December 28, 1895, in the basement of the Grand Café on the Boulevard des Capucines in Paris. Tickets cost one franc, for which a dozen strips, each running about one minute, could be seen—among them, the famous *Sortie de l'usine Lumière à Lyon*

(*Workers Leaving the Lumière Factory*). On that first day, the thirty-three audience members were dumbfounded. Thanks to word of mouth, the showings soon drew twenty-five hundred viewers a day. Their success was such that the Lumière brothers had to quickly make new films. *L'Arrivée d'un train en gare* (*Arrival of a Train at La Ciotat*) was so striking that many people, afraid the train would run them over, quickly moved away from the screen! After immortalizing scenes from daily life such as *Le Repas de bébé* (*Feeding the Baby*), in 1896 they attacked fictional comedy with *L'Arroseur arrosé* (*Sprinkling the Sprinkler*). They and their cameramen slowly learned new production and framing methods that film made possible. They were content to exploit the commercial aspects of their discovery, leaving others to explore its artistic potential.

When Film Becomes Magic . . .

A young magician who was besotted with film requested a meeting with Antoine Lumière, the father of Auguste and Louis, and tried to persuade the old man to sell him a camera. Antoine Lumière attempted to convince the young man that the process had "no future." The truth was that he wanted to ensure the exclusivity of film

production. But Georges Méliès was not easily discouraged. He went to England, where he bought a camera from the Englishman Robert William Paul, the creator of the Animatograph and several films conceived for Edison's Kinetoscope that had already been shown at the Théâtre Robert-Houdin. Méliès hired two engineers to develop a new version of the camera, or Kinetograph. According to a famous anecdote, it was by accident that he discovered his first "effect." His camera jammed while he was taking shots of the traffic around the Place de l'Opéra. Méliès cut out the destroyed section of film, repaired the blank film, and continued to shoot. While projecting it, he was amazed to discover that a bus had abruptly transformed into a hearse! Between the accidental interruption of his shooting and when he started again, the hearse had moved into the exact same spot. Méliès immediately understood the importance of the effect "by substitution."

The First Special Effects Studio

In his first film with special effects, *L'Escamotage d'une dame chez Robert-Houdin* (*The Vanishing Lady*, 1896), Méliès no longer had to use trapdoors and other theatrical mechanisms. To make the actress Jeanne d'Alcy disappear, all he had to do was interrupt the shooting and replace her with a skeleton before having her reappear. Thus, in the fantastic he had found his calling, but he still needed a studio. The double exposure and matting effects with which he was experimenting were too complicated to be produced outside in available light, as the simple passing of a cloud could ruin an effect in progress. To address his needs, Méliès designed a film studio that was the synthesis of a photography studio and a stage replete with theatrical mechanisms. Construction began in 1896 in his garden in Montreuil-sous-Bois, just east of Paris. The building, which measured fifty-six feet long by twenty-three feet wide (seventeen by seven meters), was composed of a large iron structure, frosted glass walls, and a wood parquet floor. Beneath the stage, Méliès excavated a ten-foot (three-meter) pit that he fitted with numerous trapdoors, hoisting mounts, and winches; he installed the mechanisms outside the studio. Méliès was an outstanding designer. He created scenery, trompe l'oeil painted cutouts, as well as canvases that protracted the perspective of staircases and those parts of the building depicting its volume. Once the

actors were in their proper places, the trick took off. The lighting of the trompe l'oeil elements was particularly important. Méliès devised a system of movable shutters that could block intruding sunlight. Thanks

A waxwork of Georges Méliès on display at the Grévin Museum, located in the Forum des Halles, Paris
Photo courtesy of the Archives Grévin

to an array of cords and pulleys, each shutter could be opened or shut in an instant.

In 1897, Méliès discovered and started to develop methods for double and multiple exposures and matting. The procedure common to these three effects entailed exposing the film several times, rewinding it each time in order to add a new effect. To create the appearance

of a phantom, Méliès first filmed his stage set with the actors reacting to a ghost they did not see. He then rewound the film and shot a brightly lit actress dressed in a shroud, who moved in front of a black velvet backdrop. When the film was viewed, a transparent moving silhouette was superimposed on the scenery. But the process had its limits. With each new exposure, the extraneous light that hit the already exposed portions of the image dulled and faded them. The contrast became blurred, and the quality of the composition showed the effects. Méliès then brought the concept of matting into focus. Carefully preparing his special effects, he determined, one after another, which parts of the images he wanted to film. He would make a set of cards out of black cardboard that corresponded to the contours of each scene fragment, each successive stage of the shooting. In order to reproduce himself in his film *L'Homme-orchestre* (*The One-Man Band,* 1900), he made as many cards as there were chairs arranged next to one another. Following a meticulously prepared choreography, he filmed the arrival of each of his selves, one after another, each time removing the card that corresponded to the entering character, while the others that remained protected the nonexposed areas of the film.

A model of the Méliès studio with its glass walls   Photo courtesy of Maison de la Magie de Blois

Watching the film, the viewer would see Méliès's clones sitting down and then chatting while turning right and left, before playing their instruments.

In 1902 alone, he created the first disaster film, *Éruption volcanique à la Martinique* (*Volcanic Eruption on Martinique*); the first science fiction film, *Le Voyage dans la Lune* (*Trip to the Moon*); and the first fantastic adventure

film, *Le Voyage de Gulliver à Lilliput et chez les géants* (*Gulliver's Travels*). His productions were distributed around the world. Unfortunately, Méliès was to experience many hard knocks. Most of his films were copied and illegally distributed in the United States. He was forced to open an expensive branch in New York, and in 1908, in order to distribute his films legally on American soil,

he had to affiliate with Thomas Edison's company. He obstinately persisted in producing films with painted scenery at a time when his contemporaries were already filming in natural settings and experimenting with tracking shots and aerial views. Little by little, his creations were deemed archaic. The American branch folded. Beginning in 1911, Méliès was under contract to Charles Pathé

A drawing of the mechanism constructed to control the giant in À la conquête du pôle

and working under Ferdinand Zecca, a director who over the years would plagiarize his work. This humiliating partnership demoralized him. In 1912, he filmed *À la conquête du pôle* (*Conquest of the Pole*), in which a giant snowman swallows the explorers. The enormous puppet, which could move its head, eyes, arms, and hands, was controlled by fifteen special effects technicians.

Despite the efforts taken, the film met with only mild success. In 1913, with the death of his wife, Méliès abandoned film. Financial setbacks came one after another. In 1923, a creditor bought his home at a very low price and copies of his films were sold off at market stalls. Ruined, despondent, Méliès destroyed some of his collection himself. In 1925, he married one of his former

actresses, Jeanne d'Alcy, who had a toy shop in the Montparnasse train station in Paris, and ended his professional career. In 1932, the Mutuelle du Cinéma enabled him to end his days without a care in the château d'Orly, where his admirers would come to meet him. When the father of special effects died in 1938, he knew that his art would survive him.

Film and Manipulated Reality

In the first years of the 1900s, through the use of special effects to enhance the realism of certain scenes, innovative technicians distinguished themselves from Georges Méliès's extravaganzas and comic fantasies. During the filming of *The Great Train Robbery* (1903), the American director Edwin S. Porter hung black velvet in the frame of a train carriage's open door. He first filmed the bandits as they blew up the train's safe, making sure that they never passed in front of the door. Porter then inserted a black cardboard matte between the lens and the shutter of his camera, blocking the entire image, save for the door. He then rewound the film and shot a moving panorama from a real train. The effect worked perfectly. As the safe exploded—thanks to a double exposure—the smoke blew naturally across the passing landscape. During the following years, technicians often inserted mattes and counter-mattes in their cameras, as photographers had done since the 1850s in order to create a composite shot of several models. By using such a split screen, Dorothy Phillips was able to play both twin sisters in *The Right to Happiness* (1919). First she was filmed lying in bed. Then, blocking out the contour of her face and the upper portion of the shot, the cameraman rewound the film. A counter-matte was inserted to protect the film already shot, and the first one was then removed. The actress once again lay down on the bed, this time pretending to kiss herself.

Paintings on Glass

To address the needs of the film *Missions of California* (1907), the American cameraman Norman O. Dawn invented the method of painting on glass. He asked an artist to paint the missing segments of the church arches on a plate of glass, which was then placed in front of the camera, re-creating the textures, light, and shadows of the real building. When screened, the manipulation was not discernible. This technique was then used to re-create great historical sites and to fill empty skies with beautiful storm clouds. Glass paintings were also used for interiors. When a director filmed a low-angle shot of a room, he could not help but frame the "grill," the structure on which the spotlights are suspended. By painting a ceiling and a light fixture on a plate of

The matte painting from Michael Curtiz's film Noah's Ark *(1929)*

A hobbyhorse filmed the way scenes were shot at the beginning of the twentieth century, in front of a turning painted canvas attached to rollers Photo courtesy of Universal Studios Hollywood

The making of one of the matte paintings for Raiders of the Lost Ark
Photo courtesy of Photofest

glass, an artist could fix the problem, but he had to work fast, as studios were expensive to rent. With the invention of matte painting, the problem was resolved. Before the start of filming, a black matte would be painted on a plate of glass so as to block out a portion of the image. First the scene was shot with the actors, and then the empty set was reshot, producing another hundred feet of extra film that would be cut out and used for tests. The partially exposed shots with the actors, which had yet to be developed, were transferred into another camera that was mounted on a support securely fixed into a

cement piece of flooring and placed in front of a white canvas. A clip of the test sequence (with the empty set) was developed and loaded into the camera, so it could be viewed through a reflex viewfinder. This image enabled the transfer of the black matte onto the canvas; finally, the painting completed the image. Black was painted on the part of the image that corresponded to the shots with the actors. The original negative was then exposed a second time to attain a composite of the real and painted scenery, which could then be completed through other special effects. The superimposition of flames on the painting of a half-burned building, for example, could create an impressive inferno scene.

Special Effects and the First Comedies

Beginning in 1912, producer-director Mack Sennett peppered the chase scenes in his Keystone Kops comedies with amusing special effects. Once, he asked an assistant to throw a cloth mannequin of a policeman from the top of a building, which he then filmed falling

A spectacular stunt by the Keystone Kops

and crashing to the ground. The mannequin was removed from the scene and replaced by an actor lying in precisely the same position. As the filming started again, the actor stood up unsteadily. On the screen, the policeman appeared to take a dreadful fall and then stand up unscathed! Sennett also played with the speed of shots to film a scene in which the car of the Keystone Kops crosses the railroad tracks, coming

within a hairsbreadth of a passing train. The scene was shot at seven frames per second, while the train and car both traveled at about 15 mph (25 kph). At this speed, the events were easily controlled and the risks reduced. But when the action is viewed at sixteen frames per second (the standard speed of silent films), the vehicles appeared to be charging at each other in defiance of all danger.

sequence of the parting of the Red Sea by shooting in close-up a split block of gelatin that he shook. In 1924, *The Thief of Baghdad,* directed by Raoul Walsh, depicted a "Thousand and One Nights" city by integrating shots of models with real scenes. A flying carpet moved through the scene by a system of pulleys and suspended tracks. The leaping Douglas Fairbanks, superimposed onto a miniature

The set of the underwater palace discovered by the hero in The Thief of Baghdad *was completed with a glass painting.*

The Fantastic 1920s

The 1920s was a period of phenomenal technical experimentation. In the first version of *The Ten Commandments* (1923), Cecil B. De Mille filmed the

landscape, fought a slew of monsters. At the same time, in Germany, Fritz Lang was directing the battle scene between Siegfried and Fafner in his *Die Nibelungen*. Ten technicians

Siegfried bathes in the dragon Fafner's blood in order to become invincible. One of the memorable scenes in Die Nibelungen.

filmed, director Fred Niblo could create the illusion of the whole amphitheater during the chariot race sequence.

Metropolis: The Excellence of German Special Effects

In 1927, designer Erich Kettelhut conceived of a stunning futuristic city in the German studios of UFA for Fritz Lang's *Metropolis,* and the models were constructed from his superb drawings. A number of airplanes were made to glide along invisible wires between skyscrapers that towered some ten feet (three meters), and hundreds of cars were moved frame by frame, millimeter by millimeter, to create the illusion of air and street traffic. Ten technicians working an entire day succeeded in producing five seconds of film. Lang wanted to insert his actors into these miniatures, so head cameraman Eugen Schüfftan developed the process that now bears his name. He first placed a plate of glass at a forty-five-degree angle between the camera and the model of the skyscraper and demarcated the outline of a balcony or window by looking through the camera's viewfinder. He transferred this outline onto a mirror and, using nitric acid, completely removed the part of the mirror's silver coating that

hidden inside the monster activated its head, feet, and tail using a system of cables and pulleys. When the dragon's mouth was opened, a gas flame shot out. In 1925, the dinosaurs that special effects artist Willis O'Brien brought to life in *The Lost World* stunned audiences. His forty-nine miniature monsters featured articulated metal scales (see pages 221–22). The same year, in the first version of *Ben-Hur*, by suspending miniatures above the camera as the life-size scenery was being

The stunning urban landscape of Metropolis, *in which the land and aerial traffic were animated by stop-motion*

fell outside the outline, then set the mirror at a forty-five-degree angle in front of the camera. The small part of the mirror that remained on the otherwise-transparent plate served the double purpose of concealing a section of the model and reflecting the image. Schüfftan placed the actors at the other side of the stage, some forty feet (twelve meters) away, so that they were reflected in the small mirror. The quality of the special effect—integrating actors with models—that he achieved was excellent.

The filming of a scene in Trader Tom of the China Seas, *a 1954 serial made using rear projection*

Rear Projection

The process of rear (or rear-screen) projection came to the fore in the 1930s. It consisted of placing actors in front of a translucent screen, on the back side of which a previously filmed sequence was projected. The projector was fitted with a high-intensity arc lamp that could produce extremely bright images. Electric cables attached the projector to the camera so that the two shutter actions were synchronized. This effect allowed actors to be integrated into an image slightly more blurred and faded than the foreground, but in a way credible enough so as not to disturb the audience. It was often used to film scenes of dialogue that took place in a car. The illusion of movement was completed by passing black drapes or branches in front of the

spots illuminating the vehicles. Alfred Hitchcock made great use of this method when filming exterior scenes in the tranquillity of a studio.

King Kong: Willis O'Brien's Triumph

It was in 1933 that special effects wizard Willis O'Brien made his masterpiece: *King Kong.* The giant gorilla was a model that measured thirty-two inches (eighty centimeters) tall and was covered in rabbit fur. The tyrannosaurus he encounters measured about three feet (almost one meter) tall. The miniature scenery was fitted with small screens made of stretched sheets of surgical rubber, on which stop-motion shots of the actors would be projected. Whenever contact between a human and a monster occurred,

the human was replaced by a pliant figurine. The jungle on Skull Island was depicted by exceptional models, throughout which O'Brien planted small, lush foliage. But when he watched the daily rushes of his filming, he saw that the plants were shooting up all around the dinosaurs! Their slight growth, recorded by stop-motion, became outrageously accelerated when projected at normal speed. So the real plants were uprooted, and the tropical plants and palm trees were replaced by leaves cut out of copper. Gnarled trunks, made of branches and clay covered with toilet paper, were covered with shellac and paint. Knotty vine roots and dried moss completed this reduced universe. It was all set out on top of large pine boards that had been pierced with thousands of holes, where the feet of the models

The miniature models of King Kong and the stegosaurus, placed in the miniature set. One can see the holes through which screws were set so that the models' feet could be held in place during stop-motion photography.
Photo courtesy of Photofest

were secured to screws during the stop-motion filming. Deeply influenced by the etchings of Gustave Doré, O'Brien emphasized the depths of his landscapes by manipulating the dark and light zones. The flora in the foreground was miniature in volume. Other trees, vines, and sundry plants were painted on glass plates placed in the background. A trompe l'oeil in the back of the scenery created the horizon. O'Brien was such a stickler for detail that he made tiny birds fly through the landscape with breathtaking beauty, gliding on a piano wire the thickness of a hair.

The Traveling Matte and the Optical Printer

Linwood G. Dunn, who was in charge of the optical effects of *King Kong,* used two different techniques for insertion that had been developed in the preceding years. The first was developed by C. Dodge Dunning. From a negative of the background of an image (a piece of scenery, for example), a positive would be made and then dyed orange. In a camera magazine expressly created for this process, the colored film was placed against a strip of blank film. If a blue cyclorama were brightly lit (blue being the complementary color of orange) and photographed on the blank film atop the orange positive, one would get, from the orange positive film, a duplicate black-and-white negative of the scene, the positive orange having been exposed to the light of the blue cyclorama. Using this same process, if actors were placed between the camera and the blue cyclorama, and they were lit by spots filtered with an orange gel, the actors would be integrated into the background action on the negative. The background would not become imposed upon the images of the actors as they were lit in orange, and therefore their silhouettes would block out the light of the blue film. In effect, the actors became their own mattes. The blank film directly registered a composite

Vernon L. Walker and Linwood G. Dunn pose proudly in front of the optical printer that they devised.

image upon which the actors were integrated in front of the scene previously shot.

The second process that would later be adapted for color filming derives from an invention that Frank D. Williams patented in 1916 under the term *traveling matte.* If one wanted to insert an explorer onto a miniature jungle scene, he would first be filmed in front of a blue background. A copy of this would then be made on high-contrast film—that is, a film with no gray zone, only black and white. Filtered so that only blue registered, the image of a white silhouette (the actor) on a black background was obtained. This rendition would mask the scenery. Its inverse, a black silhouette on a white background, would mask the silhouette. With his optical printer (which comprised a spot situated in front of the lens and a camera loaded with blank film), Dunn first printed the background image (the jungle scene) and then, with the black silhouette of

the actor, created a reserve. After that, he used a black matte around the white silhouette to protect the image of the scene already printed on the film, then added the image of the explorer filmed on a blue background. When the negative was developed, the composite showed the explorer inserted into the miniature scenery. This procedure was undertaken twenty-four times just to produce a single second of traveling matte.

The color blue was initially chosen because it rarely appeared on the faces or clothes of the actors. John P. Fulton, also in 1933, used the traveling matte against a black background to produce the special effects in his film *The Invisible Man.* He filmed a figure covered from head to toe in black velvet, rewrapped him with a second layer lighter in color, and then placed him in front of a black velvet background. The negative of this scene showed a black silhouette of a body with neither a head nor hands upon a light background. Fulton used the negative as a matte for the clothes, which he inserted into the background. Sixty years later, digitally generated special effects enable the use of a far more practical green fluorescent that is automatically detected by computer programs specifically designed to create the unseen insertion of mattes and counter-mattes.

Special Effects in the Serials of the 1930s

In 1912, a new form of entertainment appeared in the movie theaters: the serial. The misfortunes that befell the orphan in *What Happened to Mary* moved the audience to tears. Over the years, these twelve-episode films would become action stories with each segment ending in a cliffhanger, the suspense spurring the audience to return the following week to learn the outcome. In the 1930s, the brothers Howard and Theodore Lydecker invented an ingenious device that enabled the model airplanes used in serials such as *Dick Tracy* (1937) to fly. They managed to make a model measuring more than three feet (one meter) glide along two wires that crossed the length of the set. A third wire attached to a motor could fly the model at the desired speed for some forty feet (twelve meters). When shot in close-up, the wires could not be seen. To get the plane to spin, the Lydeckers would twist the support wires. They always filmed their models in open air, taking advantage of natural daylight. Scenes in which the models were destroyed were shot at 120 frames per second, the de-acceleration of the action creating the impression of a massive explosion. In *The Adventures of Captain Marvel* (1941), it was a mannequin of

Howard and Theodore Lydecker use models during the filming of scenes from Dick Tracy, *a 1937 serial inspired by the famous comic strip.*

the superhero that the brothers hurled through the air!

Abused Lizards

Hollywood returned to prehistoric times with *One Million B.C.* (1940) and its "authentic" depiction of the life of cavemen battling dinosaurs! Director Hal Roach and his technicians rigged baby alligators and lizards with rubber horns in order to transform them into prehistoric monsters. Placed in miniature sets, these poor reptiles were then goaded to fight in front of the cameras while being filmed at 120 frames per second. When viewed, their slowed-down motion gave them the gait of mastodons. This technique was again used by L. B. Abbott in the film *Journey to the Center of the Earth* (1959), but under the control of the

Victor Mature confronts an iguana in One Million B.C.

American Humane Society. In it, Jules Verne's explorers could be seen in encounters with giant iguanadons that were portrayed by their true descendants— iguanas adorned with crests made of latex.

INTERVIEW

RAY HARRYHAUSEN AND DYNAMATION

In the early 1950s, Ray Harryhausen (b. 1920) invented Dynamation, a method that integrated models with real images without using miniature sets. Placing his creature in front of an unpolished translucent screen, he used a black matte to mask the support into which it had been screwed. To control the interactions between the actors and his creature, he watched the composite image through the viewfinder. The lower part of the real image—the floor—was then added by using a counter-matte. Harryhausen's masterpiece is *Jason and the Argonauts* (1963), which abounds in gems, such as the appearance of the bronze giant and the battle between the heroes and a horde of skeletons. Today, hundreds of people take part in the digitally generated effects of a film. Ray Harryhausen's creations, for which he was awarded an Oscar in 1992, were the fruit of one sole artist, one of the great geniuses in the history of animation.

How did you feel when you discovered "King Kong" in 1933 at Grauman's Chinese Theater in Hollywood?

Ray Harryhausen: Kong's enormous mechanical torso was on display in the lobby of the theater. I had goose bumps when the huge curtains opened and the title *King Kong* came up. I was dumbstruck, asking myself how had they filmed those dinosaurs and that incredible fight between the tyrannosaurus and the gorilla, since they couldn't have done it with men dressed up in costumes! I taught myself about stop-motion animation and started experimenting in my garage. I produced rear projections on a screen placed behind my articulated models, with a 16-millimeter projector, in order to mix the real shots with the animated characters. I made a cave bear with a wooden structure that moved in jerks, making a rattling noise. I cut out a third of an old coat of my mother's to cover it in fur. I was relieved to learn that she didn't want it anymore, once I had already done it! These early animations were jerky, but I could see, as if by magic, my characters come to life on the screen.

What was your state of mind when you showed your films to Willis O'Brien?

Ray Harryhausen: I tried to appear serious and calm, but I was trembling! He was pleasantly surprised by my animated stories and my dinosaurs. He seemed to be thrilled to meet a teenager who shared his passion for this underrated art. He was a nice man with a good sense of humor. Later, I became imbued by his ideas when I worked with him on the production of *Mighty Joe Young.* At the time, I didn't know that he had lived through a tragedy. [O'Brien's first wife, a woman with severe emotional disorders, committed suicide after having first killed their two sons.] Darlyne, his second wife, was able to make him happy. He would come over to play golf on a nine-hole green. . . . O'Brien would draw great, large-scale illustrations in preparation for some of the scenes, and hundreds of charcoal sketches to describe the details of the action.

How did you create the Dynamation process?

Ray Harryhausen: When I made the scenes in *Mighty Joe Young,* twenty-seven layout artists worked full time making the props and miniature scenery that were placed next to the model gorilla. Four people worked on the rear projections on screens integrated with the models. We used so much painting on glass plates to link the created elements with the real shots that we also had to hire four painters. This all cost so much that after *Mighty Joe Young,* no one knocked on Willis O'Brien's door,

Ray Harryhausen in his studio in 1981, with the goddess Kali from The Golden Voyage of Sinbad

A scene from Mighty Joe Young. *The miniature gorilla reacts to the presence of a lion, whose image was rear-projected inside the model of a wagon.*

even though he won an Oscar for that movie. I wanted to simplify the "sandwiching" process that puts a model between real shots. The first time I used Dynamation was on *The Beast from 20,000 Fathoms* (1953). The budget for the film was tiny: $210,000. I just barely had enough to buy a little technical equipment, but for the first time, I was in charge of special effects. I filmed all the background images with models and actors.

How did you construct your articulated models?

Ray Harryhausen: I used two different methods. The first consisted of constructing layer by layer, following the method used by Marcel Delgado and Willis O'Brien since *The Lost World*. I began by designing the character, and then I would make a metal skeleton with ball-and-socket joints. I could adjust the pressure on the steel balls of each joint by tightening the screws. This way, the knees were able to support the weight of the model as it was made to walk. Then I made the muscles out of foam rubber, which I attached to the frame, and I covered it all in a layer of foam rubber. The second method, which I used after the movie *Animal World,* consisted of sculpting the model out of clay and then molding it. I spent many weeks sculpting and detailing complicated models like the seven-headed Hydra in *Jason and the Argonauts,* or the Gorgon in *Clash of the Titans,* so they would be credible in close-ups. The armature was made to fit inside the mold of the sculpture. It was held in place with steel wires, and the joints were protected by a thin film of latex. Then I prepared the foam rubber, injected it into the mold, and baked the whole thing in an oven. When the model was removed from the mold, it had a foam skin and a metal skeleton. Then the skin had to be painted, the hair or scales had to be added, and other features had to be made.

The Ymir in 20 Million Miles to Earth *appears to be fighting with an elephant.*

Why have you never been listed in the credits as codirector?

Ray Harryhausen: Since *The Beast from 20,000 Fathoms,* I got into the habit of drawing the principal scenes and the continuity of the most complex scenes. I had to wear many hats, since these movies were made on low budgets. The directors were there, above all, to see to the performances of the actors, but everything else was predefined. I often codirected a scene with the director. Or directed the scenes filmed with the second crew that I would be using in my special effects sequences. I always had control over the editing of the animated scenes. In truth, ever since my first movies, I should at least have been credited as codirector. Afterward, it didn't bother me anymore.

Could you explain to us what the "sextopus" was?

Ray Harryhausen: The giant octopus in *It Came from Beneath the Sea* (1955)! With our budget we couldn't give it eight tentacles, only six. So the octopus became a "sextopus"! If the budget had been even smaller, we would have had a "tripod." Everything was shot "dry." First I filmed the attacks of the octopus on the upper portion of the frame, putting the edge of the matte just above the waves. The model was then animated in front of rear projections of shots of the ocean. Then I rewound the whole scene in the camera and exposed only the bottom half of the frame, while again filming the rear projection screen. I added the double exposure of the splashing at the level of the horizontal matte line to give the impression that the octopus was thrashing in the water.

The *"sextopus" in* It Came from Beneath the Sea *attacks a ship.*

The Cyclops who appears in "The Seventh Voyage of Sinbad" (1958) is one of the most popular characters. How did you imagine his personality before animating him?

Ray Harryhausen: His personality emerged during the shooting. One pose followed another, and the character's body movements slowly evolved. His physiognomy, his physique, and your sense of observation dictated his movements. When I shot *Mighty Joe Young,* I mimicked the movements, with a stopwatch in my hand, to measure how long they lasted. Later, with experience, you sense things. You don't need to quantify.

The Cyclops in The Seventh Voyage of Sinbad, *one of Ray Harryhausen's most famous characters*

How did you come up with the unforgettable scenes in "Jason and the Argonauts"?

Ray Harryhausen animating the snake-woman from The Seventh Voyage of Sinbad

Ray Harryhausen: I let that project sit for a very long time. Beverley Cross and Jan Read wrote the screenplay based on my drawings—the gods of Olympus looking down on the mortals in a pool of water; the giant statue of Talos, which I based on the idea of the Colossus of Rhodes, whose feet straddle the entry to the port. In the original story, Talos was only ten feet (three meters) tall. I made him bigger to increase the impact of the scene. My contributions to the screenplay were never credited. "Modesty" is a big word in Hollywood!

The fight against the bronze giant, and his end

How was the sequence of the sword fight against the seven skeletons prepared?

Ray Harryhausen: We used seven stuntmen, who wore a number on their costumes. Each of them played the role of one skeleton during the filming. They practiced their moves with the actors six or seven times, and then the actors were filmed alone. The fencing master for this scene was Fernando Poggi, who played one of the Argonauts.

How did you manage alone to film these seven skeletons in a sword fight with seven actors? Did you use the filmed scene with the stuntmen as a reference while you were animating the skeletons?

Ray Harryhausen: Oh yes! That reference was indispensable. Each model had thirty-six articulations, and they had to be animated in synchronization with the movements of the real actors. I couldn't shoot more than thirteen frames of that sequence a day, which works out to be a little more than a half second of film.

The stuntmen led by Fernando Poggi incarnate the skeletons during movement rehearsals of the final fight in Jason and the Argonauts.

The finished scene—a true feat of animation

How did you film the scenes with the flying creatures, like the Harpies?

Ray Harryhausen: The models were suspended by very fine wires in front of a rear projection screen. The wires had to be painted frame by frame, to give them the same color as the background projected behind them. They were attached to a kind of wooden cross surrounded with spools that could be wound and unwound, and then braked to hold the model in place. The model had three support points. The wires reached out on the diagonal, toward the outside, to avoid any swinging.

Your daughter wanted to play with the models.

Ray Harryhausen: I gave her a rubber replica of the tyrannosaurus from *The Valley of Gwangi* when she was small. She laid it down in her baby doll carriage and took it everywhere. One day, two very proper old ladies screamed in horror to find a tyrannosaurus in her baby carriage. They gave me a furious look and said, "Why don't you give a doll worthy of its name to the poor child?"

"The Golden Voyage of Sinbad" (1974) led you to discover a six-armed statue of the goddess Kali, whom you bring to life before a sword fight with Sinbad. How did you prepare this sequence?

Ray Harryhausen: We called upon the Indian choreographer Suya Kumuri. Suya asked one of her students to plaster herself against Suya's back, and they joined themselves with a belt at waist level so they could create four-armed movements. Their dance gave me a reference for animating Kali.

Preparatory drawing by Ray Harryhausen for Kali's dance scene

Fernando Poggi again directed the sword-fighting scene. He attached three stuntmen, one behind the other, to reenact the fight with actors.

How did you create Medusa, the Gorgon in "Clash of the Titans" (1981)?

Ray Harryhausen: I thought that a woman with snakes in her hair wouldn't frighten any-one. I transformed the lower half of Medusa's body into a rattlesnake, which allowed me to use the particularly sinister sound of the rattle in the silence of her den. I borrowed the goddess Diana's bow and arrow

Opposite and above: *Medusa, the Gorgon in Clash of the Titans*

and gave them to Medusa, and I used disks with different colored gels to imitate the variable light of the torches when I was shooting.

You've sculpted many bronze statues since you've retired.

Ray Harryhausen: One of the first was an homage to *King Kong*. I depicted the battle between Kong and the tyrannosaurus. I also have sculpted Perseus slaying the Gorgon, Sinbad fighting the dragon—a dozen bronzes in total. Most of them are reconstructions of my characters, which were destroyed in order to recycle their armatures. The tentacles of the octopus in *It Came from Beneath the Sea* became the tails of dinosaurs in other films!

One of Ray Harryhausen's superb bronze sculptures: an homage to King Kong

How do you feel when people tell you that your movies captivate their children?

Ray Harryhausen: I am always honored and thrilled. Recently, an entire family came with me to a private screening. Three generations of fans! Many people have said to me that some of our films have changed their lives. I've received letters from two professors who decided to become paleontologists after seeing [the remake] *One Million Years B.C.*! I'm thrilled that our films have had a beneficial influence.

Takeoff of the ark during the final sequence of When Worlds Collide

George Pal, the Magician of Science Fiction

The Hungarian filmmaker George Pal (1908–1980) made his first foray into animation in his own country; then, in the United States in the 1940s, he created his *Puppetoons* series of stop-motion puppetry. Afterward he dedicated himself to the production of science fiction movies. In 1950, *Destination Moon* launched the genre of space adventures. The following year, in *When Worlds Collide,* a crew of experts builds a rocket to escape just before Earth crashes into a rogue planet and its star. Gordon Jennings constructed a model rocket about 4 feet (1.2 meters) long that took off by gliding in a horizontal position before nosing up along the length of a ramp leaning against a miniature mountain. Jennings also built 6-foot (nearly 2-meter) models of New York buildings to film the flooding of the city. The sequences shot with the small-scale models brought the budget of the film to $936,000, quite a sum for the time. But *When Worlds Collide* had great success and was awarded the Oscar for best special effects. The Jennings/Pal team outdid itself in 1953 with its adaptation of H. G. Wells's *War of the Worlds*. The Martian spaceships, based on the shape of a manta ray, comprised copper hulls measuring a little more than 5 feet (1.6 meters) in

One of the Martian war machines in The War of the Worlds

The space traveler in his machine, conceived by the great designer Mentor Huebner

diameter. They were attached by wires to supports that glided on suspended tracks. The force field that protected the space- ships from earthly artillery was obtained by double-exposing the image of a plastic dome using an optical printer. The flashes of the Martians' rays were pro- duced with an oxyhydrogen blowtorch and solder wire. To film the destruction of Los Angeles City Hall, explosions were set off in the 8-foot (2.4- meter) model, working from top to bottom to create the most realistic effect. Disintegration was achieved by making mattes in the form of the objects struck by the rays. Through the use of counter-mattes, a reddish glow was obtained, before a dissolve revealed the empty set. Jennings was awarded a second Oscar for his work.

In 1960, working alone, Pal directed and produced the greatest H. G. Wells adaptation:

The robot Robby, unveiled in Forbidden Planet *(1956), became a veritable science fiction icon. Its structure was made from a thermoformed plastic in order to make it lighter for the extra who had to wear it. The front and back halves were sculpted on a wood matrix by the design department of MGM. The sculpture was perforated with hundreds of holes and then attached to a vacuum system. Elements were used to heat a layer of plastic stretched on a frame. Hermetically sealed on the matrix, the soft- ened plastic hugged the contours of the wooden frame when the air was sucked away. Cold air was injected to unstick the thermoformed plastic from the matrix.*

The Land Unknown *(1957) tells of the discovery of an intact prehistoric jungle at the North Pole. The dinosaurs in this unfairly forgotten movie were depicted by extras wearing costumes, as was done in* Godzilla. *Other creatures were animated by mechanisms created by Fred Knoth, Orien Ernest, and Jack Kevan.*

The Time Machine. Stop-motion animation made it possible to depict an acceleration of time. As soon as the time traveler pushed the lever of his machine, snails (which were models) marched across the ground, leaves and fruit (all imitation and fitted with iron wire armatures) suddenly sprouted on the trees, and the dresses on the mannequins in the store windows across the way appeared and disappeared. To simulate the rapid passage of day to night, Paul Vogel, the director of photography, placed a glass disk in front of his camera. This disk was composed of four different parts, each with a different color: dawn was pink, daytime was transparent, night-fall was amber, and night was tinged blue. By turning the disk in front of the lens, Vogel created the impression that the lighting of the sets was changing. George Pal used special effects again in *The Seven Faces of Dr. Lao* (1964) and in *The Power* (1967).

A Giant Octopus in the Disney Studios

In 1954, while filming *20,000 Leagues Under the Sea*, director Richard Fleischer sustained great setbacks with the giant octopus crafted by technicians under the direction of Bob Mattey at the Disney Studios. The enormous model was made of large inflatable rubber tubes that were filled with kapok and attached by cables to a series of pulleys. A team of technicians animated the monster during its battle with the crew of the submarine *Nautilus*. When it was first filmed against a background of a setting sun, the flaccid appearance of the octopus disturbed both Fleischer and Walt Disney. Even worse, when the scene was then projected on a large screen, the cables supporting the tentacles could be seen! Disney asked Mattey for a second, even larger octopus fitted with a pneumatic system that could make the tentacles coil up. This time, the background of the set was a stormy sky, and a battery of fans let loose a storm in the studio. Drenched under the downpour, the new octopus took on nightmarish proportions. The cables were finally invisible, and the body and beak of the octopus were activated by pneumatic and

The model of the submarine Nautilus, *its marvelous design the work of Harper Goff* Photo © Disney Enterprises, Inc.

Overleaf: *The giant octopus of* 20,000 Leagues Under the Sea, *made by Bob Mattey* Photo © Disney Enterprises, Inc.

hydraulic systems. Although this second shooting took eight days and brought the production over budget by $250,000, Fleischer and Disney knew that they had created the outstanding flourish of the movie. Their efforts would be rewarded with an Oscar for best special effects.

John P. Fulton and the Parting of the Red Sea

In 1956, *The Ten Commandments,* directed by Cecil B. De Mille, presented one of the most complicated and expensive special effects scenes in the history of film. One million dollars was allocated for the sequence of the parting of the Red Sea, out of a total budget of thirteen million dollars. It was John P. Fulton who had the responsibility for its conception. He built a thirty-five-foot-tall (ten-meter) construction, a kind of barrier extended by a gently inclined ramp. Fifteen floodgates linked to twenty-four reservoirs permitted control of the flow of water that flooded down the ramp to form a cascade. This wall of water was filmed twice, so as to create the right and left liquid walls as the Red Sea parted. By completely opening the floodgates, Fulton could make the water surge and create the impression of an enormous wave. In conjunction with this construction, he used a blue background, six

The waves of the Red Sea crashing down upon the pharaoh's troops in The Ten Commandments   Photo courtesy of Photofest

An image from the Russian movie Planeta Bur *(Storm Clouds of Venus, 1962), directed by Pavel Klushantsev. The crew, accompanied by a stunning robot, explores the planet Venus.*

hundred extras, dozens of optical effects, and a stormy sky re-created with smoke machines.

This extraordinary work earned him the Oscar for best special effects.

Journey into the Human Body

In *The Fantastic Voyage* (1966), a small submarine and its crew were shrunk and launched into the body of a wounded professor in order to treat him. Twentieth Century-Fox specified that half of the $6.5 million budget would be allocated to sets and special effects, supervised by L. B. Abbott. During preproduction, director Richard Fleischer hired Harper Goff—who had already created the *Nautilus* for *20,000 Leagues Under the Sea*—to create the submarine *Proteus*. Constructed in real-life size at a cost of $100,000, it was filmed suspended from cables to give the impression that it was floating. Numerous gigantic sets were constructed to represent the various parts of the body visited by the submarine. The one depicting cardiac valves was 130 feet (40 meters) long and 33 feet (10 meters) tall. The vein into which the *Proteus* is injected was a transparent, flexible resin and fiberglass set measuring 50 feet (15 meters) in width and 100 feet (30 meters) in length, which was illuminated by amber gels and pink and purple rotary spots to depict circulating cells. For blood cells, droplets made of a mixture of Vaseline and red-dyed oil were filmed at high speed as they sank to the bottom of a tank. Images of the

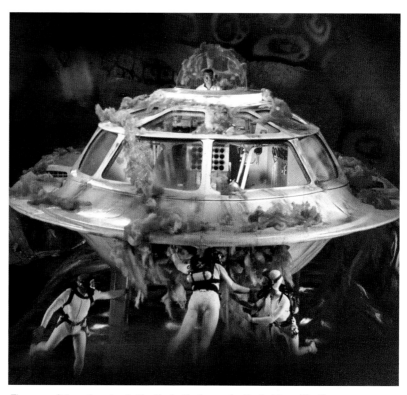

The crew of the submarine in The Fantastic Voyage *is attacked by antibodies.*
Photo courtesy of Photofest

actors dressed in wet suits were recorded on a blue background and then inserted into these shots through the use of a traveling matte. In most of the scenes, the actors pretended to swim while suspended from cables. In order to create the impression that they were moving through a viscous liquid, they were filmed at seventy-two frames per second, which slowed down their movements when projected. The attack by antibodies on the beautiful Raquel Welch was filmed in reverse, with the actress covered in strips of plastic fringe that were attached to wires. At a signal, assistants pulled on the wires, detaching the "antibodies" one by one. Projected in reverse, the scene gave the impression that the antibodies swooped down onto the actress (for which they can hardly be blamed). Fleischer's remarkable film won the Oscar for best special effects.

2001: A Space Odyssey

Made over a five-year period, Stanley Kubrick's *2001: A Space Odyssey* (1968) follows the intervention of an extraterrestrial monolith in the evolution of the human species. One of the most famous scenes shows an astronaut, thanks to artificial gravity, running through a spaceship along a circular passageway. To film the scene, Kubrick had the airplane manufacturer Vickers Armstrong construct a drum forty feet (twelve meters) in diameter. This three-hundred-thousand-dollar cylinder could spin at a speed of 3 mph (5 kph). The camera was set inside and turned on its axis while being maneuvered to follow the movement of the actor, who ran around at the bottom of the wheel at ground level. When projected from the point of view of the camera, the astronaut appeared to be defying the laws of gravity, running horizontally on the walls of the cylinder.

The visual effects of 2001: A Space Odyssey, *conceived by Douglas Trumbull, have lost none of their effectiveness.*
Photo courtesy of Photofest

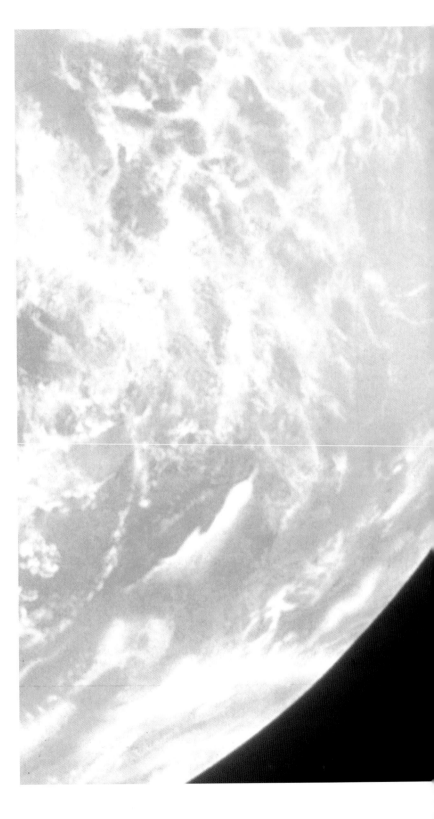

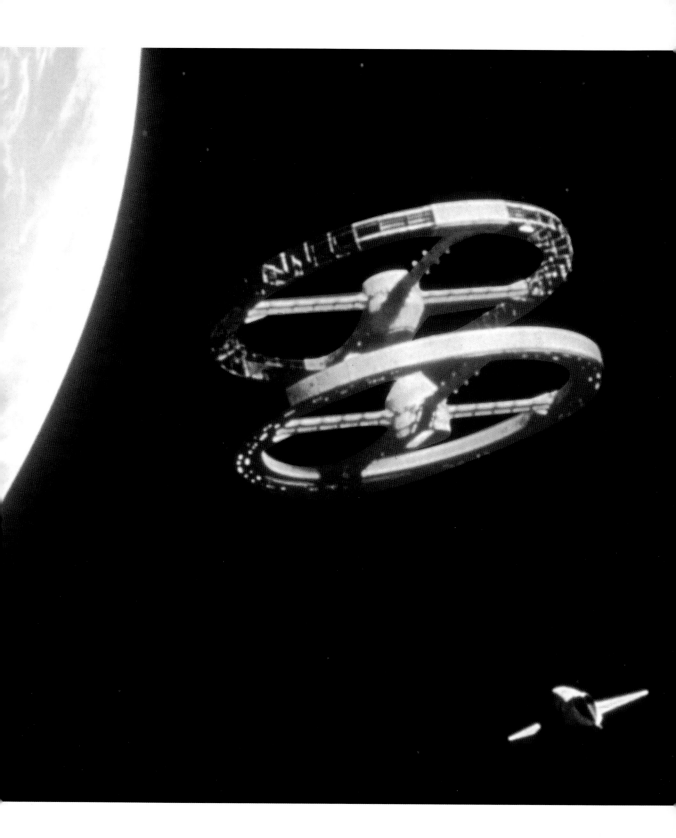

INTERVIEW

DOUGLAS TRUMBULL

Memories of *2001* . . .

Douglas Trumbull is one of the greatest creators of special effects. He contributed to the success of *2001: A Space Odyssey*, *Close Encounters of the Third Kind* (1977), and *Blade Runner* (1982), and he directed *Silent Running* (1971) and *Brainstorm* (1983). In 2001, appropriately enough, he launched a system that enabled the integration of actors into virtual sets in real time.

How did you learn to use special effects?

Douglas Trumbull: I started when I was an advertising illustrator. But I wanted my images to move. I was hired by Graphic Films, a small Hollywood studio that produced short industrial films for the U.S. Air Force and the National Aeronautics and Space Administration (NASA). The cameramen filmed drawings made with an airbrush on glass plates that were superimposed under the camera. This created an effect of depth that could be enhanced with double exposures and insertions. I learned the basics of my trade and then worked on the production of

Douglas Trumbull during the filming of his movie Brainstorm
Photo courtesy of MGM

To the Moon and Beyond, a film about space exploration. It was filmed in 70 millimeter, with ten sprocket holes, to obtain a high-definition image. The film was projected on a giant dome at the 1964 New York World's Fair. The speed of the film had to be reduced to eighteen frames per second to avoid it tearing! Kubrick saw it, and I became one of the technicians he hired to work in England on the space sequences of *2001.*

How did you prepare yourself to take up this technical challenge?

Douglas Trumbull: I started by spending six months animating the texts and logos that had to sweep across the computer Hal's screen! Today, all that you'd have to do is type on a

keyboard to make the text appear, but back then, every one of those letters had to be drawn by hand, painted, animated, and filmed in 16 millimeter. The images that appeared on the "televisions" were 16-millimeter rear projections on frosted screens mixed into the scenery. We then made an animation stand with steel tubes to prepare for the filming of the space scenes. It was composed of a backlighting table that could illuminate the elements by passing light through them and a camera fitted with an Angénieux zoom lens. This animation stand was so rudimentary that the camera couldn't even automatically be moved up and down. I came across a building kit with rods, and nuts and bolts, and constructed a mechanical mount,

The spaceship Discovery *in* 2001: A Space Odyssey   Photo courtesy of Photofest

attaching its gears to those of the camera to synchronize its movements with the rhythm of the shots. This piece of equipment allowed for multiple double exposures. Each time, the camera was focused at a different point of definition, a different depth of focus. The first space sequence, which shows the satellite revolving around Earth, was made this way, "flat" with cropped photos and back-lighted transparencies. The slit-scan, which gave the impression of going through a tunnel lit with abstract shapes, was also made "flat." The process consisted of having a back-lighted transparency move up and down behind a thin slit, while the shutter of the camera was open, and then we zoomed in. The illuminated slit, which ran vertically, thus created an image distorted into a trapezoid onto the film. We then made the rear document move with a small interval for each frame, to transform a flat drawing into a landscape that the camera seemed to fly over. We repeated the process in the other direction to create the upper part of the tunnel.

The projection effect produced by the slit-scan technique

Had you already considered preprogramming the movements of the camera at this time, even without the help of a computer?

Douglas Trumbull: Oh yes! Our insertions became more and more complex. We had to make mattes of the moving spaceships during the passages that were repeated with models in front of the camera. In order to obtain a black matte of a model, it had to be filmed in silhouette, without lighting it, in front of a white background, by repeating an absolutely identical movement with the one in the normal shot. The illuminated interiors of the spaceships were filmed separately, also in the dark, leaving the shutter of the camera open for a long time to capture the small sources of light. The differ-

ent shots were combined with an optical printer to get the definitive special effects. Wally Veevers devised several motorized systems to help us do the scenes with the orbital station, the Pan Am shuttle, and the spaceship headed for Jupiter. We used stepper motors, synchronized with the camera's motor, in order to move the models and the camera mount. These motors were hooked up to gears based on those of a car's gearbox. With a large-diameter gear, the mount moved quickly; with a smaller-diameter gear, it moved slowly. Each movement was activated by a different motor—right/left, up/down, front/back, etc. We were able to repeat the movements with great precision, as long as everything was written down. It was incredibly exacting

work. After *2001,* I returned to Los Angeles and asked some engineers to help me master this kind of equipment. We found a control system of stepper motors and put together an apparatus that enabled the recording of the pulses of the motor controls onto magnetic stereo tapes. One track was reserved for the movements of the camera mount, the other for the mount supporting the model. While the track was being read by the machine, the pulses reached the motors, which repeated the prerecorded movements. Speeding up the tape was enough to speed up the movement. This process was used for the first time filming an advertisement for True cigarettes. Later, home computers like the Apple II replaced magnetic tapes.

You were also the first to "miniaturize" the atmosphere around the models.

Douglas Trumbull: It was one idea that came to me while I was making *Close Encounters of the Third Kind*. In reality, the farther away objects are from you, the more atmospheric diffusion there is, making them appear blurry and bluish. First we made a test putting a model in an aquarium filled with cigarette smoke. We took photographs and made sure it was working well. Steven Spielberg filmed many tests with models on a large set in Burbank, but the smoke wouldn't remain homogeneous in such a space. Shots of the miniatures couldn't be slowed down to two or three frames per second without seeing the movement of the curls of smoke speed up when projected at twenty-four frames per second. So we built a fifty-five-square-foot (five-square-meter) smoke room, in which we installed a smoke machine and a photoelectric cell that measured the quantity of light emitted by a lamp placed at the other side of the room. As soon as the cell caught the slightest increase in the intensity of the light—meaning that the smoke had become less dense—the system automatically started up the smoke machine. It was in this airtight room that the shots of the UFOs and the touchdown of the mother ship were filmed.

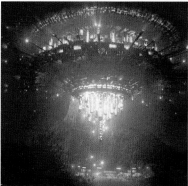

The mother ship in Close Encounters of the Third Kind, *filmed in a smoke-filled atmosphere*
Photo courtesy of Columbia Pictures

The shimmering lights that appear on the lower portion of the spaceship were created using rear projection on a translucent dome.
Photo courtesy of Columbia Pictures

The mother ship was a six-foot (two-meter) model equipped with neon tubes and incandescent bulbs, and pierced with tens of thousands of holes linked to fiber optics, built by Greg Jein. We used the same process several years later to film the scenes flying over Los Angeles in *Blade Runner,* and then again for the *Return to the Future* ride with the Omnimax system.

In Blade Runner, the talents of Ridley Scott and Douglas Trumbull led to the creation of an unforgettable vision of Los Angeles in 2017. The skyscrapers encircled by flying cars actually measured only about 50 to 65 inches (120 to 170 centimeters). They were adorned with delicate copper work cut out with acid to resemble metal girders. The windows were illuminated by hundreds of optic fibers.
Photo courtesy of the Ladd Company

The 1970s: The Age of Disaster Movies

In *The Poseidon Adventure* (1972), produced by Irwin Allen, a cruise ship is capsized by a colossal wave. The survivors must weave their way through this upside-down labyrinth to get to the keel and eventual help. L. B. Abbott and A. D. Flowers created scenery that allowed the scene to be shot while the vessel was upside down. A replica of the grand salon of the *Queen Mary,* measuring 128 feet (39 meters) long, 60 feet (18 meters) wide, and 30 feet (9 meters) tall, was fitted with an interchangeable floor and ceiling and was mounted on a platform inclined thirty degrees. The rest of the movement was simulated by tilting the cameras. During the second part of the scene, the ceiling and floor were switched to give the impression that the ship was inverted. The gallery through which the water surges was made to explode with numerous electrically triggered explosions. High-pressure pumps shot hundreds of thousands of gallons of water into the watertight set while 125 actors and stuntmen simulated panic. Abbott and Flowers received an Oscar for this new feat.

The most amazing sequence in The Poseidon Adventure: *a tidal wave capsizes a cruise ship.*
Photo courtesy of Photofest

The Glass Hell

The trio of Abbott, Flowers, and Allen reunited two years later to embark on another gigantic project: *The Towering Inferno* (1974). Abbott started off by making tests on a model composed of a metal structure and ten windows, each six inches (fifteen centimeters) high. Flowers and Fred Kramer helped by developing the pyrotechnical effects. Behind each window was placed an eight-inch-deep (twenty-centimeter) metal box, its curved upper part leaning against the window in such a way as to guide the flames toward the outside. Each box was fitted with three pipes: the first released butane; the second, acetylene; and the third, compressed air. The two gas pipes were fitted with a spark generator. When set alight, butane produces a blue flame and no smoke, while the combustion of acetylene produces an orangish flame and black smoke. By manipulating the two gases, Abbott could change the color of the flames and the quantity of the smoke. He regulated the movement of the flames with a measured inflow of compressed air. Left to move naturally, the flames would have been lethargic and thus betrayed the true scale of the models. With compressed air, Abbott could perk them up. At the end of three days of testing, he developed a formula with

which he could obtain convincing flames, filming at seventy-two frames per second. With the method proven, a gigantic model of the main tower and another of the building closest to it were constructed out of metal and fitted with hundreds of inflow gas pipes and thousands of bulbs. The tallest tower reached a height of seventy feet (twenty-one meters) and was so thin that Abbott took the precaution of securing it to the floor with four cables between takes. A mirror was placed on the floor to film the tilt-up shots. Provisions for the integration of the model into shots of the background also had to be made. During the course of a month, at dusk, when the details of the buildings were enhanced by the twilight and the night lights, Abbott filmed the San Francisco urban landscape from all angles. He kept every cut of these stock shots. In order to align the perspectives of the real settings with those of the models, he would place the cut in the slot of the camera's viewfinder, in accordance with the shots chosen by director John Guillermin and by Irwin Allen. Despite this detailed preparation, a small accident occurred when Abbott and his crew opened the gas inflow valves but the spark generators did not immediately function. Gas spread throughout the model for ten seconds before the first spark struck. An

enormous explosion sent glass and metal debris flying everywhere; however, no one was hurt. Allen, thrilled with the explosion, pressed Guillermin to keep it in the film! One of the film's first special effects showed Paul Newman's helicopter flying in a circle over the city before landing on the roof of the tower. The real part of the scene was filmed from the top of a building in San Francisco with a remote-controlled model helicopter. The film's two skyscrapers were inserted into the image through the use of a traveling matte devised by Frank Van der Veer. The passing of the helicopter in front of the two buildings was achieved with stop-motion mattes designed by Rotoscope. These mattes effectively inserted the image of the model helicopter into the foreground as if it had passed in front of the two models of the towers.

The seventy-foot-tall (twenty-one-meter) model built for The Towering Inferno
Photo courtesy of Photofest

The Big One

Also in 1974, the movie *Earthquake,* under the supervision of Glen Robinson, made use of miniaturized special effects. The audience got to see the principal buildings of Los Angeles collapse during the quake, as well as a dam burst. In order that the size of the drops of water not be noticed, Robinson had about a fifty-foot-wide (sixteen-meter) model of the dam constructed, as well as a valley with houses, a freeway overpass, and trees. A drain linked to a neighboring lake and a series of pumps were used to drive an enormous mass of water against the model, which had been designed to collapse. Numerous explosive charges were triggered just as the barrage of water struck the dam, and the result was filmed at high speed by several cameras. The landscapes, devastated by the catastrophe, were the work of Albert Whitlock, one of the greatest painters on glass in the history of film. He created twenty-two panoramas, which were either mixed in with real shots or used alone in some forty different scenes. Whitlock and Robinson would each win an Oscar. *Earthquake* also made great use of the formidable new advertising gimmick Sensurround. The process entailed the placement of loudspeakers throughout a movie theater. At a given moment, the fabric on the enormous speakers would begin to vibrate with ultra-bass-frequency

Preparation for the collapse of the dam in Earthquake, *a sequence filmed with models conceived by Glen Robinson*
Photo courtesy of Universal Studios Florida

A painting by Albert Whitlock
Photo courtesy of Universal Studios Florida

This close-up reveals the "Impressionist" technique used by Whitlock. A more precise image would not create a realistic result on the big screen.

pulsations. The vibrations spread into the air and plunged down onto the audience—at the epicenter of the earthquake!

Front Projection

Rear projection had been in use since the 1930s, but more sensitive films in the 1970s revealed the dull appearance of the backgrounds. Thus, the traveling matte and front projection, which resulted from work that Walter Thorner had embarked on in 1932, came to be preferred. The construction he devised was rather complex. First he placed a concave mirror across from a mounted camera in such a way as to throw back the projected image directly into the lens of the camera. This system could function only if the point of origin of the projection was the same as that of the camera—which is impossible. To resolve this problem, Thorner placed a semitransparent mirror in front of the camera at a forty-five-degree angle. A projector was placed to the right of the camera, also at a forty-five-degree angle to the mirror. While the projector was sending an image onto the semitransparent mirror, the image was projected in the direction of the concave mirror, reflected back toward the camera while passing the semitransparent mirror, and imprinted on the film. An actor standing between the mirror and the camera served as his own matte and appeared to be inserted into the frame.

Unfortunately, manufacturing a large concave mirror demanded an enormous investment, and no studio offered to finance it.

The Magic of Scotchlite

In the 1940s, the 3M Corporation registered the patent for a reflective material that was covered in thousands of tiny glass beads: Scotchlite. In 1951, Philip V. Palmquist, Dr. Herbert Meyer, and Charles Staffell used the material to make the screen for their new front-projection device. In a system that linked a projector, a camera, and a semitransparent mirror, the Scotchlite reflected 99 percent of the light that was pro-

The Zoptic front projection system created by Zoran Perisic enabled Superman to fly.
Photo courtesy of Photofest

came up with a solution. The Scotchlite was cut into triangular "tiles," each side in the shape of an S. These were interposed like a mosaic and then glued onto a Dacron cloth and covered with a film of Mylar. This presented a large surface furrowed with curved lines that, differing from straight lines, were undetectable by the human eye.

"You'll believe a man can fly"

In July 1978, engineer Zoran Perisic registered the Zoptic process. This system enabled the synchronization of the movements of two zooms, one mounted on a camera, the other on the projector used for front projection. This system would be put to use during the filming of *Superman* (1978). Actor Christopher Reeve was suspended before a Scotchlite screen while the camera zoom was focused to shoot at a wide angle. The zoom on the projector was then also set to project a wide-angle image on the screen. While Perisic zoomed in on the actor, who would become enlarged in the frame, the zoom on the projector, in sync, reduced the size of the image projected behind it. This gave the audience the impression that Superman was moving in front while the landscape behind him remained the same size. Perisic was awarded the Oscar for his invention.

jected onto it. If the equipment were not placed directly in front of the screen, the brightness would not be noticeably diminished, thus greatly facilitating the direction of the actors and changes in the framing. This invention was awarded an Oscar in 1968.

Screen Puzzles

Scotchlite is fragile, however; the slightest scratch leaves a mark. If a large screen were fashioned out of horizontal bands, the lines would be visible. In the 1980s, Apogee, John Dykstra's special effects shop,

Introvision

In 1981, Peter Hyams put the system of front projection to new use when he directed his space western *Outland*. The Introvision process, invented by magician John Eppolito, entailed a double front projection, one onto a giant screen, the other onto a small one. A system of mattes and counter-mattes made it possible to adjust the parts of the frame behind which the actors could disappear. Take the example of a model of a space station with a door and a gangway. First it would be photographed and developed as large-scale slides. The definition and the bright-ness of a projected slide are far superior to those of 35-millimeter film, and therefore it can sustain a minor loss of definition when reshot. Eppolito made a matte that corresponded to the part of the miniature scenery behind which the actor would disap-pear—for example, the wall situ-ated to the left of the miniature door. Using his double projection system, he would re-imprint the image of the model over this matte. The actor could give the impression of emerging from the left wall to appear in the frame of the door and then, through the classic front projection method, exit the miniature building and walk down the gangway. Used during the 1980s, Introvision became obsolete with the advent of digital effects.

An image from the movie Outland, *made with the Introvision process*
Photo courtesy of Introvision

Backstage at Industrial Light & Magic

In 1977, the special effects of *Stars Wars* turned the American film industry on its head. The film's unpredicted success proved to the big stu-dios that innovative special effects would bring audiences into the theaters.

INTERVIEW

JOHN DYKSTRA

John Dykstra founded Industrial Light & Magic (ILM), George Lucas's special effects studio. The winner of an Oscar for best special effects (*Star Wars*) and another for technical achievement, awarded for the creation of a system that ILM developed whereby the camera is steered by computer, Dykstra has gone on to lead an illustrious solo

John Dykstra at Sony Imageworks, during postproduction on Spider-Man
Photo courtesy of Columbia Pictures

career, notably responsible for the special effects of the *Spider-Man* movies.

How did you come up with the idea for a camera whose movements were controlled by computer, for filming the battle scenes between the spaceships in "Star Wars" (1977)?

John Dykstra: To start, I had worked for the University of California at Berkeley on a project for the National Science Foundation that consisted of getting a camera to move by a computer-controlled system. It was one of the first research projects in motion-control technology. All the elements of the system had to be piloted at the same time, and the interface between the motor that moved the camera mount on all its axes and the motor that moved the mount itself along the dolly tracks had to be perfect. Everything had to be controlled to a hundredth of a millimeter. We had to control the lenses when changing the focus during a shot, the forward and reverse movement of the film, to the near image, in the camera, etc. Our PDP 11 computer, which had the power of today's pocket calculators, filled an entire room! This research helped us later when I was developing the system for *Star Wars*. Al Miller made the microprocessors that simultaneously recorded the data of each motor in the ILM system. We devised a new method of working and the equipment with which one could quickly film hundreds of shots.

The camera nicknamed Dykstraflex by the special effects team of Star Wars, *in honor of its inventor*

Do you consider your work on "Stars Wars" revolutionary?

John Dykstra: No. We were a bunch of guys working in a garage! When I explained to George Lucas how I intended to create the images in *Star Wars*, I described to him equipment that functioned because of a combination of six different techniques. If even one of these elements had broken down, we wouldn't have been able to release the film on time!

Today, ILM is a highly organized studio that employs hundreds of people. What was it like when you created it?

John Dykstra: I gathered together a team of friends with the necessary abilities to create special effects, but who had no experience in film, with neither the habits nor the customs of the big studios. There was a sandal maker, a guy who worked in a hospital laboratory, a social worker, another guy who worked in a pizzeria, a metalworker. . . . Not a single one of them was an "expert" in the field of special effects, which enabled them to use original approaches to solve the problems that arose. We spent more than a year building the equipment that was used to film the special effects in *Star Wars*. The heads of the studio were afraid that we were in the process of depleting their budget. We couldn't show them the smallest finished effect, while the costs were still mounting. They would drop in, in the middle of the day. As our hangar was in the San Fernando Valley, where the heat was incredible, some of us would be in a little swimming pool filled with cold water. It was the only way to cool off after spending hours in the overheated hangar, without air conditioning. They quickly named the place the "country club" because of the pool! Of course, you wouldn't see them

John Dykstra and his team filming a shot from Clint Eastwood's Firefox (1982) in the parking lot of Apogee. In this scene, the prototype airplane comes to a halt just at the edge of an ice cliff.
Photo courtesy of Apogee

coming at three in the morning, when you could finally film with the projectors going without the temperature reaching 120°F (50°C) on the set! These kinds of things ended up in misunderstandings.

You have seen computers turn special effects techniques upside down.

John Dykstra: First you make use of it for experimental films. When I started working for Douglas Trumbull, I discovered one of the first high-resolution video systems. It was a black-and-white video camera whose very minute scanning took an insane time to compose an image on the screen. It was controlled by a UNIVAC computer, which managed only the simplest binary functions. This was prehistoric times for computers! Later, when we used computers to create virtual

images, we used the same procedures as those of motion control. First we established the position of the camera in the created virtual universe inside the computer. Then we determined the movement of the camera and the number of frames during this movement, and we animated the objects filmed during the scene. The great progress that occurred since the time of *Star Wars* is the capacity to create the surfaces of realistic objects in high-definition computer-generated images (CGI). To create a 3-D image of a glass of water is not hard. The difficulty exists in imitating the subtle details that lend a real aspect to an object: the little imperfections in the material; the curvature of the surface of the water where it makes contact with the inside of the glass. At one time, our job consisted of telling the director what he couldn't do. Today, everything is possible. Our role consists of helping them tell their story in the best way possible using the techniques that are available to us.

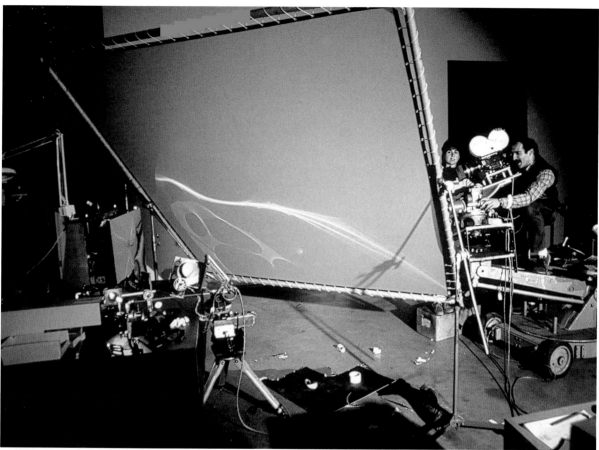

John Dykstra founded the firm Apogee to take control of the creation of special effects for productions such as Tobe Hooper's Lifeforce (1985). Here, a laser is bent by passing through a glass lens with irregular contours and hitting a translucent screen. The camera filmed the projections that evolve when the lens is moved. These effects were then inserted into real shots.

INTERVIEW

Phil Tippett

Phil Tippett is the worthy heir to Willis O'Brien and Ray Harry-hausen, who inspired him during the years he spent at ILM before founding his own studio. He made a remarkable transition from traditional techniques to virtual images, contributing to the special effects of *Jurassic Park, Starship Troopers, Blade II,* and *Hellboy.*

Phil Tippett, Peter Konig, and the creatures from the comedy Evolution
Photo courtesy of Columbia Pictures

How did you come to work on "Star Wars"?

Phil Tippett: Fortuitously. The English makeup artist Stuart Freeborn got sick during the filming in London. George Lucas couldn't film all the scenes with the extraterrestrials. Dennis Muren suggested he call Jon Berg, Laine Liska, Doug Beswick, and me, as well as Rick Baker and his assistant Rob Bottin. We developed the masks and costumes using Ron Cobb's sketches. We wore the

masks while George Lucas and Carroll Ballard filmed the cut-in shots of the bar sequence. George learned that we were animators when he discovered our studio, and he hired us to animate the holograph chess game sequence. Jon and I made several models more than George had selected in our studio. We filmed that scene in two nights in a corner of ILM. We finished it during the wrap party, while everyone was drinking and having fun!

The Snow Walkers in The Empire Strikes Back *were miniatures animated by stop-motion.* Photo courtesy of Photofest

What was the atmosphere at ILM during those first years?

Phil Tippett: George was in charge of everything when ILM was located in Los Angeles. He would meet with people before hiring them and followed the entire conception and realization of the special effects. Then I was one of the fifteen people who moved from Los Angeles to organize the work in the new premises in Marin County, near San Francisco. George was thirty-five years old, and he didn't want

to reproduce the bureaucratic structures of the large studios. We formed a tight-knit team. Our special effects sequences were developed in a lab in Washington and wouldn't arrive in San Francisco until between noon and 4 P.M. We wouldn't start working again until after we had seen them, and we would get home between three and four in the morning. We worked six or seven days a week with no complaints, because we had the chance to take part in large-budget films, seen by millions of people.

How did you animate the quadruped vehicles in "The Empire Strikes Back" (1980)?

Phil Tippett: Jon Berg collaborated with Joe Johnston developing the mechanical parts of the armatures of the Snow Walkers. The movements of the head and legs were transmitted to gearwheels and pistons on the carcass of the vehicle. The Walkers were large, rather heavy models. The action had to be minutely controlled to obtain the slow movement. It was difficult to measure them with a gauge, an instrument that Willis O'Brien was the first to use in the 1920s. Originally, the surface gauge was used by metalworkers. It looks like a pencil set on top of an articulated pedestal. Imagine you were animating a character. You would set the point of the gauge at the tip of the character's nose to establish a reference point for it in the space. Then you would remove the instrument and animate the character. You put the gauge back in the same spot, and you measure precisely the movement of the character's head. The gauge allows you to soften the movements by progressively diminishing the amplitude of each phase of the animation of the character. It also prevented some jerking. When animating an eye, you could do it without having to move the head down and then up on the next frame, which produces a visibly shaky image. The longer and more complex the character's body, the more you use gauges. This tool was used a lot before video monitoring appeared, which lets you view what you're animating in stop-motion.

You contributed to developing the Go-Motion system. How did you use it to animate the dragon in "Dragonslayer" (1981)?

Phil Tippett: The Go-Motion system was an extension of the one we developed for *The Empire Strikes Back*. We attached the snow kangaroos, the Tauntauns, onto a computer-controlled motorized dolly. We first animated the character, and the system moved it one millimeter while the camera's shutter stayed open. We got a soft-focus effect that made the lateral movement fluid and lessened any jerking due to the stop-motion animation. The purpose of Go-Motion was to generate a soft-focus effect on all fast movements, whatever their axes. Jon Berg, Stuart Ziff, Dennis Muren, and I came up with a platform outfitted with stepper motors that could animate a rod marionette. Each mount could move on the x-axis, y-axis, and z-axis, and also rotate completely in both directions. It was necessary to use as many mounts as there were principal parts in the character's body. In the case of the dragon, there was a mount for the body, a mount for each of the four legs, and, for some actions, there was one for the head and another for the tail. We also needed a track to be able to move the character. We made the first tests of the pro-

The team from Dragonslayer *poses behind the Go-Motion system, which enabled the blurry effects during the monster's fast movements.*

gramming on an Apple II computer. Gary Leo had created a program that let us arrange each gesture. The results were sometimes disconcerting. When the dragon moved forward, we had to take into account that its feet had to give the impression of remaining planted on the ground during the walking cycle, before rising up. As the platform moved forward along the track, advancing the character, the feet had to be programmed "to the ground" so they would move backward. These movements seemed wrong when you saw the motorized mounts in action, whereas they were perfectly logical! The process prefigured the programming of characters in computer-generated images. First you had to conceive of a global

The remarkably realistic-looking dragon in Dragonslayer   Photo courtesy of Photofest

animation, then divide each movement into a long series of movements, as if you were writing the musical score for a symphonic work. The program also allowed us to accelerate or slow down the programmed move-ments. As the motorized mounts automatically controlled 60 to 80 percent of the movements, we had the possibility of animating many versions of the same shot, varying the animations by hand. It was incredibly slow. For *Dragonslayer,* I had to animate and program the movements twelve to fifteen hours a day, seven days a week, over three months. And this work appeared in only a few shots!

This monoclonius is the hero of the superb short film Prehistoric Beast *(1984), directed by Phil Tippett.*   Photo © 1984 Tippett Studio

Phil Tippett reconstructed the life of the prehistoric animals in the documentary Dinosaur! *(1985). The skin of the dinosaurs, made in part with impressions from lizard skin, consisted of foam rubber attached to a musculature sculpted by Randy Dutra. This permitted the realistic details of the scales and the folds of the skin, which could be shot in very tight close-ups. This remarkable work received an Emmy Award.*
Photo © 1984 Tippett Studios

The animation sequences in "RoboCop"(1987) used the process invented by Ray Harryhausen. What modifications did you apply to his system?

Phil Tippett: Harry Walton discovered that developing less-contrasted images of the background allowed for compensation for the excess of contrast that we got when the images were refilmed in a rear projection onto a screen. Thus, we limited the differences in aspect between the backgrounds and the images of the animated models in the foreground. The backgrounds were filmed in the VistaVision format (35 millimeter and horizontally

Phil Tippett and the animation models of RoboCop

framed on eight sprocket holes) in order to get an image half as grainy. We achieved these significant improvements although we had a small budget to produce fifty special effects shots in three months. Two crews worked in parallel. When we filmed *RoboCop 2,* we noticed that the tightest framing on the characters gave us more opportunities to create soft-focus effects when following the movements of action scenes.

The animation of the robot ED 209 in front of a rear projection screen, as it appeared in the movie RoboCop
Photo © 1987 Tippett Studios

"Jurassic Park" (1993) marked a decisive turning point in your career. How did you live through that experience?

Phil Tippett: That film was an extremely traumatic experience for me. In the beginning, the dinosaurs were to be filmed in two ways: Stan Winston's animatronic characters in close-up and medium shot, while the models animated in stop-motion were to be in all the wide-angle shots. When Steven Spielberg called me, he had decided to film the majority of the shots with the life-size dinosaurs. One year later, it turned out that the animatronics weren't developed enough

for the dinosaurs to walk or run. We tested different ways to get these effects: with rod puppets; with models animated in stop-motion. We thought of constructing many Go-Motion units to animate the raptors, the T. rex, and the other dinos. At the same time, Dennis Muren and his crew worked at ILM on the sequence of the herd of gallimimus. They tried to create them through computer generation, as that was the only imaginable method to depict hundreds of animals running in a wide-angle shot. Now, the more the conception of the scene progressed, the more the frame closed in on the animals. And finally, they had to realize that their computer-generated dinosaurs came out well in wide angle. When Steven saw that, he realized that it was the technological innovation that he needed. He made the very important decision on the spot, without hesitation, but it had its consequences. When I heard the news, I was sick with pneumonia and incommunicado for several weeks!

T. rex, the human characters, and the jeep used for filming the preparatory animations for Jurassic Park

Was it Spielberg who gave you the bad news?

Phil Tippett: No! Dennis Muren, who is a friend, brought me up-to-date. We were depressed at the same time. He, because he had to achieve an enormous technical feat, and I, because I thought I was finished! At the same time, we were both filming test sequences using traditional stop-motion animation in order to develop the body movements of the dinosaurs. While the first computer-generated images of the dinosaurs were already impressive, the stop-motion sequences worked better to highlight their personality. Steven appreciated this. He wanted to use the expertise of the stop-motion animators who knew how to endow the characters with a mass, with a weight, while some of the early computer-generated characters looked as if they were floating above the ground. It

1993 Universal Studios / Amblin Productions
Photo provided courtesy of Industrial Light & Magic

The insertion of a computer-generated T. rex into the real shots of Jurassic Park *was done by ILM.* Photo courtesy of SGI

Phil Tippett and the Digital Input Device (DID), thanks to which the expertise of traditional animators could be applied to the computer-generated dinosaurs in Jurassic Park

was important to utilize this knowledge when depicting the movement of a three-ton T. rex! When the 3-D animators controlled the movements of a character, they use functions called "F-curves," each of which corresponds to the outline of a movement and the space in which the animator can work. At the time of *Jurassic Park,* these curves were managed mathematically. Craig Hayes had performed tests using a rudimentary system that enabled the phase-by-phase recording of the animation of an armature and the transmission of this data into a computer to animate computer-generated characters. Craig, my wife, and my partner Jules Roman presented the results of these tests to ILM and proposed to them dividing up the animations. Dennis Muren accepted the proposal and we made the first DID (Digital Input Device), which allowed us to create our first

3-D animations using traditional stop-motion animation methods. When we brought our data to ILM, the people in charge of animation programs were convinced that it wouldn't work because the famous F-curves were irregular. But when the characters moved because of this method, their movements appeared spontaneous, visceral. The mathematical perfection of the first computer animations gave an artificial side to ILM's first computer-generated images.

The hordes of giant insects in "Starship Troopers" (1997) were an animation tour de force. How did you create them?

Phil Tippett: We used a program that controlled the movement of each individual in the horde. Doug Abs created a program that could eliminate collisions between 3-D characters, because

Draco, the hero of Dragonheart, *has a head adorned with dozen of horns, prominent scales, and detailed claws. He is so much more complex than the dinosaurs in* Jurassic Park *that the computer artists at ILM had to devise more powerful programs in order to be able to represent him in synthesized images.*

"I tried to get closer to the facial musculature of gorillas when conceiving the design for the face," explained Tippett, "whereas the first designs by ILM were based on the heads of crocodiles. In my opinion, it would be impossible to show a crocodile speaking with Sean Connery's voice!"
Photo © 1995 Tippett Studios

they pass quickly through one another if you're not careful! The more insects you show in a frame, the more you run the risk of many of them moving in perfect synchronization and revealing the artifice of the programming. Each cycle of a galloping horse is slightly different than the others. Different from a real animal, a 3-D character always executes the same cycle of movements. To avoid synchronized cycles in the horde scenes, we projected a loop of the frames and assigned three or four people to scrutinize them, isolate the duplicated movements, remove those char-acters, and replace them with others moving to a different rhythm. This process took several weeks for each shot.

How were the interactions between the soldiers and the insects regulated?

Phil Tippett: We made a storyboard of each fight scene with Paul Verhoeven and Jack Mogiazza. We rehearsed the precise camera movements with the actors, the cameraman, and Paul Verhoeven. I carried a long stick with a yellow ball at the end to indicate to the actors, the extras, and the cameraman where the level of the heads of the insects would be. We rehearsed the scene five or six times, faster and faster, and then filmed the scene without me and the stick appearing in the frame. It took eight or ten takes to get a good one.

What are your memories of doing the special effects in the comedy "Evolution" (2000)?

Phil Tippett: This film is characteristic of a growing trend. Its preproduction, production, and postproduction took place

Previous page and above: *The giant insects in* Starship Troopers, *a new feat from Phil Tippett's studio* Photo courtesy of Photofest

simultaneously. We were still in the process of conceiving the characters when the filming started, and we animated some scenes before they were done! These are very difficult working conditions, but as the producers insist that, all the same, we manage to provide them with what they want, they are convinced that we can accomplish these feats faster and with less money than before!

How did you accomplish the spectacular fights in "Blade II" (2002) and "Hellboy" (2003)?

Phil Tippett: We scanned Wesley Snipes, and from this inert 3-D image we created an articulated model with a musculature and skin, so that the clothes would move independently from the body. This work was developed by Craig Hayes and Blair Clarke, in collaboration with Guillermo Del Toro, with whom we then worked on

the battles in *Hellboy*. Wesley Snipes's positions were animated manually, because the motion-capture systems don't allow you to get dynamic enough movements for superhuman battles. We often made use of soft-focus rapid pans to substitute the 3-D clones for actors. We used the same techniques to show *Hellboy,* who was played by Ron Perlman, fighting with creatures made from computer-generated images.

The Innovations of ILM

Throughout the 1980s, the teams at ILM continued to develop technical innovations. The ghosts that leave the Ark of the Covenant in *Raiders of the Lost Ark* (1981) are depicted by rod puppets dressed in tattered white fabric and manipulated in

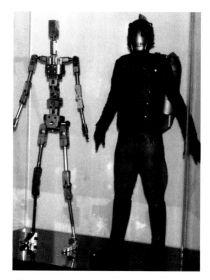

The armature and foam rubber body of the miniature likeness in Rocketeer *(1991)*

an aquarium. This idea by Richard Edlund made the phantoms' shrouds float as if they were weightless. These images were then inserted into real ones. An efficient process, it would be used again in *Poltergeist* (1982). In addition, one of the Nazis had to melt in a few seconds during the final scene of *Raiders*. Chris Walas first made a mold of actor Ronald Lacey's head. He used

a plastic cranium in which he set glass eyes. Lacey's copy was made with a multilayered colored gel mold. The head was topped with a hat and given a pair of glasses. Hot-air pistols were aimed at the head while the camera recorded at one frame per second. When this shot was projected at twenty-four frames per second, it showed the almost instantaneous liquidation of the Nazi. The firestorm that came from the Ark, sweeping away the units of German troops, was done in a live shot. A miniature replica of the set was suspended upside down and inclined, so that its highest point was positioned in front of the camera. Edlund placed a gas burner at the back of the set. As the ignited gas was lighter than air, it flattened itself to the "ceiling" (which was the floor of the inverted model) and spread upward toward the camera. Repeated in the inverse, this scene depicted a river of fire creeping across the floor.

In *Return of the Jedi* (1983), ILM devised a shot for a space battle of unimaginable complexity: three hundred different elements—spaceships, laser guns, explosions, stars—were combined using an optical printer. For a long time, this tour de force remained unequaled. In 1984, Dennis Muren confronted a thorny problem during the preparation for *Indiana Jones and the Temple of Doom:*

The animated figure of the demon in Golden Child

a major sequence of the film shows the heroes racing in a tipcart through the maze of a mine, chased by their enemies. Spielberg wanted the camera to follow the mining carts, which entailed constructing miniature tunnels large enough for the camera to pass through. A quick calculation revealed that the cost of manufacturing such a model would be prohibitive. Muren then got the idea of transforming the body of a motorized still camera into a mini-film camera linked to two small magazines of 35-millimeter film. The reduced volume of this shooting equipment meant that a smaller model could be made. The carts moved along toy train tracks, the largest gauge that could be found. Remote-controlled articulated puppets were set in the carts

during the insane race, while the camera, mounted on a flat truck, followed, filming them. In 1986, Eddie Murphy fought a stop-motion animated winged demon in *Golden Child*. Horizontal and vertical panoramic shots accompanied the action. The Tondreau system, used for the first time there, was a variation of Go-Motion. Eddie Murphy first pretended to fight alone, without the creature. Then developed shots were placed in a 35-millimeter camera on a computer-controlled

mount across from a blank screen. Using a light source, an architectural point of reference was defined, serving as the line of sight, and at the first projection, a cross was delineated on the screen. During projection of the following frames, the motorized camera mount was moved to relocate the point of reference onto the cross. With controlled motion, the camera movements were compensated for and then recorded on computer. They were then reproduced during the animation of

The battles in Return of the Jedi *were the most complex ever done with an optical printer. One of the composite shots was made with a combination of three hundred elements.*
Photo courtesy of Photofest

the demon, which could be inserted into the real footage, to look as if the creature truly walked on the set and fought Eddie Murphy.

INTERVIEW

JOE VISKOCIL

Pyrotechnician, Specialist in Exploding Miniatures

At the beginning of your career, you made the Death Star explode in "Star Wars."

Joe Viskocil: I filmed many tests of the pyrotechnical special effects for *Star Wars*. I developed the special effect of explosions in the weightlessness of a small room. The camera was fixed pointing up, in a completely vertical position, and we filmed an explosive charge attached to the end of an electric cable that triggered the detonation. The charge was placed in a black case and filmed on a black background. When the explosion occurred, the sparks cascaded down, because of gravity, but with the camera pointed upward, it looked like a ball of sparks. The illuminated projectiles flew in all directions, melting toward the camera lens, which was protected by a glass plate. You couldn't see the smoke that rose toward the ceiling. When projected, since the sparks didn't fall to the bottom of the frame, the impression was that the explosion occurred in weightlessness. I spent time finding the right mixture of

Joe Viskocil prepares a U.S. military jet for impact in a scene in Independence Day.
Photo courtesy of Joe Viskocil

components to create the explosion. In the final shot, I combined a gas explosion with an explosion of black powder mixed with a titanium powder, which produced very bright sparks. I

realized that the softer the explosion, the longer it would generate effects useful to the shot. On the other hand, the more you surround a charge in a thick, tight case, the faster the explosion.

The explosion of the Death Star in Star Wars *was filmed vertically with the camera pointed in the air; protected by a pane of glass set on trestles, it captured the sparks flying toward it.*
Photo courtesy of Joe Viskocil

Joe Viskocil inserts an explosive charge in one of the X-wing spaceships in Star Wars. Photo courtesy of Joe Viskocil

What kind of camera did you use to film your very high-speed explosions?

Joe Viskocil: Most of the time, we used a Photosonics camera that could shoot up to 360 frames per second. I could create many explosions, but the final result always depended on the combination of a good chemical formula and a good shooting speed. I chose these parameters depending upon the size of the model, the materials that I chose to make it with, the distance of the camera, and the lens that I used. I could create an explosion that was blue or green, with brilliant sparks or completely devoid of sparks. But the base is always the black powder or a special powder that doesn't produce smoke.

You made a model of a tanker truck explode in "The Terminator" (1984).

Joe Viskocil: This model measured twenty inches (fifty centimeters) high and ten feet (almost three meters) long. We filmed this scene twice. Since the character played by Michael Biehn placed an explosive behind the truck, I put forty-three different charges in the model to animate the explosion from the back to the front of the vehicle.

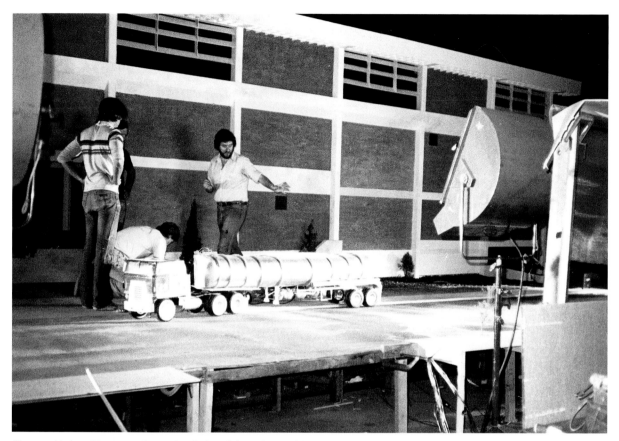

Above and below: *The preparation and explosion of the tanker truck in* The Terminator   Photos courtesy of Joe Viskocil

How do you set about filming an underwater explosion like the one of the submarine in "The Abyss" (1989)?

Joe Viskocil: Explosions conducted underwater are very special. I used black powder, but also a lot of flashbulbs to extend the duration and the glow of the explosion. The model of the first submarine destroyed at the beginning of the movie was filmed in a reservoir in Los Angeles. The problem was to reduce the size of the air bubbles and not give away the scale of the model. I did tests with effervescent pills and with champagne, but in the final analysis, it was beer that worked the best. So I put a container filled with beer inside the model, which burst during the explosion. When you see the sequence, the size of the bubbles helps make the scene very realistic. I often buy strange props. I frequently need receptacles for exploding small amounts of gasoline.

The best solution is to fill up condoms, because they are so thin that they go up immediately. The explosion disperses the gasoline, creating a beautiful ball of fire. So I have to send an assistant out to buy five or six dozen condoms! He'll come back all red and embarrassed.

How did you create the nuclear explosion in "Terminator 2" (1991)?

Joe Viskocil: I worked with a team from 4-Ward Productions, directed by Bob Skotak. That sequence was made with a number of air guns and "pre-broken" models that could implode on command, giving the impression that a nuclear cloud was sweeping through the city. You could see buses and cars just disappearing.

The sequence of the destruction of the bridge in "True Lies" (1994) is shockingly real.

Joe Viskocil: That's my favorite sequence. I did all the tests in Los Angeles, in collaboration with Stetson Services, Mark Stetson's company. We studied all kinds of materials before choosing what would be used to build the model. They built sections of the bridge and we filmed the destruction at various speeds, with different materials, to determine exactly what we

Above and opposite: *Assembling the enormous model bridge in* True Lies, *and the explosion triggered by the reduced-size model van* Photos courtesy of Joe Viskocil

needed. The elements of the bridge were erected, and then sent to Florida. We constructed the miniature bridge there, installed it in the water, and exploded it before Jim [Cameron]'s eyes, who wouldn't have missed it for anything in the world. In this scene, shot at 120 frames per second, the explosions took place ahead of and behind the truck as it was crossing the bridge. The trajectory of the miniature vehicle had to be perfectly synchronized with the explosions. And that was what activated the electrical contacts working below to get the desired effect. I had a safety button in

my hand to save the model if the truck deviated from its course.

How did you develop the special effects of the "wall of fire" and the destruction of the White House in "Independence Day" (1996)?

Joe Viskocil: The "wall of fire" is the applied inverse of the principle used in the explosion of the Death Star. In this case, it was the camera that was mounted high up, shooting downward. The model of the street was set vertically, at a ninety-degree angle. When I set

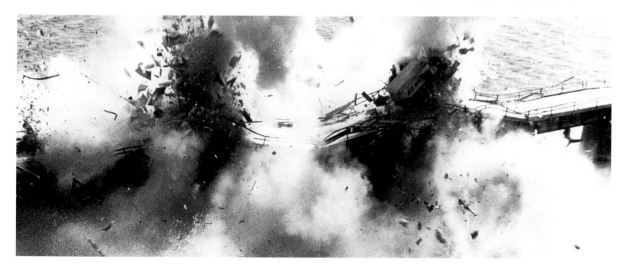

off the fire at its base, the flames spread toward the center of the street, as in a chimney, toward the camera. We used propane gas and benzil peroxide to create the magnificent flames. It was these test shots that convinced Fox to produce the film. It was a fabulous project for me—almost every day, I had a famous monument to destroy! The White House had to be constructed in plaster. As always, I shot a test using a section of the model that had been built expressly for this purpose. I decided to work with Primacord, a fuse through which the detonation passes at a speed of twenty-two thousand feet (sixty-seven hundred meters) per second. This produced no flames, no smoke, no sparks. But the destruction was effective. If the Primacord was attached high up, part of the model would be propelled upward and the debris would fly laterally, toward the camera. If it were attached toward the bottom of the model, just in from the walls, the building would collapse downward, as if it were caving in on itself. The model makers had to build three models of the White House to film this scene, but the first shot was good.

What were the special pieces of equipment that you used to precisely trigger each explosion, while you were setting off dozens?

Filming the plane flying low through a canyon in the chase scene of Independence Day. *The model glided along a cable, using a system devised by the Lydecker brothers.*
Photo courtesy of Joe Viskocil

Setting up the model of the White House Photo courtesy of Joe Viskocil

The destruction of the White House. This shot, conceived by Joe Viskocil, is one of the most famous visual effects images in the history of film. Photo courtesy of Joe Viskocil

Joe Viskocil checks the positioning of the black-and-yellow Primacord, a very powerful explosive, which will split apart the facade of the model at lightning speed.
Photo courtesy of Joe Viskocil

Joe Viskocil: I devised a programmable computer console that controlled twenty-four circuits. The intervals between each explosion could vary from 1,000th of a second to an hour. I would film a test with this console and flashbulbs, to previsualize what would produce the development of the explosion. This allowed me to fine-tune what I wanted to obtain, simply by watching this test film in stop-motion. I would correct the triggering of a 500th-of-a-second charge if it would contribute to the final impact.

INTERVIEW

MARTIN BOWER

In 1979, Ridley Scott conceived and directed one of the most oppressive universes in the history of film: the one in *Alien*. He called upon the Swiss painter H. R. Giger to bring the film's creature to life and to design the wreckage of the extraterrestrial spaceship. Model makerr Martin Bower took part in the creation of the miniatures. He describes the back-

The head of the monster in Alien, *minus its translucent dome; the human shape of the skull can be seen.* Photo © Martin Bower

The storyboard for Alien, *drawn by Ridley Scott*
Photo courtesy of Twentieth Century-Fox

The mechanisms of the Alien's head being made. The head's mechanical jaw, used during the filming of close-ups, was conceived and made by Carlo Rambaldi and Isidoro Raponi.
Photo © Martin Bower

The Alien finished off
Photo courtesy of Twentieth Century-Fox

Peter Voysey modeled the extraterrestrial spaceship derelict on the paintings of Hans Rudi Giger. Photo © Martin Bower

stage goings-on of this legendary film.

How did Giger work?

Martin Bower: I rubbed shoulders with him at the Bray studios, where the scenes with the models were filmed. Giger arrived in the morning, always dressed in black, and, without saying a word, sat down next to me at the same workbench and, with an airbrush, drew some of the concepts. The costumes for *Alien* were made from these drawings at the Shepperton studios by Peter Voysey, Patti Rodgers, and Shirley Denney. They were composed of many layers of latex and a head with mechanical jaws. Bolaji Badejo, an actor of Masai heritage, who was very thin and more than six feet six inches (two meters) tall, wore the costume. Giger worked at a phenomenal pace. I saw him paint a view of a section of the extraterrestrial spaceship wreckage in a few hours. He cut out cardboard mattes that he would put on his drawing to get clean edges. He worked without measuring, with striking dexterity. The model of the extraterrestrial spaceship wreckage was sculpted out of blocks of polystyrene by Peter Voysey, who also sculpted the extraterrestrial pilot known as the Space Jockey. He covered this plasteline form and its small details in plastic that he stuck into the material to get the identical

The Space Jockey, imagined by Giger and sculpted by Peter Voysey   Photo © Martin Bower

organic shapes that Giger had drawn, which were also painted with an airbrush.

How did you create the film's spaceship refinery?

Martin Bower: Brian Johnson contacted me regarding this film, but he was there only a short time. He had to quit the project to go supervise the special effects for *The Empire Strikes Back*. It was Nick Alder who filmed most of the special effects shots. The base of the spaceship had been built by the studio carpenters, headed by Ron Hone. We built the tower structures with the plastic rods that are on the square sector, and which are covered in detailed plates. At the beginning of the film, Ridley Scott wanted the top of the spaceship to be decorated with spires like a cathedral's. When he came to see us, he looked at what we had done, and then grabbed a chisel and a hammer to make them go flying! I remember my colleague Bill Pearson and I were horrified watching pieces of the model flying in all directions.

You were also asked to put some of the models in motion, like the "Nostromo" shuttle.

Martin Bower: Ridley wanted the shuttle to be pushed outside of the main spaceship by an arm with a claw in the shape of a

The space refinery, before Ridley Scott sent its turrets flying . . . with the help of a hammer and chisel
Photo © Martin Bower

A widened section of the Nostromo, *made so a video monitor could be inserted behind the porthole. Images of Sigourney Weaver were projected onto the screen to give the impression of a human presence in the spaceship.*
Photo © Martin Bower

hand. The shuttle was attached to an elevator carriage. The base of the telescopic arm was fixed to an immovable part of the main spaceship. The other end was simply placed on the top of the shuttle. Nick Alder hid the elevator carriage with black velvet. When the carriage moved, it went alongside the model of the spaceship while deploying the arm. Afterward, he lowered the fork of the carriage to give the impression that the shuttle had fallen off the stowage arm. The effect of the release of smoke from the reactors was done with pressurized Freon.

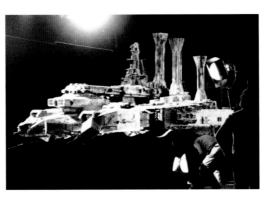

Filming the separation of the shuttle Nostromo *from the rest of the refinery*
Photo © Martin Bower

The model of the relief spaceship Narcissus
Photo © Martin Bower

Why did you install a television monitor into the wide part of the "Nostromo"?

Martin Bower: Nick Alder got the idea to film a body double of Sigourney Weaver at one end of the set on video. We built a very wide section of the front of the *Nostromo* to put this video monitor behind a twelve-inch (thirty-centimeter) window. We used the same effect for a scene where Sigourney is seen entering the evacuation cap-sule, at the end of the film. That time, we made a "squashed" version at the point of the capsule, which looked normal when viewed from in front. Nick synchronized the timing of the shutter of his camera to the movement of the video images on the monitor to prevent anyone from seeing bars crossing the screen. The result was perfect. I think it was the first time that this very simple technique was used to insert an actor into a model.

The Narcissus *emerges from under the refinery.*
Photo © Martin Bower

INTERVIEW

GENE RIZZARDI

Eugene P. Rizzardi is a model effects supervisor who has worked on many feature films such as *Apollo 13, Titanic, Mission: Impossible, Alien Resurrection,* and *Galaxy Quest,* as well as television series such as *V* and *Star Trek: The Next Generation.* He reveals to us the secrets of his art, the imitation of reality on a reduced scale.

How do you choose the material that you use to build a model?

Gene Rizzardi: According to how the model will be used. If you build a house for a simple sequence, the foundation will be constructed in wood. If you want to keep the house in perfect condition for a long time, then you would construct it in metal. You would use Plexiglas for the windowpanes and resin for the moldings and architectural details. If the house had to be destroyed, you would use a material that easily disintegrated, like plaster, and polyurethane or polystyrene foam. Everything depends on what the director wants and the available budget. When you have a small budget, you salvage materials lying around in the studio, recycling pieces from other models, and you simplify the work. Someone

Above and left: *Details of the extraordinary model of Park Avenue created for an advertisement*
Photos courtesy of Gene Rizzardi

once came and asked me to quickly make a tractor trailer. I recycled medium plywood and some small pieces. All I bought were wheels that corresponded to the scale of the model. If we had been asked to create a landscape, we would have twisted an iron wire fence around a big wooden board to quickly create the relief of the set. We would have gotten a smooth surface and covered it completely with newspaper and glue. The details would have been made out of papier-mâché, and we would have gotten the texture of the dusty surface by spraying it with plaster and water.

How do you make the elements of the model?

Gene Rizzardi: With carpenters' tools: a workbench, vises, saws of every size, files, sandpaper. We also use band saws, circular saws, even a lathe for working with metal and making complicated pieces, which are then molded in silicone and duplicated.

How did you build the miniatures for "Apollo 13" (1995)?

Gene Rizzardi: The liftoff scene required a model built at a scale of one-eighth the size of the rocket and the launchpad. The cone heads of the hydrogen engines were made of resin reinforced with plastic. The platform was a steel structure, covered in pieces of metal and Masonite. Takeoffs were simulated with flames and jets of steam. After each shot, the black residue had to be cleaned off

Ignition of the rocket engines in Apollo 13, *filmed with miniatures*
Photos courtesy of Gene Rizzardi

and the model sponged and repainted for the next take. It's always the effect that you want that determines the choice of materials. We approach it the same way whether we're asked to build a miniature boat that's set on the surface and floats, or has to sink straight down, simulating a shipwreck. If the model were too light and made of plastic, it would float like a cork. It would be better to construct a metal structure weighed down with lead, to stabilize the model.

The final composite of the Titanic *leaving port, an image that combines real shots of the pier and models with digital images of the sky and* ocean Photo courtesy of Gene Rizzardi

Could you explain the process of laser registration that you used to make some of the details of the bridge of the ship in "Titanic" (1997)?

Gene Rizzardi: The bridge on the real *Titanic* was made of large boards of pine. We ordered sheets of very fine pine plywood from a company in Texas, and then sent these sheets to a factory that cuts wood with a laser. The laser

first traced the contour of the relief on the surface of each board, and then it cut the groups of boards according to our outlines. These pieces could be intermeshed in one another, like pieces of a jigsaw puzzle. This allowed us to assemble the bridge very quickly. Even on a major production like *Titanic,* you still have to economize with time and money. The rest of the main model of the *Titanic* was

detailed with deck chairs, staircase banisters, buoys. The deck chairs were assigned to Greg Bryant. He took photos of a chair used during the filming. He then drew the outline in miniature, fabricated it in plastic at the reduced scale, and molded it in silicone to make the fabrications in urethane resin. The lateral metallic supports of the life-size wooden benches were very detailed. We manufactured a reproduction in

Close-up of the bridge of the model of the Titanic, *made of layers of pine cut by laser*
Photo courtesy of Gene Rizzardi

Final details of the enormous model
Photo courtesy of Gene Rizzardi

The miniature cruise ship being filmed "dry" in front of a red background, to be used as an insertion into the rest of the image, largely composed of synthesized images by Digital Domain
Photo courtesy of Gene Rizzardi

brass, made a mold in silicone, and produced a series of casts, having poured molten lead into the mold. We also made the little tugboats that towed the *Titanic* out of port. They were constructed in wood and detailed with sheets of pine plywood cut with a laser. We created the effects of wear and rust by spraying many coats of paint with an airbrush.

What was your role on "Godzilla" (1998)?

Gene Rizzardi: I was the supervisor of the construction of the miniatures. There were so many models to construct that several companies had to share the job: Cinema Production Services, Hunter Gratzner Industries, and Cinebar. They constructed the miniatures according to our specifications, brought them to us, and I then had the job of checking them, modifying them, detailing them a little if necessary, and taking care of them before and during the filming. We also salvaged miniatures created for other films. We repaired the facades, added details to the different interior levels of the buildings that didn't originally exist, and constructed other facades for buildings that were designed to collapse. These models made of wood were molded in silicone. The molds were used to produce plaster casts, which were

assembled and painted. Great quantities of debris were stored up inside the models, and they would come pouring out when the facades were made to collapse. The models were so fragile that we had to construct them on the set to avoid having to transport them. Assembling materials is always very delicate. The base was a metal structure designed to guide the collapse of the building. Steel

The vast miniature set made for Godzilla
Photo courtesy of Gene Rizzardi

mounts in the form of scissors supported the interior of the building during the preparation. When they were removed by folding them before the shot, the building no longer stood on its plaster framework and the articulated metal structure that would guide the fall. The destruction might be triggered in different ways. You could use a powerful hydraulic jack to pull the structure downward and make it implode. You could also drop a very heavy mass on the interior of the model. It would smash everything and produce an effect resembling an explosion. You could also use real pyrotechnical charges to get a very fine-tuned destruction. Generally, you construct two or three copies of these miniatures, in case the destruction doesn't come off as planned. But there are also times when we're asked for only one. We always arrive at the shoot with extra pieces, in case we're asked to film additional takes from what remains of the destroyed building. In those cases, we salvage the largest pieces of debris, assemble them as best we can, add some brand-new details to the foreground, and get a model that is already rather damaged but can be destroyed a second time. By combining the first and second takes, you get more shots and increase the duration and impact of the sequence.

You built a life-size cockpit for "Alien Resurrection" (1997).

Gene Rizzardi: Yes. The layout artists know how to work and mold all the materials, so they're adept at making life-size sets. The set designers on *Alien Resurrection* had built the structures of the set, which we loaded with technological details, small consoles, levers, and buttons. Many of these elements were army and air force surplus—airplane seats and control panels whose warning

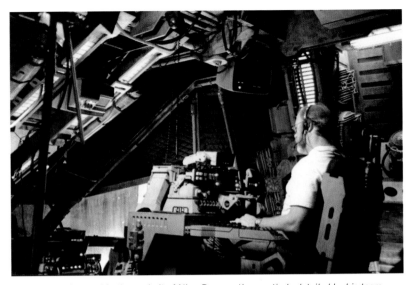

Gene Rizzardi seated in the cockpit of Alien Resurrection, *entirely detailed by his team*
Photo courtesy of Gene Rizzardi

lights we replaced with very powerful bulbs to be visible on screen. We hijacked many objects from daily life, like the racks used for drying dishes. By gluing them upside down on a wall, they became storage shelves for equipment in the spaceship's infirmary! We also transformed a woman's razor into a communicator. It's enough to modify objects that already have an odd shape to quickly create futuristic props for a science fiction movie. It's the same thing when someone asks you to make a set of a miniature living room. If you can find the elements for a model in toy stores for a television or books on a shelf, you save a lot of time. Just yesterday, I picked up a small model of an astronaut that we would use if someone asked us to build a NASA vehicle. I've assembled a great collection of

model cars and trucks on different scales. They're useful for adding props on the streets, like the ones in *Godzilla*. Unfortunately, today you can only find models of Formula 1 cars and prototypes, whereas in the sixties, there were all sorts of "normal" cars. I made molds of some of these models in order to be able to make a cast out of a single piece. We paint their windows black and place them at the back of the miniature sets, to add to the overall feel of the shot.

A miniature forest, primarily composed of plants whose shapes and textures evoke large trees Photo courtesy of Gene Rizzardi

Has the development of computer-generated images taken work away from you?

Gene Rizzardi: Oh yes! People are calling us much less often. Producers of big-budget movies know that models are always worthwhile in terms of results, manufacturing time, and cost, but most small productions think, wrongly, that you can do everything cheaply with 3-D effects. Even ILM, which claims to do everything with digital imaging, in truth uses models a tremendous amount.

When the U.S. Air Force refused to fly one of its stealth bombers for the filming of Executive Decision *(1996), Isidoro Raponi built a replica out of wood, complete with a motorized undercarriage.*
Photo courtesy of Isidoro Raponi

Isidoro Raponi is one of Hollywood's best special effects experts. After having collaborated with Carlo Rambaldi on the mechanical effects of the 1976 remake of King Kong, Close Encounters of the Third Kind, *and* Alien, *he now works alone on pyrotechnical effects, animatronics, special props, and effects scenery for dozens of big productions.*
Photo courtesy of Isidoro Raponi

INTERVIEW

ROBERT SHORT

Special Effects Supervisor

Robert Short is a multitalented creator of special effects. His work with makeup, mechanical effects, computer-generated images, and animatronic characters can be seen in such films as *Cocoon, E.T.,* and *Beetlejuice* (which won him an Oscar in 1998), and in television series such as *MacGyver* and *Star Trek: The Next Generation.*

Robert Short and Flash, whose costume he created   Photo courtesy of Robert Short

How did you create the look of the mermaid in "Splash" (1984)?

Robert Short: We first created the beauty makeup for Darryl Hannah with an eye shadow and a lipstick that was water-resistant. From a cast of her body, we then devised a tail for the mermaid that was very pliant, so she could swim easily. It was manufactured in a trans-

Darryl Hannah, the seductive mermaid in Splash, *and her translucent urethane costume*
Photo courtesy of Robert Short

parent urethane—Skinflex from BJB Enterprises—into which we incorporated an orange dye and an iridescent paint to mimic the scales of a red fish, as director Ron Howard wanted. We also prepared the filming of a single-shot scene in which Darryl walks toward a bathtub, slides into the water, and makes her mermaid tail emerge by spreading her flippers. The first part of the transformation of her legs and the appearance of the fins were achieved with prosthetics hooked up to mechanical and pneumatic systems whose cables and tubes were attached to Darryl's back with Velcro. They were concealed in her bathrobe. When she took off the robe while sitting on the edge of the bathtub, half of her back was cut off by the edge of the frame. At that precise moment,

technicians rushed over to the cables, detached the Velcro, and connected the tubes to the mechanical systems and the pneumatic pumps. Everything was controlled down to the second. We had placed a tube in the bathtub, under the water. The mermaid tail was hidden inside of it. A mechanism allowed us to get the mermaid tail out of the tube and make it appear out of the water. Unfortunately, the bathtub filled up so slowly that we had to cut the sequence during editing in order to speed it up!

You created a superb effect for "E.T." (1982): the moment when you can see the heart illuminated in the chest and beating.

Robert Short: I constructed a torso out of thermoformed transparent plastic, on which I could attach one of the mechanical heads made by Carlo Rambaldi. The torso was painted with an airbrush to appear opaque when it was not illuminated by the xenon lamp placed behind it. It was filled with inflatable translucent organs linked to tubes that delivered compressed air. Steven Spielberg had conceived of E.T. as a form of highly evolved vegetal life. So I made molds of gourds and dried fruit to give vegetal form to its organs. At the beginning, the torso only had to be used once, during the resurrection of E.T., but Steven liked the effect so much that he used it again when E.T. says good-bye to Elliott.

Carlo Rambaldi and the design model for E.T. that was approved by Spielberg

Carlo Rambaldi, the creator of E.T. A sculptor by training, Rambaldi began in the 1960s to animate imaginary creatures by using remote cables, levers, and ingenious mechanisms. He then exported his refined expertise to the United States for the filming of the remake of King Kong. *His techniques, inspired by the workings of bicycle brakes, were adopted by all the American makeup artists.*

Spielberg liked the effect of E.T.'s illuminated heart so much that he used it in two sequences instead of one.
Photo courtesy of Robert Short

During her discovery of the hereafter, Geena Davis meets Harry, who didn't survive his encounter with headshrinkers. One of the hilarious scenes of Tim Burton's Beetlejuice.
Photo courtesy of Robert Short

How did you collaborate with Tim Burton on the extraordinary special effects of "Beetlejuice" (1988)?

Robert Short: Tim Burton made sketches of each scene. The supervisor of visual effects, Alan Munro, analyzed these drawings and then divided the making of the effects among the members of the crew. Our goal was to faithfully transpose Tim's vision. It was that much more difficult since *Beetlejuice* was one of the last movies filmed without digital effects. Almost everything that you see was filmed just by the camera. The costume-carousel effect had to be decomposed in many stages. Beetlejuice first wore a hat in the form of an umbrella, which quite simply opened up to reveal the little animals hanging on the rim of the hat. Then we used a second, rigid hat attached to a mount fixed to the floor behind Michael Keaton. This second hat was motorized for turning, animating, and lighting up. Beetlejuice then spreads out his long arms, which are in the form of rolls, just plain arms padded with fabric that we made roll out on the floor. We used a complex system to make the wooden mallets that swell up at the ends of his arms appear. We inserted a disk mounted on a pneumatic jack inside each of the rubber spheres that were fixed to circular mounts. Initially, the balloons inflate normally. Then, when the two jacks are deployed inside the balloons, they elongate the balloons, giving them a more cylindrical shape. Just then, we sucked out the air from the balloons with a pump to force the latex membrane to tighten between the disk and the support circle, and we got two cylinders in the form of mallets. For the following shot, we replaced this system with two long mechanical arms, the axes of which were situated at Michael Keaton's shoulder level, and their opposing extremities crossed the wall of the set. The arms were extended by two ultralight thermoformed plastic mallets. All we had to do was lower the opposing extremities of the arms behind the set in order to animate them.

One of the most ingenious mechanical effects conceived by Robert Short for Beetlejuice. *Not a single element of this image was retouched by computer.* Photo courtesy of Robert Short

We came up with a lot of funny effects for the scene of the accidental dead. The shrunken head of the explorer was a puppet manipulated through a false wall. We created the first airbrush makeup in collaboration with Ve Neill, spraying fluorescent foundation on the faces of the phantoms, which were illuminated in black light. The elderly lady who welcomes Geena Davis and Alec Baldwin into the hereafter wore a prosthetic throat made of slices of latex foam, in which we inserted tubes. When she inhaled a drag from a cigarette, a technician blew smoke into the tubes to give the impression that smoke was coming out of her throat. We also used a false perspective to create the illusion that Geena Davis held Alec Baldwin's decapitated head. Geena was filmed standing in front of a desk. We glued a prosthesis of a cutoff neck under Alec's chin. We made a reduced replica of the front of the desk, which we placed in the foreground, in front of the real desk. Alec knelt down behind the little replica of the desk and laid his neck on it. His body was concealed by this false perspective, and you thought you saw his chopped-off head float in front of the desk!

INTERVIEW

JEAN-MARIE VIVÈS

Illustrator and Matte Painting Specialist

The paintings of Jean-Marie Vivès have been incorporated into such famous movies as *Alien Resurrection, La Cité des enfants perdus* (*The City of Lost Children*), and *Jeanne d'Arc* (*Joan of Arc*). He talks of the unique art of matte painting, from the time of optical special effects through the era of digitalization.

How did you start out?

Jean-Marie Vivès: By accident. In 1978, I designed the logo for a special effects company called Acme Films. Alain Resnais had contacted it to do the paintings on glass for *La Vie est un roman* (*Life Is a Bed of Roses*), and I got to work on the project. I painted on very large plates of glass, which were interposed between the scenery and the camera. Resnais definitely did not want anyone to try to interweave the cartoon drawings by Enki Bilal into the real images. He simply wanted to see them side by side. Later on, I learned the laws of optics to calculate the focal lengths when I made my first realistic

Self-portrait by Jean-Marie Vivès   Photo courtesy of Jean-Marie Vivès

paintings on glass. These paintings on glass were done in a studio, so the light could be regulated. The head cameraman told me what diaphragm aperture he was going to use, and I would calculate at what distance from the camera I had to place my glass plate in order for it to be right. I'd look through the camera to note the points of reference corresponding to the perspectives of the set on my plate. I then put a prime coat on the parts of the glass that I'd be painting with Krylon spray paint, normally used in auto body shops. I would wait a day or two for this prime coat to dry, and then use razor blades to scrape off the parts of the plates that had to remain transparent. It wasn't until then that I started to paint. I used alkyd oil paints that dried very fast and acrylic paints. I played with the transparency of these oils to create the blurry effects between the paint and the scenery seen through it.

Did you also use an airbrush to create other transparent effects?

Jean-Marie Vivès: Very little. An absolutely hyperrealistic drawing done with an airbrush would immediately stand out if you tried to blend it into a real image. By really studying the American masters like Harrison Ellenshaw, Albert Whitlock, Mike Pangrazio, and Craig Barron, I became convinced that the best matte paintings come closer to an Impressionist approach. These are the paintings done with strong textures and small strokes. Sometimes I reinforced the realism of my compositions by adding some

model elements in the foreground, to create a sort of multiplane effect. Different from American crews, I always work alone on a creation and the integration of a painting into the real image.

You have also used the process of three-color recomposition. Could you explain it?

Jean-Marie Vivès: When I've painted with a brush on glass, matte painting, I came up against the fact that in France, they weren't used to using the latent image technique. It's a special effect that consists of protecting a part of the image during the real shot and then filming the painting in the studio on the same film, thus reprinting the same shots using a counter-matte. I used a very soft positive to recopy the real part of the image that was to be kept, but the final result was still much too contrasty compared to what I had wanted to obtain. You could see a clear difference in the quality between the manipulated image and the first-generation image. I studied the separation of the color strips according to the Technicolor process. The negative of the original that's to be worked on is passed under a selection of blue, green, and red filters. I got three strips in black-and-white. I manipulated

my painting, filming it three times, once with a blue, green, and red filter, and afterward, I recomposed my manipulated image to obtain a final composite that was in color and of higher quality. The three-color recomposition and the integration of the painting became a single operation. During this period, I was working for Excalibur, which manufactured the components for three-color separations.

How did you manage to replicate colors and textures of the real sets onto your paintings?

Jean-Marie Vivès: I projected colored lights onto my painting to correct some shades. I also used filters. I played with the exposure time. I used different exposures to obtain a whole range of light intensity. Through many trials, I would always come upon one that had almost the identical value as that of the original image.

When did you move on to digital?

Jean-Marie Vivès: I bought my first computer in 1990. It was a Macintosh II Fx, 40 MHz with 16 MB of RAM, and I still have it. People told me, "You're crazy! Digital, that will never work with movies!" But I forged ahead and completed my first digital matte for the movie *On vit une époque formidable* (*Wonderful Times*) by Gérard Jugnot. It was a very simple shot: a building seen at night, from afar. Right after that, I worked in digital on *Les Visiteurs* (*The Visitors,* 1993). From then on, every-one said to me, "Digital, it's incredible! Why didn't we use it earlier on?"

The matte painting of the bridge and château in Les Visiteurs *(top), and the real image before being altered (above)*
Photos courtesy of Jean-Marie Vivès

Above and below: *The imaginary forest in* Le Petit Poucet   Photos courtesy of Jean-Marie Vivès

Could you explain the steps that go into making a digital painting?

Jean-Marie Vivès: I usually study the images that I'll be manipulating for a long time, immersing myself in them, and then I decide how to approach them. It also all depends on the nature of the rapport with the director. In some cases, as with *Le Petit Poucet* (*Little Thumb,* 2001), I was given carte blanche when asked to extend the image. To work on *Blueberry,* I went to Arizona and took thousands of photos, finding textures, shapes, rocks, etc.

I also created 3-D elements to make digital mattes in which traveling shots could be made, and I completed it all with drawings, since before all else, I'm an illustrator. I work on very large-size images. An image from *Le Petit Poucet,* for example, was 1,650 gigabytes! Digital allows me to get deep into things. First I compose a very small image for making the composition of a matte. Then I "blow it up" artificially, and I reenter into it to create the fine details and shadows. And I start over again many times. I also compose images directly from a supply of photographs,

re-created with a computer program called Painter. I can take the texture of a branch and use it to re-create an entire tree.

Three stages in the creation of a composite shot in La Cité des enfants perdus. *Above, the final shot. Below, the real shot and the preparation of the 3-D elements.* Photos courtesy of Jean-Marie Vivès

What are the pitfalls to be avoided when creating a good matte painting?

Jean-Marie Vivès: First, you have to avoid framing it like a classic matte painting! The manipulated shot must be integrated into the continuity of the sequence, if possible in a movement. You could go for a dramatic effect on establishing shots, but otherwise, it's better to use a subtle approach, drawing the audience's eye to where the main action is going on. In *La Cité des enfants perdus* (1995), there was an image where I put chains in the foreground to accentuate the depth. The painting's perspectives draw the eye toward the walkway where the characters cross over. I always conceive of my mattes as if there were the possibility of filming them normally, with a camera fixed on a mount. The shot of the walkway was created as if it were to be filmed from a crane. I like adding a small moving object in the foreground. Particles suspended in the air, smoke, something that brings life.

Above and below: *The making of another superb shot in* La Cité des enfants perdus   Photos courtesy of Jean-Marie Vivès

Two of the mattes made for Alien Resurrection, The wide shot is of the gangway that posed the greatest problem for Jean-Marie Vivès: "There was only Winona Ryder, one end of the gangway, and a large green background in the real image. The set designer gave me a small sketch of what he wanted, and then I worked, without a net, in my studio in France. Once the work was done, I sent it to the United States by Internet."

Paris buried under sand in the film Peut-être (Maybe, *1999)* Photo courtesy of Jean-Marie Vivès

Only the attic window is real in this image from Bon Voyage (2003) Photo courtesy of Jean-Marie Vivès

Atmospheric Effects

In film, simulating fog, rain showers, or a snowstorm is more complicated than it appears. Rain can be replicated by using fire hoses or special rain clusters that disperse drops of water over an area ranging from 325 to 645 square feet (30 to 60 square meters). When the water pressure is low, the devices spew fat droplets; when it is at full throttle, the effect is more like a spray. Hurricane winds can be simulated by using giant fans, or even modified airplane engines. Very finely ground ice can be spread to evoke a snowstorm, as can biodegradable materials such as cotton or crumpled paper. A variation of this technique was used in *Dante's Peak* (1997): tons of paper were crumpled up, dyed gray, and then, to replicate showers of ash falling on a village next to the volcano, blown about using huge fans. When filming in a studio, enormous wire mesh cylinders are suspended over the sets. Designers will fill them with artificial snow made out of fireproof polyurethane that has been finely crushed. When they need to make the snowfall, the motorized cylinders slowly start to turn, causing the fake snowflakes to escape as if through a sieve. Most smoke machines use oil-based solutions that are heated and vaporized. In order to generate blanketing smog that is heavier than air and

Water devices hidden at the top of electric poles made rainfall possible on this set at Universal Studios in Hollywood.

hovers just above floor level, dry ice is plunged into tanks of heated water. Chemical products are also used to create the impression that a given prop is self-consumed, like the pen that Parker, a character in the movie *Alien,* dips into the acid-laced blood of Facehugger, the creature undergoing an autopsy. The scene in which the blood eats away at the floor of the spaceship was gotten by projecting the chemical onto a polystyrene plate. The corrosive actions of this product, which produces fumes when exposed to humidity in the air, caused the material to dissolve.

Computer-Generated Images and the Digital Age

Computers first began to be developed in 1939, and by the

middle of the 1940s, success came with ones such as ENIAC, the first one capable of performing multiple tasks. From the beginning of the 1950s, their computing power enabled them to simulate experiments. The military took advantage of the development to determine the range of missiles and the air resistance of wings on prototype jets, as well as to decode secrets. In those days, computers spat out the data in columns of numbers, but since a picture is worth a thousand words, the machines were reconfigured to display the data in real time on the screen. Computers could register point coordinates of height, length, and depth in three-dimensional space. All that remained was to display these points in the form of an image, and then rotate that image to obtain different viewable angles. Thus, the first computer-generated images were born. After that, people worked on developing them. The points were connected by lines to create "wire" representations of objects, and more and more complex surface areas could be displayed. From the beginning of the 1960s, the U.S. Army and some large aircraft manufacturers such as Boeing used 3-D imaging to develop their equipment. Then computer imaging escaped the confines of scientific research. For example, credits on television newscasts popularized what came to be

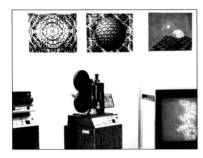

A 35-millimeter Mitchell camera attached to a Dunn imagery system: a very high-resolution black-and-white monitor. Red, blue, and green filters are placed in succession in front of three different black-and-white video images to print a single color image on film.

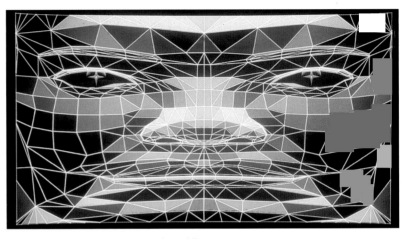

The MCP (Master Control Program) face of Tron   Image © Disney Enterprises, Inc.

known as "flying logos," the catchy name given to those letters they often showed spinning around the globe.

The First 3-D Images in Film

In 1982, the film *Tron* presented the first cinematic computer-generated scenes, which were primarily conceived by MAGI (Mathematics Applications Group, Inc.).

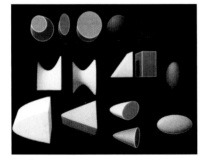

The 3-D volumes from which vehicles were made in the movie Tron
Image © Disney Enterprises, Inc.

Motorcycles, tanks, and the very simple, geometric landscapes inspired by the first video games heralded the visual revolution of the seventh art. Jeff Kleiser, cofounder of Kleiser-Walczak, had already been a part of Digital Effects, one of the four companies dating back to 1980 that were instrumental in the creation of *Tron*'s 3-D images: "We met Harrison Ellenshaw at the Disney Studios and he described *Tron* to us, and by all evidence, it was an exceptional project. Before working on *Tron,* we had bought a medical imaging device that let us record images in gradations of gray on 35-millimeter film. At the time, when you printed high-resolution video images on film, you began with many versions of the same image in varying degrees of gray and then colored them using filters. It took several superimpositions to get one single color

image—an exacting effort. This is how we made the credits for the film—effects like the pieces of a puzzle coming together—as well as the character of Bit, who accompanied the hero through the 3-D world." Throughout the 1980s, it was ILM that accomplished most of the great advances in 3-D. Riding on the success of *Star Wars,* George Lucas had the financial means to prepare the computer-generated images of the future. He recognized that the future of film lay in digital, and he began testing the first digital effects on film back at the beginning of the 1980s. Unfortunately, the technology of the time did not allow for realistic images. Lucas worked with large companies on many tests in an attempt to develop higher-performance programs, and he financed Pixar to manufacture the first computer designed to compute images. In

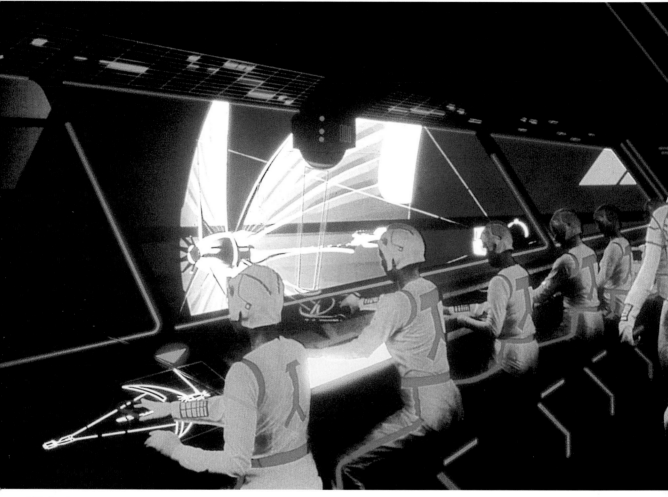

Differing from the vehicles, which were all made in 3-D, the sets and costumes in Tron *were illuminated using a series of complex optical effects that combined blocking out on celluloid, mattes backlighted on an animation stand, and the use of many colored filters. The postproduction of the film entailed hundreds of people both in the United States and in animation studios in South Korea producing celluloid mattes and counter-mattes.* Image © Disney Enterprises, Inc.

1982, in *Star Trek II: The Wrath of Khan,* the sequence of the "Genesis effect"—the transformation of a dead moon into a living planet replete with oceans—entailed the first use of mathematical fractal formulas to depict the textures of mountains and oceans.

Nevertheless, the first 3-D spaceships were not conceived by Lucas's studio, but rather by Digital Productions, a company founded by Gary Demos and John Whitney. The twenty minutes of space scenes inserted into the film *The Last Starfighter* (1984) were computed

by a Cray XMP computer, one of the most powerful machines of its day. The spaceship still looks like a hybrid, close to the imagery of the video games on which the film's script is based. In 1985, while working for ILM, John Lasseter animated the first character in a full-length

Lightcycles in which the heroes escape the tanks in Tron   Photofest © Disney Enterprises, Inc.

The first realistic CGI spaceship was made for The Last Starfighter.

feature that was completely computer-generated: it was the knight who emerged from a stained-glass window in *Young Sherlock Holmes*. The studio developed its own computer

The stunning simulation of water in The Abyss   Photo courtesy of Silicon Graphics

The glass knight animated by John Lasseter in a scene from Young
Sherlock Holmes
Photo courtesy of Photofest

programs for the morphing process, which were first used in *Willow* (1988). The first modeling of water in 3-D appeared in *The Abyss* (1989). In 1991, the liquid metal cyborg in *Terminator 2*, T-1000, was depicted by actor Robert Patrick, using a series of false heads made by Stan Winston's studio and some of the most astonishing computer-generated images to come from ILM. After a history of more than sixty years of optical manipulations, this film was the first in which the special effects were composited digitally. Douglas Smythe and George Joblove also developed a retouching program that could easily erase the cables supporting the motorcycle on which Arnold

T-1000, made in 3-D, emerges from the flames in Terminator 2.
Photo courtesy of Silicon Graphics

Schwarzenegger's double was perched during a spectacular leap. To address a problem of continuity, James Cameron asked that the scene be reversed from right to left, but the words on the street signs in the background appeared backward. With the new program,

the words were inverted so they could once again be read. Lucas used his television series *The Adventures of Young Indiana Jones* (1992–96) to test in video the digital effects that he would later use in film. He would increase the number of extras on the battlefield,

re-create historical sites in 3-D, and depict other countries—all by using virtual sets.

A page in the history of 3-D was turned in 1993 with *Jurassic Park,* when audiences got to experience the first-ever hyperrealistic digital animals on film. The team created a 3-D model for each dinosaur, layer by layer, from designs made at ILM. The character's skeleton comprised numerous joints, each accorded a specific axis of movement. The character's usage determined whether it needed one foot to be able to bend backward or its head to spin all the way around several times. The bones of the neck, feet, belly, and legs were then

covered over with an array of muscular bulk. This mass was specifically devised to lose its shape, wrinkling over itself when the skeleton changed position. The dinosaur was then covered in a stamped, textured skin digitally drawn by an artist. At this stage, the dinosaur was still lifeless. In order to animate it, its joints had to be interconnected and a hierarchy of its movements established. In other words, its legs would be programmed so that they would automatically unfold as soon as one "pulled" on the feet. The dinosaur thus became a virtual puppet that could be handed from one animator to another. In 1994, Kitty, the saber-toothed tiger in *The Flintstones,* became the first computer-generated character endowed with fur. This technique was developed the following year in *Jumanji* (1995). The monkeys in *Jumanji* were among the first 3-D characters to have hair. They had to move about in real shots that had already been filmed, as well as "act" with flesh-and-blood actors. The first stage of animation entailed positioning the character in its principal stances, those four or five "key frames" defining the primary lines of action and serving as anchor points for the trajectory of a movement. The secondary movements were added one at a time, just as is done in traditional animation, until there were twenty-four positions per second

The superb simulation of the ocean by ILM for The Perfect Storm (1999). Habib Zargarpour and John Anderson replicated the laws of fluid dynamics to control the motion of billions of particles that composed the raging waves. The collision of one single wave against the 3-D model of the boat caused the dispersion of millions of particles.
Photo courtesy of SGI

of film. The direction, color, and intensity of the lighting of the virtual characters had to correspond precisely with those of the real sequences, just as the shadows had to be cast identically onto the ground. Once the plan was approved by the animation supervisor, it was processed with the Motion Blur computer program, creating a ghost effect, or transparent blurring, on those parts of the body that move quickly. The skin of the dinosaurs in Jurassic Park were defined merely by bumpy surfaces, whereas a

single monkey in Jumanji was covered with millions of hairs that undulated in accordance with the animal's position, necessitating computations 123,000 times more complex.

Synthesized Stuntmen

The same year, Cinergy asked Kleiser-Walczak to create the 3-D flying vehicles for Judge Dredd. The company had to concern itself not only with the aerial traffic over the futuristic city of Mega City One, but also with a

chase scene involving flying motorcycles. The real shots with Rob Schneider and Sylvester Stallone were filmed in England against a blue background. In order to get the wide-angle action of the motorcycles on which the actors were seated, they would have had to shoot with a motion-control camera. But the studio did not want to put a star worth twenty million dollars next to a several-ton motorized crane! So Jeff Kleiser had to develop the first synthesized stuntmen: "We took shots of the motorcycle and cyber-scanned Stallone's and Schneider's faces. Diana Walczak sculpted half of a body in reduced scale and attached it to a mirror to verify the symmetry. That facilitated the digitalization of these complex volumes. All that we had to do was reverse the data of the left half of the body to get the right half and the whole body. Diana then dressed it in a motion capture costume, and we recorded its movements while it was being jostled in all directions on a model of the flying motorcycle, in accordance with the preplanned stunts. The data allowed us to animate the digital doubles of the actors and their pursuers."

Higher-Performance 3-D Muscles

It was in 1996 that ILM first used the CARI animation

Diana Walczak sculpted half of the miniature likenesses of Rob Schneider and Sylvester Stallone and used the aid of a mirror to ascertain the complete model. This process made it easier to scan the volumes of the sculptures. The 3-D images thus obtained were duplicated in the reverse to create the other half of each of the characters.

The synthesized stuntmen on flying motorcycles in Judge Dredd

Opposite and above: *Three key stages in the creation of Imhotep for* The Mummy
Photos courtesy of Universal Studios

program, which enabled the characters to be displayed in complete rendering (skin and muscles) during animation. It was an important step for animators, who previously had to content themselves with using "wire" silhouettes to animate. Using a program designed by Cary Phillips, the dragon in the movie *Dragonheart* (1996) was endowed with facial and muscular animations that were four times more complex than those of the T. rex in *Jurassic Park*. The next year in *Titanic,* the sky, the ocean, and the extras seen in long shot pacing up and down the model of the cruise ship, along with the albatrosses and the dolphins, were all prod-

ucts of Digital Domain computers. In 1999, ILM brought out a new, virtual version of *The Mummy*. When he first appears, Imhotep, a computer-generated character, is a tangle of yellowed bones, muscles, and skin riddled with holes and a hyperrealistic texture. By removing the organs of his victims, he manages to recover his past state. Using photographs of actor Arnold Vosloo as a point of departure, the computer artists at ILM created the phases of the character's decomposition. They made several virtual mummies with bones covered in an assortment of muscular masses and shrinking organs that could be seen

through the holes in the skin. New computer programs made it possible to animate the different masses of flesh independently, producing a more realistic impression. Once prepared, the 3-D character was illuminated "virtually" to cast shadows that correspond with the real shadows on the ground, and then it was integrated with the flesh-and-blood actors. The transition between the actor and the computer-generated character was done in stages, using a series of makeup appliances created by Nick Dudman. The facial prosthetics worn by Vosloo were fitted with black holes into which electroluminescent diodes were inserted.

Two prosthetics furnished with electroluminescent diodes were glued to Arnold Vosloo's face so the ILM computer artists could juxtapose a fake throat and a beetle in 3-D with stop-motion.
Photos courtesy of Universal Studios

These points of reference were then used to insert the mummy's computer-generated yellowed teeth and dried-up jaw muscles into the "holes." The computer artists at ILM spent hundreds of hours precisely coordinating the movements of the actor's jaw with those of the virtual teeth and muscles.

In 2000, the Sony Imageworks studio made an even more powerful modeling to create the invisible effects used in Paul Verhoeven's film *The Hollow Man*. Scott E. Anderson, the chief visual effects supervisor, first conducted extensive studies on human physiology and the re-creation of the movements of the body. His collaborators took anatomy courses at hospitals and medical schools and even attended some autopsies. Surface textures similar to those applied to the exterior of objects were often used, like a kind of skin applied onto a hollow space. Under Anderson's direction, the crew created three-dimensional objects in order to make detailed replications of muscular contractions, bones, joints, and all the body's internal movements. The 3-D character was then animated using "volume rendering," which can calculate not only its surface area, but also the surface area of all its internal details. The other difficulty of the invisiblity sequences entailed showing the effects of

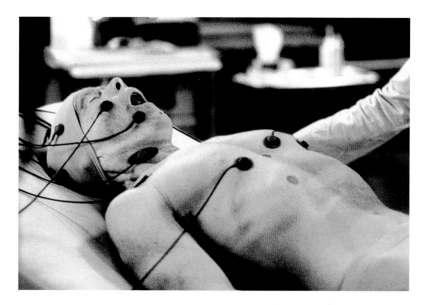

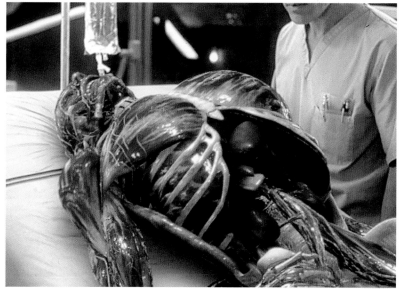

The cutaway made by Sony Imageworks for The Hollow Man *was an actual clone of Kevin Bacon. The actor spent most of the time covered in white, blue, black, and green makeup so that he could be erased frame by frame and appear invisible.*
Photos courtesy of Columbia Pictures

the presence of the formidable Sebastian Craine—the smoke that outlines his silhouette and the rain that flows over his body. To get these images, actor Kevin Bacon had to be clothed in green, blue, or black outfits, depending on the desired effects. His teeth had to be masked over, and he had to

Above, below, and opposite: *Actor Jet Li's face, reconstituted with computer-generated images, was inserted over the green mask worn by the stuntman. This was the method used to make the shots in* The One *in which Jet Li fights with his evil double.*

wear contact lenses that completely covered his eyes. The scenes were then shot normally, but they had to resort to using digital mattes to block out his silhouette. These mattes reinserted the background of the set behind his body, which had been reconstituted in 3-D and repositioned in stop-motion, in keeping with poses that had been filmed earlier. It was a long and exacting process, but one that allowed smoke and 3-D rain streaming over the invisible 3-D body of Kevin Bacon to be added and thus delineate the outline of his body. In 2001, Kleiser-Walczak once again came up with innovations in their special effects for the film *The One,* in which actor Jet Li is shown fighting himself. "We cyber-scanned Jet Li's face, then had the stuntman who played his evil double wear a green mask," explained Jeff Kleiser. "We marked reference points with Scotchlite on the mask. We put a fluorescent

The One special visual effects by Kleiser-Walczak. © 2001 Revolution Studios Distribution Company, LLC. Property of Sony Pictures Entertainment, Inc. © 2001 Columbia Pictures Industries, Inc. All rights reserved. Images courtesy of Kleiser-Walczak

light around the lens of the camera so that these points would appear luminous. They allowed us to replace Jet Li's face, frame by frame, with an identical 3-D image, which we then animated during the fight scenes. This digital face replacement technique can be a great asset when transposing the face of a star onto a stunt person who's doing some daring physical feat."

Apollo 13

In 1995, Digital Domain built an eighteen-foot (more than five-meter) model of the Saturn V rocket to film the liftoff scenes in *Apollo 13*. The fuselage was a structure made from large cardboard tubes used for pouring pillars of reinforced concrete. The tubes were cut out and then covered with plywood and sheets of polystyrene and thermoformed plastic to replicate the corrugated iron of

the fuselage. A steel tube consisting of mounts in the form of an X made the model rigid. The twenty-foot (six-meter) launchpad was even more complicated. The arms supporting the rocket were activated by stepper motors. There was an elevator that went up and down inside the structure. These enormous models made it possible to film extreme close-ups, but to get the high-angle shots that the director had planned, the camera would have had to be placed thirty-three feet (ten meters) above. Thus, the motion control dolly would have had to be put on the floor in order to function properly. To resolve this problem, the model, supported by cables, was laid on its side, as was the camera. The liftoff sequence with the Saturn V rocket combined many elements: the miniature rocket and launchpad on a green background, computer-generated images of the haze, and the gas jets and ice that fell from the tanks. The real Florida sky and vibrations added to the scene complemented these very realistic images.

Previous two pages and above: *The miniature capsule and the filming of a sequence of* Apollo 13 *with motion control equipment by Digital Domain*
Photos courtesy of Digital Domain

Gladiator

Ridley Scott brilliantly used digital effects to depict Roman antiquity in *Gladiator* (2000). He first searched for a site to reconstruct Rome and its Colosseum. Set designer Arthur Max decided to use the structures at Fort Ricasoli, in Malta, as the basis for his set. Max built a large portion of the first level of the Colosseum, measuring about a third of the circumference of the original, at a height of some sixty-five feet (twenty meters). It was in this set of a partial amphitheater that the gladiator fights were filmed. After shooting the real scenes, the Mill Film's crew, directed by John Nelson, topped off the real set with two additional computer-generated levels. Thirty-three thousand computer-generated extras were animated throughout the tiers above the two thousand flesh-and-blood extras. By using a motion-reckoning system, the perspectives of the real and virtual sets were perfectly aligned during the sweeping panoramic shots. Other synthesized buildings were added next to the Colosseum to create the general views of Rome, populated with virtual people and animated using a motion capture system. Actors wearing reference marks on their costumes moved toward the center of a circle, surrounded by a dozen magnetic sensors. The three-dimensional data gathered were then transposed onto the 3-D characters in order to animate them. Thanks to Mill Film's special effects and Ridley Scott's sense of visual composition, *Gladiator* is one of the most beautiful examples of the use of digital techniques.

Above and next two pages: *Ridley Scott's aesthetic sense, realized through digital effects by the Mill Film studio, produced some of the most beautiful visions of ancient Rome.* Photos courtesy of The Mill

INTERVIEW

Sylvain Despretz

Concept and storyboard artist Sylvain Despretz pursued his career in the United States. He speaks of the process of designing for special effects.

The spaceship from Alien Resurrection
Photo courtesy of Twentieth Century-Fox

What was your professional itinerary?

Sylvain Despretz: At sixteen, I came from France as an exchange student and lived in a small town in the northern United States. I made Super-8 movies with friends. We discovered editing, framing. After college graduation, I offered my services to ad agencies in New York. I worked with several directors, among them Ridley Scott. When, soon after, I

Drawing of the spaceship from Alien Resurrection
Photo courtesy of Twentieth Century-Fox

SYLVAIN 96 —

"THE AURIGA"

moved to California, I spent a decade or so trying to land jobs on noteworthy movies. One of the reasons I was able to break into film was that I was always interested in the politics of the trade, which is key.

How do you collaborate with directors?

Sylvain Despretz: I work with a limited number of directors, to better understand their way of thinking. Ideally, a director should draw the storyboard himself. Our collaboration depends on how he "lets go of his baby." Jean-Pierre Jeunet, for example, is very meticulous in his preparation, very private. He shows up with the first small sketches that he drew himself, and he never goes back on what he's decided to do. The passage to the image is a "clean copy" that follows the storyboard. When I worked on *Alien Resurrection*, I had the feeling that Jean-Pierre didn't want anyone to make suggestions. Ridley Scott, another example, had the opposite attitude. Ridley is a wonderful draftsman who starts off meetings with hundreds of beautiful drawings that he thinks of as idea outlines, as a way to assess the power of an image. He has a very open mind. First the scenes to be storyboarded are chosen, and then some fifty versions of the same scene are

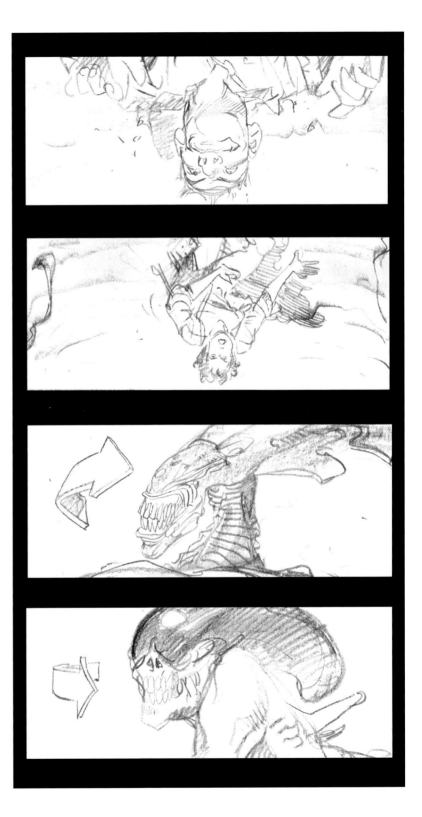

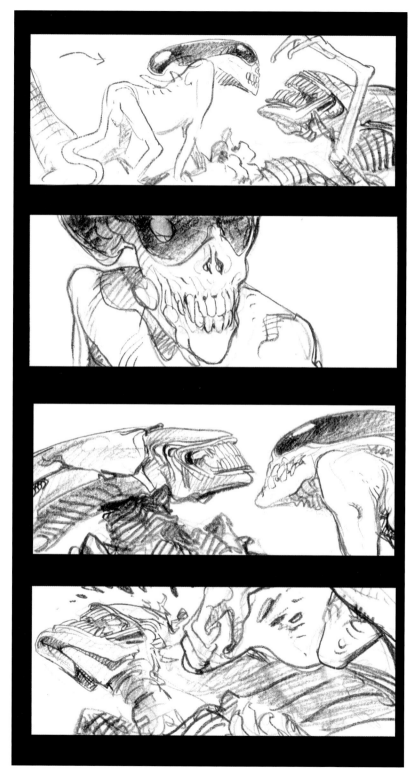

drawn, until it no longer becomes an obsession. Ridley never films exactly what has been storyboarded. He draws ideas from them to build his sets, prepare the lighting, and preconceive the dynamics of a shot, but once he's on set, he focuses his attention on his actors. Inexperienced directors often waste the storyboarding process; essentially, they render it useless, by not knowing how much to give to it.

How do you prepare special effects shots?

Sylvain Despretz: Jean-Pierre Jeunet often says that you have to avoid relying on visual effects subcontractors to visualize creative material. If someone asks a visual effects house to pre-visualize the shots, you can bet they will make suggestions that are based on making their life easy. Today, all visual effects houses are capable of both the best and the worst. It's not technology that guarantees the quality of the effects, it's the technicians, the "programmers" and digital artists. Each studio has its own little house genius, waiting for the next headhunter to call.

What are the differences in the special effects between those described in the script and those that appear in the storyboards?

Sylvain Despretz: A good director will take hold of a script and shape it to correspond with his vision. Not doing this would be a mistake, because the studio is paying him to bring his own original touch. At this stage, whole sequences are changed or dropped. The director's vision is established, and the film begins to come to life. Afterward, the budget becomes an issue, and it all turns into a narrative soup into which the special effects and the limitations are incorporated. The closer to the shooting date, the more important it is to resolve problems and make decisions to move the picture forward. If fifty special effects shots have been planned, they may drop to thirty-five before filming starts, but often, another ninety will have to be added during post-production to correct problems that arose during the shooting.

Do economic considerations have an immediate bearing on the creation of a storyboard?

Sylvain Despretz: Yes. A director as experienced as Ridley immediately finds practical solutions for bringing forth his artistic vision. By studying the model for the Colosseum in *Gladiator,* Ridley and production designer Arthur Max realized that it wasn't necessary to build it in its entirety. Even the complete circumference wasn't necessary, because the images could be flopped, or reversed optically, from right to left to simulate the opposite side of the set. Directors hate calling on subcontractors who take over the making of a shot. Ridley often says that he doesn't like computer-generated images, because he can't see the final result in camera. When you do get to see the final 3-D images, you're so pressed for time that you're practically forced to accept them as they are. The film industry is very old, very wary of CGI companies that

come and turn everything upside down and set the laws. The industry tries to keep the 3-D studios in their place as subcontractors. Ridley, for example, didn't want the entire Colosseum in the frame, as Mill Film suggested. He wanted the first sight of the building to be partial, as if seen by a passerby of the period. A large part of the effects in *Gladiator* merely consisted of adding more light and shadows to reinforce the artistic composition of the image. Not many special effects people are aware of the crucial role of the shadow in a frame. There's a magnificent shot where you see the gladiators fighting a tiger in the shadows while a diagonal beam of light showers the set. The light was filmed separately, at Shepperton studios, using the effect of suspended dust in the air to evoke the light of the French Orientalist painter Jean-Léon Gérôme. Ridley is a director who has a real sense of the conception of an image and who never delegates this aspect of the work.

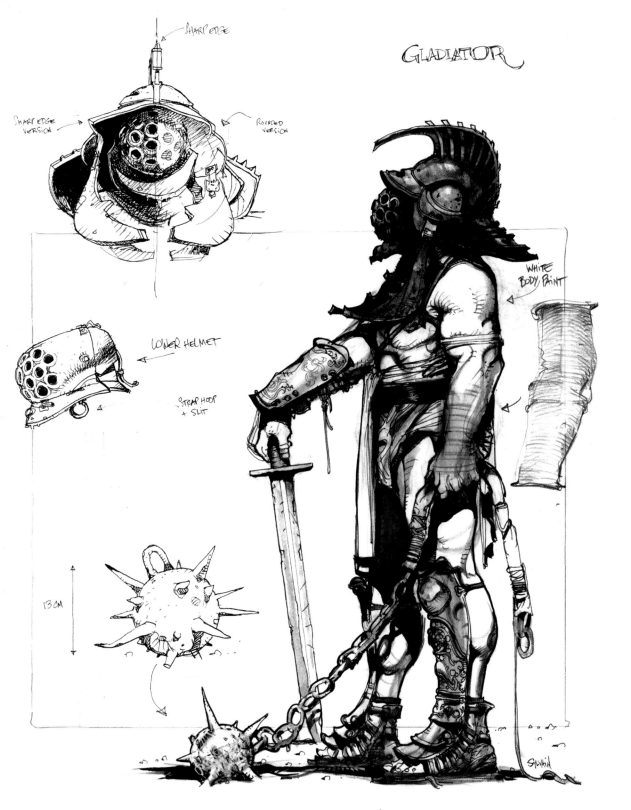

SHARP EDGE

SHARP EDGE
VERSION

ROUNDED
VERSION

GLADIATOR

WHITE
BODY PAINT

LOWER HELMET

STRAP HOOP
+ SLIT

13 CM

SYLVAIN

ABH ARENA ?

Previous page, above, and left: Gladiator, *including the storyboard of the battle between the Roman legions and Germans, as well as a sequence from the beginning of the film*
Photo courtesy of Universal / Dreamworks

Some unpublished images of a battle with a rhinoceros, at one time considered for Gladiator, *but never filmed*
Photo courtesy of Universal / Dreamworks

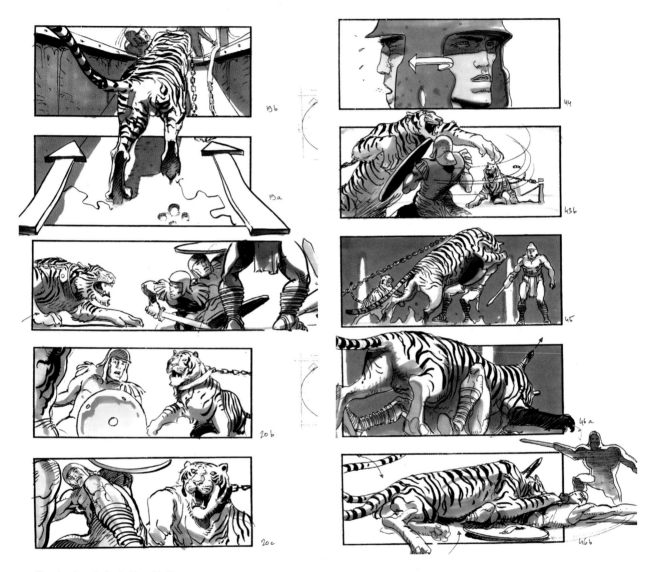

The storyboard of a battle with tigers

You worked on two projects that did not come to fruition: "Superman Reborn" by Tim Burton and "I Am Legend" by Ridley Scott.

Sylvain Despretz: *Superman Reborn* was the first of two films that I worked on with Tim Burton's crew. The second was *Planet of the Apes.* It was a big project pitched on the names of Tim Burton and Nicholas Cage, in the role of Superman. I was one of ten artists who spent months going around in circles with a script that was not going to be used. Burton rarely visited the art department, despite his aura as an artist. I think that he was frustrated working in animation, way back, and he's content with his status as a director; he doesn't seem interested in the arduous aspect of art department labor, and I can't blame him. My feeling is that the most complete study of the "Burton style" comes from Henry Selick's work on *The Nightmare Before Christmas.* I don't see Burton's drawings as being complete enough to work in three dimensions, "as is," so to speak. His production designer, however, is instrumental in making it all look coherent; he perfectly transposed Burton's style when he designed the sets and props.

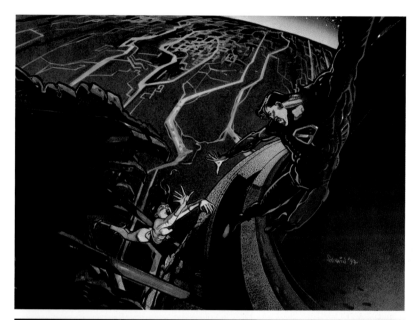

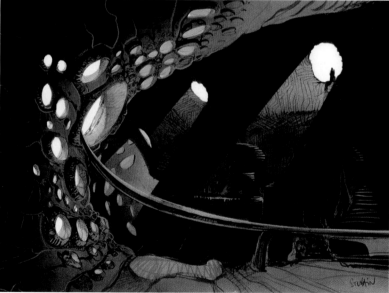

Different concepts of Superman Reborn, *worked on for more than two years by Tim Burton and then abandoned*
Images courtesy of Warner Bros.

Images courtesy of Warner Bros.

Why was "Superman Reborn" never finished?

Sylvain Despretz: The project was developed in 1997, a year during which Warner Bros. experienced poor box office returns. The top brass, who were already not overly thrilled with the script, ended up panicking. There were conflicts between Tim Burton and producer Jon Peters, who often came and offered us his "bright" ideas. One day, he showed us a fossilized skull on the cover of *National Geographic*. He wanted us to use this image for a concept of the spaceship for Brainiac, Superman's nemesis who was a supercomputer in human form. So we drafted dozens of skull-spaceships. But Peters rejected all of them, because he wanted it simply to be a skull! Since I'm black, he shouted at me, "I want every brother in the ghetto to be scared shitless!" It was pathetic! I was ready to quit when I ran into Ridley Scott in the restaurant on the lot. He asked me to join the crew of *I Am Legend,* which I did right away. It was a great project, also developed during that awful period between 1997 and 1998. The screenplay told the tale of the last man on earth, who confronts mutants called Hemocytes. Again at Warner, they panicked at the idea of a man talking to his dog throughout most of the film. They wanted to put in action and love scenes that had nothing to do with the whimsical and atmospheric story imagined by Ridley, transforming it into a kind of *Terminator* movie. We found some interesting sources of inspiration for the mutants: a book on sliced cadavers that I discovered in Paris, another book on physical ailments, and Arthur Max had a book of photos by Leni Riefenstahl on the Masai. Ridley wanted the creatures to weave their outfits from garbage bags and to draw tribal designs on their faces. Some tests for the Hemocytes' makeup were devised from our drawings. It was a great shame that the film folded, because unlike *Superman, Legend* would have been both an inspiring and provocative picture that would have invigorated a very tired genre.

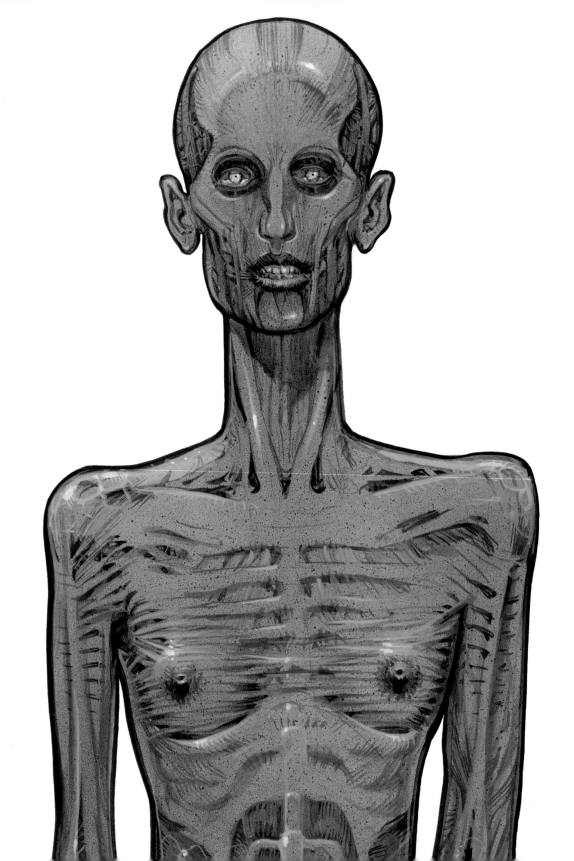

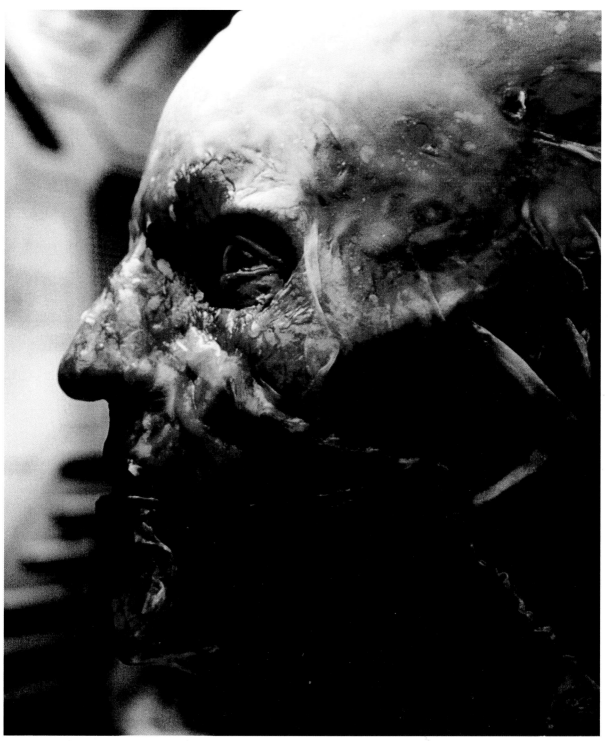

Opposite and above: *The Hemocytes, which were to appear in Ridley Scott's project* I Am Legend, *and tests of the makeup based on drawings by Ridley Scott and Sylvain Despretz* Images courtesy of Warner Bros.

Above and opposite: *Drawings for* Le Cinquième Élément (The Fifth Element, *1997) by Luc Besson*   Images courtesy of Sylvain Despretz

INTERVIEW

Nikki Penny

The Business of Special Effects

Photo courtesy of Nikki Penny

Special effects producer Nikki Penny participated in such major productions as *Gladiator* and *Harry Potter and the Chamber of Secrets*. She reveals to us the workings of her underappreciated profession.

Could you describe your daily work?

Nikki Penny: There are several cases to consider. When I participate in the filming, I'm on the set from seven in the morning and continue working after the last shot. I have to organize the work of the special effects supervisor, or supervisors, and make sure that all we have been filming is what we've needed. I also take care of negotiating or renegotiating the estimates for creating the special effects, which are submitted to the production throughout the filming. As soon as we receive new storyboards, a first estimate has to be processed and submitted to the producer and the studio, and then we

Photos courtesy of The Mill

wait to be asked for alternative solutions that are easier and less costly. It is a job that's done with the special effects supervisor and the director, as these decisions will have repercussions on the work of the set designers and the costume designers. To come back to the

filming, I have to verify that the elements of a composite shot are filmed in the right order. It is imperative that the "background image" is filmed first and that the intensity, the color, and the direction of the light sources are picked up. It is only afterward that scenes of a blue background can be filmed, by re-creating similar lighting. The other case to consider is the work that I perform only in postproduction for a special effects studio. Then my job consists of checking how the composites are created—if they are done in the correct order, on time, and if it is all assembled properly. This represents an enormous amount of work, of meetings, verifications, the fine-tuning of new estimates, and day-to-day financial negotiations.

The big American studios like to give the impression that the budget for a film is set from the first day of filming.

Nikki Penny: They would like it to go that way! In the case of *Harry Potter and the Chamber of Secrets,* there was a difference of several million pounds sterling between the initial estimate, based on an estimation from the first script, and the final estimate, based on the real requirements of the filming.

How do you renegotiate the cost of certain shots with the studios?

Nikki Penny: We reexamine the storyboards in detail with the director to determine what he really needs. In some cases, you can avoid having to resort to effects done in postproduction by preplanning an effect done in front of the camera. The first estimates for the special effects are always based on the theoretical description of what the director is going to do. But during the filming, a still shot that would have lasted two seconds may become a tracking shot lasting ten seconds. At that point, you establish a new estimate based on the materials really expended. We take into account the wishes of the director, and we negotiate with the studio. Special effects also are used to make up for things that didn't work during the filming, or to conceal an inappropriate object that someone left in the middle of a scene that does work!

During these stages of renegotiation, how do you reconcile the grandiose ideas of the directors with the economic needs of the studios?

Nikki Penny: You have to be very diplomatic. We try to preserve the director's vision, but at the end of the day, it's the studio's money. We often have to make great efforts to satisfy everyone. No one has asked me to produce a special effects shot free, but I have often been asked to do it for almost nothing, after the initial budget had been spent! The big studios know how to play the competition between special effects studios to their own advantage.

Is the competition between the special effects firms very strong?

Nikki Penny: The competition has its good points, because it forces everyone to excel. Some firms, like ILM, are known for being more expensive than other American companies and much more expensive than English companies. On the other hand, some firms have greater financial resources than others and can afford to present very tight budgets in order to win a contract.

The elf Dobby, made by teams from ILM for Harry Potter and the Chamber of Secrets
Photo courtesy of Photofest

How do you manage to finish the special effects of a film on time when the release date of the film set by the studio didn't take into account the realities of filming?

Nikki Penny: Before the problem of the release date, the first ordeal that awaits us is the preparation of the first movie trailer that the studios want to show very long in advance to entice audiences. We have to work day and night, knowing the objectives are impossible to attain. In those cases, some shots are lost. The release date is set very long in advance and is only very rarely changed. We organize all our work in terms of it, and we always allow for a margin of safety to deal with extra work.

INTERVIEW

VOLKER ENGEL

Special effects supervisor of *Independence Day, Godzilla,* and *Coronado,* Volker Engel has taken his experience with traditional special effects and combined it with the most spectacular digital effects.

How did you begin to conceive of special effects?

Volker Engel: I was thirteen years old when *Star Wars* was released in Germany. I was so blown away by this film that I decided to buy my first Super-8 camera. I had to wait one year and make my Communion at church before receiving money from my family. I invested the fourteen hundred marks that was given to me in a camera and a projector.

So you prayed for a camera.

Volker Engel: Exactly! From around fifteen or sixteen, I animated wire and clay puppets, and I wanted to make double exposures by rewinding the Super-8 film, which is incredibly hard to do. Between sixteen and twenty-one, I set up a studio in a ten-by-ten-foot (three-by-three-meter) bedroom, which was in the attic of my

Volker Engel examining the set of a miniature avenue for Godzilla
Photo courtesy of Isabella Vosmikova

grandfather's house next to his studio. I wanted to make a ninety-minute film all alone! I placed a spaceship that I had built in front of a black background. The camera was set on a graduated mount, which let me control its movement frame

Volker Engel and a model of a spaceship made for one of his amateur projects Photo courtesy of Volker Engel

by frame, return to the point of departure to identically repeat a movement, and expose the same piece of film a second time. During the spaceship's first passage, I placed an animation cel in front of the camera, on a glass plate. Looking through the lens, I marked the outline on the model, and then I blackened the interior of this silhouette with black paint to get a matte. Each exposed frame of the model filmed on the black background corresponded to an "animated" matte. During the second passage, I filmed the animated mattes in stop-motion in front of a starry motionless background. Mixing the two shoots allowed me to insert the spaceship onto the starry background. It was insane! When I realized that my film project would never get done, I filmed myself preparing the special effects, as if it were a fifteen-minute "making of." This documentary opened the doors of the Stuttgart fine arts academy to me. During my second semester, by chance, I met Oliver Scholl, who became Roland Emmerich's artistic director and who introduced me to him. After seeing my Super-8 film, Roland said to me, "I think you're nuts enough to work with us!" And that's how I got to work on the last project he directed in Germany: *Moon 44* (1990).

What special effects techniques did you use on that film?

Volker Engel: It was long before digital effects; 99 percent of the special effects were done in front of the camera. Since it was a small budget and we had to film more than three hundred special effects shots with spaceships flying over lunar landscapes, we suspended the models on wires. The installations were based on Roland's ideas. When he arrived in the morning, he would draw the system that he had imagined on a piece of paper and explain to us how it could be used. The mount for the models

Building the futuristic platform in Moon 44   Photo courtesy of Volker Engel

Preparation for the destruction of a truck in Universal Soldier *(1992)*
Photo courtesy of Volker Engel

resembled a long metal horizontal rod that could pivot on a vertical axis. One of the ends of the rod was extended by three more telescopic rods that could be lengthened or shortened according to our needs. On the first rod, we hung one of the helicopters of the heroes, and on the other two rods, their enemies' spaceships, which were

chasing them. Pivoting the large rod was enough to get the spaceships to move between the walls of miniature canyons. Obviously, the spaceships always flew in a circle, never straight! To make this less noticeable, we also filmed some shots very close up while moving the spaceships by hand like puppets. Roland taught me how to load

Volker Engel creates a model of an air base for Independence Day. Photo courtesy of Volker Engel

the film in a 35-millimeter camera, what lenses to use to get certain effects, what filters. It was a formidable special effects school. I also got to know about pyrotechnical effects and models. I built most of the lunar canyons, as well as the set with giant skyscrapers and the platform that the spaceship landed on at the beginning of the film. After many months of preparation, Roland very kindly asked me to become the special effects supervisor for *Moon 44*.

The very successful special effects in "Independence Day" didn't cost as much as those of other American mega-productions. Are you more economical than your American colleagues because you come from Europe?

Volker Engel: Absolutely! There's another thing I often hear said in the United States: the organization of the special effects filming is often done day-to-day. The organization of the shots to follow isn't planned enough in advance. Consequently, a considerable backlog builds up as

the filming progresses, and you have to call on more and more service providers to compensate for the lateness, which brings budget overruns. The lack of communication between the crews can cause mistakes and additional costs. In the case of *Independence Day*, we only had six weeks of preproduction, which wasn't anything. At the beginning of the filming, I hired Marc Weigert, whom I studied with at film school and who happened to be in Los Angeles at the time. Together, we founded the company

Uncharted Territory. Marc is an organizational genius. He created the computer program Digital Assistant for Visual Effects, which lets you organize a shoot from the preparation of the script and storyboards, through the filming and post-production. It determines the number of shots that have to be filmed each day. It will announce, "You have filmed three and a half shots today instead of six," letting you know immediately at what point you're beginning to accumulate a backlog. It's an invaluable tool to use on big productions.

The miniature effects in "Godzilla" are spectacular. Could you explain to us how you sank so many fishing boats?

Volker Engel: I wanted to build a giant model to represent the enormous Japanese boat at the beginning of the film—the size of the water drops always reveals the size of the model and that it's being filmed in a pool. The model did measure more than thirty feet (nine meters), but budget constraints kept us from going beyond that. It was mounted on a support controlled by hydraulic jacks. We put tubes in front of the boat for simulating the displacement and swell of the water while the model was motionless in the pool. It was

the movement of the camera that gave the impression that the boat was advancing. I am still dissatisfied with the result we got on that sequence. The destruction of the small fishing boats was filmed in a large pool at Universal Studios in Hollywood. This time, the model boats were large enough to resolve the problem of the size of water drops. They would stream down the sloping ramps concealed below the surface. The models were also connected to metal cables that passed through rings fixed to the bottom of the pool and were attached to the chassis of a van. On my signal, the cameras began filming at two hundred frames per second, the van moved forward a few meters, and the boats were pulled under the water.

You like to mix simple special effects and sophisticated effects to get the most impressive results. Do you think people rely on digital effects too systematically?

Volker Engel: This tendency comes from the fact that the majority of people who are now starting out in special effects have never built a model or a miniature landscape, and have never learned how to do optical effects on 35-millimeter film. It's too bad, because you get the richest images at

The filming of a scene of a bridge collapsing in Coronado, *the superb action movie produced by Volker Engel and his company, Uncharted Territory*
Coronado © Uncharted Territory

significantly lower cost when you know all the techniques of special effects. Producers and directors should learn to do some of the things. On my last project, I cowrote with the director and took the time to explain to him what you had to do with different special effects. The same process can apply to producers. In most cases, the studio hires a special effects company, which has its own supervisor. He advises them to use only the techniques that this company has mastered, but not the others. When I'm hired as a freelance supervisor, I'm free to choose several companies to participate on different sequences. After

Godzilla, I decided that I wanted to develop my own projects, and that's why I formed a production company with my partner. The fact of having received an Oscar helped me to find the financing and to develop and produce the film *Coronado,* which has more than six hundred special effects shots. We produced everything ourselves: the preparation, the filming of the real shots in high definition, the filming of the special effects, and the postproduction. We finished the film for a budget less than had been initially projected, something that practically never happens in Hollywood!

Above and below: *Volker Engel added a patina to the model of the small cave, which can be seen in its entirety in this composite shot.*
Photos courtesy of Bruno Arnold & *Coronado*
© Uncharted Territor

Opposite: *A CGI helicopter, inserted into the interior of the miniature cave, exits passing through a deluge from a waterfall, also rendered in 3-D.*
Coronado © Uncharted Territory

Principal Tools of Spectacular Films

The virtual sets of *A.I.* (2001), the synthesized cats and dogs in *Cats & Dogs* (2001), and the models of the Petronas Towers in Kuala Lumpur inserted behind Catherine Zeta-Jones and Sean Connery in *Entrapment* (1999) were digitally manipulated using the highest-performance workstations. The leader in this field is Silicon Graphics, which supplies the big special effects studios such as Digital Domain, Tippett Studios, and Cinesite. It is also in close participation with innovations at ILM, such as the computer-generated dinosaurs created for *Jurassic Park III* (2001), which is indiscernible from Stan Winston's mechanical dinosaurs filmed on set, even in close-ups. One of the most recent workstations by Silicon Graphics is the Tezro, whose very high capabilities are particularly appreciated by television and film visual effects designers.

Opposite and above: All photos courtesy of SGI, except *Entrapment* photos: courtesy of Cinesite. *Entrapment* © Twentieth Century-Fox

The Marvel Years

The beginning of the twenty-first century has been marked by numerous film adaptations of the adventures of the Marvel Comics superheroes, created in the 1960s by the scriptwriter Stan Lee. The first was *X-Men* (2000) by Bryan Singer, which was filmed in Toronto. Sabertooth, Wolverine's sworn enemy, was played by Tyler Mane, a 6-foot-10 (2.1-meter) former wrestler: "My first fight with the X-Men took place in a real, snowy forest. [The character] Storm makes a snowstorm come on that pushes me back. The technicians used giant fans to project twenty-five tons of mashed potato flakes onto me. They thought about protecting nature by using biodegradable materials, but not the actors. I got hit right in the face, at a speed of 100 mph (160 kph); my legs were buried in the snow at –22°F (–30°C)!" Hugh Jackman wore molded blades on his hands to play the fierce Wolverine, who makes metal claws shoot out from his fists. But the prosthetics often fell off during fight scenes. Digital Domain replaced them with virtual claws by superimposing 3-D models of hands over Jackman's in order to spot the correct perspectives of the blades. The actor would have preferred doing it without the real claws: "One day, I wanted to wipe my face before doing a retake. I saw my partner turn

Sabertooth (Tyler Mane) in the middle of a storm . . . of mashed potato flakes in X-Men   Photo courtesy of Twentieth Century-Fox. X-Men characters © Marvel

pale, pointing at my head. Blood was pouring down my face! Another time, I cut my thigh! The blades weren't the only problem; our leather costumes were very hot. Once, when I flew into a rage during a fight, I became dangerously dehydrated and fainted. I realized that I would have made a pitiful superhero when I woke up surrounded by the entire crew and the nurses, who were applying ice packs on the nape of my neck to lower my temperature!"

Wolverine's Clone

The final confrontation between Wolverine and Sabertooth takes place at the top of the Statue of Liberty. Thrown into the void, Wolverine plants his claws into one of the points of her crown, turns on this axis, and regains his original position. This scene marked the first appearance of a 3-D superhero clone, a technique conceived by Jonathan Egstad of Digital Domain. "We scanned Hugh Jackman to get a 3-D representation of his face. The rest of the character was sculpted by our computer artists and dressed in leather textures. The fake Wolverine appeared in three hundred frames up to the continuity with the real shots on the set." This sequence was filmed in one expanded section at the summit of the statue's head, in front of a green background. The New York skyline that was inserted around the set was a panoramic painting made by Matte World. The painting was scanned and digitally extended by computer artists at Digital Domain, then separated into many pieces of landscape and placed in a large virtual cylinder surrounding the set of the Statue of Liberty. The cylinder was composed of 2-D images of skyscrapers that were separated from one another to produce an effect of depth. Egstad's

Wolverine (Hugh Jackman) confronts Sabertooth at the top of the Statue of Liberty. The New York scene that surrounds them was a virtual re-creation. Photos courtesy of Digital Domain. X-Men characters © Marvel

In this scene from X2: X-Men United (2003), Wolverine's claws were computer-generated and added frame by frame onto real shots.

team used a laser telemetry device to take down the measurements of the studio scenery, and placed a chrome sphere in the middle of the set to obtain color references and lighting positions. These measurements were then processed by computer to obtain a 3-D image of the set, the scenery, and the reference points found therein. The angles of the real shots were also made to correspond with the perspectives of the virtual sets.

The mutant Mystique morphs into Wolverine, taking on his appearance, in this scene from X-Men. *This special effect, done in 3-D by Kleiser-Walczak, uses a real shot of a stuntman leaping in front of a blue background. Once the transformation begins, it is a likeness of Mystique, entirely computer-generated, that performs the stuntman's opening leap. The 3-D clone of Mystique was rendered from a scan of actress Rebecca Romijn-Stamos's face and body. During the metamorphosis, the scales on her body move, vibrate, and regain position. The full process was composed of eighteen stages.*

Spider-Man at the Movies

Filming began on *Spider-Man* a few months after the success of *X-Men*. Director Sam Raimi, a fan of comic books since childhood, wanted to faithfully represent the character's acrobatic postures. John Dykstra remembers the first test he made to this end: "We saw three objectives: to create a credible virtual character, to animate it so it behaved like the real actor Tobey Maguire, and to devise the environment in which he would move around, because we knew that the filming of some of the real New York sets would not be sufficient. We created a very faithful double for Maguire, and we used video takes to analyze his manner of moving. It wasn't the broad, dynamic movements that were the hardest to animate, but the small, subtle gestures, which had to appear natural." Some computer-generated images of buildings were added to real views of New York, while other views were erased. The perspectives of some shots were extended to follow the vertiginous movements of the character. "We created some parts of the city in 3-D, we filmed the camera movements in the streets, and we mixed it all to create the scenes in which Spider-Man moves very fast," added Dykstra. "In some cases, the sequence began with a real building in the foreground, in front of which we would sweep the camera at top speed, while the scenery in the middle ground and the background of the frame were entirely created by computer."

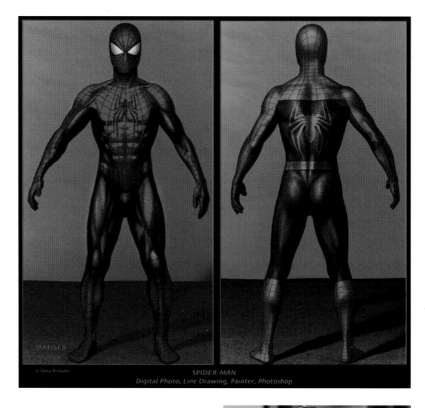

SPIDER-MAN
Digital Photo, Line Drawing, Painter, Photoshop

Spider-Man's costume, conceived by costume designer James Acheson, was composed of two layers: foam rubber musculature fixed to a costume made of a highly elastic fabric, and a second costume on which was printed the textures of Spider-Man's musculature, designed by Warren Manser. The reliefs of Spider-Man's web, made from foam rubber, were added later.
Photo courtesy of Columbia Home Video.
Spider-Man © Marvel

Overleaf: *The 3-D clone of Spider-Man swings at the end of a thread from his web, in a New York scene that was also reconstituted by computer-generated images.*
Photo courtesy of Columbia Home Video. Spider-Man © Marvel

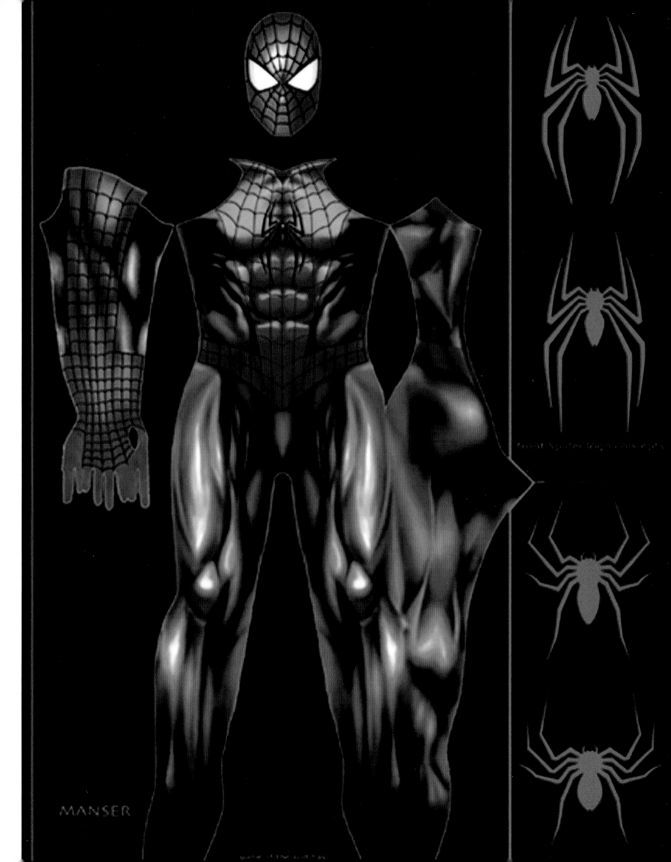

MANSER

INTERVIEW

SAM RAIMI

The Making of *Spider-Man*

Sam Raimi brilliantly transformed the adventures of Spider-Man into film. He humorously reveals the torments he endured making the special effects sequences.

Director Sam Raimi in conversation with Tobey Maguire (Spider-Man) and Kirsten Dunst (Mary Jane Watson)

Photo courtesy of Columbia Home Video. Spider-Man © Marvel

What were the images that you had in mind when you began to visualize the first "Spider-Man"?

Sam Raimi: I first thought about how I would reconstruct his movements. Spider-Man was always depicted like an aerial dancer, like an extremely graceful acrobat who moved above the city. I started by drawing a storyboard myself, which was so bad the professional artists would turn it upside down, trying to understand it! I described to them what I imagined, and they made illustrations that everyone could read. Then I worked with a small team to create the very simple, 3-D animatic sequences to define the movements that I wanted to get in each scene. A number of teams went to New York to locate the venues I'd chosen, like the Empire State Building. Then they used telemetric instruments that let them take precise measurements of the building and reconstitute it in synthesized images. They then took hundreds of photos of the building to "glue" them onto the 3-D volume of the building, thus getting a hyperrealistic surface that could be seen from all angles. This process, called Photogrametry, enabled us to re-create a complete 3-D landscape of New York, inside of which I could make all the camera movements that I wanted.

What was the most difficult sequence to film in terms of technique?

Sam Raimi: The final fight around the bridge! Mostly because I had to remember all the different images that had to be shot separately and then put together to get the final image. A shot like the one where you see Spider-Man holding Mary Jane hooked to a cable for an aerial tram suspended above a river, with a boat below, is composed of many elements: first Spider-Man filmed in the studio on a green background, or a computer-generated Spider-Man; then Mary Jane filmed on

Spider-Man leaps to catch hold of both the cable, from the cabin of an aerial tram, and Mary Jane at the same time—complicated effects that were a logistical nightmare for Sam Raimi!

Photos courtesy of Columbia Home Video. Spider-Man © Marvel

a green background; then a high-angle image of a boat I filmed in the port at Long Beach, California; then part of a bridge I filmed in New York, on the island of Manhattan; then a reconstitution of the perspectives of the bridge that had been assembled by computer from a multitude of photos shot at all angles. . . . It's like this with all the shots. It was difficult for me to keep all the pieces of the puzzle in my head. What's more, in many cases, I didn't film each of the elements myself. I had to precisely describe what I wanted to the director of the second crew. I had to say to him, "Use a 25-millimeter lens, put yourself fifty feet (fifteen meters) above the surface of the water, make sure the camera is at an angle of four degrees, shoot at a speed of forty-eight frames per second to slow down the movement of the boat a little and amplify the movement of the water." I asked him to find out how fast the boat would be moving and communicate it to me in order to adjust my shots.

But once on the film set with the blue background, other problems arose. When I asked for the camera to be placed fifty feet (fifteen meters) above the floor, the chief cameraman announced to me that the ceiling in the studio wasn't high enough! And then he said to me, "Why didn't you think of it

before?" Because I had a billion other things in my head! So we had to change the lens and take a 40-millimeter in order to "move" our subject farther back. But in doing that, we'd reveal all the rest of the set. To keep only the useful part of the frame while retaining a good definition, we had to use a VistaVision camera, which recorded each frame on a surface twice as large as ordinary 35-millimeter cameras. We then removed this piece of the frame to get one of the composites of the final shot. And this was only one shot! I don't want to enumerate the miseries of the life of a director, but the problems didn't end there. The crew that had to film in New York couldn't find a single 50-millimeter lens for rent! They called me to ask me what they should shoot with, and then I really hit bottom! This kind of problem can really make you lose your mind. Of course, I had excellent artists with me, to draw the images I'd imagined on the storyboard, and John Dykstra, who is a special effects genius. A genius is at the same time someone you want to take in your arms and thank for saving your life and, on some days, you just want to strangle! John said to me, "Oh, sure you could shoot this shot, but you'd have to shoot it by combining five elements!" When he lays it all out like that, you say to your-

self, "Great, everything's set." But then, when you realize the complexity of what has to be shot, you just want to kill!

The Spider-Man DVD contains dozens of short documentaries that detail all aspects of the visual effects production of the film. Photo courtesy of Columbia Home Video. Spider-Man © Marvel

Blind Justice and a Green Monster

Endowed with a smaller budget than the one for *Spider-Man, Daredevil* (2003) did, however, have good special effects, made by the Rhythm and Hues Studios. Here again, a virtual Daredevil was used to do the impossible acrobatics. The Houdini computer program made it possible to simulate flesh and the pleats of the leather costume on the 3-D clone of actor Ben Affleck. Rhythm and Hues also inserted virtual sets of New York's Hell's Kitchen neighborhood into shots filmed in Los Angeles. The same year, crews from ILM directed by Dennis Muren outdid themselves creating the devastating special effects of *The Hulk.* Just as in the comic strip, Dr. Bruce Banner metamorphoses into a green giant endowed with super-human strength. This double role was played by Eric Bana, using a process that transposed the expressions on the actor's face onto computer-generated images of the Hulk.

After having created the outfit for Spider-Man, James Acheson designed the red leather costume worn by Ben Affleck in Daredevil.
Photo courtesy of Twentieth Century-Fox. Daredevil © Marvel

Overleaf: *The expressions of the computer-generated likeness in* The Hulk *were animated by ILM using five hundred spot points, which were glued to actor Eric Bana's face.*
Photo courtesy of Universal Studios. Hulk © Marvel

The Legendary Trilogy of
The Lord of the Rings

The Lord of the Rings trilogy was the first special effects super-production to be filmed and produced entirely in New Zealand. The Weta Studios, founded by director Peter Jackson, magnificently carried out this colossal job, the postproduction of which took three years. The first two parts of this "fresco" each won an Oscar for best special effects. The character of Gollum, whom we fully discover in the second part, proves to be the most moving virtual creature ever created. The digital character's body movements and acting were based on those of actor Andy Serkis, who, dressed in a white, blue, or green costume (ultimately erased in the editing), incarnated Gollum in all the scenes in which he appears with other actors. Serkis reproduced his body movements at the Weta studios, wearing a motion capture suit, and then lent his voice to the creature. The 3-D face of Gollum, animated by Richard Baneham, Eric Saindon, Ken McGaugh, and Bay Raitt from Serkis's expressions, portrays emotions with astounding naturalness.

To play the dwarf warrior Gimli, John Rhys-Davies was literally covered from head to toe in creations by Weta: a facial prosthesis, a fake beard and wig, as well as a helmet, armor, and weapons devised by New Zealand artisans turned special effects designers.
Photo courtesy of New Line

INTERVIEW

RICHARD TAYLOR

Special Effects Supervisor at Weta Studios

Did you have trouble convincing Hollywood that you could produce quality special effects in New Zealand?

Richard Taylor: When Miramax sent one of its collaborators to us, at the beginning of the project, she expected to find the place housed in a trailer behind Peter Jackson's garage! Weta occupies a modern space covering sixty-eight thousand square feet (sixty-three hundred square meters) and employs 148 people full time. We are as well equipped as American studios, but it was hard to get this across! To prepare for the filming of *The Lord of the Rings*, we also hired saddle-makers to make the leather armor, and blacksmiths and coppersmiths for the weapons, helmets, and

Three stages of the addition of the 3-D characters animated with the Massive computer program, a product of Weta Digital: the background computer-generated warriors, the foreground scene filmed against a blue background in the studio, and the perfect mix of foreground and background
Photos courtesy of SGI

metal armor. We found wood sculptors, potters, and dozens of wonderfully talented crafts-people whom we trained in medieval European art.

What computer programs did your teams develop for the three films?

Richard Taylor: In his books, Tolkien describes confrontations between hundreds of thousands of monsters and warriors. To create these countless armies, we first made dozens of stat-uettes of the Orc warriors and knights. We scanned them in three dimensions, equipped with 3-D articulated skeletons, muscular mass, and details added with a graphics platform. But then we had to find the way to animate these characters on the battlefield. Since it was impossible to animate them one by one, we got the idea to give each of them an artificial intelligence and a "vocabulary" of warrior poses. Using the Massive program, thousands of characters advance in the direction we chose, acting in a realistic manner and reacting to the presence of the other characters around them like individuals with free will.

How did you develop the fight between the real actors and the Cave Troll in "The Fellowship of the Ring"?

Richard Taylor: Jackson wanted to film that scene as if it were passing before his eyes, without restricting the movement of his camera. So Weta developed a 3-D system that allowed him to see the computer-generated images of the Troll in the scenery during the filming. Peter wore glasses with video screens that played 3-D images of the Troll that had been ani-mated earlier. The perspectives of the Troll's environment were subordinate to the real perspec-tives of the setting that the scene was to be filmed in. If Peter took a step to the right, the position of the Troll changed immediately. He saw the 3-D rendering of the char-acter in motion in the room and could move it freely by guiding the movements of the actors.

How did you reduce the size of the actors playing the Hobbits?

Richard Taylor: We were con-stantly changing the technique. To film some shots, we asked Elijah Wood to kneel down while Ian McKellen stood on a small wooden crate. Scenes that show different-sized char-acters moving in the same set were filmed twice with a cam-era whose movements were controlled by computer. The actors playing the large-sized people were filmed first; then the camera's movements were reprogrammed to film a second run-through with the frame a third larger and the movements magnified likewise. The size of the actors playing the roles of the Hobbits was therefore smaller in the frame. When these two frames were digitally combined, the reduced silhou-ettes of the Hobbits had to be blocked out and inserted into the real-sized image. We also made small-sized models that we put next to the actors for some long shots—when Frodo is sitting next to Gandalf on a cart, for example.

The Orc warriors sent forth by the sorcerer Saruman during the assault on the fortress at Helm's Deep. The computer-generated images of Orcs climbing up the ladders were added to the image of the miniature fortress.
Photo courtesy of SGI

The actors playing the Hobbits were often filmed separately and reduced in size in the frame, but they were also replaced by small-sized extras, as in this scene. The background set of the mines of Moria is a highly detailed model inserted into the real image. Photo courtesy of SGI

How many miniature sets and props did you make for the three films?

Richard Taylor: More than sixty-five different sets. Along with the cities, there were the forests; the fantasy architecture, like Helm's Deep; and the volcanoes, like those around Mount Doom. These miniatures were combined with synthesized images, completing the landscape. Weta manufactured a total of 48,000 props, including 1,000 pieces of armor, 2,000 weapons, 1,800 costumes and body prosthetics,

10,000 facial prosthetics, 1,800 pairs of Hobbit feet, 10,000 bows, and 18 scanned miniature monsters! The scenery and prop departments themselves also produced tens of thousands of objects. The human props were enlarged for the Hobbits, and the Hobbit props were reduced for the large-sized people.

How was the makeup for the Orcs devised?

Richard Taylor: We produced dozens of artificial sets of eyebrow arches, noses and chins, contact lenses, wigs, and different false teeth. By combining these props on the faces of actors—who are all unique—and by using foundation makeup with different colors, you could get endless variations. In addition to this makeup, we also used latex masks that slipped on like hoods, and articulated foam rubber masks. In all, we had to create makeup for

One of the sumptuous images created by Weta that add models to real shots of the New Zealand landscape
Photo courtesy of SGI

six hundred Orcs. The made-up characters were put in the foreground. The extras with the articulated masks were farther back, and those wearing the latex masks, even farther back. We put tens of thousands of 3-D Orcs in the background during postproduction.

Retouching the makeup of an Orc warrior Photo courtesy of New Line

The performance of actor Andy Serkis was transposed by the animators at Weta in order to create the body and facial expressions of Gollum, the first truly emotionally moving, hyperrealistic computer-generated creature.

Photos courtesy of New Line

INTERVIEW

PITOF

If there's one man who typifies French special effects, it's Pitof. The director of *Vidocq* (2001), the world's first high-resolution digitally shot film, recalls his fascinating journey.

How did you learn to master special effects?

Pitof: At the beginning of my career, I worked on industrial films, whose video image I found truly vile. The image on film was for me "THE beautiful image." I had fun destroying video images, playing with them, refilming the screen. I moved through the biggest control rooms, starting with high-band U-matic tape and progressing to one-inch tape. At the time, we only had PaintBox. With analog video, the more you work on an image, the more it deteriorates from copy to copy. The settings shift. When I discovered the possibilities of the digital manipulation of images that brought about the creation of the Harry by Quantel, I realized that it was the locomotive for a new century of special effects. Initially, it was a tool for virtual editing with basic capabilities like insertion, ADO, used for reducing an image and making it move, but above all, it let you work in stop-motion.

The quality of the digital image did not degrade, even after dozens of reworks. I was able to develop a hybrid technique, halfway between optical effects achieved by an optical printer and video techniques in real time. You could immediately see what you had done, without waiting a day for it to be developed. The images were created on an analog console and then digitally mixed. It was first used for making advertisements, clips, and experimental films by artists like Michel Jaffrenou and Marc Caro.

In your opinion, what caused the delay in France's participation in the domain of optical effects?

Pitof: It was a cultural delay. France had had popular movies, action movies, for a long time, but the New Wave decreed that you had to get out of the studios and film in the streets, the camera on your shoulder. This trend was a deathblow to popular movies, and technique ground to a halt. The English and the Americans continued to explore their visual imagination. In order to be able to develop techniques, you had to have access to financial support, to new films. All the French who were interested in new special effects techniques left France to work for various companies in England or in America. And then, all of a sudden, France

was once again in the driver's seat, and I had the pleasure of participating in this progress. The first important step was made thanks to ads. Most French TV spots were filmed in England for one simple reason: the ads had to be made on a 35-millimeter base because they were broadcast using the 35-millimeter telecine installed at the technical headquarters of French television. The irony was, even when you wanted to shoot an ad on video, it had to be transferred onto 35 millimeter to be shown on TV! After great struggle, television finally agreed to broadcast one-inch B SECAM videotapes, and everything got turned on its head. Films to be shown on TV could be post-produced on video. Finally you could get back the French clients who had gone to England. At first, we only produced the insertions of titles and erasings, but then people asked us for more and more complicated things. After ads, we got back the filming of creative video clips, like those by Jean-Baptiste Mondino. Little by little, we learned how to produce more sophisticated effects and to master stage techniques, motion control, models, computer-generated images, etc. We made film tests of special effects. Duboi was the first French studio to scan a 35-millimeter negative, work on it digitally, and then transfer it back onto a 35-millimeter negative.

When did this important step take place?

Pitof: The first film that was released in digital was *Delicatessen* (1991). We didn't have a scanner and had to make a botch job using a telecine to reintegrate some fifteen special effects shots in such a way that you couldn't see a difference in resolution. The movie was filmed in 1.85 format. The trick was to manipulate the movies on a full-screen extended video format to make the most of the video definition of the telecine. When transferring onto film, you "tamped down" the image to concentrate all the resolution of the video image on the useful part of the 1.85 image. We also played with the contrast and filtering, letting us refine the image. The 35-millimeter image had been processed with a non-bleaching process developed by the head cameraman, Vittorio Storaro. The bleaching step was eliminated during the developing of the internegative and the manipulated negative. This desaturated the colors a little and heightened the contrast. The first time we made a real 35-millimeter scan from start to finish was on an ad, to be shown in movie theaters, for Peugeot scooters—a character was transformed into a tree. The person responsible for development at Duboi, Rip O'Neal, had gotten an Oxberry optical printer, mounted it on top of a medical imaging scanner, and jerry-rigged a machine. It was an in-house production, which had to be completed by writing special computer programs. Jean-Marie Poiré saw the ad, and as he was preparing *Les Visiteurs,* he contacted us. The machine continued to be used for many years. The next stage was *La Cité des enfants perdus,* which had 144 special effects shots. The main problem was the number of shots to produce. At the time, there weren't any interactive effects programs. I made my "models" of the effects shots on the Harry, and Rip O'Neal translated my manipulations into a computer script in order to steer the machine. And this is how we wrote the Dutruc special effects program, which I used to conceive the interactivity. I tried to find a way to establish a means of dialogue between the different cameramen, so they could share their data and work on the same shot. Earlier, computers were less powerful and therefore slower. The cameramen worked on small, simplified versions of the images so they could concentrate on the creation. This system also enabled the transfer of the definitive image's computations overnight.

What role do French special effects studios play in the international market?

Pitof: The French film industry doesn't allow big special effects firms to develop. To survive, the firms must be composed of small permanent teams that work with a complement of freelancers. They have to be extremely careful with their investments. Technological evolution is so fast that you can go broke buying a new machine that will be obsolete almost immediately. At home, I have an Apple G4 bi-processor that cost about 10,000 euros (12,500 dollars). It is much more powerful than the Harry that I used when I first started out and which cost almost 1 million euros (1.25 million dollars)! Prototype machines that are four or five years old are equivalent to personal computers. There is no difference between an image produced on a Silicon Graphics console and an Apple computer. In some cases, you compute an image for five hours on a Mac, while it would take thirty minutes on a Silicon. But such are the parameters of the organization and the planning of the job. Before, when using film, no one would even imagine building his own optical printer at home. Today, with personal computers, it can be done.

You employed this method on "Vidocq," the first movie entirely filmed in high-definition digital.

Pitof: Yes. All the special effects were done on PCs and Macs. The difference is appreciable regarding the budget for the equipment, but even more so in terms of quality. The problem with using very big machines is that the people who are trained to work with them don't necessarily have an artist's approach. Now people can teach themselves at home, using less expensive machines, and come on to a shoot well prepared. You can choose them solely for their talent. During the filming, I wanted to avoid innovation. I didn't want to get caught up in technique. I fixed on the quickest actor, the one who needed the most mobility, in this case Gérard Depardieu, to set all my camera movements. This is why 90 percent of the movie was filmed with a Steadicam.

Vidocq (through page 199): From a raw, high-definition video image through the final composite, which incorporates a computer-generated image of the church converted into a foundry Photos courtesy of RF2K Productions

Above and opposite: *The computer-generated images used to represent the back of the set of the church*
Photos courtesy of RF2K Productions

Would you say, being both the director and the special effects designer, that there are only advantages in filming in high-definition digital?

Pitof: For the moment, the sensors of cameras don't handle big disparities in contrast. Those who shoot outside have to choose whether to expose for the highlights or the darker regions. On the advantage side, you can enter the digital images directly into a computer, without having to scan them, as you have to with 35 millimeter. The special effects were conducted like the continuation of an artistic vision. Jean Rabasse conceived the sets in 3-D, then had them built, then completed and finalized them in 3-D. All the postproduction was done in-house with personal computers bought by the production, with the exception of the reflections of the alchemist's mask, which were produced by Mac Guff Line.

A Parisian landscape entirely re-created in CGI
Photos courtesy of RF2K Productions

Opposite and next four pages: *A superb digital matte painting depicting a nineteenth-century panorama of Paris, and the redrawn print that served as the basis for the elaborate re-creation*
Photos courtesy of RF2K Productions

INTERVIEW

Nicolas Rey

The Most Complex Special Effects Scene in All of French Film

Nicolas Rey, supervisor for 3-D special effects on the film *Le Boulet* (*Dead Weight,* 2002), explains to us how the Mikros Image team made the incredible sequence of the Ferris wheel flying off its axle, tearing through the Tuileries Gardens, and landing at the bottom of the Champs-Élysées.

How was the Ferris wheel sequence born?

Nicolas Rey: For us, the adventure of *Le Boulet* began when we were contacted by Christian Guillon of EST, which is a group that helps film producers disperse the production of their

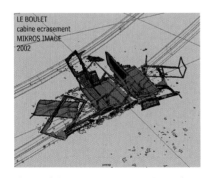

A test of the computer-generated crushing of a cabin for Le Boulet
Photo courtesy of Mikros Image & La Petite Reine

Above, opposite, and page 203: *Phases from the computer-generated rendering of the Ferris wheel whose axle becomes disengaged*   Photos courtesy of Mikros Image & La Petite Reine

special effects among different postproduction studios in order to create the effects quickly. We were contacted to make the Ferris wheel sequence. François-Xavier Nallet and I took care of

the 3-D, Krao managed the 2-D with Hugues Namur, and twenty-five other people from Mikros Image contributed to the work. We created one animatic scene by cursively modeling the

Tuileries and the Ferris wheel, but respecting all the real dimensions. This animatic allowed us to establish a rough cut of the shots, but also to get a detailed pre-shooting script, which led us to estimate the cost of the project. For two months, we polished this approach with the director and also abandoned some moves, as we only had three half-days of shooting for the scene in the Tuileries. We identified the problems that could arise during the shoot. Then we established, shot by shot, topographical readings of the sites that indicated where we had to place the camera. Of course, at the moment of filming, the head cameraman had to improve upon the preset frames. EST had prepared the shoot so as to film a minimum of scenes in the Tuileries and to make the stunt shots with a sun and similar trees at La Ferté-Alais, mixed with background images of the Tuileries.

How did the head cameraman frame the virtual Ferris wheel in the image?

Nicolas Rey: We were there on-site with a PC onto which we had loaded 3-D simulations of all the shots. We attached the video port of the 35-millimeter camera to the PC and made a double exposure of the 3-D images onto the real image. The PC allowed us to account for the head cameraman's framing changes and to alter the angle of the 3-D simulations.

Did you simulate the damage caused by the wheel during the filming, or was that added during postproduction?

Nicolas Rey: Concurrent with our work, the Versailles team had made a model at La Ferté-Alais of a one-third-scale wheel that measured sixty-five feet (twenty meters) high. Some of the crushing of the cabins and fairground stalls were filmed in real shots with this model. The Versailles team also built pre-crushed cabins on the same scale, which were brought to the shoot and placed in the trajectory of the Ferris wheel. In the beginning, we thought to do all the crushing of the cabins with the model, because we weren't sure we could properly simulate it in 3-D. So the Versailles team built a machine to crush the cabins, with power points distributed in order to guide the crushing. They built a hundred miniature cabins. The filming of the models took place in September 2001, but afterward, we succeeded in making the 3-D crushing of the cabins realistic by controlling the deformation of the shapes like the body of a character. We determined the particular articulations according to the shape of the crushing, as one would construct the skeleton of a character. We simulated the twisting of the metal as if it were the skin of a character. We could also model different phases of the crushing and have the computer make a 3-D morphing of one or another model. Finally, it was easier to use the 3-D cabins directly than to integrate the model cabins with stop-motion into the 3-D of the Ferris wheel. Rather than adding dust clouds during the filming, we preferred to ask the Versailles team to film the sand cloud in miniature on a black background. They hollowed out a trench in the ground, placed a hose at the bottom, and covered it over with dust. The hose was attached to a compressed-air valve, and the air was shot through the length of the hose. On the screen, you see a channel cave in and send up a cloud of dust! We took thousands of photos of the textures and details of the real Ferris wheel in order to create a 3-D duplicate. We had to create a computer program to manage the arrangement of the thousands of light bulbs.

Behind the Scenes of the *Matrix* Trilogy

The visual universe of *Matrix* (1999), *Matrix Reloaded* (2003), and *Matrix Revolutions* (2003), conceived by directors Larry and Andy Wachowski, was the product of work by costume designer Kym Barrett, production designer Owen Patterson, and visual effects supervisor John Gaeta. In front of the cameras, the actors wore special costumes that enabled them to perform physical feats. "Very often, the actors in *Matrix* wore harnesses that were screwed to supports attached to cranes or to cables that went up to the ceiling grid," explained Kym Barrett. "We also used ropes to violently pull them back when we wanted to simulate the impact of a shot, or to project them through a wall. We always film the new prototypes of costumes with different film stock that will be used during the filming, to make sure that it works on-screen. We also test the performance of the costumes during quick movements, and while the characters fly, and in the rain, and in front of a giant fan. We make as many versions of the costume as there are different action scenes. We start with the "perfect" costume, which is used during dialogue scenes. Then we take the actors' measurements again while they're wearing the

John Gaeta made wonderful use of Bullet-Time Photography in Matrix. *The system consists of a series of still cameras set in a circle around the actors, recording the action from all angles. Moving from one image to the next, the impression is of the camera moving at the speed of the light. If all the cameras are triggered at the same time, the succession of points of view seems to turn around the characters frozen in the midst of a leap. The set of the Metro station seen behind Keanu Reeves and Hugo Weaving was reconstituted in CGI.*
Photos courtesy of Photofest

harnesses. From these measurements, we make the costumes that will be used in the scenes where the actors are suspended from cables. Sometimes we have them wear a rubber diving suit over the harness, or a corset, to compress the flesh and make them look thinner. Thanks to this trick, the presence of the harness under the costumes is less noticeable. We make copies of the actors' outfits for the stunt people who double for them. Supports have been invented that hug the shape of the body, and onto which the harnesses and the costumes can be bolted down. This device allows the actors to be moved in all directions. In that case, the costumes are cut in two, lengthwise. A fake half of the costume is attached to the support, and I align it with the real costume. You have the impression of seeing the actor's body, while it's covered in part by the support. We also prepare costumes for the pyrotechnical scenes by plunging them in a liquid solution that makes the fabric inflammable. If someone asks us to prepare for the impact of bullets against the costume, we fatigue the inside of the fabric with razor blades so it can tear apart more easily when the little explosive charges blow up. We also make leather protectors to keep the actors from getting burned by the detonations."

Real- and Virtual-World Scenery

Owen Patterson was in charge of the real-world and virtual-world scenery in *Matrix,* which was often mixed with special effects: "In the first film, in 1999, we used a sort of giant slide called a Translight that depicted a montage of the real landscape of Sydney. We removed some buildings to make the action more visible in the foreground. This enormous composite served as a background image during the sequence of Morpheus's escape, when Neo and Trinity turn out to be in the helicopter. We created around 150 different settings in 2001 and 2002 for *Matrix Reloaded* and *Matrix Revolutions.* We started by constructing a 1.5-mile (2.5-kilometer) portion of a freeway on an old, decommissioned naval base at Alameda, [California,] in the United States. It was a replica of the 1-10, a freeway that crosses Los Angeles—there are tracks and cement walls very close to the cars. This enormous setting allowed us to film the complicated stunts without wasting time. The filming there lasted twelve weeks, with two crews working at the same time—one on the main scenes and the other on the background images that were added behind the filmed actors in the car's passenger seats, using insertions on a green background.

"We built two other sets, one of which was a temple, an enormous decorated cavern 350 feet (106 meters) long and 250 feet (76 meters) wide. We only constructed the lower portion, because of its size; the rest was completed and enlarged with computer-generated images. We had to create an uneven floor with undulations capable of bearing the weight of hundreds of extras. The other setting depicted streets with traditional New York facades. We made 147 sets in Australia. We had 240 days to shoot the two films. If you compare the number of shooting days with the number of sets, you'll understand why it was necessary to take apart and reconstruct or reassemble the sets to best use the available sites. Some sets were used only one day, and sometimes just half a day! Most of the structures were made of wood. The surfaces were laminated and covered with different layers to create the textures, and then with many coats of paint to imitate the materials we had to represent. We put openings in the ceiling of the scenery of the teahouse in Chinatown, so that the cables that allowed the characters to fly or to leap up while they fought running along the tables could pass through. It was what we had already made when we constructed the Metro station for the first film. The scenery for Zion is very complex. We had to use a lot of textures, painted

The Excesses of Visual Effects

Rewarded with an Oscar, the Bullet-Time Photography special effects created by John Gaeta have become so ingrained in the imagination that they have been reused or parodied in numerous films. Initially, this process consisted of placing a battery of 124 still cameras around Keanu Reeves and then triggering one after another at intervals of one-thirtieth of a second, in a studio entirely painted blue. The more the interval was reduced, the more the action slowed down. Using this mechanism, Gaeta could also "freeze the time" by triggering all the cameras at the same time. This way, he got a "frozen" 360-degree view of the actors suspended in place. The programming of the shots also made it possible to change the speed of the action and to control the fast-motion and slow-motion effects. Transitional images created by computer were inserted between the photos so as to prolong certain effects and obtain extreme slow motion, equal to filming at twelve thousand frames per second. But this first success had to be surpassed in the following two episodes so as not to disappoint the audience. "The experience acquired during the first *Matrix* allowed us to push the creation of the 3-D hyperrealistic environments even further,"

patinas. Geoff Darrow had designed a part of Zion that the directors really liked. I had to make a faithful transposition of it into computer-generated images. We enlarged the portion of the 3-D set that we were going to construct, in order to establish the shots. This process allowed us to precisely align the real set with the perspectives of the set added later, using digital special effects. When our sets were finished, the special effects team came and photographed them from all angles to create a database of textures and colors. They were used to "dress" the computer-generated images.

The famous scene from Matrix Reloaded *in which Neo confronts hundreds of clones of Agent Smith was made completely in CGI, from the motion capture of the actors. A new feat achieved by ESC, the studio founded by John Gaeta.*
Photos courtesy of Photofest

John Gaeta (in camouflage shirt) consults a storyboard during the filming of a freeway chase scene in Matrix Reloaded. Photo courtesy of ESC

explained John Gaeta. "We created virtual human characters that are different from the computer-generated characters you'd seen before. In the first *Matrix,* we developed a process, called Image-Based Rendering, which was used to create all the scenery that appears behind Neo during the famous sequence where he dodges the bullets. It consisted of taking a multitude of photos of a real landscape of skyscrapers, then taking down the real dimensions of the buildings. The volume of the buildings were reconstituted in 3-D and affixed on top of the photos of the landscape. We could then move the virtual camera in this space without any constraints. The result obtained is perfectly realistic, since it is a reconstitution in volume of an actual set. For the following sections, I asked my crew to look into how we could film the action scenes with actors and reconstitute them in full, in 3-D.

"I wanted this system to be able to record the most complicated actions conceived by martial arts expert and choreographer Yuen Wo-Peng, and even to amplify them, to multiply them, and to alter them beyond what one could get with real shots. The system that we developed consisted of working with the actors on a special stage that was entirely green. The images of their faces were recorded by an ensemble of five high-definition cameras, the recordings of which were not 'compressed.' There was, therefore, no more of a loss of definition than what occurred when George Lucas made his first shots in high-definition video. All this information was then transferred onto the computer-generated images of their bodies, moving in space. Thanks to this exceptional definition, we were capable of showing very close-up shots of our virtual actors without anyone being aware of the effect. All the details on their skin, the textures, their hair were reconstituted to perfection. We could also show them talking—their facial expressions when speaking were perfectly captured by the system. The body movements of the actors were recorded with the motion capture system, these being the performances of Keanu Reeves and Hugo Weaving that you see on screen. Later, 3-D replicas of their clothing were added onto the images in order to complete the virtual recording of the finished scene. It was a new way to direct superhuman powers. We also could 'show' these scenes the way we wanted to, moving the camera at another angle, changing the movements, and even completely altering the scene after a take, after filming, during the postproduction of the digital effects. We could insert a stuntman entirely in 3-D among the real actors without anyone being able to detect the differences between the two. One could imagine an entirely virtual version of *Matrix* in the coming years."

Animation: From Paintbrush to Pixel

Animation Before Film

Stories were first recounted through a succession of pictures in prehistoric caves, on Egyptian walls in the form of hieroglyphics, and on Greek urns, all long before Christ. A progressive narrative was again seen on the Bayeux tapestry, a 230-foot-long (70-meter) embroidered piece of linen said to date from the eleventh century that depicts the battle of Hastings (1066) and the ascension of William, Duke of Normandy, to the English throne. The first projection of still images did not occur for another six hundred years. Following the "magic lantern," the prototype of which was developed by the Dutchman Christiaan Huygens in 1659 and then perfected by the German Athanasius Kircher in 1671, new lanterns with two lenses made it possible to reveal two slightly different drawings in succession, thus creating an illusion of motion. In 1832, the Belgian Joseph Antoine Plateau introduced the Phenakistoscope, which split up animated motion into separate components. His device was composed of a cardboard disk with vertical slits around the perimeter. Eight or

Sketch illustrating the principle of the magic lantern by Athanasius Kircher

Engraving of a magic lantern

ten phases of a movement were drawn on the other side of the cardboard disk, between the slits. By turning the disk in front of a mirror and looking through the slits, which served as shutters, the drawings appeared to be animated. In 1834, the Englishman William George Horner perfected this principle with his invention of the Zoetrope, a rotating cylinder inside of which were tapes of paper with drawings on them. Motion could be seen by looking through the slits at the top of the cylinder. It would not be until the invention of the Praxinoscope by Émile Reynaud (discussed in chapter 1) that the first appearance of animated characters on a screen would be seen, not long before the invention of film.

A Phenakistoscope disk

A contemporary advertisement for the "Wheel of Life," as the Zoetrope was also called

ZOETROPE.

The **ZOETROPE**, or "**Wheel of Life**," is an instructive Scientific Toy, illustrating in an attractive manner the persistence of an image on the retina of the eye; it consists of a card-board cylinder, about 12 inches diameter, and 8 inches deep, with 13 equidistant narrow openings, each about 3 inches long, arranged near the top as shown in the engraving. The lower end rests on an iron shaft, rising from a substantial wood base; on strips of paper, about 3½ inches wide, 36 inches long, are printed figures of men, animals, etc., in different positions, which are placed in the cylinder. By revolving the cylinder by the hand, and looking through the openings, the images passing rapidly before the eye are blended, so as to give the figures the motions of life in the most natural manner. As many persons as can stand around the Zoetrope can see the movements at the same time.

PRICE OF THE ZOETROPE, $2.50.

The Big Screen Becomes Animated

One of the first animated cartoons on film was the Matches Appeal (1899) advertisement directed by the Englishman Arthur Melbourne Cooper. He lured British movie audiences into buying matches and sending them to soldiers mobilized during the Boer War. In the United States in 1905, Edwin S. Porter animated the title cards for the short movies *The Whole Dam Family and the Dam Dog* and *How Jones Lost His Roll,* by moving cutout letters that successively formed words and sentences. The first animation of objects was done by the Spaniard Segundo de Chomon in *El Hotel Eléctrico* (*The Electric Hotel,* 1905). The American caricaturist James Stuart Blackton amused himself by altering drawings of faces in *Humorous Phases of Funny Faces* (1906). The same year, he was the first to animate figurines in *A Midwinter Night's Dream.* He then used modeling paste to transform the objects in *The Haunted Hotel* (1907) by stop-motion.

James Stuart Blackton, animation pioneer, in 1906

An image taken from Humorous Phases of Funny Faces

The character Fantoche, created by Émile Cohl, was the first cartoon star.

Émile Cohl, a French Pioneer

After attending a showing of *The Haunted Hotel,* Émile Cohl (1857–1938) appreciated the principle of special effects by

Émile Cohl, one of the inventors of animated drawings

substitution. He got the equipment, found financing, and made the first French cinematographic animated cartoon, *Fantasmagorie* (*A Fantasy*), which was screened on August 17, 1908, in Paris. At the time, the standard rate of projection was still sixteen frames per second (the speed would increase to twenty-four frames per second in 1927 with the advent of the talkie), and so talented caricaturists such as Cohl could fairly quickly produce sequences drawn directly on paper that ran one or two minutes long. Along with creating the character Fantoche, who would appear in short comedic scenes such as *Le Cauchemar de Fantoche* (*The Puppet's Nightmare*), Cohl also

gave birth to the first cartoons, which were exported throughout the world. He was an incessant innovator: he animated puppets in *Le Tout Petit Faust* (*The Little Faust,* 1910), colored drawings on film in *Le Peintre Néo-Impressioniste* (*The Neo-Impressionist Painter,* 1910), and used cutout paper characters in *Les Douze Travaux d'Hercule* (*The Twelve Labors of Hercules,* 1910). He inaugurated morphing by transforming his drawings in *Les Joyeux Microbes* (*The Merry Microbes,* 1909). In 1911, he used "pixilation" to make *Jobard ne peut pas voir les femmes travailler* (*Jobard Can't See Women Working*); he took still shots of his actors and then filmed them in stop-motion to obtain comical animation and speeded-up effects. Cohl continued to produce short films up until the end of his career in 1923. Although most of his films are lost, his work has not been forgotten. Walt Disney paid homage to the father of animated cartoons when, in 1935, he was decorated with the Legion of Honor by the French consul in California.

Winsor McCay, the Dinosaur Trainer

Winsor McCay became famous in 1905 with the debut of *Little Nemo in Slumberland* in the *New York Herald*. This masterpiece of a comic strip was read by hundreds of thousands of people. Beginning in 1906, McCay made the most of his fame by performing in nightclubs. His Chalk-Talk Artist act

consisted of drawing characters in chalk on a blackboard while presenting an ongoing comedic commentary—too simple an exercise for this genius whose talent was equaled only by his speed. So McCay decided to produce a little animated film. He drew four thousand images on sheets of stiff paper and came up with *Little Nemo* (1911). This first attempt was a masterstroke, with its characters

Frightened by a mammoth, Gertie won't wait long to chase it away.

moving remarkably naturally. In the final scene, a dragon appears to the left of a pretty princess and opens up his mouth wide. His tongue turns into a golden throne, on which Nemo and his beauty take their places and wave to the audience. The slithering dragon disappears off into the horizon. *Little Nemo,* colored by hand, became the most beautiful animated cartoon of its time. McCay outdid himself three years later with his *Gertie the Dinosaur* (1914). He used a finer paper, and thus could trace a fixed setting behind his title character, which was animated by stop-motion. He presented the film himself at music halls. Once the movie started, sitting below and to the right of the screen, he would crack the whip he had in his hand and yell, "Gertie, Gertie!" An enormous female brontosaurus would then emerge from a cave and move toward him. McCay would ask her to concentrate and raise her her right foot and then her left foot, despite the interruption of a mammoth passing by—which Gertie would seize by the tail and hurl into the nearby lake—and the appearance of a sea serpent. At the end of the film, McCay would slip behind the screen and reappear in the form of an animated silhouette. Gertie would place her head on the ground so her

The movie poster for Gertie the Dinosaur *led people to think that the animal really appeared on the stage.*

"trainer" could climb up onto her and go off into the landscape, to the applause of the audience. This interactive presentation was an immense success. In 1918, McCay made *The Sinking of the Lusitania,* which re-created the torpedoing of an ocean liner by a German submarine. This tragedy was presented with shots at dramatic angles. The care taken with the animation of the smoke and the explosions that rocked the ship prove that McCay considered animated cartoon to be a new art form. He made six more films after this masterpiece, the last of which was *The Flying House* (1921). But it was *The Sinking of the Lusitania* that would allow him to evolve his techniques and use, for the first time, a material far more practical than paper: celluloid.

The First Celluloids

The process of painting on celluloid was developed by John Bray and Earl Hurd and patented in the United States in 1914. Characters were drawn and painted on transparent sheets that were placed on top of the scenery. Perforations ensured that the celluloids were always aligned identically. From this point on, it was no longer necessary to simplify the scenery in order to be able to recopy it on each new drawing, and backgrounds were painted with watercolors and became highly detailed. The concept of

separating the animation of the character into several zones of the celluloid also came to be appreciated: if the body were to remain stationary while the head moved, a drawing of the body would be made on a first piece of celluloid, on top of which was placed a second piece, enabling just the head to be animated.

Ladislaw Starewicz's Magical Puppets

Assisted by his daughter Irina, the Polish-born Ladislaw Alexandrowicz Starewicz (1882–1965) made some of the most beautiful puppet animation movies ever filmed. His passion for insects gave him the idea to animate some preserved specimens in *Lucanus Cervus* (1910). This first film was quite successful in Poland, and made it possible for him to film *La Belle Lucanide* (*The Beautiful Leukanida,* 1910) and then *La Cigale et la fourmi* (*The Dragonfly and The Ant,* 1911). In 1912, he moved to Moscow and set up his own studio. World War I and all the turmoil that it brought to Russia forced him to leave, and in 1924 he moved to Fontenay-sous-Bois, outside Paris. The thirteen short films he made during the 1920s are marvels of poetry and invention. Sixty years before Go-Motion computing was developed by ILM, Starewicz was already creating blurred effects with the rapid movements

Ladislaw Starewicz and his daughter Nina in his studio around 1925. They are surrounded by the puppets from his movies Amour noir et blanc, Les Grenouilles qui demandent un roi, La Reine des papillons, *and* Les Yeux du dragon. Photo © L. B. Martin-Starewicz

of characters. How did he manage to do it? If one watches his movies frame by frame, one can detect the differences in the characteristic brightness of the protracted opening of the shutter during each of these blurred or "drawn-out" scenes of movement. Did he use very fine wires or black gloves to move his characters when the shutter was open? We no longer have any precise or technically convincing information regarding his methods. If this mystery persists, the process he used to make his puppets is well known. The most complex characters had wooden armatures and ankles that were attached with screws. Their faces were covered in kidskin and could be reshaped to make different expressions. A main character would be produced on several scales so it could be placed in sets of different sizes. When he filmed his puppets, Starewicz made it seem as if the camera was moving around the set, when in fact it was the puppets, the scenery, and the projectors that moved in front of the camera. In *La Petite Chanteuse des rues* (*The Little Street Singer*, 1924), Starewicz had a real

A trick photo in which Starewicz pictures himself among the animals from Le Roman de Renard
Photo © L. B. Martin-Starewicz

actress appear with an animated puppet. It took eighteen months of work, between 1929 and 1930, for him to make the full-length *Le Roman de Renard* (*The Tale of the Fox*), the sound version of which would be released in France in 1941. The detail of the puppets in this movie was superb. The largest puppets, like the lion, measured thirty-two inches (eighty cen-

timeters). Starewicz continued to produce short films throughout the 1930s, but the advent of sound and color shook up the world of film. Financial backing became essential, and this was not available to the independent artist. In 1949, *Fleur de fougère* (*Fern Flowers*), his first color movie, won the prize for best animated feature at the Venice Film Festival. In it are some

stunning effects of the projection of the scenery at the feet of Jeannot, who appears to be running toward the camera in an attempt to flee from the monstrous creatures of the forest—a set "loop" of a caterpillar apparently moving beneath a puppet, controlled by a rigid metal rod. Ladislaw Starewicz died in 1965, but his work continues to influence animation artists.

INTERVIEW

LÉONA BÉATRICE
MARTIN-STAREWICZ

Ladislaw Starewicz's grand-daughter Léona Béatrice Martin-Starewicz has kept the work of her grandfather alive by restoring his films, exhibiting his puppets, and participating in conferences and festivals around the world.

Starewicz during the filming of La Reine des papillons *(1927)*
Photo © L. B. Martin-Starewicz

Léona Béatrice Martin-Starewicz and one of her grandfather's puppets, whose original costume she restored
Photo © L. B. Martin-Starewicz

How did your grandfather construct his film puppets with such expressive faces?

Léona Béatrice Martin-Starewicz: There were three kinds: soft puppets with iron wire armatures, puppets with wooden articulations, and "spontaneous" puppets, which were made with different materials, like modeling paste. The heads of the puppets were sculpted from pieces of cork, with the indentations corresponding to the eye sockets. The face itself was fashioned out of a piece of damp kidskin, which could be easily shaped before it dried. The iron wires were placed beneath this skin so the soft parts of the face, like the lips and cheeks, could be animated. Starewicz worked with the small pliers used by dentists to delicately animate the finest articulations and turn the eyes in their sockets. These tools were extensions of his fingers. The puppets' bodies were wrapped in cloth or fur stuffed with cotton or straw and meticulously sewn. My grandfather would place two small wooden disks that were attached with an endless screw inside the belly of some of the characters. By turning this screw in one direction and then in the other, using stop-motion, he could increase or decrease the separation between the two disks, and thus create the impression that the character was breathing.

How were the puppets' costumes made?

L. B. Martin-Starewicz: Starewicz always drew his characters. His daughter Irina took care of the dressmaking with great finesse, fashioning the cloth that was wrapped around the body. My grandmother was also extremely painstaking with the clothes she made. Some of them, like those that appeared in *Le Rat de ville et le rat des champs* (*The Town Rat and the Country Rat*), were made with thousands of little pearls. Irina worked in close collaboration with my grandfather for thirty years. She became blind in the 1950s but, despite her handicap, still managed to produce equally fine work. The broad parts of the costumes (vests, jackets, skirts) were reinforced with iron wires, so they could be animated, accompany the characters' movements, or give the impression of being blown by the wind.

The devil puppet that appears in "L'Épouvantail" ("The Scarecrow") and in "Fétiche mascotte" ("The Mascot") was fitted with eyes that were bulbs attached to a rheostat. Did Starewicz talk about his technical ideas, or did he keep them in his "inner world"?

L. B. Martin-Starewicz: My grandfather spoke little, rarely mentioned his ideas, but this silence was not ponderous. He was brimming with great benevolence. Starewicz was concentrated, totally involved in his creation. He used all sorts of materials to construct his sets, with a particular fondness for cork, which could be shaped very quickly. He also made props out of wood, like the sculpted throne in *Le Roman de Renard*. I often saw him working when I was small without truly understanding why he undertook such meticulous work with the puppets. I didn't see the movies until much later. As we always spoke in Russian, I was taken aback to learn much later that he spoke French very well!

In "Fétiche mascotte," a small dog is seen wandering along the edge of the sidewalk in front of real shots of cars. Legs animated in stop-motion pass in front of him. How did Starewicz develop this system of back projection?

L. B. Martin-Starewicz: He constructed everything himself. When he needed an instrument, he would invent it. He never registered a patent. He worked alone, with the assistance of his daughter Irina. My grandmother made the costumes and my mother, Nina, acted in the movies he filmed in France. These movies were family projects, developed in a tight circle. Starewicz constructed dozens of devices that I still have, and the function of which I don't know. He made special effects himself and developed the film in his own laboratory.

Who are the filmmakers of today that remind you of your grandfather's work?

L. B. Martin-Starewicz: Ray Harryhausen saw his puppets and found them very beautiful. He was surprised to see that they were fitted with wooden armatures and ankles, because he uses a very different, more rigid system. I also know that Starewicz's movies were viewed by some of Tim Burton's collaborators before they started work on *The Nightmare Before Christmas*. Furthermore, there is a certain resemblance between some of the devils in *L'Épouvantail* and those in Burton's movie.

Willis O'Brien: When an Animation Artist Becomes a Special Effects Genius

The American Willis O'Brien is one of the pioneers in the three-dimensional animation of characters. In 1913, he was constructing models in the offices of the chief architect of the San Francisco World's Fair. During a break, he modeled a statuette of a boxer out of clay and fitted it with a wire skeleton. One of his colleagues made another one, and they had fun modeling the different stages of a fight. O'Brien then wondered whether with this technique one could produce animated movies other than with animated drawings. Having decided to pursue this idea, he constructed a miniature landscape on the roof of a large building so as to make use of the sunlight and a real sky. He hired a news cameraman to film animation of his first two puppets—a caveman and a dinosaur, each endowed with an articulated, wooden armature and skin made of modeling paste—in stop-motion. Producer Herman Wobber liked this test and invested five thousand dollars in the filming of O'Brien's first short movie, *The Dinosaur and the Missing Link* (1915). This series of humorous vignettes recounts the misadventures of several cavemen who look for food in order to seduce a beautiful cavewoman. Enthusiastic

Willis O'Brien animating the models of his unfinished project Creation, *a sequence of which was filmed long before* King Kong

about the movie, Thomas Edison bought the distribution rights and hired O'Brien, giving him carte blanche. The animator then produced other prehistoric comedies. In *R.F.D., 10,000 BC* (1916), a postman is seen using a brontosaurus to deliver the mail, which consists of slabs of engraved stone. Edison's studio was experiencing difficulties at the time and did not have much work to offer the animator. Herbert M. Dawley, a sculptor who made statuettes of dinosaurs to be used in photographs, offered him a budget of three thousand dollars to codirect a movie. O'Brien jumped at the opportunity and filmed *The Ghost of Slumber Mountain* (1918), the story of a mountain climber who, in a dream, sees the ghost of an old hermit living on the mountain with his "magic telescope," through which one can

discover life that existed millions of years before. This sequence was the first realistic representation of prehistoric times that O'Brien directed. He took the time to study dinosaurs in the paleontology departments of museums, and his new puppets were exact replicas of prehistoric animals. He animated a brontosaurus and a diatryma (a giant carnivorous bird), and he filmed a spectacular fight between a tyrannosaurus and a triceratops.

The enormous success of the film made him the great specialist of dinosaur scenes, and in 1925 he was asked to do the animations for *The Lost World,* the first adaptation of the novel by Arthur Conan Doyle. It was the turning point of his career. O'Brien developed a technique for making animation puppets that is still used today. Working from a diagram of the skeleton of a dinosaur, he manufactured a set of metal bones that had small steel balls affixed to each end. These balls were sandwiched between plates of aluminum, drilled with holes into which the balls would become lodged. The aluminum plates were attached to one another with screws, making it possible to exert pressure on the balls and thus function as a ball-and-socket joint. With this mechanism, the skeleton could be positioned in any pose. O'Brien hired the young artist Marcel Delgado to construct the body

Previous page and right: *The scenes from* The Lost World *stunned audiences in 1925, who got to see the first realistic dinosaurs ever filmed for the movies.*

of each dinosaur, layer by layer. Delgado started by covering the metal armature with pieces of foam rubber, originally bath sponges. He assiduously cut them to form the outline of the animal. The skin was made from thin layers of the latex used by dentists. Delgado cut the plates and glued the pieces onto the foam to get a smooth surface. He then released small droplets of liquid latex, one by one, onto the skin. With the help of a hair dryer, the droplets solidified, taking on the appearance of reptilian scales. Delgado also placed in the bellies of some of the dinosaurs the

bladder from a football, which, when inflated and then deflated (filmed in stop-motion), gave the impression that the dinosaurs were breathing. The filming of *The Lost World* began in 1923. The head cameraman, Arthur Edeson, used mattes to film the scenes in which actors were confronted by the dinosaurs. He would cut a piece of black cardboard and place it in front of the camera to hide the part of the frame where the prehistoric animals were to appear, and then would use the outline of a large rock or a grove of trees to create the line of separation. If this line had to be

as precise as the outline of the rock, a large matte would be placed at some distance from the camera. For the outline of foliage, the matte would be smaller and placed closer to the camera, so as to blur the line of separation. Edeson then handed over the undeveloped original negative, with the outline of his matte within the frame of the image, to O'Brien, who would make the reverse counter-matte—one that hid the images of the actors—and filmed his stop-motion animation without the slightest room for error. The dinosaurs in *The Lost World* enchanted the

audiences of 1925. Willis O'Brien left his role as an animator to become one of the greatest special effects supervisors. Eight years later, he created his masterpiece: *King Kong*.

The First Full-Length Animation

Lotte Reiniger produced the first full-length animation film, *Die Abenteuer des Prinzen Achmed* (*The Adventures of Prince Achmed,* 1923–26), in Germany using a shadow play technique that she dubbed Silhouettenfilm. Reiniger placed black paper silhouettes on backlighted sets. The characters look like shadows moving in the foreground on an illuminated background. The costumes of these magnificent jumping jacks are often adorned with feathers and extremely delicate props, cut out with scissors and blades by Reiniger herself. A superb interpretation of *A Thousand and One Nights, Die Abenteuer des Prinzen Achmed* transposed the Asian aesthetic of shadow theater to film.

Lotte Reiniger turned cutouts into an art form. Her movie The Adventures of Prince Achmed *was the first full-length animation in the history of film.*

Oskar Fischinger and Musical Abstraction

The German artist Oskar Fischinger (1900–1967) invented new processes to make abstract shapes suddenly appear on the screen. From 1923 to 1927, he made the *Wachs Experimente* (*Wax Experiments*) series of movies, using a machine that cut colored blocks of wax into fine layers in order to penetrate ever more deeply into the material. The blocks were inclusions of elements prepared in advance—a motionless red cone pointing forward in white wax would produce the effect of a red circle that grew progressively larger. Fischinger produced startling animation by varying the shapes and colors of his inclusions. In 1925, he collaborated with Fritz Lang in working on the special effects of *Frau im Mond* (*Woman in the Moon,* 1929). Slowly he diversified his techniques, animating abstract forms in cut paper and in volume for *Komposition in Blau* (*Composition in Blue,* 1935.) He left Germany the following year to escape persecution by the Nazis, who declared his movies "degenerate works." Moving to the United States, he found work at the Disney Studios and collaborated on the sequence of Johann Sebastian Bach's *Toccata and Fugue in D Minor* that appears in *Fantasia.* Fischinger, who spoke only a few words of English, could not take part in production meetings, though his films inspired others. Isolated, he was assigned the job of a subordinate—to make the sparks of the fairy's magic wand in *Pinocchio*! Disillusioned, he quit Disney Studios and, through the curator and founder of the Guggenheim Museum, Mrs. von Ehrenwiesen, was given the means to pursue his creativity. The grants enabled him to produce several masterpieces, such as *Allegretto* (1940), *Radio Dynamics* (1943), and *Motion Painting No. 1* (1947). In the 1950s, he invented the Lumigraph, a device that made it possible to project fine beams of colored light into a space and create moving shapes on a hand, face, or object. He died before completing his project of a full-length film inspired by Antonín Dvořák's *New World Symphony.*

The Fleischer Brothers, the Rotoscope, and the Rotograph

While it is remembered that Max and Dave Fleischer were the creators of Koko the Clown and Betty Boop, their technical talents are sometimes forgotten. Their first invention was the Rotoscope, developed in 1915, which enabled them to produce their first animated cartoon in 1917. The device comprised a light source contained in a

Max Fleischer and his most famous heroine, Betty Boop

lantern that illuminated the film loaded into an adapted projector. A 35-millimeter image was projected onto a frosted glass disk, attached to which was a perforated drawing sheet. This way, the movements of the actor could be traced in stop-motion and transposed onto a cartoon character. The obtained animations appeared natural and made it possible to reproduce complex actions, which the animators took great pains to draw. The Rotoscope, for example, made it possible to replicate a dance down to the smallest detail, even the folds in the dress as the character moved. The first character animated by Rotoscope was Koko the Clown. He first appeared on-screen coming right out of Max Fleischer's inkwell, while the artist was filmed working on a blank page, and he starred in the series of shorts *Out of the Inkwell,* which debuted in 1919. In 1924, the Fleischer brothers produced *Mother Pin a Rose on Me,* their first talking animated cartoon

Drawings for the patent registration of the Rotoscope, invented by the Fleischer brothers

Fig. 1

Fig. 2

Fig. 3

WITNESSES

Frank C. Palmer

INVENTOR

Max Fleischer

using the Phonofilm system, which synchronized projection with a 78 rpm record. The process was not very reliable and quickly disappeared. The brothers created Betty Boop in 1930, then transposed E. C. Segar's *Popeye* comic strips in 1933.

It was the following year when they came up with the Rotograph, which could interpose an animated character into a real shot. The celluloid character was placed on a plate of frosted glass that served as a projection screen. With each repositioning of the celluloid, the projected image was changed. Insertion of cartoon characters into real shots proved to be of limited use, and the brothers devised a variation. The celluloid was placed vertically between two plates of glass—in order to keep it flat—in front of a miniature set constructed on a circular revolving mount. To animate the characters and give the impression that they were moving from left to right, the set was turned from right to left in stop-motion. On the screen, one saw the perspectives changing. The three-dimensional aspect was enhanced when miniature props were placed in front of the celluloid—a character might be seen walking between a tree orchard in the foreground and a vast set in the background. These "back sets," as they were called, first appeared in *Poor Cinderella* (1934), a Betty Boop adventure. The Rotograph was used to won-

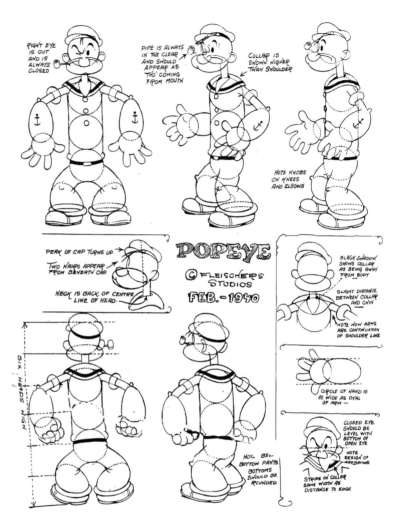

The model sheet for Popeye, transposed from the comics for the movies by the Fleischers

drous effect in *Popeye the Sailor Meets Sinbad the Sailor* (1936), the first *Popeye* in color. The cave scenery in which Popeye and Sinbad confront the evil sorcerer set the scene for such superb effects of depth that it was nominated for an Oscar. Hoping to ride on the coattails of

Walt Disney's *Snow White,* the Fleischers made two full-length films: *Gulliver's Travels* (1939) and *Mr. Bug Goes to Town* (1941). Neither of these movies saw the success of the Disney productions, which were more modern in style. Using the Rotoscope system, the brothers again, beginning in 1941, animated realistic characters in *The Adventures of Superman*. These shorts, brimming with spectacular action sequences, were to be their last success.

Walt Disney: The Eternal Innovator

At the beginning of his career, the young Walter Elias Disney made humorous drawings and advertising illustrations for newspapers. He then became interested in cartoons and sought a way to distinguish himself from others working in the field. He decided to insert a real girl into animated scenes; in 1923, he debuted the *Alice in Cartoonland* series. This form of special effects briefly captured the public's imagination, but the novelty soon faded. Disney abandoned Alice in favor of creating Oswald the Rabbit, which an unscrupulous producer stole from him. The revolution of talking movies arrived, thanks to a process from Warner Bros. that transferred sound onto film through an optical sound track. Disney decided to produce the first talking animated movie, featuring his new character, Mickey Mouse, animated by Ub Iwerks. Mickey was set to appear in two silent cartoons, *Plane Crazy* and *Gallopin' Gaucho,* but Disney decided not to release them immediately. Instead, he wrote a new script entitled *Steamboat Willie,* with sound effects gags. At the time,

sounds could not be recorded independently; rather, they were mixed and synchronized with the movie. Everything had to be recorded in a single take. Disney assembled a small orchestra and two sound effects engineers and conducted rehearsals in front of a screen onto which a loop of the animation was projected. Disney drew marks on the film to point out the principal effects. By viewing the movie again and again, the crew succeeded in recording the entire sound track as the scenes unrolled in a single take of seven minutes. When *Steamboat Willie* was released in 1928, it was a great hit. The audience roared with laughter at the comedic sound effects and gags.

Walt Disney himself created Mickey Mouse's falsetto voice, but by the 1940s, when he was snowed under with work, he passed on the role to Jimmy McDonald. McDonald was a sound effects genius, who disassembled objects such as car horns, tin cans, balloons, or

Jimmy McDonald, one of the most inventive and talented sound effects men of the golden age of Disney cartoons   Photo © Disney Enterprises, Inc.

This machine devised by Jimmy McDonald produced the sound of a machine gun.
Photo © Disney Enterprises, Inc.

Gliding along strings, these cans that McDonald stretched leather over would produce perfectly realistic frog croaks. The bigger the cans, the deeper the croaks.
Photo © Disney Enterprises, Inc.

watering hoses to build new sound effects instruments. To create the rumbling of thunder, he would roll small metal balls inside a larger rubber ball. He imitated to perfection the roar of a bear by growling into the glass bulb of an oil lamp. McDonald arranged each utensil in a cardboard box, indicating beneath the sound it produced: surrealistic labels such as Zoiing! Plop! and Blang! Having conquered sound, Disney went into an exclusive agreement with Technicolor to produce the first color animated movie. It was *Flowers and Trees* (1932), which was honored with the first Oscar for an animated picture. When others would have rested on their laurels, Disney was already conceiving a new form of animated entertainment: a full-length movie. Some critics declared that audiences would never stand "those vivid colors and grotesque characters" for a long duration. They forgot that Disney intended to entertain and move the audience with characters as endearing as actors. But before anything else, he would develop a revolutionary camera that was to distinguish this kind of production from all that had come before it.

The Creation of Multiplane

Walt Disney developed the multiplane camera in the middle of the 1930s. This innovation made it possible to animate different cels of a frame independently and thus create a sense of depth. Disney described it by saying, "Imagine walking on a country lane, at night, in the beam of a full moon. The moon doesn't grow larger as you walk forward, any more than it recedes as you walk away. The problem that presented itself was to give a drawing the same characteristics. This was impossible, since we were filming a flat landscape, in two dimensions. Therefore, we came up with plans for a new animation camera that allowed us to rem-

edy this. The different elements of a scene were separated into many layers of drawing superimposed on glass plates, according to the distance in terms of the audience's point of view. We positioned the moon on the plane farthest from the camera. By breaking down our original image in this way, it was possible to control the relative speed at which each part of the scenery approached or drew away from the camera, without changing the size of the moon or moving it. Since this camera used many planes, we called it a multiplane camera." The short feature *The Old Mill* (1937) marked the first use of the multiplane, which would be employed extensively during the following year on Walt Disney's big project *Snow White and the Seven Dwarfs,* the first full-length animated movie. Disney used a plate of glass specially made by a craftsman to animate the surface of the river next to which Snow White sings with the animals of the forest. The scenery depicting the surface of the water was viewed through the glass. When the plate was moved laterally in stop-motion, its delicate textures and irregularities of thickness altered the still picture depicting the water. A second still setting of trees and the riverbank was cut out and placed in front of the glass plate, thus remaining unaltered. Celluloids of the characters were placed on this third layer of

scenery. When the sequence was projected, the impression was of seeing the swirling waters of the river. The same special effect was used to distort the mask that appears in the wicked queen's magical mirror.

Armed with this experience, the multiplane camera operators accomplished a true achievement in 1940 during the filming of *Pinocchio,* in which the little wooden puppet is seen going to school for the first time. The audience sees the clock tower that overlooks the town, and then doves flying around it. The camera pans over the rooftops and then down small streets to show the activities of townspeople—a mother kisses her son; a group of children are hurrying off. A pan to the right ends this sweeping movement, bringing us to the door of Gepetto's house as he is opening it and saying good-bye to Pinocchio. The simultaneous movements of different planes of scenery and different animated characters were computed and then executed with extreme precision, just as were the progressive changes in focus, made by stop-motion. This one technical feat came at a price—forty-eight thousand dollars, or the cost of two cartoons! Disney always took things one step further. He hired the best

Walt Disney and his technicians with the famous multiplane camera used to create the effects of depth and relief for the sets of animated cartoons
Photo © Disney Enterprises, Inc.

high-fidelity sound experts to develop the first projections of synchronized stereophonic sound, dubbed Fantasound for the occasion. Disney imagined making *Fantasia* into an ongoing concert, with sequences regularly being replaced by new ones and the movie always kept in the public's eye. Produced at great cost, *Fantasia* was a resounding failure when it was released in 1940. Walt Disney had to dream up projects that were more easily accessible, such as *Dumbo* (1941), to pull his company out of bankruptcy.

The Disney Method

Walt Disney and his collaborators established the basic procedures for making an animated film. Once the script was approved, the actors who would lend their voices to the characters were chosen and all of the dialogue was recorded. Analyzed syllable by syllable, a twenty-fourth of a second by a twenty-fourth of a second, the dialogue was then transcribed onto large-format pages. Animators would refer to these exposure sheets when making a character's lips move, drawing by drawing, and when giving them the expressions suggested by the script. Following this decoding, each sequence was then transposed into small drawings that were pinned onto large panels, or storyboards. With them, one could see in a glance

the continuity of a scene and find those passages that were too slow or not very interesting. Also tested were the values of the shots best adapted to the narration of the story: long shots, medium shots, dolly shots, etc. Once a sequence was approved by the director and the producer, the shots were assigned to the animators. Each supervising animator was responsible for one character, deciding its postures and gesticulations. He would then supervise four or five other animators who would work on the same character. The editing of the movie would begin before filming. The still drawings that made up the storyboard would be filmed and synchronized with recordings of the actors' voices. This interim editing provided an idea of the rhythm and both the merits and shortcomings of the movie. At this point, changes in the action would be made and a scene that was deemed unsatisfactory would be replaced. The still drawings were then replaced by the first line animations, which in turn were replaced by full animations and by colored and manipulated scenes. The editing slowly transformed itself into a movie.

Alexander Alexeieff and Claire Parker's Pin Screen

From the 1930s, film animation artists latched onto the oddest materials to express their

creativity—pastels, chalk, sand, colored powders. One of the oddest techniques presaged the pixels that form computer-generated images. This was the pin screen, invented by Alexander Alexeieff, a Russian-born Frenchman, and put to use with the help of his partner and later wife, Claire Parker. The screen was made of a framed piece of honeycombed cloth through which a half-million double-pointed pins were stuck. Alexeieff illuminated it laterally. When the pinpoints were stuck into the cloth without going all the way through, they would be invisible and the resulting image would be white. If the pins were pushed through, they would cast hundreds of slanted shadows. The more the pins stuck out, the longer and more visible their shadows. The two artists then

A close-up of the screen with three pins pushed through, casting long, diagonal shadows

made their design using the shadows of the pins and the whiteness of the cloth. Alexeieff positioned himself in front of the screen to see the positive image. He would then guide Parker, who

Alexander Alexeieff and Claire Parker at work on either side of the screen. They used their wide variety of tools to compose images from shadows and light.

Tableaux d'une exposition (Pictures at an Exhibition, *1972*)

The perfect depiction of this tobacco jar, created by thousands of shadows, prefigured the first computer-generated images, composed of tens of thousands of pixels.

sat behind, telling her where to put the pins to darken parts of the image, on which he would add touches of light. Alexeieff and Parker used small wheels, curtain rings, painting knives, and all sorts of other tools to push their pins and create their designs. Using a tire from a toy, they could make notches in the surface of the fabric, which let them replicate a stalk of wheat or the branch of a pine tree. A round lid pressed on the bias against the pins would leave an impression like a crescent moon. They created magnificent black-and-white designs that were reminiscent of the engravings Alexeieff had made at the beginning of his career. This unusual technique was wonderfully employed in *Night on Bald Mountain* (1933). Despite the difficulties of his technique,

Alexeieff succeeded in rendering very complex animations— animals running and advancing in perspective, landscapes changing subtly. In *En Passant* (1943), the facade of the church slowly blurs into reveal- ing all of the details of the interior. Among the most beautiful achievements of the Alexeieff-Parker duo must be the screen credits for the Orson Welles film *The Trial* (1962) and their own *Three Moods* (1979).

Norman McLaren's Brainstorms

When the Canadian Norman McLaren became head of the animation department of the National Film Board in 1943, he invented "cameraless animation," which entailed working directly on the film. He would lift off the gelatin to obtain a transparent material on which he would draw his designs, scratching on the black film to make luminous shapes appear. He even scratched the optical track to produce artificial sounds. His movie *Begone Dull Care* (1949), made on scratched film, presents pictorial references inspired by the music of the Oscar Peterson Trio. McLaren also used the technique of "pixilation" in his renowned short-length movie *Neighbors* (1952). In it, his live characters are animated in the way they brawl, move around with their feet remaining stationary, and flit about like butterflies. He was able to get this effect by having his actors leap into the air with their arms extended and taking the shot just as their feet left the ground. McLaren continued to innovate through his last film, produced in the 1980s just before his death.

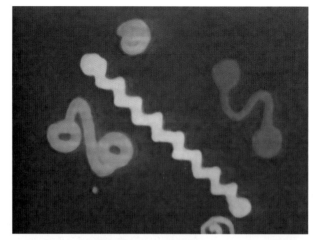

Some stunning effects obtained by Norman McLaren

McLaren used multiple exposures to produce these images in Pas de Deux.

The Fantasy Worlds of Karel Zeman

The Czech director-animator Karel Zeman (1910–1989) explored all techniques of animation in his films, which are masterpieces of poetic whimsy. He started by making advertising movies featuring articulated puppets. In his first short film, *Vanocni sen* (*The Christmas Dream,* 1945), a small cloth doll moves about in a real room amid inanimate toys. Zeman then created the character of Mister Prokouk, a puppet with an enormous nose and a bristly mustache, who made his sensational debut in 1947 in *Pan Prokouk Byrokrat* (*Mr. Prokouk the Bureaucrat*) and returned for seven more tales of misadven-

One of the dinosaurs in Karel Zeman's Journey to the Beginning of Time

The superb images in The Fabulous World of Jules Verne *were inspired by the engravings in the Hetzel collection and the universe of Jules Verne.*

ture. Zeman combined puppets and animated cartoons in his first full-length movie, *Poklad Ptaciho Ostrova* (*The Treasure of Bird Island,* 1952). The educational adventure *Cesta do praveku* (*Journey to the Beginning of Time,* 1954) relates the journey of four young explor-ers who travel up "the river of time" and find themselves con-fronted with prehistoric beasts. The animals are largely repre-sented by articulated puppets, filmed in stop-motion, but Zeman also used various sizes of hand puppets, as well as models animated by simple mecha-nisms, such as one for the mammoth that greets the explorers by raising his trunk. Zeman invented an ingenious method for depicting a herd of prehistoric antelopes and giraffes. These animations were drawn on thick paper, painted in great detail, and then cut up. The cutouts were placed in the miniature set, as was done in the Fleischer brothers' Rotograph process, and then replaced frame by frame. The result was all the more realistic because bushes set in the foreground partially hid the animated cutouts during the pan shots. Zeman's second full-length movie was an adaptation of *Face au drapeau* (*For the Flag*) by Jules Verne: *Vynalez zkary* (*The Fabulous World of Jules Verne*, 1958). Zeman drew direct inspiration from the Pierre-Jules Hetzel collection of engravings of Verne's works, drawn by artists Benett and Riou, and staged his movie adaptations of these large-scale adventures in the small studio measuring 1,500 square feet (140 square meters) that he had in Gottwaldov. The false-perspective sets, the animated models, the props, and the actors' costumes were composed of fine black-and-white layers, so they could be mixed better with cut-up engravings inserted into the image. Upon its release, *The Fabulous World of Jules Verne* was hailed as a masterpiece and brought a new life to the celebrated works of art in the Hetzel "Fantastic Journeys" collection. Zeman would again use a mix of illustrations and real shots in *Baron Prasil* (*Baron Munchhausen*, 1961) and *Na komete* (*On the Comet*, 1970), his second adaptation of a Jules Verne work. Zeman made his scenery from old, hand-painted postcards dating from the beginning of the

twentieth century. Karel Zeman devoted the end of his career to animated cartoons such as *Pohadky tisice a jedné noci* (*Fairy Tales of a Thousand and One Nights*, 1971–74).

The Meeting of the Real and Animated Cartoons

Leaping out of the pens of Max Fleischer in 1919, Koko the Clown became the first "toon" to coexist with these strange, three-dimensional beings known as humans. By the end of the 1930s, the development of the traveling matte made it possible to fine-tune these encounters. Among the principal movies in this category are the Disney Studios' *Reluctant Dragon* (1941) and *Anchors Aweigh* (1945), directed by George Sidney, in which Gene Kelly dances with cartoon cat and mouse Tom and Jerry. In 1964, the Disney Studios used the process of a sodium traveling matte to deftly insert the actors in *Mary Poppins* into the animated universe. One of the most complex sequences was the dance number that Dick Van Dyke improvised with the penguin-waiters to entertain Mary Poppins (Julie Andrews). The actors, the floor, the table, and the two chairs are the only real elements in this scene. The background of the image was a drawing inserted behind the actors. The penguins' animation was drawn over the live-action

shots, to be synchronized with the actors' movements and then inserted over the first manipulated image. This technique was used again in *Bedknobs and Broomsticks* (1971) and *Pete's Dragon* (1977).

In 1988, *Who Framed Roger Rabbit* by Robert Zemeckis proved not only that animating characters of the golden age of cartoons was still a known skill, but also that they could be given a three-dimensional appearance. The process was developed by ILM—each toon was animated to correspond with the movements of the real actors and then transferred onto film and painted. The animators responsible for the special effects then drew two mattes following the outline of the morphology of each character— one corresponding to the light, the other to shadows. If the primary light source were situated to the left, the light matte served to further illuminate the left portion of the character. The middle portion of the character would retain a medium intensity, while the right portion would become slightly darker because of the shadow matte. It was through this complex optical special effect that Jessica Rabbit's curves, enhanced by the insertion of sequins, were accentuated. Ed Jones recalls the production: "When I worked on the special effects of *Roger Rabbit,* I manipulated a lot of films with an optical printer, crossing my fingers that the 35-millimeter composite image would correspond with the effect that we wanted to get. I remember working on a particularly complex scene during which a character made a lamp attached to the ceiling spin around. The angle of the light and the shadows had to be modified with each frame, and we had to juggle the length of exposure of each element and each matte. It was an absolutely hellish job! Today, with digital, you can see what you're doing in real time. You test different effects and then refine them. It's an enormous advantage."

Ed Jones, a special effects veteran of Who Framed Roger Rabbit, supervised the digital effects of Space Jam. Behind him can be seen some of the thousands of digital tapes on which the visual effects for the movie were recorded.

On a computer screen at Cinesite, the movements of Michael Jordan, filmed on a green background, were mixed in with the structures of a computer-generated set.

Space Jam: The Era of the Digital Toon

Space Jam, directed by Joe Pytka in 1996, was a cinematographic UFO as only Hollywood can produce. In it, Michael Jordan is seen going off with Bugs Bunny to confront some extraterrestrials in the course of a basketball game. The reason Warner Bros. invested $160 million in such an idea remains a mystery. Perhaps the heads of the studio did not assess the difficulties attached to such a project. To make real actors coexist with animated characters is a Herculean undertaking. First, one shoots a normal film, then an equivalent full-length animation, and finally, the two are mixed to produce a single film for the price of two. Ed Jones, then responsible for special effects for film at Cinesite, projected Michael Jordan into the

universe of Looney Tunes: "Most of the time, Michael had nothing more than a green cyclorama with a grid of reference points in front of him. These points were used to align the real perspectives of the studio with those of the virtual sets and animated characters." During the filming, director Joe Pytka made his camera move in the space all around Jordan. The animation of the characters were computed by the marks on the floor and on the elements of the set using digital photographic enlargements, perforated like animation sheets. The animator then took frame 1, frame 11, frame 25, etc., and set down the groundwork of his animation, according to changes in perspective. These drafts were then passed under a camera to check

the rough animation. The animator made the changes that were essential and then drew the "breakdowns"—the drawings placed between extreme poses of the character, producing an effect of dynamism, acceleration, or a break in the rhythm of a given animation. The chief animator created the cartoons with complex movements himself, while "in-between" assistants saw to the easier transitions. The animated scene was then tested, approved, and scanned. The toons were then colored before being sent again to the assembled artists in the special department for tone mattes, the place where the colored shadows and the lighting effects that created the illusion of a model on a 2-D cartoon were animated.

Virtual Sets

Ed Jones and the Cinesite team also created one of the first virtual film sets, the stadium in *Space Jam:* "We added the actors and the definitive animated characters on a green background. We used a grid with points to align the real perspectives with those of the virtual stadium set. This was how the movements of the 35-millimeter camera were able to link perfectly with the point of view of the virtual camera." Digital insertion on a green background is so precise that it even made it possible to lift a real shadow of

On a computer artist's screen, Michael Jordan, with some reference points plotted on the background; inset: a final image from the movie

Michael Jordan and transfer it onto the synthesized set. The tiers of the virtual stadium were then filled with thirty thousand animated characters capable of reacting to what takes place on the court. In reality, this crowd was made up of only about one hundred different characters. Some of them were animated in the traditional way, applauding,

One of the finished digital manipulations
Photo courtesy of Cinesite

booing, whistling, and jumping up with joy, while others were created in 3-D. They were colored and shadowed using digital effects and then placed throughout the stadium in such a way that it is impossible to perceive that they have been multiplied. When the digital effects were completed, an optical printer used red, green, and blue high-powered lasers to transfer them onto a very fine-grained 5244 film. Ed Jones and his colleagues worked for two years on *Space Jam,* producing twelve hundred effects shots, some of which were composed of a hundred different elements. In 2003, Joe Dante directed a new coexistence of humans and toons in the movie *Looney Tunes: Back in Action.* This second attempt was to be the good one—the director of *Gremlins* and *Small Soldiers* knew how to handle parody, as well as digital effects. The search for the Blue Monkey Diamond was the pretext for a great chase through Hollywood, Las Vegas, Paris, and a fantasy jungle. The effects that integrate Brendan Fraser next to Bugs Bunny and Daffy Duck bring to mind the best of the Warner Bros. cartoons.

Will Vinton and Claymation

It is the rare animation director who wins an Oscar for his debut movie. Will Vinton was one. His movie *Closed Mondays* (1975), codirected by Bob Gardiner, saw the first use of his process called Claymation. While an architecture student, Vinton studied the organic creations of the great Spanish artist Antonio Gaudí. He was struck by the idea of animating modeling paste, using stop-motion to create fluid moving shapes. The forest set in *Closed Mondays,* constructed in paste, is swept up in a whirlwind of kneading and metamorphoses into a volcano. The success of this first movie led Vinton to patent his technique. He created his own studio to produce other amazing shorts, such as *The Great Cognito,* with a long shot that starts with the entry of a music hall impersonator, pictured in the frame from his head to his shoulders. His face transforms itself into caricatures of historical figures and the stars that he enacts. The impersonator becomes in turn Roosevelt, Churchill, John Wayne, the Andrews Sisters, and then the American and Japanese combatants at the battle of Iwo Jima! In his next movies, the puppets that Vinton filmed full-length were fitted with an aluminum wire armature, of which some parts (arms, forearms, legs, and torso) were

The renowned California Raisins created by Will Vinton, inventor of Claymation, a method of animation that uses modeling paste
Photo courtesy of Will Vinton Studios

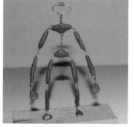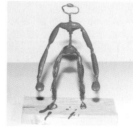

The step-by-step production of a Claymation character: The iron wire armature is first covered by a basic shape and modeled with a paste that dries with heat. It is then covered over with conventional modeling paste, mixed to be easily applied in several layers, and finally the character details are modeled by hand by Marc Spess.
Photos courtesy of AnimateClay.com

wrapped in a rigid material that was used to support the modeling paste applied onto it. The animators who work with Vinton are, like him, highly skilled sculptors capable of remodeling a face to change the expression in a few minutes. Will Vinton produced his first full-length movie in 1982: *The Adventures of Mark Twain*. The sets are superb, and the puppets of Tom Sawyer, Huckleberry Finn, and Becky Thatcher are marvelously animated. Among Vinton's most celebrated characters are the dinosaurs Herb and Rex and the California Raisins, who notably appear in *Meet the Raisins* (1988), a wonderful parody of a rock documentary, and the multicolored candy stars of dozens of TV commercials for M&Ms. Vinton also produced the remarkable animated sitcom *The PJs* (2000), conceived by Eddie Murphy and depicting the life of a black family in a disadvantaged neighborhood, as well as the series *Gary & Mike* (2001). The inventor of Claymation adapted to the evolution of technology, and by the end of the 1990s, he was also producing commercials with computer-generated images.

Nick Park animates a scene from The Wrong Trousers, *one of the mad adventures of Wallace and Gromit.* Photo courtesy of Aardman

Nick Park: The Imprint of a Paste Master

The Englishman Nick Park is the worthy heir to Will Vinton's technique. He developed a personal style, one defined by an impeccable sense of timing. He made his first animation with modeling paste, *Archie's Concrete Nightmare* (1975), when he was seventeen years old, and then studied animation from 1980 to 1983 at the National Film and Television School in Beacons-field, where he created the famous characters Wallace and Gromit. He started filming their first adventure, *A Grand Day Out,* while still in school and finished it in 1989, five years after having joined the Aardman animation studio. This first adventure of the inventor in slippers and his dog, which involves a search for cheese on the moon, was a great success. Already present are subtle jokes and the depiction of a universe of domestic comforts turned upside down with the eruption of some bizarre characters. In 1990, Nick Park animated zoo animals, using the voices of real people who were questioned about their own habitats. This idea, initiated by David Sproxton and Peter Lord, led to *Creature Comfort,* which walked off with the Oscar for best animated picture. The next Wallace and Gromit short, *The Wrong Trousers* (1993), followed by *A Close Shave* (1995), would prove that the magicians at

The wonderful Wallace and Gromit Photo courtesy of Aardman

Aardman studios were capable of making astounding action sequences. The chase scene in a miniature train in *The Wrong Trousers* and the one in a sidecar in *A Close Shave* are directorial gems. Each movie won an Oscar. After such a success, the next step could only be a full-length movie. When Park was sixteen years old, he worked ten hours a day packaging chicken at a factory so he could earn enough money to buy the camera of his dreams. Thus, the origin of *Chicken Run* (2000), which he developed in collaboration with Dreamworks, Steven Spielberg's studio. The action takes place on a chicken farm that looks like a World War II military prison. Its owners are obsessed with developing a machine that can produce chicken pies by the thousands. Ginger, a hen, decides to make an escape with her friends and solicits the help of Rocky the flying rooster, an acrobat she has seen on a poster.

A scene from the hilarious Creature Comfort
Photo courtesy of Aardman

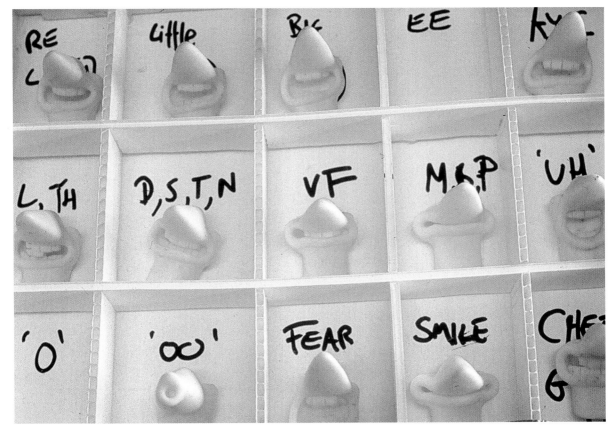

Beaks made of resin for the animation of Chicken Run   Photo courtesy of Dreamworks

Aluminum Chicken Bones

All of the chickens in *Chicken Run* contained a metal armature that was articulated with ball-and-socket joints. Different from Wallace and Gromit, who were made out of plasticine, Ginger and her friends had much lighter bodies made of a stiff silicone. Only their heads, wings, and in some cases feet were sculpted from modeling paste. The junction between the malleable parts and the rigid ones was concealed by a collar of feathers or a scarf that the chickens wore around their necks. Nick Park and Peter Lord came up with the idea of making a mold of the semirigid heads and hands of their characters to make sure the proportions did not vary during the filming. To construct a new element, the animator simply sandwiched the metal armature between two layers of modeling paste, closed a mold over it all, and got a near-perfect sculpture that needed only a few details touched up. Hundreds of thousands of heads, wings, and feet were made throughout the duration of the production. To gain time, the beaks were sculpted in advance and molded in resin. Each character had some forty to sixty different-shaped beaks to correspond with the sounds it made and its basic expressions. The eyes were simple plastic white pearls that could be repositioned by merely inserting a pin in the little hole in the iris. With their legendary sense of detail, Park and Lord even created several types of chicken "extras." They manufactured a series of detached pieces—heads, beaks, bodies, wings, feet—for these "secondary roles." The mean farmers were afforded special treatment. Mr.

Rocky the rooster and the hen Ginger, heroes of Chicken Run   Photo courtesy of Dreamworks

Tweedy's cardigan sweater was knitted by hand, which required three weeks of work, as did Mrs. Tweedy's dress. Iron wires were added to her dress in order to accentuate her austere presence. The Tweedys' faces were composed of two sections of molded plasteline—their brow ridges and their mouths. With each frame, the animators would replace one or the other half of the features to match the text. They would remove the piece of paste that was no longer useful and make the new half of the face by using first the molds, and then modeling

tools to conceal the seams. Rocky, Ginger, and their feathered friends were cloned and distributed among a dozen animation teams, who worked separately. Each chicken was made in two different scales: scale A was used when the chickens talked among themselves, and scale B, which was smaller, was used when they were filmed with humans or to create false perspectives in the background of the set. Aardman studios thus made 300 A-sized chickens and 130 B-sized chickens. The forty animators were separated into two teams

led by the two directors and Lloyd Price, the supervising animator. Some days, when twenty-eight different sets were being used simultaneously during the filming, the teams worked together to produce 240 frames, or 10 seconds of film! The enormous success of *Chicken Run* paved the way for other full-length features such as *The Great Vegetable Plot* (2005, projected) and *Tortoise vs. Hare* (2006, projected).

Overleaf: *The hens at dawn reveille. The smallest models of the hens were crafted to be used in scenes next to the farmers.*
Photo courtesy of Dreamworks

INTERVIEW

NICK PARK AND PETER LORD

Directors of *Chicken Run*

Peter Lord
Photo courtesy of Dreamworks

Nick Park
Photo courtesy of Dreamworks

What were the challenges that you faced while directing "Chicken Run," your first full-length movie?

Nick Park: The simple fact of successfully completing this gigantic undertaking. We were simultaneously filming on twenty-five to thirty different sets a day, for a year and a half. At times, all the sequences of the film were in the process of being filmed at the same time! We had to run from one stage to another to talk with the different animators and to make sure that everything was going OK. Making the film kept us locked up in a hangar the size of a football pitch that we had in Bristol. That's where we built the sets and where the filming took place. Like the chickens, we had to accomplish a super-human task to get ourselves out!

Explain what a typical workday for the directors of "Chicken Run" was like.

Peter Lord: In the morning, we'd be stressed out thinking about the sequences filmed the day before, which we'd have to

approve or reject. On a regular shoot, it's easy to do five or six takes with the actors, and then you can choose which one you want. But with animation, the long and painstaking work only lets you produce a single sequence. If you're leaning toward rejecting it, it's not only hard for the animator, but it also slows down the rhythm of the production and creates a delay that will have to be compensated for at the cost of additional work. So a day began with making decisions that held heavy consequences. We then visited the different animation stages to check on the direction, the camera movements, the atmosphere created by the lighting, and the way the puppets were being

made to "act" using stop-motion. It was the best part of the day. We constructed a small video booth to film ourselves copying the characters' postures. It was the easiest way to get the animators to understand what we wanted. At the end of the day, we focused on the mixing and the final selection of the recorded dialogue. All these simultaneous responsibilities were exhausting at the end of eight to ten hours of work.

Which were the most difficult sequences to create?

Nick Park: The ones with the chickens! (*Laughs.*) All the scenes were complicated,

The chickens' escape plan is discovered.   Photo courtesy of Dreamworks

because the characters had to act well. The scenes in which Rocky and Ginger talk on the roof of the chicken coop were filmed in close-up, with puppets that were barely eight inches (twenty centimeters) tall. The animators had to work with great finesse to succeed in expressing the subtle emotions.

It became apparent that there was an ideal size for these puppets made from modeling paste. If they were too small, your fingers would be too big to sculpt them, to animate the details. If they were too big, they would become too heavy and you'd have more trouble controlling the appearance of

the surface of the paste. I'm always amazed when I see Ginger's face—she was only one and a half inches (four centimeters) tall—filling the entire height of a movie screen and looking good!

The hero of Underground Robot
Photo courtesy of Webster Colcord

Webster Colcord uses an animation gauge during the filming of Underground Robot.
Photo courtesy of Webster Colcord

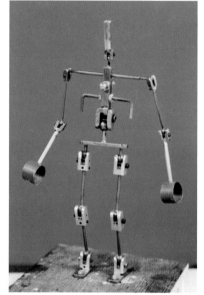

*The ball-and-socket armature used in
Webster Colcord's short feature*
Underground Robot

Animated Disney Cartoons in the Digital Age

The production of *The Little Mermaid* in 1989 marked the last time the Disney Studios would use celluloid. In 1990, the system called CAPS made it possible to digitize cartoons drafted on paper and then to color them. The painted sets were also digitized, rectifying the physical limitations of shots taken with a caption camera or with the venerable multiplane. The full-length feature *The Rescuers Down Under* (1990) was the first movie to benefit from this digital treatment. With the development of the Deep Canvas process in 1996–97, another important stage was forged. This computer program made it possible to layer hundreds of drawings of sets onto geometric shapes spread throughout a 3-D space. In the movie *Tarzan* (1999), the camera freely moved following the ape-man as he leaped from branch to branch. At the open-

ing of *Treasure Planet* (2001), Jim Hawkins flies across the sky on his solar surfer. Because of Deep Canvas, the camera could spin alongside him with a stunning fluidity.

Backstage with Disney's Special Effects

Andy Gaskill and Neil Eskuri assumed the roles of artistic director and artistic coordinator for many full-length Disney features. Gaskill worked on *The Lion King, Hercules,* and *Treasure Planet,* while Eskuri worked on *Fantasia 2000, Dinosaur, Treasure Planet,* and *Gnomeo & Juliet.*

INTERVIEW

Andy Gaskill and Neil Eskuri

Photo © Disney Enterprises, Inc.

Could you explain the evolution of the CAPS animation system?

Neil Eskuri: The acronym stands for Computer Animation Production System. Initially, it was primarily used to link the elements that composed an image: the characters, the different layers of scenery, the special effects, etc. We'd scan the line drawings of the characters one by one, and then the scenery, which had been done traditionally. The characters could also be colored using a large variety of colors that could easily be controlled. The digital cels were numbered to follow one another in each sequence, which facilitated the management of the documents.

Would you say that this system was also the 3-D transposition of the functions of the multiplane?

Neil Eskuri: Yes, with the advantage of no longer being restricted by the real dimensions of a drawing or by the range of the movements of the multiplane. CAPS also made it possible to control the blurry effects that you can't get in reality, to change the nuances of color the way you wanted, to speed up or slow down the action, to enhance the sense of depth in the sets. Multiplane only lets you control four or five levels of the set. With CAPS, you can control hundreds.

CAPS also made it possible to color in the outlines of the characters and eliminate the black lines due to the photocopying of the touched-up drawings onto cels.

Andy Gaskill: Yes. As you know, the cels of full-length features before *One Hundred and One Dalmatians* (1961) were drawn by hand, with the outlines colored in. After this period, you could resort to photocopying to speed up the process of making the film and you'd put up with the black outline, which over the years became brown, more discreet. Now a colorist starts with a touched-up drawing and scans and chooses the color that he'll assign to each outline of the character. For example, the outline of a blond hair will be orange, while some black clothing will have a blue outline. This way, you get a silhouette that is at the same time readable and composed of several shades. To color the remainder of the character, you choose a tone and then click on the zone to be filled in. Once the model for the character is established, the colors are saved in memory and reproduced from one drawing to another by the colorists. The system can't automatically color drawings, because the lines are difficult to interpret from one drawing to another— for example, when a character curls up in a corner. The folds of his pants touch his jacket, and the machine can no longer differentiate where the outlines of the shirt stop and those of the pants start. The artists also define the different color models for a character, scene by scene. The entire gamut of colors are changed for a sequence that takes place at dawn, with an orange light, and one that takes place at night, in a bluish setting.

The mechanical body parts of John Silver in Treasure Planet *were animated in 3-D, from 2-D animations conceived by Glen Keane* Images © Disney Enterprises, Inc.

A-70

70

The computer-generated characters in Dinosaur were integrated into real landscapes.
Image © Disney Enterprises, Inc.

Neil Eskuri: You can, however, manage to index the references of all the colors of a character. There've been times when we've changed the hair color of a character during production. Using CAPS, this modification was done automatically, saving us thousands of hours of work. Changes in the model colors of characters would also be done automatically by the system that would eventually replace CAPS.

How did you incorporate the shades of color on a character's face?

Andy Gaskill: Let's take the example of Princess Jasmine's cheeks in *Aladdin*. The animators traced a very small triangle on each cheekbone to indicate the spot where a shade had to appear. The colorists would shade it in pink and then use the CAPS system to blur it and spread it out.

How do you create a 3-D environment using the Deep Canvas system?

Neil Eskuri: You start with drawings of the face, the profile, in a high angle and a low

angle of the set. You model each of the elements, and you apply digitized paintings onto these volumes. You put the drawing of a wood texture onto a door, the drawing of a rocky surface onto the walls of a cave, etc. When this process is done, the set resembles a black-and-white 3-D version of the set designer's original drawing. You then move onto the colorization phase and then onto the lighting of this set.

In the past, when the scenery for an animation was drawn flat, you had to take into account the movement of the characters within the frame of the image to simplify the elements that would appear behind them for the entirety of their trajectory. How do you control the readability of characters when they evolve in a 3-D set in which it's the camera that moves?

Andy Gaskill: Moving a camera in a 3-D environment makes it possible to separate the character from the background of the set better. We could enhance the sets without diminishing the readability of the action. In the past, you could predict where the character would be moving, because you could immediately see which were the parts of the image that had been cleaned up. With 3-D, we could also change the colors, the angles, and the intensity of the light sources to produce vibrant or mysterious daytime or nighttime atmosphere.

There was a time when one had great difficulty depicting clouds and water with synthesized images. What difficulties do you still encounter?

Neil Eskuri: Water is still difficult to depict correctly, because it's a reference we have in front of our eyes every day. The animation of water that you pour into a glass and that of a wave crashing against a rock have nothing in common. These are effects that you have to conceive of differently. The clothing of 3-D characters is also very difficult to depict. You have to find a way to distress the fabric in order to produce pleats that appear natural. On *Dinosaur* (2000), we spent a year and a half developing the fur of the lemur characters. We used the method to animate the blades of grass in some of the 3-D settings. I remember that the first rendering of a lemur took eighteen days of computations. Two years later, you could do the same computations in eighteen minutes! That gives you an idea of how fast things have progressed. The images that are created with particle effects, like smoke, fire, sand, and water, are always problem-

atic to control, particularly when there are interactions with characters. In *Gnomeo and Juliet,* we told the story of Romeo and Juliet, and had 3-D garden tools integrated into the set of a real garden. We photographed the real set from all directions and measured it using telemetric readings in order to reconstitute it in 3-D. This is how our characters/tools were integrated into the real shots. They could move around in a 3-D setting exactly identical to the real setting.

Do you think that 3-D will be used to transpose complex, animated movie characters more easily into TV series? It's often difficult to reproduce them "to model" with a much reduced budget and production time.

Neil Eskuri: Absolutely. We animated an experimental 3-D version of the robot B.E.N. from *Treasure Planet* for a television broadcast. This animation was produced in real time with the motion capture system developed by Jim Henson's company. The results were amazing. The beauty of the system is that the data are transmitted by telephone to the Disney Studios, where they can replicate a rendering of the character. I think this technique will have multiple applications, particularly in the domain of animated television series. The computer will control the characters' proportions, and the animators will be able to concentrate on the subtler animations.

The superb sets of The Road to El Dorado *(2000) combined real drawings on paper, digital effects, and computer-generated effects in order to animate elements like the surface of the water, pictured here.* Photo courtesy of Dreamworks

3-D Characters: Experimental Films with Synthesized Actors

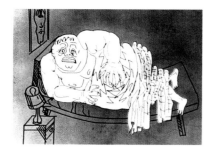

La Faim, *directed by Peter Foldes*

The Hungarian-born French filmmaker Peter Foldes was one of the first creators of animated, computer-generated characters. In his movies *Metadata* (1970) and *La Faim* (*Hunger,* 1975), he appropriated this technique in an original way, transforming in succession 2-D images in order to give them a 3-D graphics aspect in movement. This hybrid process produced fascinating images, blending the artist's strokes with metamorphoses generated by computer. The first 3-D characters that appeared in the 1980s were objects or very schematic human characters. At the end of the 1980s, the firm of Kleiser-Walczak produced the first disarming *synthespians*.

The main characters of Shrek, *jointly created by Pacific Data Images and Dreamworks, became the heroes of delicious parodies of fairy tales.*   Photo courtesy of Dreamworks

Photo courtesy of Kleiser-Walczak

This neologism—an amalgam of *synthesis* and *thespian*—would, from this point on, be used to refer to synthesized actors. But at that time, the realistic representation of a human posed such difficulties that most companies specialized in cartoon-style characters. Pacific Data Images produced the charming short film *Locomotion* (1989), in which a small, stylized train manages to cross a partially destroyed bridge. The volume of the locomotive and the cars was animated to distort, as it would in a hand-drawn cartoon. The very funny *Gas Planet,* made by Eric Darnell in 1992, depicts spluttering creatures whose 3-D rendering imitated pencil sketches. In 1996, Pacific Data Images signed a coproduction agreement with Dreamworks and had a huge success with the full-length movie *Antz.* PDI's real triumph would come in 2001 with *Shrek,* which won an Oscar. Nevertheless, the competition was on with its

great rival Pixar. The character
for *Sextone for President*
(1988), one of the first synthespians, was created by the firm
of Kleiser-Walczak. "At that
time, almost all 3-D objects
were created either using architectural computer programs or
from computer-assisted concep-
tions intended for the industry,"
recalls Jeff Kleiser. "You only
found basic, rectangular shapes.
Complex, organic shapes were
very difficult to make. We
bought a Polhemus magnetic dig-
itizer, with which we could digitize points in a 3-D space. My
partner Diana Walczak, being a
sculptor, devised the volumes
that we drew grids on. By placing the stylus of the machine at
every line intersection, we could
record a 3-D object as a complex structure. Our first synthes-
pian, Nestor Sextone, was made
in 1988. We created a special
computer program to reorder the
polygons of the many expressions that had been prerecorded.
We could go from an open mouth
to a closed mouth, from a smile
to a frown. Using Diana's sculptures of the face, which took
into consideration the anatom-
ical reality of a face and the
presence of bones and muscles,
we could animate the movements of speech. This made our
animations look more realistic
than other 3-D animations of
the time, which were restricted
to distorting the simple surfaces
mathematically."

*Dozo, the virtual singer in a video, "Don't
Touch Me" (1989), created by Kleiser-
Walczak*

Pixar's Debuts

At the beginning of the 1980s, George Lucas recruited Dr. Ed Catmull, who had directed the computer graphics laboratory at the New York Institute of Technology. He was asked to develop computers and programs specifically geared to the production of cinematographic images. At the time, the industrial processors that were being used to run factories and nuclear facilities, such as the Cray XMP/48, had been appropriated. Catmull's team already included John Lasseter and director William Reeves, who was placed in charge of the development of animation programs. The team made its debut with some 3-D special effects sequences (completed by ILM): the "Genesis effect" in *Star Trek II: The Wrath of Khan* (1982), in which a dead moon is transformed into a planet covered with green mountains and oceans; then the holograms of the Death Star in *Return of the Jedi* (1983); and the amazing scene of the glass knight who springs from a stained-glass window in *Young Sherlock Holmes* (1985). George Lucas also made many short tests, such as *The Adventures of Andre and Wally B.* (1984), one of the first 3-D cartoons and the directorial debut of John Lasseter. Lucas had already wanted to substitute 3-D images for models and optical

The characters in The Adventures of Andre and Wally B., *one of the first experimental 3-D cartoons, was animated by the master of the art, John Lasseter.*

effects in *Star Wars,* but he was disappointed with the first models of the X-wing spaceship, and in 1986 he sold Pixar to Steve Jobs, the cofounder of Apple. Jobs quickly found financial backing, making it possible for Pixar to excel.

How to create 3-D hyperrealistic images was still unknown. No problem. Pixar would specialize in computer-generated cartoon images. From the very first year, it proved itself with the formidable short *Luxo Jr.,* the story of a large desk lamp and a small desk lamp that have fun with a ball. The parent-child relationship, the sense of rhythm, and the humor are marvelously expressed by these two odd characters. In a single movie, John Lasseter demonstrated that he was one of the geniuses of animation. *Luxo Jr.* was honored with twenty prizes worldwide and became the company's lucky charm—the little lamp graces the titles of all Pixar movies.

Each new production was more sophisticated than the preceding one. *Red's Dream* (1987) relates the dream of a motorcycle abandoned in the back of a shop. *Tin Toy* (1988) depicts a tin toy pursued by an incredibly animated baby. This artistic and technical feat was awarded an Oscar for best short picture. In 1989, Pixar produced its first short feature in 3-D—*Knickknack*, the adventure of a little toy snowman who tries to escape from his plastic snow globe to join the pinup on the calendar. Once again, Lasseter's sense of humor is right on target. Attracted by Pixar's potential, Disney suggested a partnership. Steve Jobs signed a contract to develop five full-length movies, which gave Pixar complete independence while letting it take full advantage of the Disney name and its distribution network. In 1994, *Toy Story* entered the annals of film history. The first entirely synthesized full-length feature was an undeniable success and was awarded a special Oscar. Every Pixar production thereafter was a resounding success. *Geri's Game,* which depicted a very expressive old man, brought in an Oscar in 1997. The following year, *A Bug's Life* once again confirmed Pixar's excellence and capacity for ever-original ideas. *Toy Story 2,* initially projected to go straight to video, was distributed to movie theaters in 1999, riding on the

Buzz and Woody, heroes of the first full-length CGI movie, were a big hit once again in Toy Story 2.
Image © Disney Enterprises, Inc. / Pixar Animation Studios

strength of Tom Hanks (who lent his voice to the cowboy Woody). It would prove to be a triumph, just as would *Monsters, Inc.* (2001) and *Finding Nemo* (2003).

The Birth of the 3-D Stars

It is in Emeryville, a suburb of San Francisco, that you'll find the headquarters of Pixar. A typical California cool reigns over this ninety-eight-million-dollar building. While the technical studios are replete with the last word in 3-D equipment, the animators' offices are overflowing with model toys of superheroes, robots, and crazy characters. Even some of the hallways have been reinvented by the occupants of the adjacent offices and decorated like a Mexican village, or the entry of a saloon, or a lemonade stand . . . closed due to a shortage of lemons. The Ping-Pong tables and the Hawaiian shirts could make you forget how hard everyone works. In a big room on the second floor of the studio, ideas are born. John Lasseter—cofounder of the studio and the great guru of 3-D cartoons—and Pixar's decision-making staff gather there to review pitches of possible future projects. Alternatively, stories are presented in just a few sentences that have to be convincing. If one of these ideas is judged strong enough to become a film, it moves on to the protracted phase of script development. The story is then minutely dissected, every angle analyzed, transformed, and reassembled over a period of months, even years. Once the script is approved, the dialogue is recorded by actors. The direc-

The reception area of the new Pixar studios in Emeryville, California

Work studios and meeting rooms are situated above an open area devoted to relaxing.

tors then attack the storyboards. It takes about forty thousand illustrations to establish the first sketch of the movie. And it is here that most of the visual jokes are born. At this point, the creative art department develops the ambience of the sets and the personalities of the characters. Thousands of drawings and models and sculptures are created in order to define the universe of the movie. The sculptures are attached to a mount that resembles a rotisserie spit and then scanned to create the 3-D volume of the characters, which are then fitted with a skeleton, muscular mass, and skin.

Once the sets and the 3-D actors are ready, the animators bring them to life. Animator Glenn McQueen has some hundred different control commands at his access to animate a virtual character. If he pulls on a character's hand, its arm will rise up. He can also command the various muscles that control a character's ability to smile, or create extreme expressions by combining several actions. Following this long and arduous animation work, the images are passed on

A preliminary cartoon from Monsters, Inc.   Image © Disney Enterprises, Inc. / Pixar Animation Studios

to the special effects department, where Tom Porter works: "All the movements that appear in *Toy Story, Toy Story 2,* and *A Bug's Life* were created by the animation department, which was responsible for the movements of the characters and the objects, clothes, and props they carried or wore. *Monsters, Inc.* was a turning point, because we freed the animators from the jobs that could be controlled automatically by our new computer programs. A program adapted from the Maya program made the simulation of all sorts of fabrics possible. Using this program, the fabric would move automatically when we moved a character's body, the pleats of the cloth falling naturally. We also made great advances in the creation of enormous sets, like the door-stocking system in *Monsters, Inc.* and the seascapes in *Finding Nemo.* We were successful in improving fog and atmospheric diffusion effects, using an 'automatizer,' so they were more subtly rendered." The penultimate stage takes place in the lighting department. As in a real studio, light sources are placed one by one in the 3-D space, and are directed and subtly colored. The final stage is the computation of the images in the "rendering farm," a big room in which the air conditioner roars, pushed to the max, twenty-four hours a day, to cool the three thousand processors lined up like hens in a chicken coop. This is where the countless pixels of the movies in the process of creation are gathered, at a rate of four hundred billion computations a second. The array of machinery costs fifty million dollars and must continually, component by component, be replaced every two years to stay abreast of technological developments.

INTERVIEW

John Lasseter

Director, Cofounder, and Vice President of the Creative Department at Pixar

John Lasseter and Mike the Cyclops

Pixar seems able to make any 3-D character emotionally moving, even when it's an object like the little lamp of your logo. What's your secret for managing to do that?

John Lasseter: When you imagine a character, you not only have to address its personality, its design, and its 3-D articulations, but also manage to create the illusion that its movements reflect its thoughts, its emotions. This gives the impression that the character is reflecting. That's *my* definition of the animation process of a character!

We do a thing with the inanimate objects—you immediately define where the head's going to be. No matter if the object doesn't have two eyes and a nose. You choose the part of its "body" that will follow the action, like the head, which will be "looking," will be dictating all the other positions. It's enough even if it bends over to pick something up, or turns when there's a noise, and the audience will accept that this object has become a character. In the case of the little architecture lamp in *Luxo Jr.,* we had the advantage that the articulated object already resembled a neck, and its form, a slightly curvaceous body. In the case of *Monsters, Inc.*, the character of Mike was a real tour de force of animation. When you have to animate a humanoid character, you make extensive use of the neck and shoulders to mimic basic expressions: joy, sadness, fear, suspicion, etc. But Mike was nothing more than an eye with arms and feet! There was no neck and, even less, shoulders. To make him alive, we gave him asymmetrical expressions. We had other difficulties to work around with the fish in *Finding Nemo* and with the superheroes in *The Incredibles.* Each character requires a different, carefully thought-out approach.

A sculpture of an early Buzz design
Used by permission from Disney Enterprises, Inc. / Pixar Animation Studios

I was struck by the friendly atmosphere that reigns over Pixar's offices. It's a very familial atmosphere, as you find in your movies.

John Lasseter: Is that what you feel? I'm thrilled, because I think that the work atmosphere always shows through in a movie, in one way or another. Being one of the directors of Pixar, I don't only try hard to assemble the best artists and technicians who exist, but also to create a place in which everyone can feel at ease and express themselves in the best conditions. We try to create good projects, but also remain open to what's going on around us. Our experiences, our relationships with close ones, our children, what makes us laugh or moves us can always be found in our movies! In a sense, it's as if all our life could be used as tax write-offs! (*Laughs.*)

How did the Pixar studios manage to retain its personality while becoming so big?

John Lasseter: We haven't made the slightest effort to avoid becoming businessmen or bureaucrats—we just aren't! We've evolved by continuing to do what we like. I was the first animator at Pixar. Pete Docter (codirector of *Monsters, Inc.*) was the third, and Andrew Stanton (codirector of *A Bug's Life* and writer-director of *Finding Nemo*) the second. At the beginning, no one knew how to make a full-length animated film with computer-generated images. We learned stuff at Disney, and we also invented procedures all along the way. We hired people we felt close with and, each time, asked ourselves the question, "Do I like this person enough to eat dinner with him? Do I like him enough that my family will go on vacation with his family?" For me, it's the test that lets me be sure that we will come to understand each other during the long years it takes to develop a movie. There's a minimum of politics in the studio.

Pete Docter is the second animator at Pixar, after Andrew Stanton, to make his directorial debut. You embarked on a fruitful collaboration with Brad Bird on "The Incredibles." Are you in the process of training others to succeed you?

John Lasseter: Yes. Pixar has set a goal of producing one new animation movie every year. It's a long-term goal, which we haven't met yet. If you make a simple calculation, taking into consideration that it takes four years to produce a full-length movie of synthesized images, it's clear that I can't make all of Pixar's movies. In the future, I'll direct only one in three of Pixar's movies.

Are you considering also developing stories that use more realistic-looking characters?

John Lasseter: The point of departure for all our movies is a good story that lends itself to computer animation. Toys lent themselves perfectly to this medium when we started out, because the synthesized images tended to give a "plastic" side to the objects! Ever since I've worked in this branch of film, it's always been said that the Holy Grail in terms of synthesized images is to succeed in creating perfectly realistic human beings. In fact, that's

not of great interest. What interests us is the fantastic. Putting in a little dose of realism in our sets or some effects in our universes is enough to make all the fantasy that goes on around it. We don't want to draw the audience's attention to a particular effect to the detriment of the story.

Overleaf: *The four phases in the creation of the characters Sully and Mike: wire frame, volume, early fur rendering, final image*
Images © Disney Enterprises, Inc. / Pixar Animation Studios

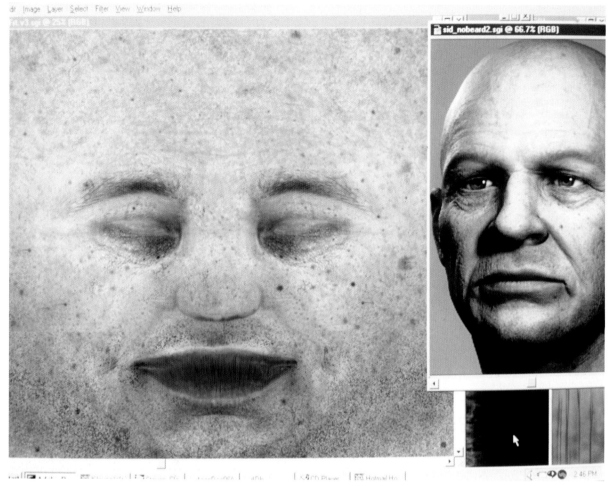

The "flattened" image of Dr. Sid, a character in Final Fantasy, *reveals the attention paid to detail—the pigmentation of the skin, the pimples, the veins.* Photo courtesy of Columbia-TriStar & Square Pictures

The Synthetic Actors of *Final Fantasy*

When *Final Fantasy: The Spirits Within* was released in 2001, an old dream was accomplished: hyperrealistic virtual actors appeared on the screen for the first time. This adventure began two and a half years

earlier. The shareholders of Squaresoft (creators of the video game *Final Fantasy*), of the Japanese company Gaga-Humax, and of the American studio Columbia-TriStar put up seventy million dollars for this project, not imagining that the costs would eventually double. The movie was produced in

Honolulu, on the Hawaiian island of Oahu, halfway between Japan and the United States, to facilitate the comings-and-goings of the participants from the two countries. Andy Jones, a veteran of the computer-generated images in *Titanic* and *Godzilla,* was named the supervisor of the animated

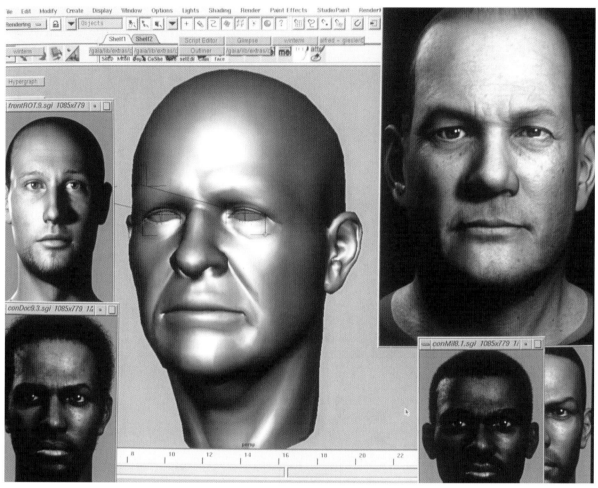

More examples of the very realistic faces created by the team at Square Pictures
Photo courtesy of Columbia-TriStar & Square Pictures

sequences. Square Pictures studios, having acutely set its sights, recruited the best computer artists in the world. The goal was to discover a way in which to reconstitute an utterly realistic living being. The equipment they assembled was commensurate with the challenge—the animators had access to 200 Octane SGI workstations, with ten terabytes of memory for the 3-D data and five terabytes for the 2-D data. The images were computed by 960 Red Hat Linux 6.2 workstations. From the start, the team did not circumvent any problems. The 3-D faces would be appearing in very tight close-ups, so they had to be replete with subtle imperfections and small details that rang true, like the beard hairs on the soldiers who surround the heroine, Aki Ross. According to Hironobu Sakaguchi, the director of the movie, "the realism of the characters is due to an accumulation of small details. The

Real actors wearing costumes covered with reference points during the filming of a scene with the motion capture system Photo courtesy of Columbia-TriStar & Square Pictures

transparency of the skin, the small defects in pigmentation, the degree of the brightness and different shades of color of the teeth, the watery appearance of the eyes. In short, everything you perceive without paying attention to it when you look at a real human being." The rendering of the characters is quasi-photographic, yet everything was re-created from A to Z, through patience and the insertion of many 3-D layers that mixed the effects of brightness, transparency, and the opaque drawn and "mapped" surfaces. Aki Ross was composed of about one hundred thousand subdivided polygons. Her hair comprised sixty thousand modeled and individually animated hairs. The representation of the hair was so complex that it required 25 percent of

the computing time of each frame in which she appeared. Her body was animated using the data collected by the Motion Analysis capture system. The movements of an actress were recorded in 3-D, using sixteen cameras spread throughout the film stage. Aki's facial expressions and hand movements, on the other hand, were programmed by the animators. Unfortunately, when released, *Final Fantasy* was not the success it was expected to be. The acting abilities of its synthetic actors still remained virtual. The most expressive and most convincing character turned out to be Dr. Sid, one of the last synthespians developed during the production of the movie, but he had only a secondary role.

The film division of Square Pictures folded, and the studio concentrated on the creation of special effects. Square Pictures did, however, produce the remarkable "Last Flight of Osiris" segment of *The Animatrix* (2003), a series of short films. The expressions of the characters were decidedly more natural. Square Pictures has not said its last word.

Above and left: *Aki Ross,
the most complex
computer-generated
character created to date*
Photos courtesy of Columbia-
TriStar & Square Pictures

INTERVIEW

Sylvain Chomet

3-D and *Les Triplettes de Belleville*

Photo courtesy of Les Armateurs

Sylvain Chomet developed a very appealing graphic universe in his first full-length movie, *Les Triplettes de Belleville* (*The Triplets of Belleville*, 2003), in which he deftly incorporated digital and 3-D effects.

The endearing universe of Les Triplettes de Belleville. *The champion's bicycle was made in CGI, as was his grandmother's tricycle.*
Image courtesy of Les Armateurs

The racers in the middle ground were entirely generated in 3-D, while the spectators on the sides of the road were animated in 2-D.
Image courtesy of Les Armateurs

Your graphic universe is very far removed from everything that's technological; however, technology helped you direct "Les Triplettes de Belleville."

Sylvain Chomet: Using 3-D let me give more than body to the movie. When dealing with the Tour de France, you don't try a trick to circumvent the difficulties in animating bicycles. There's a lot to show. The crowds were animated in the traditional way, but the pack of riders also had to be depicted. Initially, we thought we'd only use the 3-D animation for the bicycles, but we decided to model the cyclists in 3-D and have them appear in very wide shots. They're small in the frame, so it worked well with the rest of the animation, of which we're very proud. You can't bring emotions to an object, like a bicycle, and it was an absolute nightmare animating the spokes of a wheel. From the start, 3-D was a necessity, not an aesthetic choice. In *La Vieille Dame et les pigeons* (*The Old Lady and the Pigeons,* 1997), I didn't have to show a crowd or lots of vehicles. In *Les Triplettes,* in order to depict Belleville, it was crucial to show the streets packed with vehicles. While I was familiarizing myself with the 3-D, I discovered that you could use it for creating emotional images and animations, and loads of other things that I never thought about before. When you think about the look of a Citroën van and all the support lines on its body, you have no choice but to represent it in 3-D.

The stretch two-horsepower vehicles of the French wine Mafia were made in 3-D.
Image courtesy of Les Armateurs

You used 3-D to get a graphic effect on all the objects, which were demarcated by their outlines.

Sylvain Chomet: Yes, we used a special program to get that. The modeling of the vehicles made it possible for us to control the volumes of the effects, with the shadows, the gradations, but these images wouldn't have been in keeping with the global style of the movie. So we had to control the solids, the contours, and the effects of mapping in order to "dirty" the surfaces of the vehicles. I remember one day a 3-D animator said to me, "This 3-D, it's fantastic, it lets you do everything . . . except make shit!" With 3-D, there's also the tendency to become a slave to true perspective, even though I prefer odd-shaped sets and asymmetrical tiles on a kitchen floor. I didn't want to lose the flavor of this purely graphical universe.

You can see a landscape rolling by, which was constructed from real shots, on the screen of the infernal machine at the end of the movie.

Sylvain Chomet: Yes, these are images that were filmed in France, on high-definition video, with the camera attached to the roof of a car. All of these images were reworked with Photoshop, using the "water-color" function, which lets you manipulate the image to give the impression that it was com-posed with daubs of paint, like a watercolor.

Monkey Island, *the first animated cartoon by Kenzo Masaoka made on celluloid*

The Treasures of Japanese Animation

For a long time unrecognized in the rest of the world, Japanese animation is now exported and distributed and considered in the upper echelons of the genre. One of Japan's animation pioneers was Kenzo Masaoka (1898–1988). With his *Sarugashima* (*Monkey Island,* 1930), he became the first filmmaker to abandon the paper cutout technique in favor of using animation on celluloid. In 1933, he produced the first talking animated picture in the country, *Chikara to onna no yononaka* (*Strength, Women, and the Ways of the World*), and in it can be seen his mastery of fluid and harmonious movement and images inspired from

the finesse of Japanese woodblocks. During World War II, Masaoka produced *Kumo to churippu* (*The Spider and the Tulip,* 1943), the story of a ladybug that hides in a tulip to escape a horrible spider. He mixed several techniques to emphasize the dramatic and comedic effects of this chase: hyperrealistic sets, double exposure of scratched film to depict rain, and impressive animation on celluloid. *Haru no genso* (*The Cherry Tree* or *Spring Fantasy,* 1946), a superb illustration of traditional Japanese landscapes and women, is another masterpiece. Befelled by visual problems, Masaoka died without having produced the full-length picture that he had dreamed of: *The Little Mermaid.*

Traditional Monsters and Technical Wonders

Up until the 1950s, Japanese animation drew its inspiration from animist religious beliefs and folklore legends. Nature was peopled with all kinds of spirits that directors would evoke using paper cutouts, animated puppets, Chinese shadow techniques, and animated cartoons. The supernatural fox in *Ugoki ekori no takehiki* (*The Fox Versus the Raccoon*), directed by Ikuo Oishi in 1933, is characteristic of these tales about phantoms who change their appearance and can emerge in human form, as warriors. During World War II, Japanese animated film abandoned fantasy tales and began producing propaganda. After the war, the rapid technological advances made by the Japanese contributed to the popularizing of science fiction stories. Osamu Tezuka (1928–1989), an important creator of comic strips and animation, created the little boy robot *Tetsuwan Atom* (literally, *Powerful Atom*), known in the west as *Astro Boy*. This series appeared in 1963 on the Fuji TV network and saw an enormous success. Astro Boy became an icon of animated science fiction. Series and full-length features in which robots were the heroes came one after another. Fantasy and horror were equally represented. The movie *Akira,* made in 1988 by Katsuhiro Otomo, marked a turning point in

Japanese animation. This science fiction story for adults mixed animation on celluloid with 3-D effects. The themes of political manipulation and the amoral application of science are wonderfully illustrated. The character Akira lets loose his powers in scenes of apocalyptic destruction. The policemen controlling the giant robots in *Kidoh Keisatsu Patlabor* (*Patlabor II,* 1993), directed by Mamoru Oshii; the androids with a conscience in *Kukaku kidutai* (*Ghost in the Shell,* 1995) and in *Innocence* (2004), also by Oshii; and the rebels who contest the given order in the city of Rintaro's *Metropolis* (2002), derived from Tezuka's comic strip, count among the characters marking a Japanese animation that unceasingly proves its technological and artistic virtuosity.

The amazing Ghost in the Shell, *one of the best animated science fiction movies ever made* Image courtesy of Fox Pathé Europa Video

BioHunter, *an excellent OAV (Original Animation Video) made by Yuzo Sato, based on a comic strip by Fujihiko Hosono. A scientist and his contaminated friend try to stop the spread of an insidious virus.* Image courtesy of TF1 Video

The famous Tetsuwan Atom, *known in the west as Astro Boy*

Vampire Hunter D: Bloodlust: *A particularly successful segment of a fantasy cult saga. The drawings of the characters overflow with details, the sets—a mix of 2-D and 3-D— are superb, the action scenes surprising, and the characters extremely moving. A truly great animation movie.* Image courtesy of TF1 Video

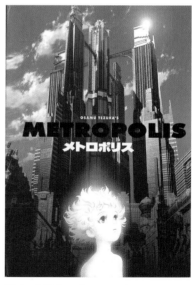

Rintaro's Metropolis: *a superb adaptation of a comic strip by Osamu Tezuka, the creator of Astro Boy* Image courtesy of Columbia Tri-Star Home Video

Opposite and above: *The dazzling* Laputa, The Castle in the Sky   Image courtesy of Studio Ghibli

Miyazaki the Enchanter

If a single filmmaker had to be selected to epitomize Japanese animated cartoons, it would be Hayao Miyazaki. *Kaze no Tani no Naushika* (*Nausicaä of the Valley of Wind,* 1984) was Miyazaki's first full-length fantasy film, and in it he painted a land devastated by war and pollution. The heroine, Nausicaä, makes contact with insect-like beings that hold the key to survival for their fellow creatures. With his associate Takahata, Miyazaki founded the Ghibli studio and produced his first masterpiece: *Tenkuu no shiro Rapyuta* (*Laputa, The Castle in the Sky,* 1986). Aside from Walt Disney, no other filmmaker has used the multiplane to such great effect as has Miyazaki. The adventures of the young Sheeta and her friend Pazu lead them to discover a flying city whose buildings are anchored into the roots of a gigantic tree. The discovery of the lost city in the midst of a sea of clouds, with its gardens tended by a rusted robot, is a vision of beauty that takes one's breath away. The depth effects of the 2-D sets prove to be more moving than if they had been the best synthesized images. *Tonari no Totoro* (*My Neighbor Totoro,* 1988) repeated this achievement. The film tells the tale of two young girls who, during

Another image from the stunning Laputa,
The Castle in the Sky
Image courtesy of Studio Ghibli

vacation, go to the countryside with their father while their mother is recovering in a hospital. They discover Totoro, a fat animal with magical powers, and the kindly forest spirits. Nature has rarely been so well depicted in an animated cartoon. Simple double exposures with bright highlights made it possible to animate an astonishingly realistic waterfall. Totoro speeds up the growth of the plants in a dreamlike sequence that would do no dishonor to Winsor McCay. Two more masterpieces, *Mononoke Hime* (*Princess Mononoke,* 1997) and *Sen to Chihiro no Kamikakushi* (*Spirited Away,* 2001; recipient of the 2003 Oscar for best animated picture), gave Miyazaki the opportunity to depict spirits from Japanese mythology, this time availing himself of the subtle effects of 3-D perfectly mixed with delicate graphics. After announcing his retirement, Miyazaki thrilled his fans when he adapted a classic of children's literature: *Hauru no Ugoku Shiro* (*Howl's Moving Castle,* 2004). The movie recounts the surprising adventures of a young girl transformed into an old woman by the evil spells of a witch.

Spirited Away: *The exploration of an imaginary universe, done with incredible radiance and depth*
Image courtesy of Studio Ghibli

My Neighbor Totoro, *one of Miyazaki's most poetic movies*
Image courtesy of Studio Ghibli

Wonderful Days: A Korean Surprise

The Korean movie *Wonderful Days* (2003), produced by Tin House and directed by Moon S. Kim, is one of the most complex animated movies to be undertaken in Asia. Director of animation Young-Ki Yoon, set designer Soug-Youn Lee, and digital effects supervisors Young-Min Park and Sung-Ho Hong mixed 2-D characters with computer-generated images, models of sets, and digital effects to create images of great beauty, a feat that required four years of work. *Wonderful Days* takes place in the distant future in a civilization ravaged by war and pollution. The rich and powerful have taken refuge on a Pacific island and established Ecoban, the last city on the planet. They mercilessly banish the irradiated people flocking to join them, who in turn create their own city on the floating island of Marr. Cade, an influential resident of Ecoban, would like to destroy Marr and the rebels led by Shua. After writing the script and designing the characters and sets, the team devised an extremely precise storyboard for *Wonderful Days*. Models of the principal sets were built and then filmed, using a high-definition camera attached to a motion control mount. The Frasier lenses used an independent Milo system computer program that controlled the camera

Director Moon S. Kim in the miniature set of Wonderful Days
Photo courtesy of Tin House

mount. A special program was developed to combine these two programs during the shooting, after which the computer artists started to work on the images of the models. As needed, they would digitally alter the colors and lighting, lending them a more graphic appearance, or partially redesign them with synthesized images. It was only then that the 2-D animations, made on celluloid, and the props and vehicles in 3-D were added. For numerous reasons, this mixing turned out to be extremely difficult to achieve. The scenes filmed with the models and the synthesized images were shot at a speed of twenty-four frames per second, while initially the animation was only twelve drawings per second. In order to accommodate the difference in the rate of movement, intermediate animated images were added, some of which were drawn, others digitally created. Harmonizing the textures also proved to be problematic. The 3-D images have a very precise, almost metallic appearance,

while the 2-D images seemed too flat. The team altered the appearance of the first models, repainting them to look more graphic. "Texture mapping" was used to transfer the realistic textures onto the 3-D surfaces, and the light, the shadows, and the dominant colors of the 2-D drawings were reworked to create modeled effects that perfectly integrated the characters into their universe. The most complex scenes of the movie were the crowds of demonstrators in the city of Marr and the knife-throwing scene in the restaurant. The camera movements and the great number of characters who are in the miniature sets are the fruit of relentless toil that demands admiration.

A sketch of the restaurant set

A shot with the model of the restaurant

An image of the model of the restaurant, lightly retouched, recolored, and shaded
Photos courtesy of Tin House

Clockwise from left: *A drawing of the set of the street; the filming of the model; the rendering of the model*
Photos courtesy of Tin House

A 2-D animation, made according to the perspective of the set as filmed earlier

The 3-D motorcycle

Above and left: *The final frame, and the model of the stained-glass window*
Photos courtesy of Tin House

The chase through the tunnels
Photo courtesy of Tin House

The Art of Metamorphosis

"Bigfoot," created by Brian Penikas

From Fake Noses to a Robotized T. rex: The Evolution of Makeup Special Effects

The Heritage of the Theater

Actors in the theater have been using makeup ever since ancient times. The first foundations were a mixture of animal fats and vegetable- or mineral-based pigments. Egyptians were the first to make human-hair wigs, in about 140 B.C. The art of producing colored powders made from rice, and eye makeup to emphasize the gaze, developed over the centuries. Actors explored the art of trompe l'oeil. They would highlight facial lines with a brushstroke and erase the rings from under their eyes with lightening makeup. Soon wigmakers had devised small crochet hooks for knotting hair onto shaped pieces of tulle and light-colored leather skullcaps to simulate a monk's tonsure. Fake noses, first made of cardboard and later of moldable wax, appeared on the scene. But in the theater, the distance separating the actors from the audience let them use crude methods. The great technical revolution in makeup came with the birth of film, when the camera zoomed

The makeup worn by Boris Karloff on the Broadway stage in 1950, playing Captain Hook in Peter Pan

in and actors were filmed in extreme close-ups.

The First Makeup for Film

The first great film makeup artists were escapees from the theater. Cecil Holland, an English actor who had immigrated to Hollywood, shaved the top of his head and half of his eyebrows, and then drew lines on his face, in order to portray General Sherman in *Crisis* (1916). He pursued his experiments by making false teeth out of latex, which he implanted in gums made of pink wax that had been softened in hot water, then wore them over his real teeth. Holland continued with his innovations, creating the makeup for a blind man in *The Love Light*

Cecil Holland creates the makeup for the movie Grand Hotel *(1932).*
Photo courtesy of Universal Studios Florida

(1921), for which he removed the white skin adhering to the inside of the shell of a hard-boiled egg and cut it to form two disks, each three-quarters of an inch (two centimeters) in diameter. He placed them on actor Raymond Bloomer's eyes, giving them the appearance of having turned white from disease. In 1927, Holland established Hollywood's first makeup department, at the MGM studios. He drew Boris Karloff's eyes back by gluing pieces of celluloid in front of his eyelids and thus transformed him for his title role in *The Mask of Fu Manchu* (1932). In 1937, he perfected this technique with Luise Rainer for the movie *The Good Earth*. He would continue to do the makeup for numerous stars until the 1950s. At the beginning of his career in makeup, Cecil Holland was dubbed "the man of a thousand faces." He was to pass along this moniker to the actor/makeup artist Lon Chaney.

Lon Chaney's makeup kit, which famously was always with him
Photo courtesy of Universal Studios Florida

The makeup of Quasimodo
Photo courtesy of Scott Essman collection

The features of the Phantom of the Opera   Photo courtesy of Scott Essman collection

Lon Chaney: Human Chameleon

Leonidas F. Chaney was born in 1883 in Colorado Springs to parents who were deaf and mute. He communicated with them by means of gesticulations, an experience he would make use of later on. He experimented with acting in the theater run by his brother, learned to do his own makeup, and then tried his luck

in Hollywood. Hearing that someone needed a gangster, he would appear before the casting director with a scar and be hired on the spot. Soon he went nowhere without his makeup case, which contained cotton, makeup and grease pencils, moldable wax, modeling tools, colored powders, and a flask of collodion. This medical substance, also known as nitrocellulose, was a mixture of cotton powder, alcohol, and

ether. Applied to the skin, it forms a film that serves as a temporary bandage. Chaney used it to make wrinkles, scars, and burn marks, enabling him to change his face at will, and it was this that landed him the role of Quasimodo in *The Hunchback of Notre Dame* (1923). Chaney made himself up with cotton and collodion attached to the arches of his eyebrows, a deformed eye, and a latex hump weighing forty

Mr. Wu *(1927): A startling metamorphosis*
Photo courtesy of Scott Essman collection

pounds (eighteen kilograms). His embodiment of the pathetic monster made him into a star. He then interpreted the role of Professor Echo, the ventriloquist in *The Unholy Three* (1925), who disguised himself as a woman to trick his victims. And after that, as Erik, the Phantom of the Opera, for which he disfigured himself with a fake skull, with cotton and collodion prosthetics to make his cheekbones jut out, with pointy false teeth, and with a piece of fish skin glued to his nose in such a way as to make it point upward. Chaney enacted other odd characters, such as the amputee beggar in *The Penalty* (1920), whom he depicted by pinning his

ankles to his thighs. He performed his only speaking role in the 1930 remake of *The Unholy Three,* a few months before he died of cancer.

Jack Pierce, The Father of Monsters

In 1914, Jack Pierce was an assistant cameraman at Universal Studios who also, when asked, made props. In 1927, he was assigned the job of transforming Jacques Lerner into a chimpanzee for the movie *The Monkey Talks.* Pierce used modeling wax covered with kidskin to form the ape's muzzle; glued hairs onto the actor's cheeks, neck, and hands; and constructed a wig fitted with large ears. He won the congratulations of studio directors who were considering adapting classics of fantastic literature. From this point on, they knew whom to contact. In 1930, Jack Pierce conceived of the terrifying features for Dracula—but Bela Lugosi insisted on looking his

Portrait of Jack Pierce
Photo courtesy of Scott Essman collection

best! And so his face was simply made up with a greenish foundation and his hair reshaped. The following year, Pierce was asked to create the Frankenstein monster. As there is no precise description in Mary Shelley's novel, he referred to brain surgeries during which doctors cut open the top of the skull; in accordance with that, he flattened the top of the monster's head and added metal staples to heighten the effect. The actor chosen to enact the role was William Henry Pratt, an English gentleman who changed his name to Boris Karloff. Pierce seated him in a comfortable chair, covered his hair over with a skullcap, and set about constructing a square forehead, layer by layer, with cotton soaked in collodion. The process took six hours. Pierce attached the metal clips to Karloff's ears a little too well, leaving him scarred. The actor felt he still looked a little too alive, so Pierce made him wax eyelids. When Karloff finally lifted himself out of his chair, with his deadened eyes, his stiff limbs, and his sunken face, he had become the incarnation of Mary Shelley's monster. *Frankenstein* was a box office triumph, bringing in some twelve million dollars. Universal had struck the mother lode.

The next year, Universal reunited the Karloff-Pierce team and breathed life into *The Mummy.* Pierce baked strips of cloth in an oven to make them brittle and appear old. He swathed Karloff's

Pierce's most famous makeup: the Frankenstein monster
Photo courtesy of Scott Essman collection

The Wolf Man
Photo courtesy of Universal Studios Florida

The resurrection of the Mummy
Photo courtesy of Scott Essman collection

body, crisscrossing it in three layers of the cloth strips, which he then covered with a layer of clay reinforced with glue; finally, he covered Karloff's face in thin layers of cotton soaked in collodion. Pierce asked Karloff to stretch his face while the collodion dried. While in repose, deep wrinkles formed around his mouth, as if the skin had mummified. Karloff's hair was pasted down with a mixture of clay and loam. When the mummy comes back to life in his sarcophagus, the clay-covered strips of cloth can be seen falling from his hands and turning to dust before the camera. During the 1940s, Pierce re-created the Mummy's makeup three times for Lon Chaney Jr., who had taken on all of the studio's monster roles. Pierce's final great creation would be the metamorphosis of Lon Chaney Jr. into a werewolf in *The Wolf Man* (1941). As he needed to be in the same position during each stage of his transformation, the actor was immobilized. His hands were encircled by dozens of small nails,

Molds of sculptures by Jack Pierce and the Frankenstein makeup re-created for Lon Chaney Jr. in the 1940s
Photo courtesy of Universal Studios Florida

and his head was propped up by a hidden support. Pierce first applied extensive werewolf makeup but then replaced it with a toned-down version that consisted of a less prominent muzzle and less hair. This process of reduction was repeated twenty-one times, with the final rendition being filmed twenty-two hours later! With reverse projections and scenes linked by fade-ins and fade-outs, this transformation of a man into a werewolf astounded audiences. But at the end of the 1940s, monster movies were no longer being produced so frequently. Universal united Dracula, Frankenstein, and the Wolf Man in a B movie, before transforming them into foils for the comedy team of Abbott and Costello. Since the advent of foam rubber prosthetics, makeup can be constructed and applied much more quickly. Although Jack Pierce's techniques had become outdated, he still held on to his cotton

and collodion. Universal Studios brought their twenty-two-year collaboration to an end. Bitter, Pierce began working in television. The man who was one of the greatest creators of fantasy characters died in 1968, largely forgotten.

Makeup for the Wizard of Oz (Frank Morgan)
Photo courtesy of Scott Essman collection

The Magical Makeup of the Land of Oz

In 1939, Jack Dawn revolutionized makeup techniques by fabricating the first foam rubber prosthetics, for *The Wizard of Oz*. Until then, this industrial product, developed by the Dunlop Corporation, was used only for making puncture-proof tires and mattresses. Jack Dawn, with his associates William Tuttle, Charlie Schram, Emile LaVigne, and Josef and Gustaf Norin, founded the first makeup laboratory.

Together, they modified the formula of the industrial foam and managed to make it softer. Their process is still being used today. Dawn started by making a mold of the face of Bert Lahr, the actor who was to play the role of the Cowardly Lion. He protected Lahr's hair with a latex bald cap and put Vaseline on his eyebrows and over his skin. He then applied several layers of plaster of Paris to his face, taking care not to obstruct his nostrils. (Today, the actor's face is cast in a mold made of the polymer alginate, which is then covered over with plaster strips.) The mold produced a plaster replica of Lahr's face, on which the lion's muzzle and jowls were then modeled in clay. This rendition was in turn molded, and when the clay was removed, the empty space between the two molds defined the outline of the prosthetics. What remained was the foam rubber preparation. Dawn and his assistants used an electric kitchen mixer to blend a foaming agent and a curing agent into a highly concentrated liquid latex. After a few minutes, the latex became foamy and filled with tiny air bubbles. A gelling agent was added, and the mixture was applied with a brush to the inner walls of the mold. The mold was then filled entirely and closed. Once the foam had gelled in the mold, it was placed in an oven and baked for two hours at 212°F (100°C). Carefully removed from the mold, the foam rubber

The Tin Man (Jack Haley)
Photo courtesy of Scott Essman collection

Scarecrow encountered Dorothy (Judy Garland) on the set, they had no way of knowing they would become the most endearing characters of a masterpiece.

The Enchanting *Beauty and the Beast*

A few years later, it was in France that another masterpiece, Jean Cocteau's *La Belle et la Bête* (*The Beauty and the Beast*), was born. But in 1946, French makeup artists were not using foam rubber, and so the challenge facing Hagop Arakelian was that much more demanding—how to trans-

form Jean Marais into a frightening beast, whose kindness would win over the heart of a young girl. Marais suggested to Pontet, the chief wigmaker for the movie, that he might get inspiration from his dog's coat. So a mask was created like a wig, composed of three parts with stripes radiating from the brow and disappearing back into the beast's mane. Each morning, five hours were spent applying the makeup: three for the face, and one for each hand. Arakelian first applied a black polish on Marais's teeth to give them a sinister look, and dental prosthetics were fitted with long

The face of the Beast (Jean Marais)
Photo courtesy of Scott Essman collection

appliance was cleansed of any chemical residue, dried, and glued to Lahr's face with spirit gum. Carried away by the lightness of the mask, Lahr became disillusioned when he discovered that his tailor-made lion fur weighed fifty-five pounds (twenty-five kilograms)! Silver paint and blue powder makeup transformed his costar Jack Haley into the Tin Man. And just like a suit of armor, Haley's costume was welded shut! For Ray Bolger, who played the Scarecrow, Jack Dawn carved the folds of a sack into a cast of the actor's head and then transferred the reliefs onto a coarse cloth. When the Cowardly Lion, Tin Man, and

The mutant Metaluna in the movie This Island Earth *(1955)*
Photo courtesy of Universal Studios Florida

The Creature from the Black Lagoon
Photo courtesy of Universal Studios Florida

canine teeth attached by gold hooks. The three sections of the mask were then glued together. Photographed to perfection by Henri Alekan, Jean Marais brought life to one of the most beautiful characters of fantasy films.

The Costumes of the 1950s

At the beginning of the 1950s, Hollywood studios competed with television by producing 3-D movies such as *Creature from the Black Lagoon* (1954), the story of a fish-man caught in the Amazon. Sculptor Chris Mueller and make-up artist Bud Westmore created a foam rubber costume and a mask detailed with thousands of scales and painted with iridescent high-lights. Because of all the time spent in the water, the costume deteriorated. Repairing it and continually crafting new pieces brought the cost of the creature to fifteen thousand dollars—a small fortune at that time. But the amphibious monster drew hordes of avid sensation seekers. In Japan, an actor encased in another rubber sculpture portrayed a gigantic monster. Special effects master Eiji Tsuburaya filmed *Godzilla* (1954) at 120 frames per second, with the monster trampling on models of the streets of Tokyo. On the screen, with the movements slowed down, it looks as if the creature is enormous. Its extraordinary success spawned more giant monsters, such as Rodan the

The indestructible Godzilla
Photo courtesy of Toho

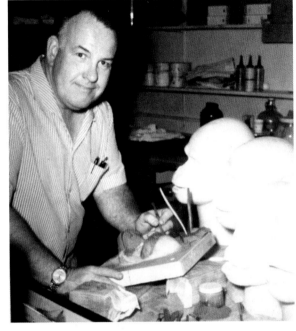

John Chambers sculpts the face of a young chimpanzee during preproduction on Planet of the Apes. *On the worktable are latex masks before being painted to be worn by extras in the background.*
Photo courtesy of Brian Penikas

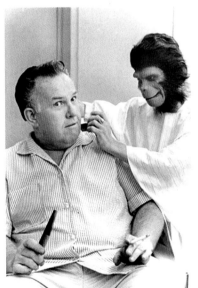

A reversal of roles during a makeup session; one of the superb life-size replicas of Cornelius made by Brian Penikas and sold to the delight of collectors
Photo courtesy of Brian Penikas

pterodactyl, Mothra the moth, and Gamera the flying tortoise!

The Planet of John Chambers

Not all the great makeup artists had artistic training. John Chambers acquired some of his knowledge by studying the fabrication of dental prosthetics while in the army. He then worked at Fitzsimmons Hospital in Denver, where he made all sorts of prosthetics to help disfigured soldiers regain a more normal appearance—noses, false hands, false legs, false eyes fitted into glasses with thick lenses, prosthetic palates to help the wounded speak, etc. He experienced great joy when the patients he "repaired" dared to face the look of strangers. During this time, he made countless experiments with different plastics and glues. Hired by the National Broadcasting Company in 1953, he brought to Hollywood his mastery of medical materials, which had never been used to create makeup appliances before. In 1962, he signed with Universal Studios. The following year, *The List of Adrian Messenger,* directed by John Huston, gave him the opportunity to create ten different sets of makeup. Kirk Douglas played a killer who disguises himself in order to murder distant relatives and inherit a vast fortune. Burt Lancaster appears disguised as a woman, and Frank Sinatra as a Gypsy! Between films, Chambers would work in

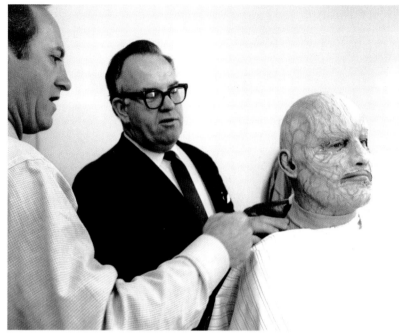

Dan Striepeke and John Chambers working on the makeup of a mutant for Beneath the Planet of the Apes, *the second movie in the series*
Photo courtesy of Brian Penikas

The "humanimals" created by Chambers for The Island of Dr. Moreau

television. He created the futur-
istic being played by David
McCallum in the famous episode
"The Sixth Finger" from the
series *The Outer Limits,* and he
made the pointed ears for Mr.
Spock on *Star Trek.* His moment
of glory came in 1967. Producer
Arthur P. Jacobs tried to convince
Twentieth Century-Fox to finance

Planet of the Apes, but a problem
arose: would the ape makeup be
credible, or would audiences roll
in the aisles laughing? Chambers
suggested radical transformations. He sculpted the face of a
gorilla and another of a chimpanzee, and then split them into
two parts: the forehead, the
arches of the eyebrows, and the

snout constituted one section,
while the chin was independent.
The snouts were fitted with false
teeth, making the apes' mouths
protrude more. Charlton Heston
believed in the project and
agreed to participate in a screen
test with two made-up actors.
The result was so impressive that
Fox gave it the green light.

Zira and Cornelius, the most famous of Chambers's characters, continue to delight audiences forty years after their creation.

Chambers assembled a team of collaborators who oversaw eighty makeup artists. He made two kinds of prosthetics for the gorillas, for the chimpanzees, and for the orangutans. The principal actors, such as Roddy McDowall, Kim Hunter, and Maurice Evans, wore prosthetics made from molds of their faces. Interchangeable prosthetics were assigned to members of the secondary cast in accordance with the size of their face. Transposed from one morphology to another, the prosthetics made it possible to create very different ape personalities. Latex masks covered in fur were given to the extras relegated to the background. Using a spray gun, Chambers painted the prosthetics with a porous mixture of plastic, pigments, and glue that did not obstruct the cells of the foam rubber, and thus let the actors' perspiration pass through the makeup. The makeup artists used a greasepaint foundation to hide the lines where the mask and skin met, and they shaded the area with toned makeup. This innovation reduced the makeup time from five hours to four hours and fifteen minutes. Chambers also sprayed the inside of the prosthetics with glue, to save a little more time. But the big problem remained the amount of prosthetics that had to be made to ensure each day of shooting. Chambers came up with a way to recycle a portion of what had already been worn. He developed a mixture of acetone and alcohol that could dissolve the glue residue without damaging the edges of the prosthetics, which were then washed, disinfected, and repainted to be used again—this time, however, in the background. McDowall and Hunter, in their roles as Cornelius and Zira, the chimpanzees who befriend Taylor (the astronaut played by Heston), had great presence on the screen. *Planet of the Apes* was released in 1968 and was an enormous success. In 1969, John Chambers received a special Oscar, which was presented to him by Walter Matthau—and a chimpanzee! Fox made the most of the apes' popularity, producing four more movies and finally ending their career in 1974 with a thirteen-episode TV series. The man-beasts in *The Island of Dr. Moreau* (1977) were Chambers's final creations. When he died on August 25, 2001, his family revealed that he had created sophisticated makeups for CIA agents working undercover, just as the Rollin Hand character does in the *Mission: Impossible* TV series. He is also believed to be the person who made the costume for "Bigfoot" in the supposedly authentic 8-millimeter movie shot in 1967 by Roger Patterson and Bob Gimlin. Rumors or reality—it doesn't really matter. The extraordinary talents of John Chambers made him a legend.

INTERVIEW

DICK SMITH

The Generosity of a Genius

Dick Smith is a true legend in the world of makeup. He invented many revolutionary techniques and taught them to his peers throughout his prestigious career.

Photo courtesy of Dick Smith

Who were the makeup artists who influenced you the most as a teenager?

Dick Smith: I first became interested in makeup when I saw *The Hunchback of Notre Dame,* starring Charles Laughton, in 1939. That was designed by Perc Westmore. It fascinated me. The next year, when I was a freshman at Yale, I found a book on sale that helped me learn the basics of stage makeup. The first I did was based on the Spencer Tracy makeup in *Dr. Jekyll and Mr. Hyde.* After that, I did the Hunchback, and then I did the Jack Pierce makeups. All these experiments made me feel that this was what I wanted to do. A great inspiration to me was Maurice Seiderman, who was the man who did the wonderful, innovative makeup on *Citizen Kane* in 1942. Not only did he invent some makeup products for this historic makeup, but he

also later invented one of the two soft contact lens formulas and even participated in eye surgeries. I did not actually meet Maurice and become his friend until he was in his seventies, still wonderfully inventive.

Can you describe the early makeup experiments you undertook in an attempt to obtain thinner prosthetic edges?

Dick Smith: I worked for NBC from 1945 to 1959, then I worked for two years freelancing for David Susskind on television dramas. He then hired me to work on his *Requiem for a Heavyweight* with Anthony Quinn. I had always been told by movie makeup artists that film makeup was way more difficult than television makeup, because the image was enlarged on the cinema screen. This terrified me. I had to

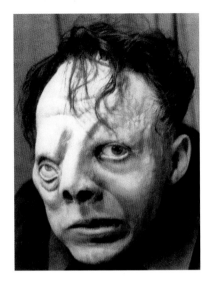

One of Dick Smith's first amateur makeup jobs, done in 1942, based on The Hunchback of Notre Dame
Photo courtesy of Dick Smith

Another metamorphosis, this time inspired by Dr. Jekyll and Mr. Hyde
Photo courtesy of Dick Smith

Anthony Quinn transformed into an aging boxer in Requiem for a Heavyweight
Photo courtesy of Dick Smith

create eleven makeup appliances for Quinn. He was to look like an old fighter with a lot of bruises, but each time the edges of my molds were too thick! I seriously considered quitting, but I asked to do a test makeup one week before the shooting to have some time to somehow correct the problems. So I did the first makeup with appliances with thick edges. And the next day, I was trembling when I went to see the screen test. The first shot that came in was this full-face close-up on Tony. And it was perfect! You couldn't see any edge! And then I thought, "Those sons of bitches lied to me! This is a piece of cake!" If it had been on television, I would have seen the defects, but on film, because of the film process, the details were simply not there. Once I relaxed, I realized that I had made the molds so well that they were closing up all around the edges, and the excess foam was creating a

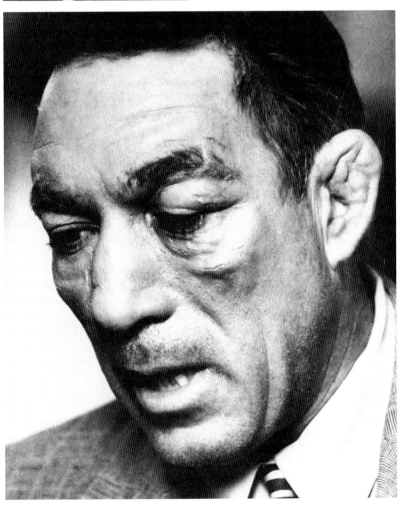

pressure that held the two halves of the mold slightly apart. So I drilled a hole inside the mold of the face, releasing the excess foam. This hole did not affect the outside look of the appliance, and the molds were closing perfectly.

The makeup you created for Dustin Hoffman in "Little Big Man" to age him into a 121-year-old man was the result of several innovations, such as overlapping appliances.

Dick Smith: I had already done makeups that were often in separate pieces, but they were just bits here and there. So making separate appliances was well known and done by several people. But when it came to doing an extensive makeup like that one on Dustin, it was customary to make an entire mask covering the whole face. The last great old-age makeup was done by George Bau in 1948 or 1949, for an NBC show called *The Lost Moment,* starring Agnes Moorehead as a 110-year-old lady. I knew that full-face masks shrank and were hard to get on, because I had done some for stuntmen. This is why I decided to use several appliances for Dustin's makeup. I painted a thin coat of urethane on the life mask. I secured it with some dental adhesive, and I sculpted the

whole thing over that. And then I carefully pried it off, cutting the material into sections. I was able to peel the rubber behind the plasteline sculpture sections and transfer those plasteline pieces to smaller sections of the life mask, like a duplicate of the forehead, a duplicate of the chin, etc. I then blended off the edges and retouched the details of the sculpture before making the final mold. There is not a wrinkle that I sculpted on this makeup that I had not seen on real people during my research. In the 1960s, film stock became much more sensitive, and it became more difficult to hide the artificiality of makeup on screen. Directors then became reluctant to use extensive makeups in films, fearing that it would look phony. So people like Johnny Chambers and I had to convince them that there were ways to make it work and look believable. *Little Big Man* and *Planet of the Apes* revolutionized the industry at that time.

You spent a lot of time on details such as Dustin Hoffman's eyelids.

Dick Smith: Oh yes! Before that, eyelids were sculpted like little visors over the eyelids. When the actor with the old-age makeup would look down, his

real eyelids would appear from underneath the appliance. I had sculpted these very delicate foam rubber pieces that were paper-thin in the middle area, and I had them pleated like an accordion so that when they were actually glued up by the eyebrow itself and at the bottom just above the eyelashes on the eyelid, Dustin could actually open and close his eyes naturally.

Unfortunately, the hard contact lenses we had to use fell out each time he blinked. After the first day of filming, we rushed to an oculist to regrind the lenses somewhat. And so, on the other two days, Dustin was able to wear the lenses, but he was very careful not to blink because it did move them around. On some occasions he did blink on camera, but not a single one of those shots made it into the edited film!

You added some realism to his aged skin by painting lots of little spots on it. How did you maintain continuity on this day after day?

Dick Smith: Well, years ago, it was customary to simply put a basic greasepaint skin color all over an appliance and then stipple some red on top of it with a rough sponge. I noticed that this often produced a "mask" effect, and I always tried to use

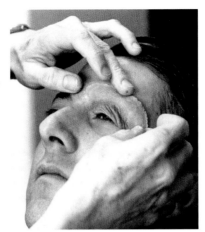
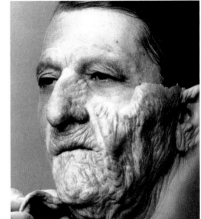

Above, below, and right: *Dustin Hoffman prepares to become an old man for* Little Big Man; *the placement of appliances onto his eyebrows and eyelids; the appliances placed one by one, covering his whole face; close-up of the articulated lids, eyes closed; the penultimate stage; the final makeup.*   Photo courtesy of Dick Smith

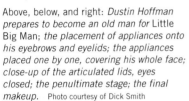

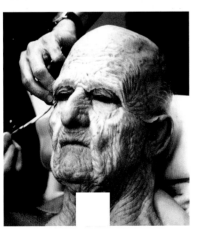

richer combinations of colors to produce a better effect. I learned something from Johnny Chambers. In order to save time on the *Planet of the Apes* make-ups, he found a kind of a rubber cement material into which he could incorporate colors and use it to pre-paint his appliances. I took his basic formula and used it to color Dustin's appliances and paint the veins, the spots, and everything. I simply put the most important spots always at the same place. But I learned from experience that continuity details like this really don't show. People would not notice them except if they were extremely obvious. Like when hairstyle varies from a shot to another.

You created a remarkable old-age makeup on Marlon Brando for "The Godfather," despite the fact that he had refused to have prosthetics applied on his face.

Dick Smith: Marlon is a nice guy. Before we shot the film, I went to England to meet him and discuss what I was going to do. He seemed to agree with my plans to use appliances, but when he came to New York he wanted a simpler makeup. For a test video that [Francis Ford] Coppola had made months earlier, Marlon's makeup man, Phil Rhodes, had put cotton in his cheeks, gray in his hair, and

painted in some wrinkles. When they saw the video, the Paramount Studio executives did not recognize him and therefore agreed on having him cast as the Godfather. Marlon was so nice; what could I say? So I used old-age stipple to create wrinkles on his skin. It is a mixture of natural latex, gelatin, some pigments, and some material that stiffens the product. It has been used since the 1930s. Marlon had his blond/white hair dyed black except for the temple area, which looked more natural. I had dental "plumpers" made for him. They are like removable bridges that fit over the lower teeth, with little pads that push his cheeks out. It is not realistic, but it gets by. It only took me one hour and twenty minutes to prepare him, as opposed to three to four hours if I had to use appliances. I did also put a shoulder pad on his shoulders and a belly pad to age his body.

In "Taxi Driver," you created bloody makeup effects for the shooting scene, but also Robert De Niro's half-shaved head and a sophisticated bullet wound on his skull.

Dick Smith: Actually, I created the first "makeup effect" for *The Godfather*. It was a false forehead piece on Sterling Hayden that had a little

Marlon Brando's makeup in The Godfather *was simplified at his request.*

Contrary to what is often said and written, Marlon Brando never stuffed cotton in his mouth to play the Godfather in the film. Shown here are the dental prosthetics made by Dick Smith to create the jowls.
Photos courtesy of Dick Smith

Despite how it appears, Robert De Niro did not shave his head for scenes in Taxi Driver. *He wore a bald cap conceived by Dick Smith.*   Photo courtesy of Dick Smith

explosive squib under it, opening up a bullet hole and causing blood to pour out when he is shot in the face. The effects appearing in *The Exorcist* opened up a whole new dimension in makeup and revolutionized the industry. After this, everyone wanted to incorporate makeup effects in their films! To come back to *Taxi Driver,* I wanted to perfect the look of the bald cap Robert De Niro would wear to make it look as if he had been recently shaved. For this, I devised a way to spray on very finely chopped real hair onto the adhesive covering the cap. I used a medical atomizer that was used some time ago to spray powder directly into the throat. Spraying the hair very evenly was very difficult to do, but a lot of people were fooled into believing that De Niro really shaved his hair. The wound was created with ethyl methacrylate, which is a plastic that I used to create appliances with a passageway for fake blood. I put a small piece on the side of his neck, with a little "plug," a piece that fitted into the mound, making it look normal. Then I would attach a very fine line to that plug. A hidden tube running to his costume, attached to some kind of pumping device, pumped artificial blood. So on cue, when the bang went off, someone would pull the line that would open up the wound and at the same time would pump the blood.

One of your most memorable creations was Linda Blair's makeup in "The Exorcist."

Dick Smith: Billy Friedkin, the director, was an extraordinary man to work with. A perfectionist, but he brought out the best in me. He gave you all the time and whatever budget you needed. The only problem with Billy was the fact that he had no sense of diplomacy, no tact. If he did not like something, he would just say so bluntly! And when I first met Linda Blair, I thought, "Oh my God, how am I going to turn this sweet-looking apple-cheeked girl into a monster?" We went through a series of makeup tests that Billy would look at and criticize. The look we picked was rather frightening. The first scene that was shot with this makeup was a scene with a psychiatrist. And because her appearance was changed so much, the things they said in that scene did not make any sense. At the time, I

was disappointed, because I liked this design, but I realized that it had to be changed. I then tried to emulate the look of a strange sickness on Linda.

How did you create the "help me" message appearing on the girl's stomach?

Dick Smith: I knew the stomach was going to be a large, thin appliance with ribs, going from her neck down to her crotch. I thought of mechanical devices, but nothing seemed to be organic looking. Then I remembered an old trick played on a makeup apprentice on the production of *The Wizard of Oz* back in 1939. Makeup men gave an apprentice carbon tet [trichlorethylene] instead of acetone to clean some old appliances. Because this product is a petroleum distillate, it attacked the foam rubber and

One of the makeup tests for The Exorcist
Photo courtesy of Dick Smith

Another makeup test, rejected
Photo courtesy of Dick Smith

Linda Blair's final makeup
Photo courtesy of Dick Smith

made it expand instantly. I made some tests on various foam rubbers, and I noticed that in some cases, when the foam dried, the expansion would disappear without leaving a trace. I got the idea to film the whole thing in reverse. During the shooting, we first starched her clothes so that they would not move when the heat gun above her would blow hot air on the appliance. I would trace the letters with a brush on the appliance to make the foam expand, we would then roll the camera while the heat gun was on, and the letters would disappear within a minute. When the film was run backward, the effect was great. But Billy thought it ran too long and inserted a cutaway, and I thought it sort of made it look like it was faked. The other problem was the vomit coming out of her mouth. Billy wanted

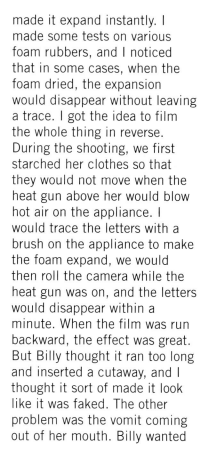

The mannequin of Linda Blair, with the head that turns 360 degrees
Photo courtesy of Dick Smith

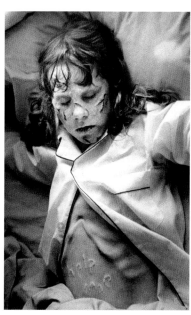

The message "help me" on Linda Blair's stomach   Photo courtesy of Dick Smith

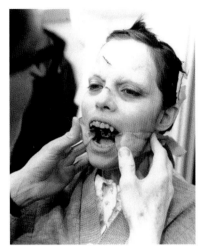

Dick Smith adjusts the vomit-projecting mechanism on Eileen Dietz, Linda Blair's double. Photo courtesy of Dick Smith

Max von Sydow without makeup. He was a little over forty when he starred in The Exorcist. Photo courtesy of Dick Smith

Max von Sydow as he appeared in the movie Photo courtesy of Dick Smith

Dick Smith: Billy warned me that he did not want to use any lens diffusion to shoot the scenes with Max, but he gave me the opportunity to make three full makeup tests on camera before shooting. I started off by using three different greasepaint base colors: on the forehead, the midsection, and the neck. Then I did stipple colors on top of that. I painted veins, freckles, liver spots, and so on. That was the most detailed coloration that had ever been made until that time. The appliances were rather thin. They covered the sides of his jaw and cheeks, up to the cheekbone area. There was a tiny appliance on his upper lip, a larger piece on his lower lip and chin, and there was also a wattle underneath his jaw. All the rest was done with the old-age stipple. Of course, his hair was painted white. I even used some old-age stipple on my neck and later molded the wattle it formed to create the mold for this appliance.

You are really into your work.

Dick Smith: (*Laughs.*) Very good! The second time we did it, Billy asked me to cut Max's hair short in the back, as if he had been to a barber. I told him that it was not a good idea, since the old-age stipple would

to see it coming straight at the camera. I had to devise a whole rig of thin, flat tubes molded to fit the sides of her cheeks, connected with a pipe that went through her mouth, like a bit in a horse's bridle, and then connected with the tubes behind her head to a pump, pumping hot pea soup. Later on, I found out that Billy changed his mind and matted in straight jets of vomit over my carefully planned effects! There is still one scene in the film when you can see Linda Blair with her head on her pillow, with lava-like vomit oozing from the corner of her mouth. That is the effect working in that scene.

Max von Sydow's old-age makeup was so natural-looking that many people did not realize he was only forty-three years old then.

get caught in the thin hair and look terrible. But he did not change his mind. I did cut Max's hair nice and short, and I tried to put old-age stipple as close as I could to the hair without getting in it. And it left a tiny little line of separation there. Then Billy arrived. I had worked hard all day on Linda's makeup and then on this make-up. And the first thing Billy says is, "That's awful!" And I said, "Billy, I told you that this was going to happen!" And then he said, "Don't raise your voice to me!" And I said, "That's it," and quit! And my assistant quit as well. I had been working seven days a week for months. To make a long story short, I came back the next day and said that I wanted to finish the show but needed to have some time off because I was too exhausted. Billy and I eventually made up and he gave me a full screen credit on the film. And we have been good friends ever since.

How did you invent PAX, the flexible coloration for appliances?

Dick Smith: During my television days, I had to create a Mark Twain makeup on Hal Holbrook's face and hands, and since he was wearing a white shirt and suit, greasepaint would have left marks on the

The Hunger: *David Bowie, with a light makeup that gave him the appearance of a 45-to-50-year-old*
Photo courtesy of Dick Smith

Second transformation: 60 years old. Bowie wore a wig, prosthetics on his forehead, and a shaved beard applied over cheek prosthetics.
Photo courtesy of Dick Smith

David Bowie wore prosthetics covering his face and hands to look 90 years old.
Photo courtesy of Dick Smith

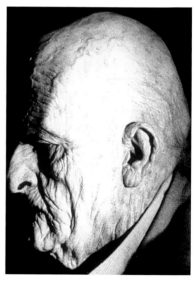

The final makeup: David Bowie at 150 years old
Photo courtesy of Dick Smith

Top to bottom: *Dick Smith flattens down F. Murray Abraham's hair at the start of a makeup session for* Amadeus; *prosthetics were applied onto his head, cheeks, and neck; the application of bags under the eyes; Dick Smith retouches the shaved beard that he'd glued onto the prosthetic.*

Opposite: *Salieri's final makeup*
Photos courtesy of Dick Smith

clothes that would have been clearly visible. I had the idea to mix latex with acrylic artist paint. It stuck well but was barely satisfactory. When I tried Pros-Aide [a medical adhesive] on my hand and saw how resistant and flexible it was, it only seemed natural to mix acrylic paint with it to see how it would work. I had no time [because I was busy working on *The Hunger*] to make further tests on this mixture that I later called PAX. I received a phone call from the makeup lady who was working in England with Tony Scott, the director of *The Hunger*. She told me that Tony had asked Bowie to grow a beard for the scenes just prior to his old-age transformation! "Oh no! How am I going to put a stubble beard over grease-paint? It will be a mess!" Before I left for England, I took the precaution to take some of that Pros-Aide and PAX with me. The first day I did the makeup on Bowie, I just used PAX on the area where I would glue the stubble beard with an adhesive, but it worked so well that each day, as I applied the same makeup, I would use it more and more, until I used it on the whole face! Now PAX has become an industry standard.

The Salieri old-age makeup is another remarkable achievement. You even donated a few of your own wrinkles to create Salieri's forehead appliance.

Dick Smith: I am not the only one to use this "donor" technique. Greg Cannom did it as well. It sometimes gives you some little natural details that are difficult to sculpt exactly right. When I realized that F. Murray Abraham's forehead and mine had the same size and shape, I thought that making a mold of my own forehead would work well. I then "printed" my wrinkles into the plasticine sculpture and later created a very thin appliance that worked even better with his own facial expressions. Ironically, the compliments I would get from this makeup would often be, "Oh, and the forehead was so wonderful!" (*Laughs.*)

Could you explain how the professional makeup course you have created works?

Dick Smith: I always wanted to write up my findings and so forth. I had worked on a film called *Everybody's All-American,* in which I nearly came to a fistfight with Dennis Quaid. He called me outside the makeup trailer, and we were going to fight. He would have probably killed me! It was the

Dick Smith receives his Oscar for best makeup for the aging of F. Murray Abraham in Amadeus.

worst on-set experience I ever had! At that point, I decided that I didn't need to work like that. So I wrote my life's work. I came up with a written lecture on the basic things that we do. I sell the Advanced Professional Makeup Course for $1,995 to people who are ready to take it, who know basic makeup. And I am available as a teacher to all these students, to answer their questions via phone or e-mails. I sold this course to students in thirty-four countries all over the world. I also created a Basic Makeup Course, which is only $350, to help students get started without paying an expensive makeup school. I have a new protégé named Michael Fontaine, who has my course and who is going to be an important makeup artist one day. When I first talked to him on the phone, he was only eleven years old. He still had his little voice then. And he said, "I became interested in makeup when I was three, but I only got serious about it when I was six!" (*Laughs.*) Isn't it great?

What were the greatest joys of your career?

Dick Smith: Well, receiving an Academy Award was extremely nice, but I also have many other fond memories. Working with Laurence Olivier was an experi-

ence that I will treasure all my life. When I first met him, he was going to play in *The Moon and Sixpence,* a story based on the life of Gauguin. And the character winds up dying of leprosy. Here I was, overwhelmed with the prospect of dealing with Laurence Olivier, one of the greatest living English actors, but also known to be a nut about makeup, making himself up all the time very expertly. I was terrified! I had prepared some preliminary drawings, and when we first met, in two minutes we became like two old buddies. He was all excited about the makeup, just like a kid! I was so relaxed by his total openness. We had a rough taping—twenty hours a day or so. And at the final stages of his leprosy makeup, at about three in the morning, as I finished the makeup and as he looked at it in the mirror, he turned to me and said, "Dick, it does the acting for me!" And years later, when I worked on *The Marathon Man,* he went to see the director, John Schlesinger, to tell him, "Dick and I worked together before, and he created a makeup that did the acting for me!" After all those years, it was still in his mind. He was an absolutely wonderful human being.

Information regarding Dick Smith's advanced makeup course can be found at his Web site: www.dicksmithmake-up.com.

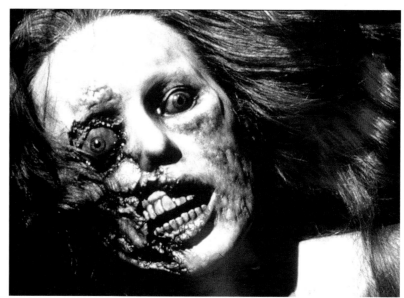

Clockwise from top left:
This supernatural appearance in Ghost Story *(1981) was cut from the final edit.*

A mechanical head created for Ghost Story

A giant head made for a hallucinatory sequence in Altered States *(1980)*

The makeup of a leper applied onto Laurence Olivier for the television film The Moon and Sixpence *(1959)*
Photos courtesy of Dick Smith

Rick Baker (with the beard) not only created the creatures in Men in Black, he also crossed to the other side of the camera.
Photo courtesy of Columbia-TriStar & Amblin

Rick Baker and the Search for the Perfect Gorilla

Dick Smith's young assistant on *The Exorcist* accomplished an extraordinary journey. A fan of fantasy movies, he decided when he was ten years old to become a "monster maker." His father taught him the basics of sculpting and modeling, and when Baker was twenty years old, he was offered the job of making the octopus-man for the TV movie

The monster in the TV movie Octaman

Octaman (1971): "Since we didn't have either the time or the money to model and mold a costume, we applied the foam rubber directly on the plaster mold of the actor. We printed the veins and the textures into the foam once it had hardened. We baked it by constructing, around it, a plywood oven that was covered in aluminum foil!" Fascinated by the great apes, Baker first made the creature for the comedy *Schlock* (1971), and then a gorilla with two heads for *The Thing With Two Heads* (1972). The following year, he devised the unusual effects for the James Bond movie *Live and Let Die*—a replica of the actor Geoffrey Holder's head, which raises its eyes skyward at the moment a bullet breaks open his skull, and a copy of Yaphet Kotto's face that swells up like a balloon. In 1976, he offered his services to Dino De Laurentiis, who was preparing a remake of *King Kong*. The Italian producer had thought to transform Kong into a primitive man! Ignoring that idea, Baker made a low-budget gorilla costume. At the same time, Carlo Rambaldi produced the costume of a creature described by director John Guillermin as "a $200,000 disaster." Baker's approach was kept, but he was obliged to collaborate with Rambaldi. He sculpted three expressions for Kong: calm, tense, and with his mouth wide open, ready to roar. The three heads were mecha-

The mechanized mask of King Kong (1976)

nized by Rambaldi, with the assistance of Isidoro Raponi. Rick Baker volunteered himself to wear the Kong costume, cover his eyes with hard contact lenses, and extend his arms with the mechanical hands, but filming was over before he was able to create the perfect gorilla costume.

He did win his first Oscar in 1982 for creating the metamorphosis in *An American Werewolf in London* (1981). Baker affixed several appliances onto David Naughton's face to depict the start of his transformation. The following stages were realized with three mechanical heads made of resin and fiberglass, covered over with a foam rubber skin. Baker had assimilated some of Rambaldi's techniques—when assistants pulled on the levers, metal cables would transmit the movements

Two mechanized heads from An American Werewolf in London, *and the animatronic mask in* Harry and the Hendersons
Photos courtesy of Universal Studios Florida

to the articulated heads, in succession. Through editing, Naughton's mouth became elongated and turned into the snout of a wolf. Long hairs were implanted into a skin made of foam rubber, so that they went straight through the material. During the shooting of close-ups, Baker gently pulled the hairs until they disappeared into the skin. By reversing the shot, the hairs seemed to shoot up suddenly. The final transformation was, in fact, a mechanical wolf animated by ten people. In 1984, Baker created the horde of gorillas for *Greystoke: The Legend of Tarzan, Lord of the Apes.* His costumes and mechanized masks were worn by mimes trained to move as apes. In 1987, he was awarded another Oscar for Harry the "Bigfoot" in *Harry and the Hendersons.* "My interest in animatronics

came because you couldn't transform a human face beyond a certain point," explained Baker. "If you glue a foam rubber appliance that's too thick onto an actor's face, his facial movements will be so inhibited that the character can't be expressive. You have to use an animatronic mask. Director William Dear wanted Harry to be imposing, so I designed a big head, inside of which we installed servomotors that animated the face. Before this film, we animated heads using cables that came out of the back of the character's neck. Ten technicians had to work together to activate these movements, which used a system based on bicycle brakes. They'd pull on a lever, and the metal cable would glide within its sheath and activate the mechanism. Using servomotors, Harry was animated

by Kevin Peter Hall, who wore the costume, and the three adjusters (of whom I was one). He had to freely come and go within the set, and be able to react to the other actors."

Baker reaped his third golden statuette in 1994 for transforming Martin Landau into Bela Lugosi in Tim Burton's *Ed Wood.* In 1996, he turned Eddie Murphy into a 550-pound

The five different makeups created for Eddie Murphy in The Nutty Professor
Photos courtesy of Universal Studios Florida

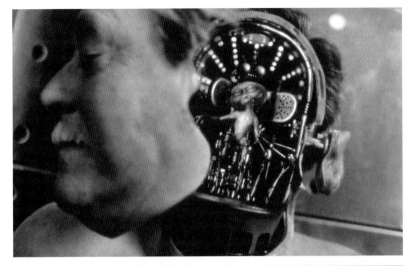

An animatronic miniature in Men in Black
Photo courtesy of Columbia-TriStar & Amblin

The "Worm Guys" in Men in Black
Photo courtesy of Universal Studios Florida

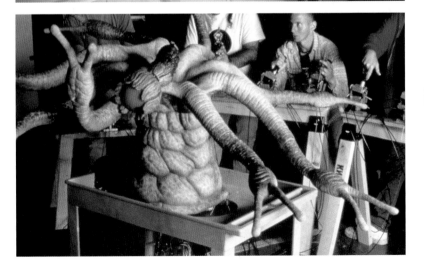

*The manipulation of the extraterrestrial
octopus in* Men in Black
Photo courtesy of Columbia-TriStar & Amblin

(250-kilogram) Nutty Professor (in the film of the same name) with the help of applications and a special wardrobe. He also devised the disguises that let Murphy play the other four members of the Klump family. This quintuple tour de force won Baker his fourth Oscar. His fifth came for his extraterrestrials in *Men in Black* (1997). He pursued his quest for the perfect gorilla with his creation of the colossal ape *Mighty Joe Young* (1998). He created three giant robots that were animated by hydraulics and the costume worn by John Alexander, a specialist in gorilla roles. Alexander moved through the miniature sets placed in front of the camera in proper alignment with the perspectives of the real sets. These scenes were filmed at thirty-two frames per second, in order to slow down the more than sixteen-foot-tall (five-meter) gorilla's movements. And Rick Baker collected his sixth Oscar for his makeup for *The Grinch* (2000), in which Jim Carrey wore foam rubber appliances on his face, a wig, enormous contact lenses, and a costume made of several layers of foam and Lycra with implanted, green-dyed yak hair. A team of sixty makeup artists transformed the noses and ears of the 125 residents of Whoville. But Baker was not done with apes: "I made myself up as a chimpanzee to make a screen test during the time when Oliver Stone was to direct a new version of *Planet of*

Jim Carrey's makeup in The Grinch
Photo courtesy of Universal Studios Florida

the Apes. It didn't work very well, because I have a rather big nose. Later I suggested to Tim Burton that he choose actors with small noses and brown eyes, like the apes. And naturally, he chose actors with blue eyes, and then Tim Roth, who has a nose bigger than mine! We had to lower the upper lip of the ape he was playing and bring forward the snout in order to camouflage his nose. Once these appliances were affixed to his face, we glued a wig on his head and hairpieces on his cheeks. Then we glued hairs one by one between the edges of the hairpieces and the rest of the mask." Rick Baker left the apes to return to the familiar universe of *Men in Black II* (2002). "We had forty-five days to prepare everything. Rummaging through my drawers, I found two man-birds that I had designed thirty

years earlier when I was assisting Dick Smith on the effects for *The Exorcist*! I designed the other characters on Photoshop, and my team transposed them in volume." In 2003, *The Haunted Mansion* presented him with the opportunity to pay homage to the famous attraction at Disneyland: "The characters in the *Haunted Mansion* were made to be seen from afar, in half-darkness. You wouldn't be able to use them as they were in a movie. I told the director that I wanted to improve the details of the characters and re-create them so that they resembled the memory we have of them." Also in 2003, Baker adapted the characters from Mike Mignolia's comic strip *Hellboy,* in which Ron Perlman plays the title role, proving once again Baker's masterful ability to conceive of spectacular creatures.

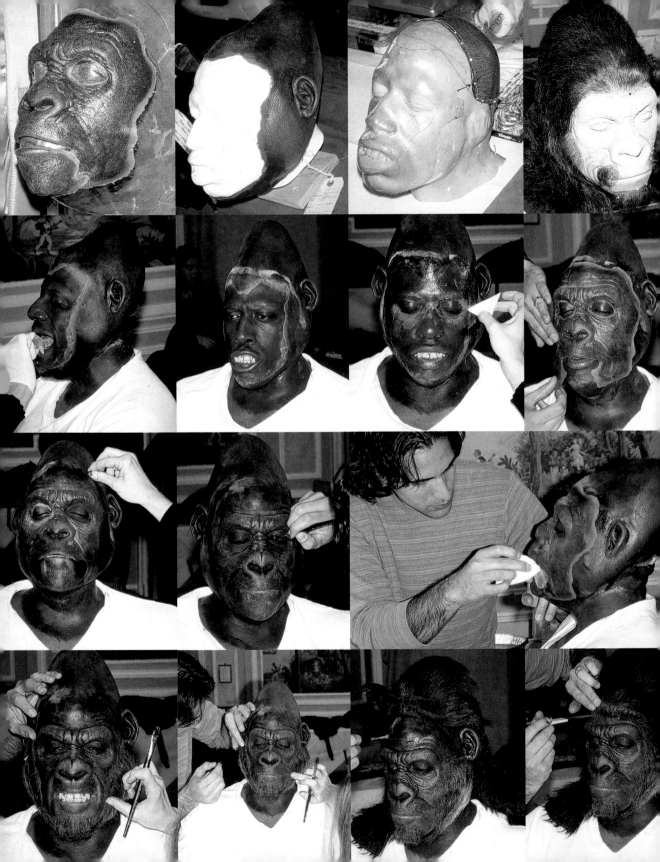

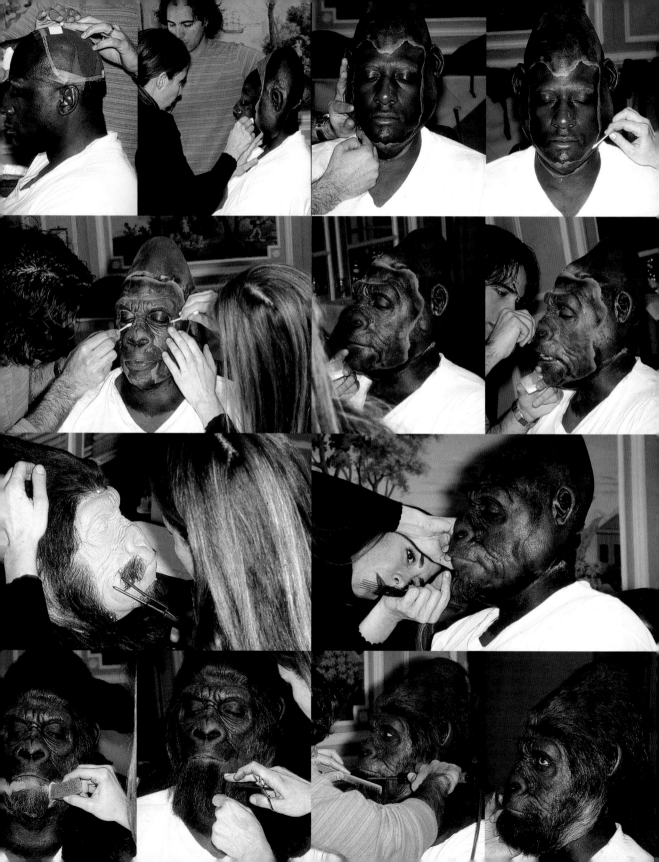

Previous pages and left:
Actor Kevin Grevioux is
transformed into a gorilla
soldier in Planet of the Apes
(2001), after a two-and-a-
half-hour makeup session.

INTERVIEW

STAN WINSTON

The Journey of a Makeup Giant

Photo courtesy of the Stan Winston Studio

Stan Winston's creations, from the Alien queen to the Terminator and the Predator, have become film icons. When you find yourself in front of one of his animatronic velociraptors capable of bending over at lightning speed to snatch up a piece of paper between its teeth, you understand why Steven Spielberg called him "Mr. Wizard."

At the beginning of your career, you were an actor. Did this experience help you once you became a makeup artist?

Stan Winston: I did admire made-up actors like Spencer Tracy in *Dr. Jekyll and Mr. Hyde,* Charles Laughton in *The Hunchback of Notre Dame,* and Boris Karloff in *Frankenstein.* The sequins and champagne side of Hollywood fascinated me. I wanted to be famous, to become friends with famous people. This was neither realistic nor a worthy motivation. I only realized my dreams by approaching my craft with the respect it deserves, having been influenced by Dick Smith and John Chambers.

You created the remarkable aging effects for the TV movie "The Autobiography of Miss Jane Pittman" (1974).

Stan Winston: First I worked with Tom Burman and Del Armstrong on the TV movie *Gargoyles,* produced by Bob Christiansen and Rick Rosenberg, which earned me my first Emmy Award. The following year, Bob and Rick asked me to work on *Miss Pittman* along with Rick Baker, who had assisted Dick Smith on *Little Big Man.* I had the job of supervising all the makeup

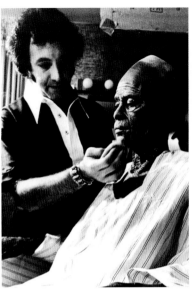

The remarkable aging in the TV movie The Autobiography of Miss Jane Pittman
Photo courtesy of the Stan Winston Studio

artists and creating Jane Pittman's look at age 110. Rick took care of the preceding aging stages. He was the one who taught me the technique of overlaying appliances that Dick Smith had developed. I was set on the goal of aging Cicely Tyson without making her unrecognizable.

Who gave you the idea of using gelatin to create the robot's appliances in the movie "Heartbeeps" (1981)?

Stan Winston: I wanted to give a translucent plastic look to the faces of Bernadette Peters and Andy Kaufman. These appliances were revolutionary, but

The gelatin appliances worn by Andy Kaufman in Heartbeeps
Photo courtesy of the Stan Winston Studio

The endoskeleton in Terminator
Photo courtesy of Universal Studios Florida

The reduced-size model of the Alien queen
Photo courtesy of the Stan Winston Studio

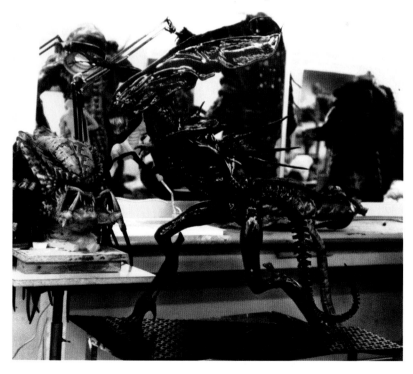

also very difficult to maintain because the heat on the film set would make them melt. The parts around the mouth had to be replaced after meals, because of the damage caused by chewing and perspiration.

How did you collaborate with James Cameron on "Terminator," the turning point in your career?

Stan Winston: Jim contacted me to create the makeup for *Terminator,* with the chrome skull that appeared through the wounds on the face. He had planned to film all the scenes of the endoskeleton with a miniature animated in stop-motion. I'd wanted to use puppetry techniques ever since I saw the documentary on the making of *The Dark Crystal* (1983). I admired Jim Henson

Stan Winston directs a test sequence on video from an animation idea for the Alien queen suggested by James Cameron. Inside this mock-up made of wood, cardboard, and black garbage bags are two stagehands, stretched out on their stomachs next to each other. The one on the right controls the right limbs; the one on the left, the left limbs. Photo courtesy of the Stan Winston Studio

Preparation of an extraterrestrial for Predator 2
Photos courtesy of the Stan Winston Studio

a lot. James Cameron approved our making the endoskeleton in real size; the body was handled by puppeteers, while its neck, head, and eyes were animated by remote-controlled servo-motors. We succeeded in quickly shooting many close-ups, despite the fact that this first endoskeleton was heavy and difficult to handle. We had used too many steel pieces. For *Terminator 2,* we lightened the character's structure by using resin, fiberglass, and carbon fibers. We covered these pieces in chrome to give them the look of metal. Ever since then, my collaboration with James Cameron has been founded upon the mutual respect of two creators. When he came to see me to offer *Terminator,* he had already designed the endoskeleton. When he came back to see me for *Aliens,* he showed me his wonderful sketches of the Alien queen that my studio and I would construct and animate for the big screen.

How did you conceive of the extra-terrestrial in "Predator" (1987)?

Stan Winston: Producer Joel Silver and director John McTiernan contacted me, because the monster they had used during the first part of the shooting didn't work for them. Joel showed me a painting of a Rasta warrior with dreadlocks.

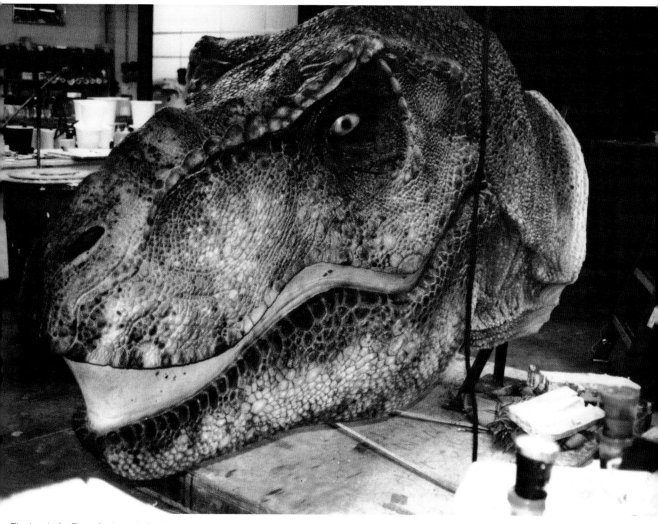

The head of a T. rex for Jurassic Park   Photo courtesy of the Stan Winston Studio

At the same time, I left for Japan with James Cameron to participate in a conference on *Aliens*. Jim was seated next to me on the plane. When I made some drawings of the Predator in a sketchpad, Jim leaned over to me and said, "You know what I've always wanted to see on an extraterrestrial's face? Mandibles!" I lengthened the character's jaw with mandibles,

and I liked the result. So there's also a little James Cameron in the Predator!

Could you explain the evolution of your technique in the "Jurassic Park" saga?

Stan Winston: The first *Jurassic Park* gave us the opportunity to

learn how to animate an enormous T. rex by means of hydraulic jacks. At that time, the velociraptors were mechanical puppets controlled by cables and maneuvered by ten animators. In *The Lost World: Jurassic Park* (1997), we animated the velociraptors using fifteen external hydraulic motors attached to the characters with hoses and fifteen

The sculpture of a velociraptor costume on the mold of an actor's body. The shape of his feet can be seen at the bottom of the mold.
Photo courtesy of the Stan Winston Studio

The crafting of the velociraptor's eyes
Photo courtesy of the Stan Winston Studio

The finished raptor
Photo courtesy of the Stan Winston Studio

The final touches on one of the raptors in Jurassic Park III. *The resin and fiberglass structure can be seen under the foam rubber skin.*
Photo courtesy of the Stan Winston Studio

Trying out the bottom of one of the raptor costumes used to film close-up shots of the feet walking on the ground
Photo courtesy of the Stan Winston Studio

other motors located inside the skeleton of the raptor. The manipulation commands, which came through a telemetric system carried by a puppeteer, were transmitted to a computer, which interpreted them and then relayed them to the character, in order to control the fluidity of the movements. In

Jurassic Park III, the velociraptors had thirty-four independent movements, controlled by smaller, more powerful hydraulic motors implanted directly into the character's body, near the joints, to obtain more direct movements. The operators who animated the dinosaurs were members of the Screen Actors Guild, because the performances entailed real acting. The gestures of the raptors were powerful, quick, natural. In a word, these dinosaurs became the best actors!

The T. rex in the first and second movies weighed nine tons and had a three-hundred-horsepower force. The spinosaur in *Jurassic Park III* weighed twelve tons and had a one-thousand-horsepower force. It could pierce through a jet fuselage with its snout. When the actors found themselves inside these sets, they were really in danger! When we constructed the T. rex of the first movie, I asked Steven not to sprinkle, because water would damage the mechanisms and electronics. And of course, the attack of the T. rex was filmed in a lashing rain. In the second part, the T. rex passes his head through a waterfall. And in the third episode, the spinosaur emerges from a lake and remains in the water! (*Laughs.*) These mechanisms were devised like those on a submarine. Actors will tell you that there's nothing worse than to act in front of an empty space.

Sculpting and painting a spinosaur for Jurassic Park III—the largest creature ever made for a movie

Photo courtesy of the Stan Winston Studio

Construction of a costume for the ptero-dactyl in Jurassic Park III
Photo courtesy of the Stan Winston Studio

The prototype of the baby triceratops, prepared for a sequence ultimately cut from Jurassic Park: *the two kids playing with the baby dino and riding on his back*
Photo courtesy of the Stan Winston Studio

If the dinosaurs hadn't been made in synthesized images, the actors would have lost their spots, and some scenes wouldn't have been able to be filmed.

How did you construct the spinosaur, the largest creature ever made for a movie?

Stan Winston: I had to raise the ceiling in my studio at Van Nuys so we could sculpt it life-size. It was forty feet (twelve meters) long from the end of its snout to the tip of its tail! The hose that contained the oil for its hydraulic circuits were more resistant than those of the T. rex. They were reinforced with Teflon, which made them more flexible and more resistant to pressure. Consequently, the spinosaur had a wide range of motion and could move fast. Its tail whipped the air. When we finished constructing it, we realized that it was too big to get through the garage door of the studio! We had to destroy the wall above and around the workshop door to get it to the film set on a trailer.

What did you do to ensure the actors' safety while they acted next to the dinosaurs?

Stan Winston: We set up clearly visible tapes marking off the

dangerous area. We sounded an alarm as soon as the large dinosaurs started to move, and lit red lights. No one was allowed to come near between shots. These animals were controlled by computers, and, as you know, these machines regularly crash. It's best not to find yourself next to a dinosaur that suddenly makes unplanned gestures.

"Terminator 2" had a number of memorable scenes, but one of the most surprising is the one in which Arnold Schwarzenegger fires on the T-1000 frozen by liquid nitrogen.

Stan Winston: The character used in that scene was a puzzle made up of hundreds of pieces. We made a mold of Robert Patrick with his costume on, and his helmet and his glasses, to create this frozen likeness. We cut it into small pieces, in the middle of which we strung Primacord, a very powerful explosive in the form of a long tape. The explosive was placed in a way to make the statue implode, to suck the debris from the exterior to the interior. We also put metal bits inside. The scene was filmed by several cameras at a very fast speed, from several angles.

*The animatronic T-1000
during preparation for the
filming of the final battle of
Terminator 2*
Photo courtesy of the Stan Winston
Studio

*Manipulating the T-1000
puppet of Terminator 2*
Photo courtesy of the Stan Winston
Studio

Amy, the animatronic gorilla in Congo

One of the superb animatronic lions in The Ghost and the Darkness *(1996)*

Sculpture of the giant crocodile in Lake Placid
Photos courtesy of the Stan Winston Studio

You made many life-size likenesses of Arnold Schwarzenegger for "Terminator 2." Was it difficult to make them move like the real Arnold?

Stan Winston: Extremely. I look upon what we did with a very critical eye. The replicas of Arnold that we constructed for *Terminator 3: Rise of the Machines* (2003) are superior to those of the first two movies. They imitate his body language better. We used all the techniques available—animatronic characters, recording and telemetric replication of Arnold's movements, the retouching of his clone with synthesized images, in order to get spectacular images. This is how we were able to create the most severe scarring effects on his face and body.

What difficulties did you encounter when constructing the giant crocodile that operated in water for "Lake Placid" (1999)?

Stan Winston: We had already constructed some hippopotamuses that attacked boats in a scene in *Congo* (1995). This experience was helpful at the time of *Lake Placid* and, later, on *Jurassic Park III*. Mechanisms that operate in water must withstand the pressure that's exerted on them during the movements. So you have to resort to hydraulic power. The other difficulty consisted of detecting leaks inside the electronic boxes in time. One single drop of water could cause a short circuit and seriously damage the robot. But the water also tended to soften the mechanical appearance of the movements, making them more natural. So there were advantages and inconveniences.

The crocodile being lowered into the water

The crocodile, animated by hydraulics, rises to the surface.

Photos courtesy of the Stan Winston Studio

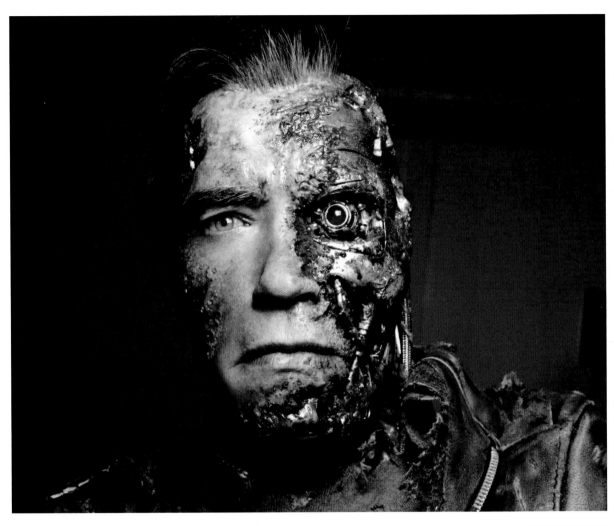

A mechanized replica of Arnold Schwarzenegger's face in Terminator 3: Rise of the Machines

Photos courtesy of Photofest

One of the T-105s in Terminator 3
Photo courtesy of the Stan Winston Studio

*An animatronic likeness of the
Terminatrix in* Terminator 3
Photo courtesy of the Stan Winston Studio

Jonathan Mostow, the director of
Terminator 3, *with Arnold
Schwarzenegger. The parts of the
actor's body and face covered in
green fabric or makeup were erased
by computer artists at ILM who then,
using stop-motion, inserted the outline of the endoskeleton.*
Photo courtesy of the Stan Winston Studio &
Columbia Pictures

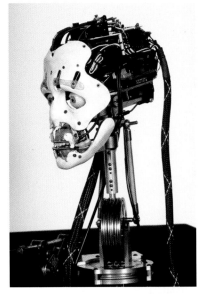

Above and above right:
*Preparation of robots for
A.I.: Artificial Intelligence*

*The telemetric system
used to animate the
arms of Teddy, the
little robot's companion
in A.I.*

*Working the cables that
enabled Teddy to walk*
Photos courtesy of the Stan
Winston Studio

What were the principal innovations of "Terminator 3"?

Stan Winston: The effects that revealed large parts of the endoskeleton under Arnold's skin. These techniques were developed in the scene in *A.I.: Artificial Intelligence* in which the babysitter robot turns its head and reveals its open skull box. We combined several techniques: the digital erasure of parts of Arnold's body and face, animatronic appliances attached to him, and special effects makeup. This is how the final scenes were made. We also developed the Terminatrix, with skin made of liquid metal that covered a skeleton of solid metal. We gave it the appearance of being both feminine and unnerving at the same time—like the Alien queen. The T-1s were also innovations. In the script, they were described as the first prototypes of the Terminators, developed before the T-800 played by Arnold. The robots of the first two movies were animatronic characters, whereas the T-1s were true robots, animated by telemetric systems. We also recorded some performances that the robots reproduced to the millimeter. With the progress of technology, we could answer all their demands.

INTERVIEW

Patrick Tatopoulos

The Success of a French Designer in Hollywood

The matte painting of Bram Stoker's Dracula *in which the design of the castle appears. The building evokes the image of a man seated on a throne.*
Photo courtesy of Patrick Tatopoulos Designs

Patrick Tatopoulos in front of the giant robot of Godzilla used in the filming of many shots of destruction, with models
Photo courtesy of Patrick Tatopoulos Designs

Patrick Tatopoulos's original approach led him to become one of the most appreciated designers and creators of makeup special effects. His work can be seen in *Stargate; Independence Day; Godzilla; Dark City; I, Robot;* and *Van Helsing.*

What has been your artistic trajectory?

Patrick Tatopoulos: I studied for one year at the School of Decorative Arts in Paris. After my military service, I decorated sailboards in Greece. Then I discovered the creatures in American movies in the magazine *Cinefex.* I sculpted and painted a dozen monsters in order to put together a photo

album, and I went off to Los Angeles. Unfortunately, my portfolio got stuck in Amsterdam during transit. I didn't get it back until two days before I left. By chance, I was hired by Makeup Effects Lab. I started by creating designs for *Beastmaster 2* (1991), a B movie. Then our team was nominated for an Emmy Award for the creature in the episode "Conspiracy" from *Star Trek: The Next Generation.* I learned to do the artistic direction and to design storyboards and props on another small film, *C.H.U.D. II* (1989).

How has a Frenchman been accepted at the heart of the American special effects community?

Patrick Tatopoulos: Aside from a few hostile reactions, the welcome has been very warm. The first designer with whom I worked loved France. In the United States, you sell yourself as much by the quality of your work as by your charisma. My first major job was the conception of the creatures and a main street for *Super Mario Bros.* (1993). The making of the creatures was divided up among three different studios. I quickly recognized that you couldn't supervise a job like that from a distance. I designed concepts for *Last Action Hero* (1993) and *Demolition Man* (1993), but I wanted to get rid of my pencils and work on a film stage. Working with the great designers like Eugenio Zanetti, I realized

The design of Dracula's chapel, which also adorned the labels of Francis Ford Coppola's own winery
Image courtesy of Patrick Tatopoulos Designs

that it was vital to understand the politics that existed on a production or in a studio. I had a disappointing experience on Coppola's *Bram Stoker's Dracula* (1992). I wasn't listed in the credits because I didn't have a green card, which would permit me to work in the United States, and I wasn't a member of a union. Coppola reproduced my drawing of the chapel, where Dracula kills himself, on the labels of his own wine bottles. I discovered that everyone received a bottle with this label—except me, lowly employee that I was! From that point on, I decided I would no longer work under somebody else's rules and would sign my creations. And I always make sure that my collaborators are listed in the credits.

"stargate"

Images of the warriors and the pharaoh in Stargate
Images courtesy of Patrick Tatopoulos Designs

Was it by seeing "Stargate" (1994) that the wider public discovered your work?

Patrick Tatopoulos: Yes. Roland Emmerich had liked the visual concepts of *Dracula*. I collaborated with Oliver Scholl on the film sets, and then Roland assigned the conception of the soldiers and the pharaoh to me. I'd seen thousands of images of

Above: *A creature from* Stargate; above right: *Graphic concepts and the extraterrestrials in* Independence Day
Photos courtesy of Patrick Tatopoulos Designs

ancient Egypt and drew upon my recollections to conceive these characters. If I had copied Egyptian works, the design wouldn't have been personal or homogeneous. When Roland approved my concepts, he also agreed to have me craft the characters. It was a formidable opportunity.

How do you prepare your designs?

Patrick Tatopoulos: First I picture the global look of the movie. In the case of *Independence Day,* the physique of the creatures determined the rest of the environment. The extraterrestrials had diamond-shaped heads. This was also the shape of the little spaceships that confront the U.S. Army jets. When I create large sets, I often use a

small object as a point of departure—as if I were an archaeologist discovering the trace of some unknown civilization.

Who helps you develop a major design?

Patrick Tatopoulos: The creative process is rather mysterious. When Roland asked me to think about a new design for Godzilla, I first went around in circles. One fine morning, I woke up relaxed, I sat down at my drawing board, and right then and there, I drew the definitive design for Godzilla.

Did you keep in mind that a man would be wearing the Godzilla costume when you were making that first drawing?

Patrick Tatopoulos: Godzilla has anthropomorphic characteristics, so he's always played by an extra in a costume. I kept it in mind without having it inhibit my creativity. His chin, for example, was based on the tiger Shere Khan in the Disney version of *The Jungle Book* (1967). When Toho, the owners of the rights to Godzilla, approved my model, we reproduced it around the mold of an actor's body. This human-sized Godzilla was scanned in order to make the 3-D model of the character. The team of computer artists at Centropolis Effects enormously enriched the textures for the close-up shots of his body. We sculpted baby Godzillas according to the same principle and modeled the giant bust of the robotic Godzilla, which was used to film the

The original design of Godzilla Image courtesy of Patrick Tatopoulos Designs

The image of Godzilla's progenitor
Image courtesy of Patrick Tatopoulos Designs

shots of the destruction of the model. Our team had two hundred people on it; that's twice the size of those for the mechanical dinosaurs in *Jurassic Park*.

How do you manage the conception of a small-budget movie like "Dark City" (1998) by Alex Proyas?

Patrick Tatopoulos: *Dark City* was filmed in Australia with extremely efficient and thrifty teams. I had complete confidence in them, and we succeeded in creating enormous sets on the available budget. Some American producers who go to Australia or Canada try to impose Hollywood methods that just don't fit. At the end of the week, the entire crew of *Dark City* enjoyed a picnic together to discuss the project outside of working hours. In Los Angeles, when crews leave the set, everyone goes their own way.

How did you conceive of the sets?

Patrick Tatopoulos: With models. You can easily cut out an element that you want to remove and add another. When I'm talking with a director, I put a mini-camera in the model to spot the angles of the shots. He can visualize his camera movements,

The lush set of Alex Proyas's Dark City
Image courtesy of Patrick Tatopoulos Designs

decide if one part of the set isn't needed, and if it wouldn't be better to make another part larger. The director of photography also uses the model to think about his lighting and how to distribute it throughout the set.

How do you choose the materials you make your creatures out of?

Patrick Tatopoulos: Everything depends on the desired effect. I wanted the skin of the extraterrestrials in *Independence Day* to be translucent. So I used silicone, which is a heavy and fragile material. If it tears during the filming, the glue I use to repair it doesn't set for twenty-four hours. Foam rubber is opaque, but it is much lighter and more solid. If it tears, you can glue it in five minutes. But it poses other problems. When we filmed the giant robot of Godzilla in the rain, water leaked into the foam like a sponge. The computer-controlled hydraulic mechanisms were set to function with the initial weight of the robot, but not with water-drenched skin. We dried off Godzilla with towels after each shot.

Actors heavily perspire when wearing these creature costumes. How do you control that?

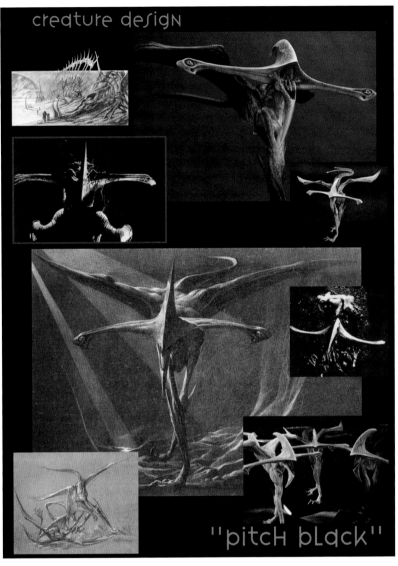

creature design

"pitch black"

Creatures from Pitch Black   Image courtesy of Patrick Tatopoulos Designs

Patrick Tatopoulos: You can install soft tubes inside, through which a liquid refrigerant flows that will cool for an hour or two. When the liquid becomes warm, you hook it up to a machine and rechill it. It's practical, but you risk pneumonia by going from cold to hot within the damp interior of the costume. Some actors refuse to wear the "cool suits," and the acidity of their perspiration erodes the foam rubber. You can clean the costume a little with soapy water, but the foam rubber shrinks and becomes hard when it dries. You have to

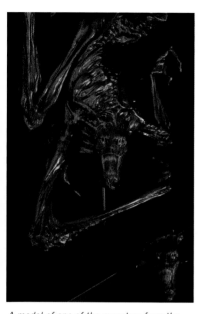

A model of one of the monsters from the movie They *(2002)*
Photo courtesy of Patrick Tatopoulos Designs

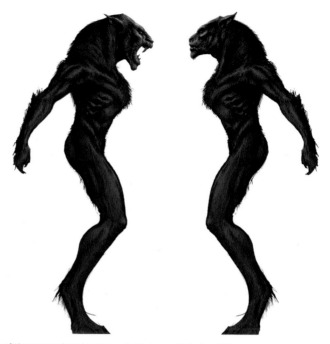

Images of the werewolves in the movie Underworld *by Len Wiseman*
Images courtesy of Patrick Tatopoulos Designs

prepare many copies of a costume, which are used in turn. We made twenty-five Godzilla costumes, with different head animation mechanics. We also constructed forty-five baby Godzilla costumes, as well as the skin of the giant robot, which cost seventy-eight thousand dollars. The foam rubber skin sections, which each measured seven by seven feet (two by two meters), had to be baked in enormous bakery ovens!

You create original concepts, but do directors and producers sometimes ask you to take a more clichéd route?

Patrick Tatopoulos: Yes. The less creative producers and directors can even push you to using direct references to other artists, which I refuse to do. I thankfully have had the pleasure of working with imaginative directors like Roland Emmerich, Alex Proyas, and David Twohy, with whom I collaborated on the design of the creatures in *Pitch Black* (2000). It was a small budget, but the creative work was incredible. In Hollywood, you have to try to collaborate on the big projects to benefit from their success at the box office. This lets you, from time to time, choose the small projects that tug at your heart.

The animatronic head of a werewolf
Photo courtesy of Patrick Tatopoulos Designs

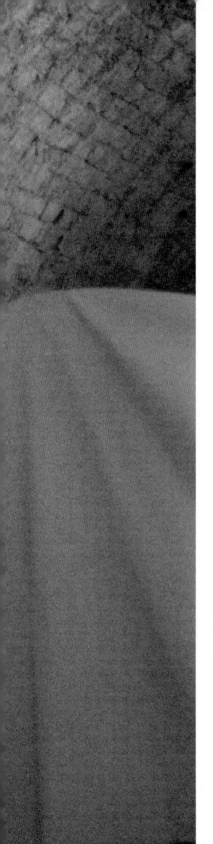

The impressive makeup of the old vampire in Underworld
Photo courtesy of Patrick Tatopoulos Designs

A werewolf as it appeared in the movie
Photo courtesy of Patrick Tatopoulos Designs

The vampire/werewolf hybrid in Underworld
Photo courtesy of Patrick Tatopoulos Designs

INTERVIEW

MILES TEVES

Miles Teves is one of the most talented artists in Hollywood. Through his drawings and sculptures, he has helped bring life to many famous characters.

Drawings of the witch, Meg Mucklebones, who appears in a sequence in Legend
Images courtesy of Miles Teves

Photo courtesy of Miles Teves

The final makeup of the witch, created by Rob Bottin
Photo courtesy of Miles Teves

Could you explain your collaboration with the makeup artist Rob Bottin on movies such as "Legend" (1985) and "RoboCop"?

Miles Teves: I met Rob Bottin in 1982, when I was eighteen years old. I showed him my portfolio filled with bad drawings, and one year later he asked me to come work on *Legend*. I learned more by myself drawing many hours a day than if I had studied theory at art school. Rob taught me to refine my drawings and to push them to the limit, and not to fall in love with the first idea that came out of my pencil. I drew in a little room without a window, away from everyone else. Rob wanted to be sure that the creative process developed only between him and his illustrator. The rest of the team had to content themselves with doing precise drawings on paper. Rob and I sort of highlighted the minutest details, in a way so that everyone understood how they'd have to be adapted for three dimensions. Darkness, the devil in *Legend,* was the first character I worked on. At that time, he had a very large head and short horns like a bull. His eyes had to be animated mechanically, and the volume of his head had to be determined by the amount of space occupied by the servomotors. When Rob decided to remake him with makeup, I tried hard to give him a demonic elegance and beauty. Rob pushed me to make the horns longer and more graceful. I drew the curve perfectly on a large piece of paper, to guide the work of the sculptors. When Rob decided to color Darkness's skin red, I made a painting of the character on which we applied different versions of eyes and teeth, so we could change the shape and color as needed. I even mixed the colors of the foundation makeups that were used to prolong the color of the applications used on Tim Curry, who played Darkness. His clothing, as well as his legs that are shown in close-up, were conceived and made in England, without our collaboration.

How was Meg Mucklebones, the incredible witch in the movie, born?

Miles Teves: She was inspired by a character drawn by Alan Lee in the book *Fairies,* and

The mutant Quatto, produced in the studios of Rob Bottin for Total Recall
Photo courtesy of Miles Teves

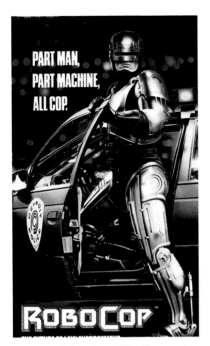

Another collaboration of Miles Teves and Rob Bottin: the character RoboCop
Image courtesy of Miles Teves

The magnificent devil in Legend
Photo courtesy of Miles Teves

also by the witch in Walt Disney's *Snow White*. We gave her a look as out there as possible, covering her with wrinkles and twitching skin and pimples and horrible details! When we were satisfied with the design, I drew Meg from all angles, using the silhouette of the mold of an actor—full face, profile, from behind, and three-quarters. These drawings were extremely detailed, textured, and shaded. Her head and hands were designed separately, in close-up. Rob would often bring the sculpture of a character to my office for me to make corrections. We collaborated in the same way on *RoboCop*, *Explorers* (1985), and *Total Recall* (1990).

How did you sculpt the animatronic characters and masks?

Miles Teves: Unfortunately, sculptors are often asked to put up with predetermined mechanical shapes. The servomotors are extremely big and must be ingeniously placed. The top makeup studios don't make this mistake. They insist their engineers place their devices inside the envelope of the character, once its design has been approved.

How are the costumes of superheroes, such as Batman, created and sculpted so that they don't inhibit the movement of the actors wearing them during the action scenes?

Miles Teves: I only sculpted the costume for Robin that appeared in *Batman Forever* (1995), but it was conceived the same way as Batman's. We started by adding a one-fifth-inch (five-millimeter) layer of wax around a resin and fiberglass mold of an actor, to take into account that he would be wearing a neoprene leotard. We covered the wax with modeling paste for sculpting the muscles. Large volumes of foam rubber tend to shrink during the baking of this material, so I had to exaggerate the volume of the most prominent muscles to be sure that the foam rubber casts would be the size we wanted. These sculptures could unnoticeably change shape during extreme movements, as we had inserted narrow, tapered forms in the parts that bent a lot.

A drawing of a costume for Robin in Batman Forever

The sculpture of Robin's costume on a body cast of actor Chris O'Donnell

Robin's final costume
Photos courtesy of Miles Teves

A version of Batman's armored costume that appeared in Batman Forever
Image courtesy of Miles Teves

A superb drawing of Batgirl's costume, with an especially clever low neck design
Image courtesy of Miles Teves

Pearl, the enormous vampire in "Blade" (1998), must have been extremely difficult to sculpt.

Miles Teves: I first sculpted a model out of resin, which was then cut into dozens of sections that were measured and then reproduced in polystyrene foam, in order to serve as a guide for making a structure in plywood. Iron wire mesh and plaster tape were applied to this structure. I modeled the body in two weeks, in clay. The mold of the actor's head stopped at neck level. The arms and legs were sculpted separately in plasteline, in order to produce fine details. I only wish I'd had more time to animate this puppet.

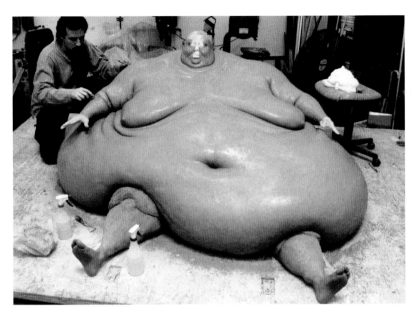

The sculpture of Pearl Photo courtesy of Miles Teves

Do you get irritated when you see flagrant mistakes in a sculpture?

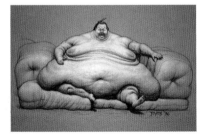

A drawing of Pearl, the enormous vampire in Blade
Image courtesy of Miles Teves

Miles Teves: I often see actors wearing appliances that are too thick. Their head is so big that the illusion is destroyed. When I make a sculpture on a face, I only add very light volumes. You have to know how to choose where you have to add thickness and where you have to glue onto the skin so you don't impede the movement.

Do you use special tools?

Miles Teves: I make most of my tools, and I often adapt those that I do buy for carving out material. I create organic shapes with what I call "buckle-rakes." These are tools com-posed of a handle and a steel buckle that I drill to create shapes looking like the teeth of a saw. I trace my textures in clay with tools of all shapes, and then I soften the reliefs with a paintbrush soaked in alcohol. I choose clay when I have to work on a large-sized character. It is easy to model, but you have to hurry when working with it before it cracks as it dries. I choose plasteline when I have more time and when I am making a thinner sculpture.

A drawing by Miles Teves for one of the extraterrestrials in Joe Dante's movie Explorers
Image courtesy of Miles Teves

One of the cenobites in Hellbound: Hellraiser II *(1988), whose makeup was sculpted by Miles Teves*
Photo courtesy of Miles Teves

Above: *The makeup concept for Tom Cruise in* Interview with a Vampire

The sculpture of a dried-up version of Tom Cruise made by Miles Teves at the Stan Winston Studios
Photo courtesy of Miles Teves

The final makeup
Photo courtesy of Miles Teves

*Another concept of the
final scene, not used*
Image courtesy of Miles Teves

*The concept of the demon that appears at
the end of the movie* Bless the Child
(2000)
Image courtesy of Miles Teves

INTERVIEW

Matt Denton

Twenty-First-Century Puppeteer

The robot in Lost in Space

Founder of Micromagic Systems (www.micromagic-sys.com), Matt Denton is an animatronic and remote-control system specialist.

How did you animate the robot in "Lost in Space" (1998)?

Matt Denton: It was piloted by a device on the exoskeleton, a sort of armor equipped with sensors at each joint. When the operator extends the robot's arms to pick up an object, the potentiometers located on the shoulders, the arms, the elbows, the wrists, and the hands record all the motion data and transmit them toward the robot's actuators, and the robot executes the same gesture. This piloting makes it possible to shoot a scene live with the actors, but it is also used to record an animation on a microprocessor and reconstruct it later. You can also combine prerecorded movements and live, piloted ones. This is a way to film physical interactions in complete safety, as in the scene where the robot hits Gary Oldman. We repeated the robot's actions at a slower speed and very close up, with the stuntman doubling for Gary. The robot was animated two times faster during filming, and everything was filmed in a few takes. You have to be careful when handling a robot that weighs a ton and a half!

What kind of actuators do you use?

Matt Denton: The engineers who constructed the robot used a computer-assisted conception system to calculate the weight of each moving part. The two enormous arms were animated by rotational and linear hydraulic jacks. The electro-valves made so much noise that we had to put them outside the studio. The other arms and the head were moved by little electric motors, as well as two enormous one-kilowatt motors, hooked up to batteries that were needed to move the caterpillars. When I conceived of the robot's piloting, I equipped each joint with a potentiometer that made it possible to control the execution of the movements. We installed a process that prohibited abrupt arm gestures—the robot was so large and so heavy that its joints could become dislocated. During the filming, my programming console was placed sixty-five feet (twenty meters) from the action, behind the cameras. The supervisor of the robot and the four operators stayed on the film stage, next to the director. The supervisor had an emergency stop button in his hand, and I had another on my console. The first day, the robot had to appear to be destroying the spaceship's control panels. I hadn't slept for sixty-five hours, and I supervised the sequence in which it very

quickly goes up a ramp just a little larger than itself. We had no room for error—if the robot was situated incorrectly, it would have fallen over to the right or to the left, ruined itself, and destroyed the set. I trembled when I saw the cameraman position himself right next to the ramp to film the robot in a tilt-up shot. The operators directed the robot perfectly, but my heart lost a beat when the director yelled, "Cut, it's a take!" A little later, someone had the brilliant idea of unplugging our piloting console and plugging in his drill. The robot's "brain" was dead, but not his limbs! He became uncontrollable for a few seconds, the time it took to cut the hydraulic and electrical power. We quickly installed a safety device to

A robot with six feet

prevent this type of incident. We constructed and programmed two identical robots in three months. Halfway through the filming, we modified one to construct the second model that appeared in the movie.

How would you explain the progress of animatronics?

Matt Denton: Equipment has been miniaturized to control more movements in a more limited space. When I worked on *Pinocchio II,* the Henson Company had succeeded in placing twenty-two servomotors inside Pinocchio's small head, so he could express subtle emotions. The head was animated with a Waldo, a device that looks like a glove. A different function, or a set of functions, is assigned to each finger on the right hand. Moving the thumb up and down, you animate the cheeks. Moving the thumb to the right, you make the mouth round. Moving it to the left, you give the impression that the character is pronouncing the letter "E." Several servomotors would automatically become positioned to produce this shape of the mouth. When the operator's thumb did not move, all the motors in the face would slowly return to a position of repose. You could also get expressions of fear, sadness, tiredness, and laughter, and combine them naturally. The index and other three fingers were used together to change the shape of the mouth. Movements of the wrist would produce other actions. The operator also held a joystick with his left hand. The handle could go up and down, and right and left, but also could go in a circle, adding five more actions. Most of the time, one operator animates the face, while a second one pilots the movement of the body. It takes a lot of training to manage to make the characters move naturally next to actors.

Matt Denton working with a remote-control glove that permits the animation of animatronic heads. The character in the background is Tev, who appears in the series Space Precinct *(1995). This glove system is also used to animate computer-generated characters live.*

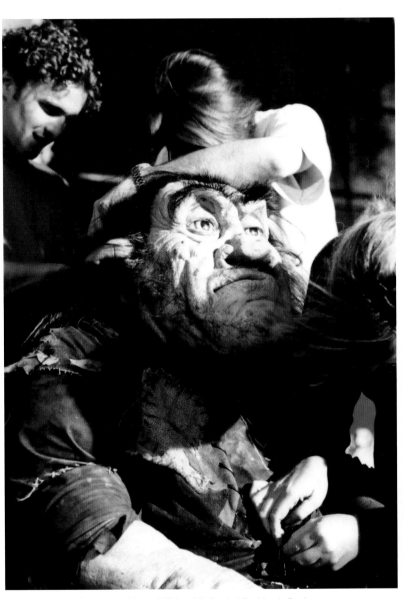

An animatronic giant created for a 1994 publicity shot for Lloyds Bank

INTERVIEW

BRIAN PENIKAS

The New Generation of Monsters

Brian Penikas is the creator of the makeup for Mini-Me, who first appeared in *Austin Powers:*

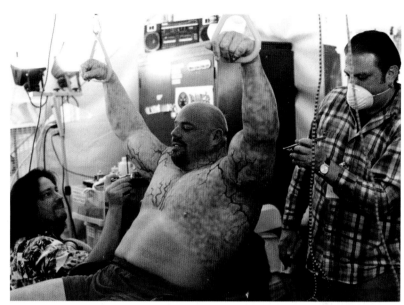

Brian Penikas in the company of the Creeper (Jonathan Breck) from Jeepers Creepers   Photo courtesy of Brian Penikas

The Spy Who Shagged Me (1999), and of the monster in *Jeepers Creepers* (2001).

How did you create the character of Bane in "Batman & Robin" (1997)?

Brian Penikas: It was makeup done with an airbrush that I conceived with Rick Stratton. We made an enormous tent to suck out the paint fumes. We

would start by painting Jeep Swenson's body at three or four in the morning, because the process took four hours to complete. We painted a version of the makeup references on a model of his body. We recopied

Bane's makeup, created with an airbrush for the movie Batman & Robin
Photos courtesy of Brian Penikas

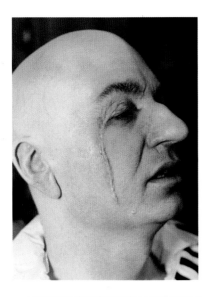

The head of the mannequin of Mini-Me, used in some of the action sequences
Photo courtesy of Brian Penikas

The makeup for Dr. Evil (Mike Myers) and Mini-Me (Verne Troyer) in Austin Powers: The Spy Who Shagged Me
Photos courtesy of Brian Penikas

this model day after day to ensure perfect continuity.

How did you reconstitute the makeup for Tony Clifton, the alter ego that comic Andy Kaufman created in the 1970s, in the Milos Forman movie "Man on the Moon" (1999)?

Brian Penikas: We got hold of some video recordings and some old photographs. Ken Chase's original molds had disappeared.

Instead of copying the 1970s makeup, which was rather basic, we made an interpretation that was more realistic and more agile. Furthermore, we avoided gluing the appliances to Jim Carrey's neck, so as not to inhibit the movements of his head. In addition to Tony Clifton's makeup, I came up with an appliance to hide the splint that Jim wore for five weeks. He'd sprained a finger in an accident. I made a splint and a false skin out of foam rubber to cover his finger.

Let's talk about your work on "Austin Powers."

Brian Penikas: We produced all the appliances for Dr. Evil and Mini-Me for the second movie of the series. Mini-Me's makeup was particularly complicated. We completely altered the shape of Verne Troyer's head. He wore a bald cap on his head, false eyebrows, a false nose, and appliances on his cheeks, chin and ears—thirteen appliances in all, I think. They were all made from gelatin, to get a translucent look.

How do you put on gelatin appliances?

Brian Penikas: We use a water-based adhesive to glue them onto the face, and we smooth edges with hot water or distilled witch hazel to gently melt the surface.

Why were you so intrigued by the movie "Planet of the Apes"?

Brian Penikas: I was very young when I discovered these apes. They terrified me, because I took them for the real thing! Later on, I found them extremely moving. My friends at Apemania and I would often have a good time showing up at parties dressed in ape masks and costumes. Then we got the idea to give John Chambers a surprise for his birthday. We appeared, dressed in the make-up and costumes, at the retirement home where he was living, as an expression of our admiration for him. He was profoundly touched. We often went back to visit him. The pictures from his birthday were published in the press, and hundreds of fans

A replica of Milo, the lead ape character from Escape from the Planet of the Apes *(1971)*
Photo courtesy of Brian Penikas

wrote to him. The walls of his room were covered with notes that warmed his heart. He could see the extent to which his creations had been appreciated, at a time when his health was declining. Twentieth Century-Fox got word of our little impromptu party and contacted us to take part in the thirtieth anniversary of the movie. And then we collaborated on many products derived from *Planet of*

the Apes: resin statuettes, masks, life-size mannequins, which were very popular with the collectors who owned the original costumes used in the movie. We also made busts and replicas of the costumes.

You've created a new great fantasy film monster for the horror series "Jeepers Creepers." How did you conceive him?

Brian Penikas: Director Victor Salva and artistic director Brad Parker wanted the face of Creeper to be covered with weird wrinkles and to open in two. I thought that would look too much like Predator, and I suggested that his whole head open up like an umbrella when he gets angry, and that when it recloses, he ends up with an essentially normal appearance. For the sequel, we uncovered his torso, which was part costume and part foam rubber musculature, and his feet, which had a thumb at the level of the heel, so he could grasp his victims as he was flying.

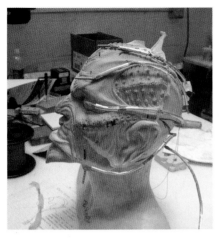

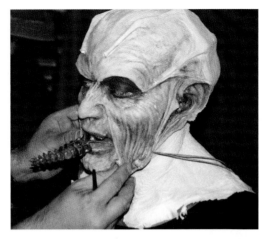

The mechanism that enabled Creeper's face to deploy

The tongue mechanisms, activated by cables and remote-control

The wings deployed

Sculpture of the clawed foot

Creeper's face opened

The final makeup
Photos courtesy of Brian Penikas

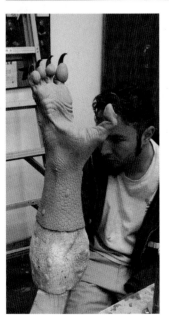

INTERVIEW

WALT CONTI

Master of Marine Animals

The orca in *Free Willy* (1993) and the giant snake in *Anaconda* (1997) are two creations by Walt Conti, one of the great animatronic specialists. His robots of whales, orcas, and dolphins are capable of swimming freely, like real animals.

Walt Conti at work on the animatronic dolphin in Flipper
Photo courtesy of Walt Conti / Edge Innovations

How did you come to specialize in the fabrication of animatronic replicas of marine animals?

Walt Conti: I studied robotic engineering at Stanford University, as well as took drawing and design courses. One day, Nilo Rodis-Jamero, who worked at ILM, offered me a job working on the humpback whales that were to appear in *Star Trek IV: The Voyage Home* (1986). He asked me to make miniature whales that could swim underwater, something I had never done, and he gave me carte blanche for six months. I watched hundreds of hours of documentaries to study how whales moved and defined the essential movements that enabled them to swim. Since I couldn't reproduce their entire anatomy, I simplified them without

The filming of the miniature whales in Star Trek IV: The Voyage Home, *which could swim freely through the use of radio-controlled mechanisms*
Photo courtesy of Walt Conti / Edge Innovations

altering the external appearance of the movements. The
reduced-scale whales measured
4 feet (1.2 meters). They had
to be watertight to protect the
mechanisms, and stabilized
under the water, without the
head or tail pointing toward the
surface. This was very difficult.
The internal space was filled
with motors, mechanisms, and
electronic equipment. As these
pieces were heavier than water,
they tended to make the whales
sink. We managed to distribute
the weight of this equipment
throughout the structure, and
we chose material that floated
to compensate for the weight of
the mechanisms. The skin was
molded from urethane. It's a
material that's very soft, but
very solid. The remote-control
servomotors that are used to
guide Korean missiles were
what we maneuvered the
fins with! Once finished, the
miniature whales could dive,
reascend to the surface,
turn around, and even turn
underwater.

The enormous mold of the orca in Free Willy
Photo courtesy of Walt Conti / Edge Innovations

The animatronic replica of Willy
Photo courtesy of Walt Conti / Edge Innovations

The floating workshops and the family of animatronic orcas in Free Willy 3: The Rescue *(1997)* Photo courtesy of Walt Conti / Edge Innovations

You created replicas of the orca Willy for the three movies in the series. How did you develop the techniques, and how did they evolve during the two sequels?

Walt Conti: An orca weighs four and a half tons. Each stage of the construction is a challenge. Willy's skin alone weighed one ton. We not only had to figure out the way to construct it, but also to remove it from the mold and work with it without causing damage. The molds were made from resin and steel-reinforced fiberglass. My team of twenty people and I spent a long time rehearsing the procedure that would let us make the skin. We started by dyeing a ton of urethane black. We mixed the component that

releases the catalyst of the product throughout the material, and then, in less than thirty minutes, we poured it all into the mold. Any longer than that, the urethane would have solidified. The conception of the mechanisms was complicated, as each character had to react naturally in emotionally charged scenes. By filming the real Keiko, we learned to recognize his state of mind. When he was sad, he would swim on his side with his head down. When he was happy, he was lively and energetic. And we used this as a base for animating our "clone." Unlike the shark that had been built for *Jaws,* our orca was not attached to a submergible platform. Its movements were fluid, because it moved freely through the water.

We constructed many replicas of Keiko. The one-quarter-scale miniatures were used on shots when it was seen swimming fast through the water. Sections with a real-sized head were used in scenes when the boy was talking to it. The full orca was attached to many hydraulic valves by a three-hundred-foot (ninety-one-meter) "umbilical cord." We directed it using joysticks. The umbilical cord was also a security measure—a remote-controlled character can pick up some radio interference by accident. Our robotic orca was so powerful, it could cause damage or hurt someone if it made any unforeseen movements. Depending on the shot, we could attach this umbilical cord under the orca's belly or on its side, so it wouldn't be seen. The two sequels benefited from digital erasing techniques—the cord was erased frame by frame. In the first *Free Willy,* our orca was only a double for Keiko. In the second, most of the scenes were filmed with our animatronics and a few stock shots found in documentaries. We developed a system that made it possible to move the orca's center of gravity, so it could pitch and roll on its side. In the third movie, our orca and the robots that played his brothers and sisters were used in 99 percent of the shots.

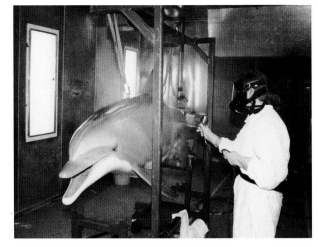

Painting the animatronic dolphin for Flipper
Photo courtesy of Walt Conti / Edge Innovations

Filming Flipper *with the artificial dolphin*

since real dolphins aren't dangerous. The reason is simple—dolphins have a limited attention span. They're very attentive for ten minutes or so, do the routines they've rehearsed with their trainers, and devour the fish you give them as a reward. When their stomachs are full, they no longer feel like making the effort. That's when you're glad you have an animatronic dolphin on hand! The calmer scenes are filmed more easily with a robot than with a real dolphin. A real animal distracts the actors when it does something unpredictable, like swimming away in the middle of a scene, while the actors are still delivering their lines!

You also made the dolphins for the TV series "SeaQuest DSV" and for the movie "Flipper" (1996). What's the secret for making a realistic animatronic dolphin?

Walt Conti: A dolphin's skin is so smooth that you'd immediately see the lines from the mold in a close-up shot. We had to make the molds absolutely perfect so the lines couldn't be seen. The color of the skin is also very particular. We started by

dyeing a mass of urethane, and then added many coats of light silver paint on the surface to get the desired effect. We added some imperfections and scars resembling those that male dolphins get when they fight. The salt water and sand quickly deteriorated our robots. They constantly had to be repainted. Our two Flipper replicas were animated with extremely powerful servomotors that we had built ourselves. We were often asked why we built animatronic dolphins,

Sharks in movies often have a fake look about them. But when you observe real sharks, they also have a fake look about them! How did you get around this problem when you depicted them in "Deep Blue Sea" (1999)?

Walt Conti: The eyes of a real shark are essentially dull, lifeless. We took the liberty of giving them very dark irises and pupils. We also modified the color of their skin by adding some silvery blue tones.

The artificial gutted swordfish in the movie The Perfect Storm
Photo courtesy of Walt Conti / Edge Innovations

The animatronic swordfish in the fishing sequences of "The Perfect Storm" (1999) were strikingly true-to-life. How did they work?

Walt Conti: They were 550-pound (250-kilogram) remote-controlled robots whose skin had been painted with iridescent highlights. Swordfish are very fast fish. Our robots could writhe and wriggle out of water. The mechanisms and the skin had to be very strong, because the actors would catch them with hooks and then would hurl them onto the bridge of the boat. We studied the moves of fishermen to prepare for the scenes in which the swordfish are gutted, and then we spent a lot of time thinking about how to replicate the meat that would be cut up. We mixed hundreds of little capsules of blood into the silicone. The skin was made out of urethane, and the blood would shoot up as soon as the skin and meat were cut. The internal organs were molded out

of silicone. Only 10 percent of these effects were in the final cut of the movie, because they were considered too realistic!

How did you construct and animate the giant snake in "Anaconda"?

Walt Conti: Normally, the animals we're asked to reproduce will have enough volume to be able to use hydraulic jacks and commercial valves. The snake's body itself was so narrow that each piece had to be custom-made. We copied the shape of the vertebrae of a real snake. The hydraulic joints that replaced the vertebrae could move up and down, and right and left. The snake's body had 120 axes of motion. But we still had to find the way to simultaneously maneuver them in order to replicate a sinuous movement. We constructed a joystick that was a one-quarter-

scale reproduction of a snake, which made it possible for us to maneuver the snake. Using a computer program, we were then able to save several key shots and link them together and compose a fluid movement. Most of the animations of the body were recorded before the filming, but the head and eyes were always animated live, interacting with the gestures of the actors. We controlled the speed of the prerecorded movements by turning a dial. Turning it slowly would slow down the animation of the snake; turning it faster would speed up its reactions. This hybrid recorded animation plus live animation system let us pilot 120 simultaneous movements while adapting to what was taking place on the stage. We constructed two anacondas. The larger one weighed two tons, was forty feet (twelve meters) long, and was two hundred horsepower. The "small" one weighed fifteen hundred pounds (seven hundred kilograms), was fifteen feet (four and a half meters) long, and was seventy-five horsepower. The snakes were attached to the ground at a midpoint on their bodies. They couldn't actually move forward, but their head, body, and tail could be animated at the same time in a single shot. The electric cables for the jacks were concealed in the scenery. The shots in which the snake moved forward on the ground were done with synthesized images created at Sony Imageworks.

How do you transport such a heavy, giant snake?

Walt Conti: We constructed a kind of long stretcher in which we could fold the two halves of the snake. Arranged like this, it would take up a space five feet (one and a half meters) wide and twenty feet (six meters) long. The problem was that it was limp. It was a little like trying to grab a giant spaghetti! It took all the members of my team coordinating their efforts to manage to roll it into its container. We also made a kind of giant sock that protected the snake during rehearsals. The skin was only in contact with the ground during the filming. We always added some dust or water to minimize the friction during its contact with the ground.

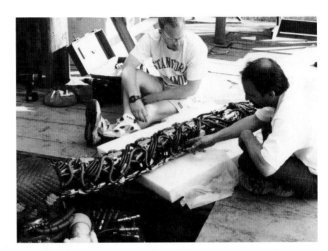

The mechanisms for the snake are the most complicated ever made for an animatronic creature.
Photo courtesy of Walt Conti / Edge Innovations

The snake during the filming
Photo courtesy of Walt Conti / Edge Innovations

The spectacular end to the giant anaconda
Photo courtesy of Walt Conti / Edge Innovations

INTERVIEW

MARK COULIER

From Miniseries to Superproductions

Mark Coulier adjusts Poseidon's costume in the miniseries Jason and the Argonauts.
Special makeup effects by Mark Coulier

Mark Coulier is one of the best English makeup artists. He collaborated on several prestigious Hallmark miniseries before working on *Star Wars: Episode 1—The Phantom Menace* (1999) and *Harry Potter* movies.

The aging of Sam Neill for the miniseries Merlin *was honored with an Emmy Award.*
Special makeup effects by Mark Coulier

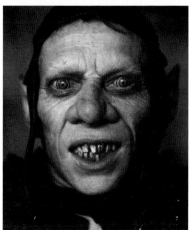

Top: *The elf Frik (Martin Short) in* Merlin

Bottom: *Another elf in* Merlin
Special makeup effects by Mark Coulier

When starting out, you worked on the TV miniseries "Merlin" (1998). Was that work very different from what you do on movies?

Mark Coulier: The Hallmark production team saw to it that the sets, the makeup, and the special effects were as beautiful as those in a feature movie, but they only had a tenth of the budget. My first job as an inde-

pendent makeup artist entailed aging Sam Neill, who was playing Merlin, and transforming Martin Short into an elf. I sculpted Merlin's aged face in three and a half days, after having submitted many designs to the director. That left me only two weeks to make the molds and as many copies of the prosthetics as there were days of filming, since they were not

reusable. My work was well received, and Hallmark asked me to do the makeup for *Arabian Nights* (2000), notably the one for the completely red devil, who had horns, intricate tattoos, and prosthetics that were conceived, sculpted, and readied in nine days. Just for comparison, I worked for twelve weeks, with a three-person team, on the makeup tests for

Silicone makeup for the goblins in Harry Potter and the Sorcerer's Stone
Special makeup effects by Mark Coulier

the centaur in *Harry Potter and the Sorcerer's Stone* (2001)! And after a long delay, the production chose to realize the character entirely in 3-D.

You also worked on "Harry Potter and the Chamber of Secrets" (2002).

Mark Coulier: Yes. I'd founded my own company, but also collaborated with Nick Dudman on *The Fifth Element* (1997), *Star Wars: Episode 1—The Phantom Menace, The Mummy Returns* (2001), and the *Harry Potter* movies. On *Harry Potter and the Chamber of Secrets,* I worked on "petrified" replicas of the children and of John Cleese. We molded them in alginate and then cast plaster positives that had been corrected. During the molding, an actor's expression can sometimes be tense. The weight of the alginate would compress the features a little. So the positive had to be reworked, removing any air bubbles and defects. The corrected positives were remolded, and these negatives were used to produce silicone faces that were dyed in bulk and had the transparency of human skin. Makeup was applied to the replicas, and we implanted hair to get hyperrealistic results. Silicone was also used to fabricate prosthetics like the ones for the goblins in the first

Harry Potter. We also made a silicone makeup appliance for Voldemort, but that scene was considered too scary and was cut.

You created a very impressive Poseidon for the TV miniseries "Jason and the Argonauts" (2000).

Mark Coulier: It was a very complicated foam rubber costume. In order to emphasize the colossal tail, Poseidon was filmed shooting up from the water with a lens that could take macro shots. We started by making a mold of the actor playing Poseidon. This resin-and-fiberglass cast of his body was covered with clay. The minute details had to be sculpted into his face, his hands, and his body to make it appear that he was made out of craggy rocks covered in algae. This sculpture was molded in fiberglass. Then we slipped a Lycra costume over the body mold and placed the entire thing inside the mold of the original sculpture. When we injected the foam rubber into the space between the molds, it adhered to the Lycra. Once it was baked and removed from the mold, we ended up with a very solid foam rubber costume. Since Poseidon was supposed to be nearly 500 feet (150 meters) tall, we spent two weeks gluing little bits of lichen

and foam onto the surface of the costume, to create miniature vegetation. We constructed two costumes and made seven sets of prosthetics for this character. Playing this kind of role is exhausting for an actor, because the foam rubber costume stays wet all day long; it becomes very heavy and, once the character emerges from the water, very cold. So we conceived of a costume that the actor could take off in twenty minutes at lunchtime and during breaks out of the water. We had prepared the seams at the neck, since the facial prosthetics remained in place throughout the day.

You also transformed John Leguizamo into a genie for the TV miniseries "Arabian Nights."

Mark Coulier: There were two versions of his makeup. In the "thin" version, he was covered in tattoos, and in the "heavy" version, he was pale and had a small goatee and a mustache. Here again, it was a race against the clock. I sculpted the first mask on Saturday, the second on Sunday, and my team had to rush the making of the rest of the prosthetics. If you have enough experience, working under such strained conditions can produce good results. You make drastic

The two types of makeup for the genie in Arabian Nights, *played by John Leguizamo*
Special makeup effects by Mark Coulier

choices that sometimes give the character a greater efficacy. You have to know how to manage the unforeseen. John Leguizamo was supposed to shave his head to play the role of the genie, but then he

The red genie in Arabian Nights
Special makeup effects by Mark Coulier

changed his mind. At the last minute, I hid his hair under a false skullcap.

How do actors carry themselves once they're made up?

Mark Coulier: John Leguizamo couldn't keep still. On day, he got the idea to launch into a demonstration of break dancing, spinning like a top on the false skullcap I'd just put on! Martin Short followed the warnings not to ruin our work. He had an icy sense of humor that I loved. Sam Neill is also very funny.

What are the memories you preserve from "Star Wars: Episode 1—The Phantom Menace"?

Mark Coulier: It was Nick Dudman who offered me the job. George Lucas had hundreds of extraterrestrial concept drawings that he had approved hung up on a wall. I chose one that was named Orn Freeb Ta. He had blue skin and tentacles that came from his head. The actor had to wear false teeth, contact lenses, an enormous false neck with a triple chin, and a very complicated costume to make him look obese. The character, which took me three months of work, was on-screen for only a second! I had hoped to see a bit more of him in *Star Wars: Episode 2—Attack of the Clones* (2002), because I knew that an Australian make-up artist had reused my prosthetics. But there again, he only appeared for a second! (*Laughs.*) I also played the role of Aks Moe, one of the extra-terrestrial pilots in the race sequence. George Lucas directed me by saying, "Walk here. . . .

Look straight ahead. . . . Turn your head. . . ." It was unbearably hot in Tunisia. Being closed up in such a dense costume was hell. What's more, the head was extremely heavy, because it was animated by dozens of servomotors. I regularly had to take the head off to avoid suffocating. They had put thimbles inside the latex gloves to secure the finger extensions I wore, and the metal got so hot that it burned my skin!

The final makeup of Orn Freeb Ta, who appeared for one second in Star Wars: Episode 1—The Phantom Menace
Special makeup effects by Mark Coulier

The character Shuna in Clive Barker's movie Nightbreed *(1990)*
Special makeup effects by Mark Coulier

The costume for the mummy of Ank sun Amon in The Mummy *(1999). The production decided to digitally erase this character's eyes after the costume had been made. As the budget for digital corrections had already been used up, the facial makeup created by Mark Coulier was covered with strips of cloth!*
Special makeup effects by Mark Coulier

A stunning effect of a shark attack made for the movie The Beach *(2000)*
Special makeup effects by Mark Coulier

INTERVIEW

ED FRENCH

Ed French is a makeup artist whose multiple talents can be seen in film, on television, and in the most arresting advertising spots of recent times.

Makeup created for a Toyota commercial, "The Three Little Pigs"
Special makeup effects by Edward French

Edward French during a makeup demonstration
Special makeup effects by Edward French

How are advertising spots made?

Ed French: The means are always there, but on the other hand, we're always given less and less preparation time. You have to assemble a big team to finish a complicated job in ten days or so. Sometimes it's so short that it almost becomes impossible. I sometimes feel that I'm the special makeup effects emergency medical service—they only call me when it's almost too late!

What are the metamorphoses you like to do best?

Ed French: The ones that go unnoticed. I had the pleasure of transforming a group of young dancers into very old ladies for an ad. When you saw them, you wouldn't have thought that they'd do a triple back flip a few seconds later! More and more directors are using digital effects to produce these types of manipulation, but some of them prefer to have total control of the images they're shooting during the filming. With digital effects, you only discover the final results two or three months later.

How did you create the makeup for the stuntman who replaces Arnold Schwarzenegger in the dangerous scenes of the theme park attraction "Terminator 2: 3-D" (1996)?

Ed French: I'd previously worked with the second makeup team on the movie *Terminator 2* in the company of Jeff Dawn, Arnold's makeup man. That's when I had the occasion to develop some stuff to make the effects for Arnold's doubles and to embark on a collaboration that continued through *Terminator 2: 3-D* and *Jingle All the Way* (1996). The work consisted of first taking a mold of Arnold's face in order to make a positive in plaster that was used as a reference. Then the stuntman's head was molded, and we compared the two sets of facial structures. After a while, we spared Arnold from having

Arnold Schwarzenegger with his double on the set of Terminator 2: 3-D, *an attraction at Universal Studios* Special makeup effects by Edward French

The extremely unusual monster that appears in Hal Hartley's No Such Thing *(2001)*
Special makeup effects by Edward French

to be molded by making a three-dimensional scan of his head. A molding takes about forty-five minutes, whereas you can make a scan in one minute. The scan generates a 3-D image, the measurements of which are used to carve a block of plastic. The bust you get is less precise than a mold, but it can be refined afterward, correcting and adding the details that it lacks. I used different procedures for the stuntmen's makeup. If they resembled Arnold a little, I only used some appliances. If they didn't, I used a mask to transform the whole face. All it needed was that their head be a little smaller than Arnold's. That was the case with Billy Lucas, who played his double in the filming of *Terminator 2: 3-D.*

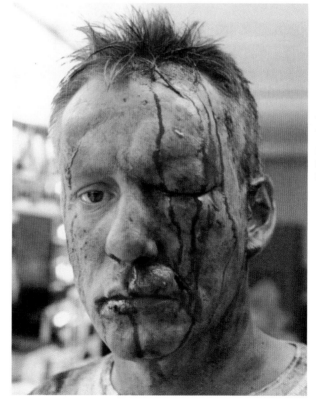

James Wood in poor shape in the movie Killer: A Journal of Murder *(1995)*
Special makeup effects by Edward French

Pierre-Olivier Persin: The New French Generation

Pierre-Olivier Persin is one of the most talented young French makeup artists. He partakes in all the artistic and technical stages of a special effect, a pyrotechnical effect, and a metamorphosis. He acquired this expertise after many years learning to master the use of such materials as alginate, plaster, resins, urethane, and all types of silicones, as well as the affixing of foam rubber and translucent silicone appliances. Persin has also become a specialist in pyrotechnical effects produced on actors. He has created spectacular bullet-impact effects for French television series such as *Les Redoutables* and movies like *Roberto Succo*.

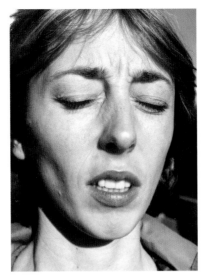

The making of a replica of an actress's face, to be used for an effect of a bullet shot in the eye, for the French TV series Les Redoutables
Photos and makeup courtesy of P.-O. Persin

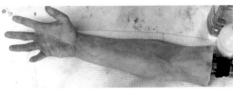

An effect with pneumatics, used to deflate an arm in a few seconds for a scene in Bloody Mallory
Photos and makeup courtesy of P.-O. Persin

Steve Wang: The Airbrush Wizard

Steve Wang is not only a make-up artist and sculptor of great talent, but also the most sought-after airbrush painter in Hollywood. The airbrush is a small paint gun the size of a fat pencil that is attached to a compressed air hose and emits a fine spray of mixed colors, often made from an acrylic or vinyl base. Using this tool, Wang enhances the reliefs on a creature's skin, attributes new textures, suggests the presence of veins, and creates the trompe l'oeil effects that give a translucent look to an opaque material. Wang also made the stunning texture and color effects on creatures conceived by other makeup artists, such as Stan Winston, Rick Baker, and Patrick Tatopoulos.

The character Mohawk in the movie Gremlins 2: The New Batch *(1990). The painting and texture work is especially remarkable.*

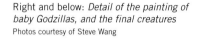

Right and below: *Detail of the painting of baby Godzillas, and the final creatures* Photos courtesy of Steve Wang

Characters created for the movie Guyver 2: Dark Hero *(1994), also directed by Steve Wang* Photo courtesy of Steve Wang

Nimba Creations: The Birth of a T. Rex in Banbury

Siobhan Hall and Tom Lauten are the founders of Nimba Creations, a makeup and special effects studio in Banbury, England, near Pinewood and Leavesden Studios. They make masks, appliances, special props, and mechanized characters. The most complicated of all the animatronic characters

Reduced-size model of the T. rex

ever conceived by Nimba Creations is a life-size tyrannosaurus that has been installed in an outdoor set at a theme park. They began by making a reduced-size model of the dinosaur, which was cut into fine slices. Each slice was enlarged and reproduced in polystyrene pieces, which were then used to produce the life-size sculpture. The finished sculpture was then molded in order to make a casting of the skin and sections of the body in

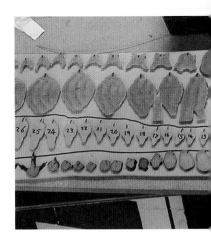

resin and fiberglass. The team at Nimba Creations made computer simulations to determine where best to place each jack, based on how much weight it would have to move. The mechanized armature of the T. rex was first assembled at the Nimba studio and then disassembled and remounted at the site. This superb T. rex was designed to remain animated throughout the year as an outdoor attraction in a region with inclement weather.

Siobhan Hall and Tom Lauten are the founders of the makeup and special effects studio Nimba Creations, located in Banbury, England. Among their most ambitious projects was the fabrication of a tyrannosaurus that was installed outdoors at a theme park.

The large cut-up slices in polystyrene

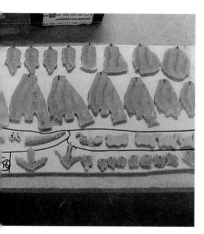

Casts of the skin

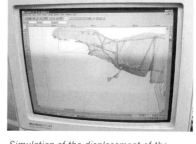

Simulation of the displacement of the weight and placement of the hydraulic jacks

The model was cut into thin slices, which were reproduced and enlarged to create the life-size sculpture.
Photos courtesy of Nimba Creations

Molds of the sculpture

The sculpture

The mechanical armature

The magnificent T. rex—
completed and animated

Christopher Tucker: The Great English Innovator

The aging of Derek Jacobi in the BBC miniseries I, Claudius. *This work was particularly innovative for the late 1970s, when actors commonly wore white wigs and used latex to add wrinkles to their face in order to appear older. Christopher Tucker had so many prosthetics to make for this production that he rarely left his studio. The prosthetics were applied by the make-up team at the BBC.*
Photo courtesy of Christopher Tucker / BBC

Christopher Tucker is one of the most renowned English makeup artists. Following a career as an opera singer, Tucker was taken by a passion for makeup. He started by creating false noses and theatrical prosthetics. The television network ITV approached him during its preparation for the miniseries *The Strauss Family* (1973), which required sophisticated aging concepts. This complicated work was a veritable technical revolution in the history of English makeup. The agings were accomplished with foam rubber prosthetics, based on methods devised by Dick Smith. The real Johann Strauss Jr. had dyed his hair when he got older, which did not make Tucker's job any easier! His work had such an impact that Tucker became one of the most respected makeup artists. The British Broadcasting Corporation (BBC) contacted him to do the aging for its miniseries *I, Claudius* (1976). At the time, to age themselves,

The aging crafted with foam rubber prosthetics for the miniseries The Strauss Family *revolutionized makeup production in Great Britain. The real Johann Strauss Jr. (played here by Stuart Wilson) dyed his hair as he aged, which complicated Tucker's work.*
Photo courtesy of Christopher Tucker / ATV

actors often merely wore a white wig and had latex wrinkles created onto their skin. Tucker's approach was radically different. He decided to create dozens of foam rubber prosthetics to produce the various stages of aging for Derek Jacobi (the actor who played the title role). All the principal charac-

ters were aged in the same way, progressively, representing a period of years. This colossal effort forced Tucker to remain in his laboratory, and so his prosthetics were applied—with varying degrees of success—by the makeup team at the BBC. Tucker then aged Lee Remick in the PBS miniseries *Jenny*, which recounted the life of Churchill's mother. The actress was made up with prosthetics composed of a plastic material that Tucker had specifically developed. According to the desired effect, it could be as flabby as silicone implants or made relatively rigid. Tucker had developed this material to replace foam rubber, which, at the time, could not be ordered in containers of less than 500 pounds (230 kilograms)!

The Strange Adventure of *The Elephant Man*

One of the most famous of Christopher Tucker's achievements was the impressive reconstruction of John Merrick, alias the Elephant Man, for the 1980 film. The production team first contacted Tucker for the addresses of makeup suppliers. He then fortuitously learned that director David Lynch had put himself in charge of producing the makeup and intended on using polyurethane foam—a rigid material! Following some catastrophic attempts, the production went back to Tucker and literally pleaded with him to make himself available and do the makeup as quickly as possible. As the head of the real John Merrick was almost twice the size of a normal head, Tucker was forced to create two layers of foam rubber makeup placed one on top of the other. The first layer was used to "deform" John Hurt's bone structure, and the second layer comprised a series of prosthetics attached to the contours of his eyes and mouth. Body prosthetics were also constructed for those scenes in which John Merrick is seen partially nude. The production insured the indispensable Christopher Tucker for two million pounds sterling in case an accident befell him during the filming!

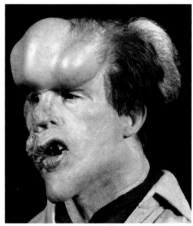

The application of the makeup for The Elephant Man, *seen here for the first time in color (the movie was filmed in black and white)*
Photos courtesy of Christopher Tucker

© CHRISTOPHER TUCKER 2003

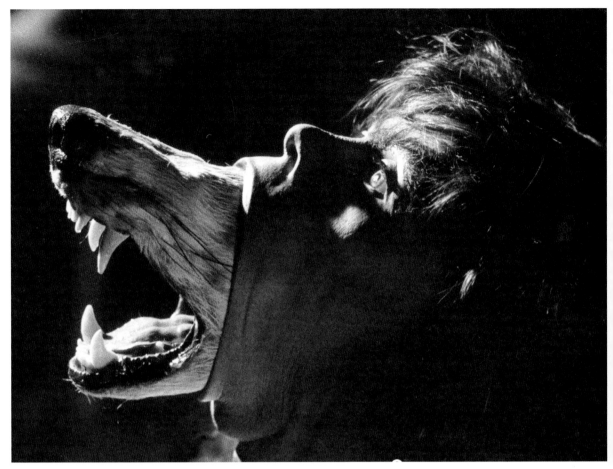

One of the transformations of the werewolves in The Company of Wolves—*an original approach that was utterly different from the metamorphoses seen in earlier American movies. Chris Tucker based his idea on a snake shedding its skin.* Photo courtesy of Christopher Tucker

Shock Images

Since the 1980s, Tucker has taken pleasure in giving an original twist to the most classic metamorphoses. Inspired by how snakes shed their skin, he reinvented the werewolf's transformation for *The Company of Wolves* (1984). When he was contacted by the Monty Python comedy team to conceive of an enormously fat man, Tucker developed the unforgettable makeup of Mr. Creosote, the star of the shock-humor sequence in *Monty Python's The Meaning of Life* (1983). The jowls and triple chin worn by Terry Jones were made of foam rubber. Creosote's enormous belly, constructed by costume makers, was fitted with an iron wire armature that was filled up with a helium balloon to make the structure lighter, and then set on a wheeled trolley so Jones could take a few steps in his opening scene. The scenes in which Mr. Creosote vomits up his meal were done by using a high-pressure pump to project baby food. Unfortunately, the filming took place in the summer during a heat wave, and the baby food, spread all over the place, fermented quickly. The heat of the projectors also hastened the process. By the end of the filming, the stench was as realistic as the special effect! Christopher Tucker has also worked on such movies as *Quest for Fire* (1981) and *Dune* (1984), as well as in countless advertisements in which his original creations often play the starring role.

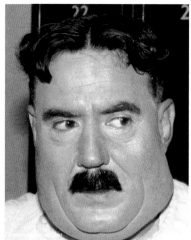

Left and above: *The repulsive Mr. Creosote in* Monty Python's The Meaning of Life. *The makeup worn by Terry Jones was made of foam rubber.*
Photos courtesy of Christopher Tucker

Delightful makeups in a TV commercial
Photo courtesy of Christopher Tucker

Grand Illusions on the Small Screen

Dinotopia © Hallmark

The Feat of Live Broadcasts

When it first made its entry into the family rooms of the late 1940s, television offered entertainment based on radio broadcasts—singers and artists performing live on a stage similar to a music hall. The first dramatic programs were stage plays, comedies, and original dramatic works produced live. (The first professional videotape recorder, manufactured by Ampex, was marketed in 1956.) Camera movements, the placement of the actors, the arrangement of the props, and the special effects were all carefully prepared. Complicated effects (storms, wide-angle shots of models, explosions) and exterior shots were filmed in advance on 16-millimeter or 35-millimeter film and then would be broadcast live by a telecine, slipped in at the desired moment between scenes being taped on video. Eventually, networks began producing progressively more ambitious dramas. In 1955, George Roy Hill directed *A Night to Remember* for the American show *Kraft Television Theatre*. It reenacted the sinking of the *Titanic*—live! A model of the ship was filmed in a half-light that sufficiently camouflaged the narrowness of the pool used to

Dick Smith in 1950, five years after the founding of the makeup department at the television channel NBC
Photo courtesy of Dick Smith

depict the ocean. This period of technical experimentation proved to be fascinating not only for the prop masters, but for the makeup artists as well, such as the young Dick Smith: "When I started at NBC in 1945, I was the first salaried makeup artist at an American network. Television grew so fast that only five years later, my makeup department consisted of myself and twenty assistants. I learned everything from teaching others! The most complicated makeups had to be prepared in two days. The directors were forgiving, because they were also learning their job. We couldn't make any tests. You could see your makeup on the video monitor during rehearsals and make adjustments. I remember desperate moments during those 'live' days. I had made a heavy

makeup with melted vinyl—jowls, nose, and chin appliances that I had to put onto the character actor Vaughn Taylor. And suddenly I saw his chin was coming loose. I did some touch-ups during the sixty-second commercial break, and we both ran back to the set. I kept my fingers crossed that the damn thing would hold until the end. He didn't restrain himself at all—waving his head around! I could see one of the edges coming off. That was so scary that I gave up using that particular material and the glue I used, and desperately taught myself how to make foam latex!"

The First Science Fiction Series

The first science fiction series appeared in the 1950s in the United States. These adventures intended for children, such as *Captain Video and His Video Rangers* (1949) and *Space Patrol* (1951), were broadcast live. Other programs, such as *Rocky Jones, Space Ranger* (1954), were filmed in 16 millimeter. The DuMont network then used an Electronicam camera—a video camera coupled with a 16-millimeter camera—to produce the montage of *Captain Video* on film. The effects were filmed directly on 16-millimeter

Filming a special effects sequence in the series Captain Video and His Video Rangers *(1949). The model of the* Galaxy 2 *rocket was created by gluing together the lower halves of two jet airplane model toys.*

Actor George Reeves played the man of steel in The Adventures of Superman *(1952–57).*

would loosen at the desired speed. Framed in a close-up, the *Galaxy 2* appeared to be traveling through space. The planetary landscapes were papier-mâché mountains and sand covered in colored pigments. Some of the episodes from this series have been preserved in Kinescope—the format in which the image is filmed directly from the television screen on 16-millimeter film. The shutter speed of the camera is synchronized with the movement of the video images, thus preventing the appearance of vertical bars on the image.

Superman on Television

The Adventures of Superman (1952–57) heralded the arrival of the comic book superhero on television. Actor George Reeves wore a padded leotard that gave him the look of an athlete. Vying with the "Man of Steel," the technicians had to use their ingenuity to simulate his powers on a budget of only fifteen thousand dollars per episode. A diving board was installed on the set so Reeves could leap and fly through a window—only to land six feet (two meters) away, on some mattresses backstage. A wind sound effect was added to complete the illusion. Superman's airborne scenes were more complicated to film. The prop people constructed a rigid support out of resin and fiberglass from a mold made of the actor's

film. The *Galaxy 2,* the spaceship in *Captain Video,* was a thirteen-inch-long (thirty-three-centimeter) plastic rocket that was suspended from wires. It was composed of two lower halves of model jets, which were glued together and then painted with a silvery paint. The spaceship was hooked up in front of a canvas that was painted black and sewn to form a loop. Small holes had been pierced into this canvas to depict stars. A wooden roller was set on each of the four vertical axes to form a rectangle, and one of them was mounted on an electric motor controlled by a regulator. With the fabric stretched out from roller to roller, and the projector placed in the center of the rectangle, the stars were made to shine. By controlling the regulator on the motor, the fabric loop

torso and thighs. This "stomach shell" was furnished with grooves, through which metal cables could be slid. Reeves would stick this shell against his chest before slipping into his leotard and then would stretch out on his stomach. The two cables threaded through the support, in the front and in the back, were hidden inside his leotard. Reeves was then hoisted up in front of a blue background, his legs kept horizontal by the support. He was inserted into the aerial shots through the use of the device known as a traveling matte. The close-up shots were simpler, entailing only a sky blue background in front of which the actor was filmed prone and in profile. He was asked to stretch out his arms and look up at the ceiling while the camera was laid on its side so as to frame his body on the horizon. And so Reeves appeared to soar through the air with the greatest of ease.

The extraterrestrial creature discovered by Professor Quatermass in Quatermass and the Pit, *a six-part dramatic series that made British television audiences shiver.*

K-9, Dr. Who's famous cybernetic dog, during a small checkup of his remote-control mechanisms at the BBC special effects workshop

Bernard Wilkie: The Pioneer at the BBC

In 1954, Bernard Wilkie (1920–2002) and Jack Kine founded the special effects department at the BBC. In 1955, Wilkie created a formless monster that perished in a refinery in the TV movie *Quatermass II.* The models of the refinery and the creature were both improvised during a lunch break, using an empty jelly jar, a small ladder taken from a toy, dry ice, and latex to cover Wilkie's hands. Traveling to the BBC on a bus the day after the TV movie was broadcast, Wilkie overheard the laudatory comments of the passengers— they'd been terrified! Three years later, he would make the floor roll under the feet of the actors in *Quatermass and the Pit.*

Wilkie had spread out Ping-Pong balls attached to wires under a carpet covered with soil. All he had to do was to pull on the wires to create an unnerving effect. But the one image that struck the audience more than any other was the Martian with the throbbing eyes. Wilkie had used a mannequin with inflated condoms in the eye sockets! The BBC special effects department first started working on science fiction sets in 1963 with *Dr. Who,* making spacesuits, laser guns, and models of spacecrafts and robots that were to become the new icons of Great Britain. Even today, the extraterrestrial Daleks' mini-tanks and Dr. Who's dog-robot, K-9, remain in the collective English imagina-

tion. Wilkie and Kine then took great pleasure in blowing up dogs, making a life-size puppet of Princess Margaret, and conceiving outlandish props for *Monty Python's Flying Circus* (1969–74). They also reconstructed historical sites from ancient Rome for the prized series *I, Claudius,* a striking evocation of the power struggle during the reign of the Caesars. Until it was shut down in 2003, the BBC special effects department continued to draw inspiration from its creativity and pragmatism, albeit while using animatronics and sophisticated digital effects. Examples of this work can be seen in its dramas, its documentaries, and the science fiction sitcom *Red Dwarf,* which debuted in 1998.

Preparation of a simple but effective visual effect: models depicting the top of a cliff and a spaceship were placed in front of the camera in alignment with a real landscape.

The character Zaphod, of the parodic series The Hitchhiker's Guide to the Galaxy, *was endowed with a second head, animated by remote control.*

One of the countless spaceships constructed by Mat Irvine and Bill Pearson for several BBC science fiction series

This spaceship was filmed in front of a blue background over an image of a starry sky.

Construction of a model of a building designed to be destroyed in the drama Ghost Sonata

The Great Anthologies

The 1960s saw the beginning of anthologies—series in which each episode was independent and the protagonists were different. The connecting thread could be a famous presenter such as Alfred Hitchcock, who made his delectable appearances at the opening of each *Alfred Hitchcock Presents* (1955–62), or a personality associated more closely with a series, such as Rod Serling, the creator and principal writer of *The Twilight Zone* (1959–65). His stories kept viewers in suspense right up until the last minute. Effects were employed with restraint, so as not to intrude on the subject of the episode. An example of this is "The Howling Man." A lost traveler finds refuge in a monastery. Night falls, but howling keeps him awake. He finds a man locked up in a dungeon who tells him that the monks have held him for years as a prisoner for no reason. The monks explain that the imprisoned creature is none other than Satan! The following night, the traveler opens the cell door. He understands his mistake when he sees horns bulging from the forehead as the prisoner flees the dungeon. This metamorphosis takes place when the character walks behind a row of pillars. During the editing, director Douglas Heyes used each interval between the pillars in the foreground as a transition

The freed prisoner reveals his true face in the Twilight Zone *episode "The Howling Man."*

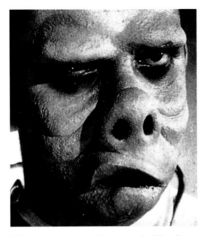

The doctor's face in the episode "The Eye of the Beholder"

Agnes Moorehead is terrified by strange creatures coming from outer space in the episode "The Invaders."

that let him insert, step by step, the progression of makeup. Viewed straight through, this scene is delectably frightening. In the episode "The Eye of the Beholder," a young girl with a bandaged face waits to learn if her plastic surgery has been successful. The doctors and nurses remove the bandages and cry out in horror when they see her beautiful face. We then see them for the first time in full light—and they're monsters with piglike snouts and deformed lips. The action's taking place on some other planet! These foam rubber makeup applications by William Tuttle remain the most famous of the series. In the episode "The Invaders," an old woman lives in a cabin that is invaded by tiny beings dressed in silver spacesuits. She succeeds in killing quite a number of them before we realize that they are astronauts from Earth, exploring a world of giants! The tiny spacesuits were hand puppets made of foam rubber. The

prop people slid their fingers into the legs to make the earthlings walk, while the prop people's arms, covered in black velvet, disappeared into the dark recesses of the set.

The Twilight Zone was a great hit every Friday at 10 P.M. CBS rubbed its hands and tried to hold the television audience a little longer with a second fantasy series that night called *Way Out* (1961). The presenter of the series was the formidable English writer Roald Dahl, who had agreed to adapt his black comedy short stories for television, and Dick Smith imparted his exceptional makeup work. In the episode "Soft Focus," a photographer played by Barry Morse discovers a magic liquid that lets him change the real appearance of a person by retouching a photograph of him. The photographer uses the process to take revenge on his cheating wife and transforms her into an old lady so that her lover will abandon her. He then uses it to make her

turn young again, but his wife realizes what he's done. Enraged, she pours the vial with the magic potion onto a photograph of her husband, erasing half his face! "I wanted to give the impression that Barry Morse's nose had disappeared," recalls Dick Smith. "I made a mold of his face, having flattened his nose with adhesive tape. Then I sculpted a mask from this mold. It was smooth on one side, and had a glass eye on the other. It was sculpted to look as if the remaining part of his face was in a shocked, odd expression. The mask virtually covered Barry's entire face." (The actor breathed through a hole in the fake mouth.) Unfortunately, these fantastic stories were deemed too macabre. Ratings for *Way Out* fell in three months, and the series was canceled after fourteen episodes.

One of the incredible makeup jobs created by Dick Smith for the Way Out *anthology series* Photo courtesy of Dick Smith

The Creatures in *The Outer Limits*

"There is nothing wrong with your television set. Do not attempt to adjust the picture. We are controlling transmission. If we wish to make it louder, we will bring up the volume. If we wish to make it softer, we will tune it to a whisper. We will control the horizontal. We will control the vertical. We can roll the image, make it flutter. We can change the focus to a soft blur or sharpen it to crystal clarity. For the next hour sit quietly, and we will control all that you see and hear. We repeat: there is nothing wrong with your television set. You are about to participate in a great adventure. You are about to experience the awe and mystery which reaches from the inner mind to . . . *The Outer Limits*." This monologue began the opening credits of television's first adult science fiction series, *The Outer Limits* (1963–65), with most of the episodes written by writer-producers Leslie Stevens and Joseph Stefano. Stefano was a master of the unsettling story—it was he who wrote the extraordinary screenplay for Hitchcock's *Psycho,* heightening the tension of the original book by Robert Bloch. But the words came up against the harsh reality of producing a television series—the budget for each episode was limited to $120,000. Stevens and Stefano gathered an exceptional team including Conrad Hall as

Joseph Stefano next to one of the amphibious creatures in the Outer Limits *episode "Tourist Attraction"*

director of photography, first-rate actors such as Cliff Robertson, Robert Culp, and Robert Duvall, and special effects experts as talented as they were speedy—a necessity, as a new, strange creature, nicknamed "The Bear," was to appear in each episode. Contacted by the producers, director Byron Haskin (*The War of the Worlds*) agreed to anonymously supervise the conception of the monsters, which would be manufactured by Wah Chang, Gene Warren, Tim Baar, Al Hamm, Paul LeBaron, Ralph Rodine, and Jim Danforth, his collaborators at Projects Unlimited. Makeup artists Fred B. Phillips and John Chambers were hired to create makeup appliances that could quite easily be fitted around each creature's mouth. They played with facial proportions by placing the creature's glass eyes either above or below the actor's eyes. The actor could see by

looking through slits hidden in the textures of the mask. In other cases, stuntmen Janos Prohaska and William O. Douglas would disappear inside the foam rubber costumes. The most complicated of these was that of Thetan in the episode "Architects of Fear." He was an extraterrestrial with long, apelike arms and three-jointed legs. Prohaska's feet were inserted into the rigid sections of the legs, which ended in paws, while he manipulated the stilts that served as his arms. Hundreds of TV stations deemed the creature too frightening and refused to air the episode, while others substituted a black screen for the close-ups of the monster or rescheduled the broadcast at the end of the evening! *The Outer Limits* disappeared after two seasons, but as Stephen King has often said, it remains "the best science fiction series ever produced for television."

James Shigeta and John Anderson, who is wearing the makeup of the Ebonites in the episode "Nightmare"
Photo courtesy of Festival Channel

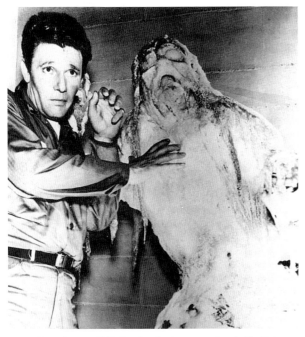

Harry Guardino and Chill Charlie, the frozen creature in the Outer Limits *episode "The Human Factor"*

The monster animated in stop-motion by Jim Danforth in the episode "Counterweight"

In the episode "The Winged Avenger" from The Avengers, *John Steed (Patrick Macnee) and Emma Peel track down a comic book character that has come to life. During the final confrontation, everybody fights while walking on the ceiling! The fantasy, as well as the restrained but effective special effects, contributed to the inimitable charm of the series.*

The robot accused of murder in the episode "I, Robot"

Banished creatures on the ground in the episode "The Zanti Misfits." These articulated puppets were animated in stop-motion.

One of the extraterrestrials from the episode "The Keeper of the Purple Twilight," and replicas of these cult characters

Photos courtesy of Festival Channel and Sideshow Toys

The Pyrotechnical Effects of *Combat!*

The series *Combat!* (1962–67) described the journey of an American patrol in Europe during World War II. A. D. Flowers was in charge of simulating the impacts of shells and the explosions of grenades that peppered each episode. He would start by digging a hole in the ground and in it would place an iron pot that held a charge of black powder wrapped in plastic and adhesive tape. A small fuse attached to an electric wire was put in the middle of the charge. Flowers then stacked sheets of cork over it, followed by pieces of synthetic sponge that looked like lumps of earth. He managed to camouflage the hole by covering it with organic foam and dirt that was sifted to remove any pebbles. The electric wire that ran along the ground was also camouflaged. When the director gave the signal, Flowers would explode the charge with a single electric impulse. Because of the flared walls of the pot, which worked like the stock of a cannon, the fragments would be projected upward. No one was hurt by the falling fake rubble, as it was very lightweight. Other pyrotechnical effects made it possible to shoot scenes of fires without causing damage to the sets at the MGM studios, where the series was filmed. Flowers would spread out a network of

Pyrotechnical effects created by A. D. Flowers for the series Combat!
Photos courtesy of the Earl Parker estate

gas burners on top of roofs or behind the walls of buildings. All he had to do was turn the valve on a butane canister, and flames would instantly surge or become extinguished. Smoke producers placed throughout the set and some charred props in the foreground completed the illusion. The impact of bullets was achieved in two ways. The traditional method entailed

inserting a small explosive charge in a hole that had already been drilled into a wooden board or the wall of a set. The hole would be filled in with putty and painted over. The explosion would be electrically triggered. To simulate the impact on walls that could not be destroyed, Flowers would use an air gun to project gelatin capsules filled with dust. As opposed to small fights, large battles are very expensive. One episode of *Combat!* portrayed the annihilation of a French village by German troops. During the preparation of this sequence, Flowers had twenty assistants working with him. They worked for two days distributing fifteen thousand bullet holes, at $1.30 apiece, throughout the set. Three hundred thousand feet (ninety-one thousand meters) of electrical wire were used in order to set off the charges from a distance. Adding the costs of supplies to the salaries of the employees ($25,000), the budget for the gun battle reached $44,500. Other scenes were less complicated. Projectiles shot from air guns made it possible to simulate bullets being shot at the Jeeps at a lower cost. A gelatin capsule filled with a transparent gel and a small black disk crashing into the windshield would simulate the appearance of a hole in the glass. Aluminum powder mixed into the same transparent gel would give the impression of stripping the paint off the metal chassis without actually doing any damage to the vehicle. Toward the end of his career, A. D. Flowers would create the effects for some major motion pictures such as *Tora! Tora! Tora!* (1970) and *The Poseidon Adventure* (1972), each of which won him an Oscar for best special effects.

The famous Batmobile in the series Batman *(1966–68) was created by George Barris, one of the great specialists of custom-made cars completely fabricated for television and film. Barris created two more Batmobiles, for the movies* Batman *and* Batman Forever.

Photos courtesy of George Barris

The original robot of the series Lost in Space *(1965–68), which can be seen at the Powerhouse Museum in Sydney, Australia. It is made of resin and fiberglass and was animated by an actor.*

The Robinson family's exploration vehicle is attacked by an improbable monster in an episode of Lost in Space.

Photo courtesy of Fox Television

Hal Holbrook played legendary writer Mark Twain in the show Mark Twain Tonight *(1967)*. The actor wore foam rubber prosthetics on his face, and latex wrinkles were added to his hands. Dick Smith developed a paint that had a liquid latex and acrylic base to cover these prosthetics. Once dry and powdered to give it a matte finish, it protected Holbrook's white suit from becoming stained. This complicated makeup won an Emmy Award.
Photo courtesy of Dick Smith

The hideous face of Dorian Grey, made by Dick Smith for a TV production of The Picture of Dorian Grey *(1961)*
Photo courtesy of Dick Smith

The crew of an experimental spaceship crash-lands on a planet populated with giants in the series Land of the Giants *(1968–70)*, produced by Irwin Allen. Each episode required complex optical effects and the construction of giant props, such as this butterfly net and these laboratory materials.
Photos courtesy of Fox Television

The cargo spacecraft Thunderbird 2 *exits its secret hangar on Tracy Island.*   Photo © ITC. Licensed by Carlton International

Liftoff of the Thunderbird 1 *rocket*
Photo © ITC. Licensed by Carlton International

A Super-production in Miniature

In September 1965, new TV credits captivated young English audiences. Marionettes were seen driving futuristic vehicles in a setting similar to that of a disaster film. The off-camera voice intones, "5 . . . 4 . . . 3 . . . 2 . . . 1 . . . Thunderbirds are go!" while a montage gave a glimpse of the dangerous rescue they were embarking upon. The superb series *Thunderbirds* was the creation of Gerry and Sylvia Anderson. It took place in 2026. Jeff Tracy, a former astronaut who had become a millionaire, retired to an island in the Pacific, where he built a lavish home in which he lived with his five sons, Scott, Virgil, Alan, Gordon, and John. This paradisaical setting was also the headquarters of International Rescue, a secret organization founded by Tracy to conduct all sorts of rescue operations. The

underground hangars on the island housed impressive supplies: rockets, a cargo jet, and a submarine invented by "Brains." The English agent at International Rescue was Lady Penelope, a pretty blonde who went around in a six-wheeled pink Rolls-Royce, chauffeured by her majordomo, Parker. The television audiences that followed the adventures of the marionettes immediately fell under the spell of their miniature world. The sets, the costumes, and the props were remarkably crafted. The characters' lips were animated by electromagnets and automatically synchronized with the actors' prerecorded sound track. The vehicles were conceived and filmed by the wonderful Derek Meddings, who later would create the visual effects for *Superman*, *Batman,* and several James Bond movies. Controlled by metal wires, the models of the *Thunderbirds* were equipped with

small motors that deployed their wings and their landing gear at the right moment. Flames and plumes of smoke would erupt from their engines during liftoff, activated by pyrotechnical charges triggered by an electrical impulse that traveled the length of the supporting wire. Each episode cost on average twenty-two thousand pounds sterling (forty thousand dollars, thirty-three thousand euros), an investment in quality worth paying for. Twenty-two inches (fifty-six centimeters) long, the Thunderbird marionettes count among the great stars of television history. They appeared in the movies *Thunderbirds Are Go!* (1966) and *Thunderbird 6* (1968), as well as dozens of TV commercials and music videos, including *Calling Elvis* by Dire Straits, and inspired the live-action *Thunderbirds* movie released in 2004.

The rocket Thunderbird 3 *draws up alongside the orbital base* Thunderbird 5, *which picks up all the distress signals from Earth. This image is a superb reconstruction of a scene from the series, photographed and staged by Martin Bower, using his models.*

Scott Tracy at the commands of Thunderbird 1

Virgil Tracy, *pilot of* Thunderbird 2, *welcomes Brains (left) and Gordon (right) into his vehicle.*

Lady Penelope, *the most glamorous star of* Thunderbirds

Lady Penelope's *fabulous six-wheeled pink Rolls-Royce had a bevy of formidable gadgets.*

Parker: *chauffeur, majordomo, and bodyguard to Lady Penelope*

Filming a casino scene forced the handlers to work in a very limited space. Their task here was more difficult than when filming the marionettes in close-up, as each gesture had to be extremely precise.

The brilliant Derek Meddings, who conceived of the amazing Thunderbirds *vehicles, is an indisputable master of miniature special effects.*

INTERVIEW

TERRY CURTIS

Backstage with "Supermarionation"

Terry Curtis and reconstructions of some of the marionettes he created for the series Thunderbirds *and* Captain Scarlet
Photo courtesy of Terry Curtis

Terry Curtis at work in the puppet studio of Anderson Productions
Photo courtesy of Terry Curtis

Sculptor Terry Curtis was a member of the team that created the marionettes for the celebrated series by Gerry and Sylvia Anderson: *Thunderbirds, Captain Scarlet,* and *Joe 90.*

What sort of mechanisms did you install in the heads of the marionettes in "Thunderbirds"?

Terry Curtis: There was a support placed in the center of the head, between the eyes. The eyes were orbs one inch (two and a half centimeters) in diameter that could pivot on their axis. The screws that jutted out behind the orbs were linked by a small joint. By pulling on the

two wires, a mechanism made it possible to move the eyes left and right. The mechanism controlling the lips functioned by an electromagnet attached to a small mount that was activated by a 50-volt impulse. The tungsten wires that we used to carry the current up to the head didn't conduct properly. The upper ends of the wires were plugged into 75 volts, so that the electromagnet at the other end would receive 50 volts.

Did you have to sculpt the shape of the heads to take into account the space occupied by these mechanisms?

Terry Curtis: There were two types of heads: the heroes' heads, which were sculpted in plasticine, molded, and then cast in resin and fiberglass, and the

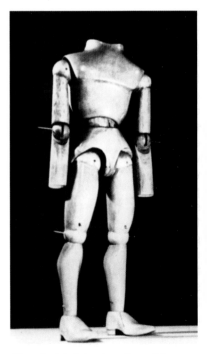

The articulated structure of one of the characters in Thunderbirds
Photo © ITC. Licensed by Carlton International

Storing Thunderbirds *marionettes*
Photo © ITC. Licensed by Carlton International

heads of the background characters that only appeared in one or
two episodes, in different roles,
and were made of polystyrene
sculpted with a sharp blade and
covered in a thin coat of smooth
plasticine. Once the sculpture
was finished, three coats of
paint were applied, and once it
dried, it was lightly sanded and
then got two more coats of an
oil-based paint. Once it was
completely dry, the exterior surface of the face was solid
enough to withstand light hits
without flaking. The lower lip
was attached to the chin by a
piece of leather painted the
same color as the rest of the
face. All that remained was to
glue the fake eyelashes onto the
upper lid and paint lashes onto
the lower lid. When we had to
simulate a two- or three-day
beard on the characters, we
used a little bit of ocher and
burnt sienna paint and, using a
pretty dry paintbrush over the
bottom of the face, made strokes
to imitate the hair texture.

*Are there different versions
of the heads of the principal
characters?*

Terry Curtis: Yes. The heads of
the heroes were sculpted in
plasticine and molded with silicone. We made six resins and
fiberglass casts of each head.
Each copy had a specific role.
Two heads were used for normal
shots. Another was kept in
reserve for extreme close-ups.
It had to be perfect to the
minutest details. We made a
fourth head with a smiling
expression, using the original
cast as a base and then modifying the shape of the mouth. The
fifth head was nicknamed the
"worrywart" because it had to
express the tension of the characters in danger. We sculpted
knitted eyebrows, eyes somewhat less open, and a pursed
mouth. The sixth head was a
"blinker," which is to say it had
very delicate leather eyelids
that could open and close. This
head was used to film scenes in

which the characters were
asleep or knocked unconscious.
The teeth came from stores that
sold dental prosthetics. We
used teeth from the lower jaw,
the smallest that we could find,
to create a character's full dental structure.

*How many different bodies
did each principal character have?*

Terry Curtis: Two or three. Each
pilot had a body dressed in an
International Rescue uniform
and a body dressed in a comfortable outfit that it wore when
relaxing on Tracy Island. Once
in a while, a third body would
be dressed in a tuxedo or some
special attire. The bodies of all
the pilots were interchangeable,
so Virgil's uniform or tuxedo
could be worn by Alan or Gordon
in another scene. Occasionally,
accidents happened. I remember one day when several wires
of one marionette broke at the

same time during a tracking shot. The marionette fell under the wheels of the dolly (the rolling camera mount) and was crushed. Another time, some characters hit their faces against a part of the scenery and had to be repaired very fast so they could be filmed the following day.

Weren't you also asked to do the "makeup" for the marionettes during the filming?

Terry Curtis: Absolutely! When a character had to appear tired, we drew in dark rings under his eyes with a colored grease pencil that could easily be removed without damaging the base color. We also had to simulate small cuts and bruises, and we would spray a mixture of water and glycerin to imitate perspiration. The makeup became much more sophisticated in series like *Captain Scarlet,* where the characters were of more realistic sizes.

Who chose the look of each character?

Terry Curtis: Sylvia Anderson. She would come see us and say, "This character must have a rather square jaw and a rather hard expression." Or she would mention a celebrity whom we'd have to use as inspiration, but not copy. I was inspired by Sean Connery's face when I created Paul Travers, the captain of spaceship *OX* in the movie *Thunderbirds Are Go!*

Why do you think the Thunderbird marionettes were so popular?

Terry Curtis: Their charm is due to their unrealistic proportions. From head to toe, they measured twenty-one and a half inches (fifty-five centimeters), but the head alone measured four and a half inches (eleven and a half centimeters). So the head was almost two times larger than normal. All that changed when we started working on the following series, *Captain Scarlet.* The marionettes became more realistic, and everything was changed from A to Z—the bodies, the heads, the mechanisms, etc. They became miniature humans and lost the inherent charm of the marionettes. I also worked on the two series *Joe 90* and *Secret Service.* Following that, I worked on a test character for a project that was to take place on Atlantis, but it never got developed beyond that because Gerry had already embarked on the production of his first movie with real actors, which was

entitled *Doppelgänger.* When the filming of the Supermarionation was finished, we simply turned the page. Since we were used to seeing these marionettes every day, constructing them, repairing them, they were not at all sacred in our eyes. When the filming was over, Gerry and Sylvia Anderson wanted to keep them, but the rest of the team had no interest. I was one of the few people who took the opportunity to save some, but for the most part, they were thrown into the garbage can. The studio, which was an old factory, was bought by a company and returned to its original use. We had to quickly empty the place and get rid of all the sets and props. Most of the spaceships and engines were saved, but practically everything else disappeared, even the molds. No one imagined these characters would become pop culture icons, and that each marionette would be worth a fortune!

You've made limited-edition replicas of some of the marionettes.

Terry Curtis: Yes. I re-created the Paul Travers character from the movie *Thunderbirds Are Go!* and I was able to find one marionette of Captain Blue from *Captain Scarlet.* The little

boy who salvaged it had added
a scar to make it look like
Action Man! He had taken off
the original hair and glued on
some of his sister's hair any
which way and had blackened
the teeth! I cleaned it and completely took it apart, and made
new molds from these pieces.
Before the auction, Christie's
had estimated the value of
these first two marionettes at
between 5,000 and 7,000
pounds sterling (9,000 to
12,700 dollars; 7,500 to
11,000 euros). Each character
takes two hundred hours of
work, not counting the problems associated with the reconstruction process. The hands of
the original marionettes were
made of vinyl. A company made
them by injecting the material
into metal molds. When I asked
a doll producer to make fifty
pairs of hands, he told me it
would cost 15,000 pounds
sterling (27,000 dollars;
25,000 euros)! I had to go
through all sorts of experiments
to make one good pair of hands.
The mouth and eye mecha-
nisms worked, but I didn't put
electromagnets in the marionettes, because no one had a
70-volt electric current source.
I also made replicas of Captain
Grey, whom I had sculpted at
the time.

*Captain Scarlet was
also manipulated from
below with cables dur-
ing the filming of
extreme close-ups.
The upper wires gen-
erally used to animate
the puppets would
have been obvious in
such tight framing.*
Photo © ITC. Licensed by
Carlton International

Characters in Captain
Scarlet *had realistic
proportions.*
Photo © ITC. Licensed by
Carlton International

Star Trek: The Special Effects of a Cult Series

In 1964, screenwriter Gene Roddenberry imagined a series with the look of a space western: *Wagon to the Stars*. He fine-tuned it into the idea for *Star Trek,* and NBC agreed to produce the pilot episode, entitled "The Cage." Roddenberry wanted to make his portrayal of the twenty-third century credible, so he consulted scientists at NASA, who convinced him that the engines of the spaceship *Enterprise* had to be placed far from the living

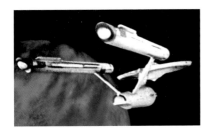

The starship Enterprise *in orbit around a planet* Photo courtesy of Paramount Pictures

Two matte paintings from Star Trek. *Visual effects meant it wasn't necessary to construct expensive sets to represent the surfaces of visited planets.*

quarters, at the ends of independent mounts, to reduce risk in case of malfunction. Military people helped him establish the hierarchy within the spaceship and the functioning of the United Federation of Planets, to which it was connected. Howard A. Anderson and artistic director Matt Jeffries closely collaborated on the design of the *Enterprise*. They constructed three models: one 3 inches (7.62 centimeters) long, another 36.5 inches (91 centimeters) long, and a third 14 feet (4.26 meters) long, which

would be used in all the shots of it approaching. The spaceship was supposed to travel several times faster than the speed of light, a difficult concept to depict in images. Anderson decided to work more on the background than on the movements of the model of the spaceship. He had large white panels made on which were painted black points. These panels were filmed over several takes in a series of tracking shots of varying speed. The points that became magnified in

the frame the fastest gave the impression of being closer, while those that moved slower appeared to be farther away. With an optical printer, these different shots were combined into a single film. The negative of this composite image thus showed hundreds of white points—stars—that moved in the darkness of space. With a traveling matte, the *Enterprise* could be inserted into this starry background. The final effect showed the spaceship traveling so fast that the stars shot past it.

The famous teleportation effect in Star Trek   Photo courtesy of Paramount Pictures

"Beam Me Up, Scotty!"

Roddenberry simplified the arrival of his heroes on unknown worlds thanks to the system of teleportation. Rather than filming the landing scenes with models, he contented himself with shooting the actors on the set of the *Enterprise* and then had them appear in the middle of the otherworldly landscape made in the studio. Anderson would use a simple fade to depict the teleportation, but he wanted to develop an effect that would become one of the visual references of *Star Trek*. He would start by filming the actors taking their places on the teleporter contacts and then, having them remain perfectly still, would slowly close the diaphragm of the camera to obtain a black background. The actors then left the set, which was filmed a second time, now empty. Anderson also made use of a negative copy to draw mattes of the actors' silhouettes. These black outlines on a white background were filmed to generate a negative countermatte—that is, white silhouettes on a black background. Anderson would then film aluminum flecks that he sprinkled into a very brightly illuminated beam. With

an optical printer, he could insert the images of the silvery flecks into the outlines of the silhouettes, using the matte produced earlier. The sparkling effect would appear and disappear during the fades. And one of the most famous special effects on television was born! Other effects came about in the actors' dressing rooms. Makeup artist Fred B. Phillips asked John Chambers to conceive of pointed ears for Mr. Spock. Phillips first lightly attached Leonard Nimoy's ears onto his neck before gluing on the foam rubber appliances. Nimoy also shaved the outer half of his eyebrows, which were then extended upward with hairpieces. In the pilot episode, Captain Pike (Jeffrey Hunter) is abducted by extraterrestrials who collect beings from far-off planets. His kidnappers are endowed with hypertrophic foam rubber skulls, on which their pulsing inflatable veins can be seen. Fred Phillips accentuated the oddness of these characters by suggesting the casting of two actresses with tiny faces whose voices were replaced with male actors' voices in editing. NBC liked the pilot but considered its plot "too intellectual" and Spock's look much too diaboli-

cal—the Vulcan had to go! Roddenberry made some concessions but refused to throw out Spock, declaring that he'd be one of the most popular characters of the series. NBC was swayed and requested a second *Star Trek* pilot episode to fine-tune the details. As Jeffrey Hunter had other commitments, William Shatner became the captain of the *Enterprise*. The second pilot, "Where No Man Has Gone Before," was accepted by NBC and broadcast in 1966. In all, seventy-nine episodes were broadcast. *Star Trek* left the airwaves in 1969, only to reappear first as an animated series, then at the movies, and finally with more than one "New Generation" replacing the original crew on the small and then the large screen.

Mr. Spock (Leonard Nimoy) and Sulu (George Takei), in conversation aboard the Enterprise. *Spock's famous pointed ears were created by John Chambers.*
Photo courtesy of Paramount Pictures

A drawing of the Star Trek: The Next Generation *set, with a cyclorama and a false-perspective lake*   Drawing by R. Delgado

Extraterrestrials in the pilot episode "The Cage"   Photo courtesy of Paramount Pictures

The first version of the Enterprise, *which appeared in the eponymic series that took place in the near future.* Opposite: *The new* Enterprise *used in* Star Trek: The Next Generation
Photo courtesy of Paramount Home Video

Mission: Impossible: A "Story Within the Story" of Special Effects

Another important series debuted in 1966: *Mission: Impossible*. Television audiences were fascinated by the exploits of Daniel Briggs and Jim Phelps, the successive heads of the team of secret agents that included Barney Collier, an all-around engineer; Cinnamon Carter, the polymorphic high-fashion model; Willy Armitage, the strongman; and Rollin Hand, the makeup wizard. During the credits, a rapid-fire montage showed the ingenious special effects that would soon be used to trick an array of dictators, unscrupulous businessmen, and all sorts of criminals. Paradoxically, the series used real special effects to realize some impossible effects, such as the transformations of Rollin Hand (Martin Landau). Landau's first on-screen metamorphosis was a believable presentation of makeup procedures: the application of foam rubber appliances created by John Chambers. Landau took on the look of a South American dictator, rigged out with a soft plastic fake skull and wig, false teeth, and a series of appliances to give him bags under his eyes, a double chin, and a new nose, all underscored by a thin mustache.

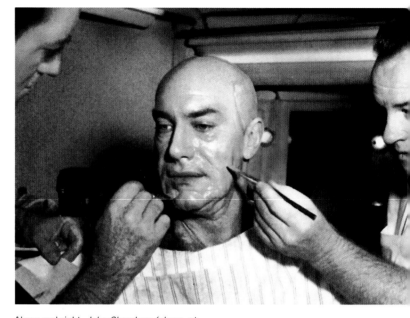

Above and right: *John Chambers (above, at right) transforms Martin Landau into a South American dictator during the filming of the pilot episode of* Mission: Impossible
Photo courtesy of Paramount Home Video

The Impossible Missions Force team all together
Photo courtesy of Paramount Home Video

In subsequent episodes, the makeup sessions were simplified to the point of absurdity. Rollin Hand would merely pour some liquid, flesh-colored rubber into a mold and then remove a latex mask, which he would glue onto his face in a matter of seconds. The rigid rubber turned into an

Willy (Peter Lupus) blows up an inflatable mannequin of Torin Thatcher, made by Bob Dawn. Photo courtesy of Bob Dawn

The exploits of Steve Austin, the hero of The Six Million Dollar Man (1974–78), were often shown using trampolines, slow motion, and fixed props that actor Lee Majors could easily destroy. Photo courtesy of Universal Television

incredibly malleable material and Rollin became the villain's double, whatever the shape of his face! Obviously, the actor whose face was depicted by the mask would replace Martin Landau through an editing effect. It was also through editing that the famous "mask pull-off" shot was achieved. The actor who played the role of the disguised Rollin Hand would pretend to grab his neck, hiding his face with his forearm. A cutaway shot showed the person who was watching him do this. Then the real Martin Landau, his face covered by a latex mask in the likeness of the other actor, would appear in the following shot, immediately pulling off this mask. The trick was played!

The most outlandish makeup job ever to appear on *Mission: Impossible* was prepared by Willy. He was shown spraying the contents of an aerosol can over the face of some unconscious villain stretched out on the floor. The product transformed into a rigid plastic mold, which was then easily lifted off. Willy poured in the contents of a small vial and quickly got a perfectly malleable mask, replete with eyebrows. . . . John Chambers, Dan Striepeke, and Bob Dawn, the makeup artists for the series, would certainly have been thrilled to have such products at their disposal! Other wonderful effects were actually conducted in front of the camera, such as the inflatable mannequin created by Bob Dawn from a mold of actor Torin Thatcher. The interior wall of the latex likeness was outfitted with inflatable reinforced rings. The flaccid character took shape as soon as Dawn released air into the rings. It was seen in the episode "The Numbers Game," in which the Impossible Missions Force places this plastic double inside an oxygen tent so that those close to him will not realize he has disappeared. The "stage" effects conceived by Jonnie Burke were also astounding. In an episode entitled "The Mercenaries," Barney drills a hole into a strong room filled with gold and inserts an apparatus that opens up like a metal umbrella. The gadget gives off such tremen-

dous heat that the gold bars melt and pour through the hole directly into a series of molds that return them to their original form! In reality, the gold ingots were ice cream bars covered in gold paint that Jonnie Burke melted with actinogens. Just like doubles of the secret agents, the *Mission: Impossible* special effects team would achieve great feats behind the scenes throughout the run of the series, which ended in 1973.

Jim Henson's Magical Puppets

Thanks to television, a genius named Jim Henson revolutionized the art of puppetry forever. Like Walt Disney in his realm of animation, Henson was a tireless innovator, capable of giving life to the nuttiest of characters. He made his first hand puppets, the cloth faces of which would lose shape in funny ways, when he was seventeen years old. In 1954, he was hired by television station WTOP in Washington, D.C., where his stylized characters excelled in comical improvisations. Moving on to WRC-TV in 1955, Henson created the show *Sam and Friends,* which was a laboratory of ideas. The hand puppets moved around in sets placed above the extended arms of the puppeteers. The sketches and song routines were identifiably the precursors to *The Muppet Show.* Henson made the first Kermit from an oval piece of cardboard folded in half to form the mouth, a piece of cloth cut from one of his mother's coats, and two halves of a Ping-Pong ball. This simplest of puppets would become the most famous one in the world. Henson was not content merely to repeat this formula. He tested new materials, animated puppets with cables and mechanisms, and directed ever more complicated routines on his show and then in com-

mercials, where the spontaneity of the Muppets worked wonders. Don Sahlin then invented a sewing method—which came to be known as "the Muppets seam"—that made the seams in the cloth invisible. He also came up with the concept of the walk-on character made of detachable pieces: a smooth head with a mouth, onto which eyes, a nose, and a little wig could be quickly attached with Velcro. Rowlf the dog was the first Muppet to be handled by two people. Jim Henson placed his left hand in the head and his right hand in the dog's right paw, while an assistant animated the left paw. The doggie pianist was a triumph on *The Ed Sullivan Show,* the most famous television variety show of the 1960s. The Big Bird character, an eight-foot-tall (two-and-a-half-meter) yellow bird was created for *Sesame Street* and handled by Caroll Spinney, who hid inside the costume. His left arm animated the bird's head, and his right hand the right wing. He could see only through a small window in the yellow tulle, which was partially hidden by the feathers. As the filming of a scene demanded great precision, a small television monitor was set into Big Bird's belly so its movements could be better controlled. Later, Snuffy the elephant, who was handled by two people, would become the largest of all the Muppets.

In 1975, Henson asked Michael K. Frith to construct the puppets for a new sequence on *Saturday Night Live,* using the glass eyes that taxidermists work with. Although the sequence lasted only one year, it gave Henson the desire to create more realistic characters. Following the triumph of *The Muppet Show,* he made the movie *The Dark Crystal* (1982). The main characters were fitted with remote-control facial mechanisms that made it possible for the handlers to concentrate on the more important body movements. It was during this period that Jim Henson's Creature Shop was born, where more and more complex animatronic puppets were manufactured. At the same time, producer Gary Kurtz asked Henson to help him conceive Yoda, whose face would be sculpted by makeup artist Stuart Freeborn. Henson's experience and the talents of Frank Oz as a puppeteer would make the Jedi master one of the most outstanding characters in *The Empire Strikes Back.* George Lucas was impressed and in 1986 decided to coproduce, with Henson, the movie *Labyrinth.* The Creature Shop next expressed its expertise in the remarkable series *The Storyteller* (1987), which presented original versions of stories and myths from ancient Greece and other parts of Europe. Marvelous mythological creatures appeared throughout this production, which Henson considered to be one of his most successful achievements. His last effort was *Muppetvision 3-D* (1990), a superb attraction presented at the Disney-MGM Studios theme park in Florida and at Disney's California Adventure park in California. Following his death on May 16, 1990, his collaborators and family remained loyal to his vision and sense of innovation. That same year, the Creature Shop invented the Henson Performance Control System, a prerecorded computer data transmission system that, by remote control, animated the animatronic masks in *Teenage Mutant Ninja Turtles*. The turtles' "pronunciation" movements (jaws, upper and lower lips, rounding and elongating of the mouth) were synchronized with the prerecorded dialogues. During filming, the turtles spoke to a playback of their voices, allowing their handlers to activate their expressions live, by remote control. This technique was awarded an Oscar in 1992 and has been used in movies such as *The Flintstones* (1994) and *Cats & Dogs* (2001), as well as in the television series *Dinosaurs* (1990). A transposition of this system was used to manipulate the computer-generated characters in real time. Branches of Jim Henson's Creature Shop in London are located in Los Angeles, New York, and Sydney.

Dave Goelz, Jerry Nelson, Jim Henson, and Frank Oz during a recording of The Muppet Show. *One can see how all the sets were elevated to correspond with the height of a puppet held at arm's length.*

INTERVIEW

JIM HENSON

Jim Henson and the Muppets

Jim Henson, who died on May 16, 1990, was one of television's great innovators. Here is a previously unpublished interview conducted with him in 1983, at the time of the release of his movie *The Dark Crystal*.

Were you fascinated by puppets from a very early age?

Jim Henson: Oddly, I never played with puppets when I was a child. I created my first char-acters in the hopes of getting a job in television! I thought up Kermit in the 1950s, when I was seventeen years old, for a show on a Washington station. I didn't study the works of the French, German, and Swiss pup-peteers until two years later. It was then that I fell in love with this extremely rich art form that allows for the expression of a vast array of emotions.

You've always used the latest techniques to animate the faces of your characters.

Jim Henson: Yes. Ever since we debuted on television, our char-acters were filmed in close-up. We had to find the means to ani-mate their faces to make them interesting. At the beginning, their heads were simply cloth envelopes bent out of shape by hand. Over the years, we used more complicated mechanisms and other materials—sculpted polyurethane foam and then foam rubber. With the help of Dick Smith, we learned how to use it to create whole characters.

It's amusing to think of Dick Smith, who created the terrifying makeup for "The Exorcist," help-ing you make these wonderfully funny puppets.

Jim Henson: Maybe one day we'll make a parody of *The Exorcist,* with Miss Piggy as a possessed pig. (*Laughs.*)

Were you surprised by the extraor-dinary success of "Sesame Street" (starting in 1969) and then "The Muppet Show"?

Jim Henson: Yes. *Sesame Street* was a show made on a very low budget, but it immedi-ately captivated young children. We were proud to contribute to their learning to read and do arithmetic while being enter-tained by our jokes. I have a particular fondness for charac-ters like Ernie, Bert, and Big Bird, who was our first giant puppet, constructed with very light structures. As for *The Muppet Show,* it was an innova-tive concept that we tried in vain to produce in the United States. We had to construct raised sets that concealed the puppeteers in the lower portion of the frame, but could let the guests appear in the upper por-tion with our characters. It was thanks to Sir Lew Grade that we found the financing for this series in England. Its worldwide success went far beyond our hopes.

Kira and Jen, the heroes of the movie The Dark Crystal *(1982), codirected by Jim Henson and Frank Oz, riding on Landstriders*
Photo courtesy of ITC Entertainment

How did you come up with Kermit, Miss Piggy, and your other characters?

Jim Henson: Most of them came about spontaneously, for no apparent reason. I was still a kid when I made the first Kermit, who still wasn't yet a frog. It was just . . . a thing! Miss Piggy's personality evolved little by little. She first appeared as a secondary character and ended up a star, thanks to Frank Oz's acting performance. All these characters, little by little, attained a depth of credibility that we never predicted.

Will Miss Piggy one day receive the Oscar that she covets?

Jim Henson: As it's a given that my friend Frank Oz animates Miss Piggy, the Academy will have to decide whether to nominate her for best actor or for best actress!

You used complicated video effects in the series "Fraggle Rock."

Jim Henson: Yes. The characters in this series, the Fraggles, evolved in large subterranean sets. The puppets were about six inches (fifteen centimeters). Some of them were radio remote-controlled. You could see them drive the construction site equipment and build the structures. Others were controlled by handlers entirely dressed, masked, and gloved in blue in front of a blue background. The puppets could then be inserted into the set that had previously been filmed. You could see different Fraggles animated in different ways evolving in the same image.

Two characters in the episode "Hans My Hedgehog" from the sublime series The Storyteller, *which Jim Henson considered his most beautiful creation*
Photo © 2003 The Jim Henson Company

Did you record the performances of the handlers on video during the rehearsals?

Jim Henson: Yes, with several cameras in order to get close-up shots and wide-angle shots. It's indispensable to have an overview of all that's going on simultaneously on the stage. It's only afterward that we could give cues to the puppeteers.

You seem to have a weakness for ugly characters, like the Skekses of "The Dark Crystal," but you avoid the cliché "ugly equals nasty." Often your most attractive characters are blessed with outrageous mugs.

Jim Henson: I love to play with the clichés laid down by film and television. When the witch Aughra appeared for the first time in *The Dark Crystal,* she took her eye into her hand to look through it like a periscope! This classic appearance of a witch didn't keep her from being the generous character who saved our heroes.

Have you already envisioned animating some characters by stop-motion?

Jim Henson: We dreamed of using the Go-Motion system created by ILM to animate the quadruped waders—the Landstriders. Ultimately, we built stilts, on which the handlers dressed in costumes made them move. A live performance always brings an additional human warmth. I think this is what characterizes our work.

Space: 1999: The Legacy of *2001: A Space Odyssey* on Television

After having produced their puppet series, Gerry and Sylvia Anderson came up with the major science fiction series of the 1970s: *Space: 1999* (1975–77). The first episode, "Breakaway," introduced us to Moonbase Alpha, which had a large nuclear waste dump. On September 13, 1999, an accident occurred: an atomic explosion propelled the moon out of orbit, far from Earth. The small community at Alpha started off on a long float into space, encountering unlikely threats and creatures that always spoke English. *Space: 1999* was endowed with a budget of $6.8 million during its first season, which ended up being the better of the two. The quality of the sets and effects is exceptional. Brian Johnson, the special effects supervisor, once again put to use the expertise he had acquired working on *2001: A Space Odyssey*. The sequences with the actors were filmed in 16 millimeter, but Johnson filmed the scenes with the models in 35 millimeter to take advantage of the stability that a film with double perforation affords. It was an essential feature for making effects that were based on double exposure. The miniatures of his *Eagle* spaceships were furnished with

The famous Eagles, *spaceships of Moonbase Alpha*

A space battle in the episode "Wargames"
Photos © ITC. Licensed by Carlton International

crossed metal bars that extended from one side to the other. The spaceships could then be hooked to mounts in the front, the back, and the sides. To film the flight of an *Eagle* through space, Johnson first attached the model to a mount concealed behind a piece of black velvet, and then placed it in front of a black background. The camera, mounted on a dolly, tracked toward the nose of the spaceship in order to create the impression that the rocket was moving toward the camera. A matte was used to block out that part of the frame in which the vessel did not travel. Johnson then fashioned a counter-matte to block out the trajectory of the spaceship,

rewound the film in the camera, and shot some stars and part of the planet in those sectors of the frame that were still empty. The composite he got was a first-generation effect. Differing from the visual effects on *Star Trek,* which were the product of several copies of a given image made using an optical printer, and were thus often grainy, the visual effects shots in *Space: 1999* were perfectly sharp and flawless. Johnson also used the *2001* approach to film the miniature landscapes at Moonbase Alpha. The buildings located in the foreground were wooden models covered in plastic from model kits sold in toy stores. The crater and the lunar surface were made out of plas-

ter. The mountains that appear in the background were photographs cut out and arranged on three planes of depth. They give the impression of a far-off horizon. The depth effect created with this photographic montage, quite similar to a multiplane installation, also made it possible to film vertical tracking shots, such as the one that was used during the famous nuclear explosion scene in the first episode. The 1976 television audience was so impressed by Brian Johnson's special effects that George Lucas, who was in the midst of filming *Star Wars,* would tell his crew that he hoped they would create effects "at least as good as those in *Space: 1999!*"

A set created for the second season Photo courtesy of Martin Bower

Brian Johnson and Nick Alder holding different-scaled miniature models of the lunar jeep in Space: 1999. *Seen behind them, mounted vertically, is the model of Moonbase Alpha.*
Photo © ITC. Licensed by Carlton International

Martin Bower and one of the twenty-two-inch (fifty-five-centimeter) Eagles constructed for the second season
Photo courtesy of Martin Bower

INTERVIEW

MARTIN BOWER

Martin Bower is one of the greatest specialists in spaceship models. His creations have appeared on television in the series *Space: 1999* and at the movies in *Alien, Flash Gordon,* and *Outland*.

How did you come to be a specialist in the construction of science fiction models?

Martin Bower: When I was a child, I was deeply affected by the marionette series on TV called *Supercar* and by Ray Harryhausen's *First Men in the Moon* (1964). I was fascinated by those creatures and by the sphere the explorers used to get to the moon. I became a lover of science fiction models for the rest of my life, to the great disappointment of my father, who thought I should have chosen a serious field! I started out by making replicas of the flying car in *Supercar* and the rocket from another series by Gerry Anderson, *Fireball XL5*. When I was fifteen years old, I filmed little Super-8 movies, which made me want to make manipulated photographs with models.

Bower today, with the shuttle from Outland, which he recently found and repaired.
Photo courtesy of Martin Bower

In 1969, Martin Bower already had a passion for model making. He constructed this rocket and liftoff pad largely from recycled objects.
Photo courtesy of Martin Bower

How did you start working on "Space: 1999"?

Martin Bower: I read an article that made a reference to a new series Gerry Anderson was about to produce. I wrote to him, and his secretary responded by suggesting I meet with Brian Johnson. Brian invited me to visit him at the Bray Studios. I filled up my car with models of spaceships in all sizes. The largest was more than 8 feet (2.5 meters). It was a rocket based on the *Discovery* in *2001: A Space Odyssey*. Brian seemed impressed and promised to call me. He kept his word; he sent me the first script that depicted extraterrestrial spaceships. Space Models workshop had already constructed three versions of the *Eagle* (the main spaceship in the series) on different scales. There was one that was 3.65 feet (1.11 meters), another 22

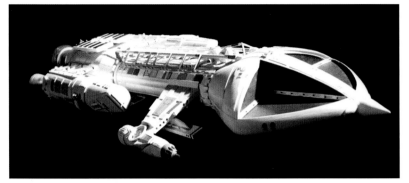

The spaceship Hawk *took on aspects of the* Eagle *spaceship of* Space: 1999.
Photo courtesy of Martin Bower

inches (55.8 centimeters), and the third 11 inches (27.9 centimeters). Brian asked me to make many additional sketches. When he saw them, he said to me, "I want one like this that's 5 feet (1.5 meters) and another like that that's 30 inches (75 centimeters). You have two weeks." I went back from the studio in such a state of elation that it took me a moment to realize that I had to make these models in no time! They were the first of the eighty-six miniature models that I made for *Space: 1999.*

Did Brian Johnson ask you to include a metal structure inside your models so they'd be able to be suspended?

Martin Bower: At the beginning, he merely drilled holes straight through for inserting the screws and nuts that were used to suspend them. Later he asked me to insert a steel tube in the center of the models in such a way that they could be attached to a mount in the front. He called me while he was preparing the special effects for the first

episode, "The Alpha Child," to ask me if he could buy my old spaceship model based on *2001,* which had fallen to pieces. I can't tell you how proud I was to see it suspended, lit, and filmed by the whole crew. Later I had the opportunity to construct some enlarged parts of the *Eagles,* like the top of the cockpit, which was equipped with a trapdoor from which emerged a laser gun. I also constructed a foot that was used for landing and liftoff scenes. I didn't make any complete models of the *Eagle* until the second season of the series—one version that was 21.6 inches (55 centimeters) and a very small version that was 4.9 inches (12.43 centimeters), which could be "swallowed" by the enormous machine in the episode "Collision Course."

How did you manage to construct these detailed models in such a short amount of time?

Martin Bower: By working day and night! The theme of the series inspired me enormously.

One of the episodes that required the most work from me was entitled "Dragon's Domain." In it, an exploration probe discovers a spaceship cemetery. I constructed two versions of the main spaceship: one 5.97 feet (1.82 meters) and a second 35.8 inches (91 centimeters), an enlarged section of the forward part that had to be on the same scale as the largest model of the *Eagle,* and the mechanisms that enabled this capsule to become detached and ejected. What's more, I had to conceive of five wrecks of spaceships. I worked from 7:30 in the morning until midnight for four weeks in order to make these six models. I tried to save time by recycling objects. This is how I created the living quarters for the episode "The Exile." I spotted in a store some dustbin lids that interested me. I said to the salespeople, "I love the shape of this dustbin. I want six of them!" They started laughing, convinced that I was completely crazy!

What kind of wood did you use to sculpt the basic form of your models?

Martin Bower: Jelutong, a species of rubber tree that produces latex. It's a wood that's very easy to saw and sand, very light, but much more solid than balsa. You get a superb rendering with a good painted finish.

Have you ever recycled parts of toys or models to create some missiles, like the lunar tanks in "Space: 1999"?

Martin Bower: I had a limited budget, so I was forced to use, as a base, store-bought toy tanks that I covered over with plastic butter dish lids! I always chose the model kits with the most details that I could rearrange my own way. I also used many disposable plastic razors and all sorts of objects that I bought in vast quantities. I would glue them in succession on my models to compose interesting shapes.

ADVENTURE IN THE FUTURE

Bower conceived an exciting new project: the series Starguard, *which he wants to produce using traditional techniques (puppets and models) to re-create the very special atmosphere of cult series. It would prove a breath of fresh air, in light of the omnipresence of computer-generated images.*

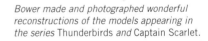

Bower made and photographed wonderful reconstructions of the models appearing in the series Thunderbirds *and* Captain Scarlet.

The Igloo Base, buried beneath the ice at the North Pole; one of the clever miniature sets designed for Starguard
Photo courtesy of Martin Bower

Battlestar Galactica: The Techniques of *Star Wars* Applied to a TV Series

In 1977, Hollywood was caught off guard by the triumph of *Star Wars*. Producer Glen A. Larson pulled out from the back of some drawer an old science fiction project entitled *Adam's Ark*. The directors of the ABC television network seized the opportunity to capitalize on the box office success of the moment. They approached Larson for a three-hour miniseries, and he contacted John Dykstra, the visual effects supervisor on *Star Wars,* and offered him the position of co-producer to convince him to translate his techniques for television. Dykstra assembled a team consisting of Ralph McQuarrie, the graphic designer of *Star Wars'* spaceships, Joe Johnston, Richard Edlund, and many other former colleagues at ILM. He simplified his methods to adapt them to the constraints of a television budget. Each shot was conceived as a potential stock shot, to be reused several times. It was during this time that Dykstra founded Apogee, his special effects studio, where he perfected his motion control equipment. This system made it possible to film spaceships against a blue background using a camera mounted on a motorized crane that moved along a dolly. The computer-controlled system could identically repeat movement and thus film different effects, which could be combined

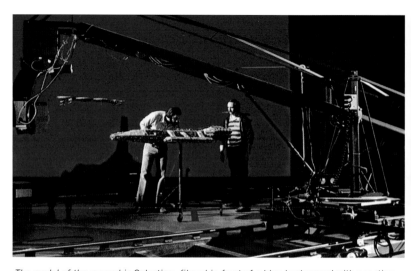

The model of the spaceship Galactica, *filmed in front of a blue background with a motion control system*   Photo courtesy of Universal Studios

by an optical printer, to create a composite shot. The model of the mother ship was made from a wooden structure covered over with pieces from store-bought model kits. Thousands of little holes were pierced into the fuselage, through which optic fibers were threaded. Neon tubes were specially shaped to mesh within the contours of the model. As they did not emit much heat, they would not damage the wood or plastic. The glaring neon illuminated the ends of the fiber optics, lighting up the entire surface of the spaceship with brilliantly luminescent spots. Dykstra also made a number of test shots for the space scenes, carefully enlarging the size of the stars so they would be visible on the small screen. The effects looked as spectacular as if they had been created for a big-budget movie. When the executives at ABC viewed the first scenes of *Battlestar Galactica,* they immediately decided to change it to a weekly series. Since it had been filmed

on 35 millimeter, they also decided to release the pilot in movie theaters all over Europe, which proved to be quite a success. In 1978, following a sensational debut on the small screen and despite the quality of its special effects, *Battlestar Galactica* saw its ratings drop. After only one season, its banal story lines bored audiences.

One of the full-scale *Viper spaceships used for filming shots with actors*
Photo courtesy of Universal Studios

The 1980s and the Diversion of Chroma-Key

Chroma-key is the simplest effect used in television. This electronic effect makes it possible to substitute a blue background, in front of which a weatherperson stands, for another image—a weather map, for example. The procedure functions by detecting the level of brightness, or light intensity, isolating the one image from all others, and replacing it with a different video image or a monochrome background pro-duced by a color generator. This effect makes it possible to create titles quickly, isolating the letters from the rest of the image. While it does work well with tones and basic light levels, it is less efficient with actors, whose skin colors and clothing run a gamut of thousands of hues. Shadows can be confused with the blue background, causing the appearance of holes in silhouettes and detailed outlines, such as static hair. New equipment was soon capable of more keenly isolating blue, orange, and green, but very high-precision keying did not appear until the end of the 1970s. The Ultimatte process made it possible to bring out fine details, such as the outline of hair, shadows, a plume of smoke, or the transparency of a glass placed before a blue background. The first effects produced this way in the 1980s were so exceptional that they rivaled the traveling mattes used in movies. No one imagined then that this technique, applied to digital images, would one day supplant insertions on film.

Different stages of a chroma-key insertion effect, produced by Bob Kertesz with the Ultimatte system
Photo courtesy of Bob Kertesz / Bluescreen LLC

Cosmos: The Wonders of the Ultimate

In 1980, astrophysicist Carl Sagan coproduced and presented the documentary series *Cosmos,* which in thirteen episodes explained the great stages of the discovery of space. From the very start of preparations for the series, Adrian Malone, the executive producer, knew that the images furnished by NASA would not meet his needs. He would have to produce spectacular views that would captivate the audience during Sagan's long presentations. Malone hired freelance technicians who had worked on *Star Wars.* He decided to represent the voyage into space by creating a "spaceship of the imagination," a set of translucent structures that were backlighted by 252 computer-controlled projectors, so as to reflect the colors of the galaxies that appeared through the gigantic porthole. The special effects depicting the space travel were rear-projected onto a screen installed at the back of the set, and used a custom-made 35-millimeter system designed by Charles Lux. The projection speed was set at thirty frames per second, to be compatible with the new, hypersensitive RCA TK-47 cameras that shot these scenes on video. The spaceship was very dimly lit, in order to accentuate the brightness of the images on the screen. These space travel scenes were made

Preparation and filming of scenes from the TV series Cosmos, *in which Carl Sagan was inserted into a model of the great library of Alexandria*
Photos courtesy Cosmos Studios

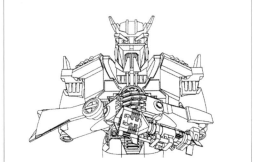

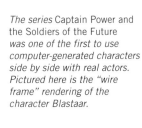

The series Captain Power and the Soldiers of the Future *was one of the first to use computer-generated characters side by side with real actors. Pictured here is the "wire frame" rendering of the character Blastaar.*

by shooting airbrush drawings. The spiral movement of a galaxy were done by shooting several "layers" of drawings, superimposed by multiple exposures. Greg Andorfer, the visual effects supervisor, made a long series of zooms over dozens of different drawings to depict the crossing of a nebula. They also used animated drawings to depict pulsars, black holes, and the explosion of a supernova. The

greatest technical feat of the series was the reproduction of the great library of ancient Alexandria, through which Carl Sagan meandered. This effect was achieved using the Magicam system, which is based on the establishment of a master-slave relationship between two pieces of video equipment. Camera A filmed Carl Sagan as he moved about a large stage set painted blue. All the manipulations (pans, trackings, zooms) were reproduced identically by camera-periscope B, which was mounted on a dolly installed over a model of the great library. The sensors placed on the wheels, the column, and the head of camera A all furnished data that were reflected—in real time or with a delay—onto camera B. The tracks were further muddled by the placement of life-size props within the large blue set. When Sagan climbed the staircase and then placed his hands on a globe that he spun, television viewers could not distinguish between the life-size props and the miniature set. It took two years of work to develop the special effects for the series. It was a tremendous success when it was first broadcast, and in 1980 it was awarded the first Emmy for best special effects.

The cyclorama and the pool set up in a small studio for the filming of an episode of The New Twilight Zone. *Director John Milius directs actor Martin Kove in a murder scene that takes place during a hunt. Backlighted and drenched in fog, the set is strikingly realistic.*

The costume of the superhero in the series Flash *was made by Robert Short and comprised two parts, separated at the waist, at the level of the character's belt. The pants and the boots formed a single element. The boots were fitted with openings on the undersides so John Wesley Shipp (who played Flash) could wear sneakers and run as fast as possible. The upper part comprised the torso, arms, and hood. Only the gloves could be slipped on separately. The whole costume was composed of twenty-one pieces of foam rubber that were assembled and glued onto a Lycra surface. The red fibers that were projected onto the costume stuck straight into the glue, thanks to static electricity. The costume ended up looking like red velvet.*

The Babylon 5 *base*   Photo courtesy of Warner Television

Babylon 5: The First 3-D Spaceships on TV

The *Babylon 5* TV series, which appeared in 1993, related the adventures of a community of humans and extraterrestrials who lived together aboard a gigantic space station. It was the first time that computer-generated spaceships appeared on television. They were conceived by Ron Thornton and Foundation Imaging. The computer artists used Lightwave 3-D software to compose rockets in the shape of seashells, starfish, and fish. The space battles required the development of choreography that took into consideration the movement of the vessels, the shots from lasers, the impacts, and the explosions of the defeated spaceships. The animators could envision trajectories and movements on any angle and at any speed, and could quickly alter them to improve the impact of a given shot. At this stage, the spaceships were rendered only as "wire frame" images, to enable the computer to display the complete animation sequence at twenty-five frames per second. The texture of the Vorlon spaceships was obtained through a fractal effect, disproportionally enlarging the yellow-colored components. A touch of authenticity was added by also imitating the reflective interference of real lenses. The 3-D images of a spaceship's flight in front of the sun seemed that much more credible.

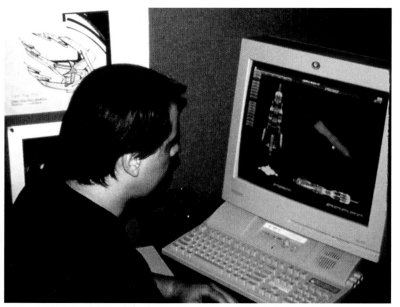

A computer artist works on the modeling of a new spaceship for Babylon 5.

The light beams were drawn frame by frame with a graphics platform.

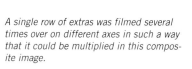

A single row of extras was filmed several times over on different axes in such a way that it could be multiplied in this composite image.

The Extraterrestrials of *Babylon 5*

The extraterrestrials of *Babylon 5* were conceived and produced by John Vulich. The makeup for G'Kar was the most sophisticated ever to have been created for a main character in a science fiction series. The prosthetics covered Andreas Katsulas's entire head and neck. Makeup appliances of this sort are generally composed of dozens of pieces and take four to five hours to apply. Vulich, however, brilliantly simplified it. His makeup appliance had only two parts—a foam

The "hood" and mask of the Narn ambassador in Babylon 5

rubber hood that was not glued on and which incorporated the neck and head, and a pre-painted facial prosthetic that covered the oval of the face. This makeup could be applied twice as fast, as Vulich's assistants had only two prosthetics to glue and thus so many fewer seams to conceal. The marks spread over the face and heads of the Narns were painted with an airbrush, using thermoformed plastic mattes. While the hoods were reused four or five times, the very delicate edges of the facial prosthetics did become damaged when removed and therefore had to be replaced with every day of shooting.

The Digital Rotoscope

The combat scenes with laser guns were made with a graphics platform that used a digital Rotoscope process. The electronic stylus made it possible to draw the rays emanating from the laser guns, to surround a character in sparks, and to create fantastic distortions, but it also could erase parts of a frame and replace them with other parts. Some of the sets were digitally enhanced to appear as if they had a second level. The same sector of the stage would be refilmed in a high-angle shot from a different height, thus creating a crop in which the upper level appeared. The longest view was inserted into the shortest view, in keeping with the laws of

perspective, which gave the impression of two stages instead of one. The special effects memory bank retained the colors, the shapes, and the basic animations of the laser rays and the planets that reappeared throughout the series. In 1994, it was still difficult to simulate explosions in 3-D, so the special effects team used a 35-millimeter camera to film the pyrotechnical effects at 120 frames per second during the night in a studio parking lot. These images were added during postproduction onto the computer-generated images of the spaceships as they were being destroyed.

Optic Nerve Studio: When Television Makeup Rivals Film Makeup

Optic Nerve Studio is hidden away in a dull landscape of Los Angeles amid warehouses and small office buildings. You pass through the door and discover a

Actor Lee Whitaker transformed into a demon in the episode "The Prom" from the series Buffy the Vampire Slayer
Photo courtesy of Optic Nerve

veritable museum of fantasy creatures from television. The extraterrestrials from *Babylon 5* sit side by side with creatures from *The X-Files* and vampires, demons, and werewolves from the interconnected series *Buffy the Vampire Slayer* and *Angel*. Some fifteen sculptors, mold makers, painters, and makeup artists are working under the supervision of John Vulich. When asked how he had managed to make makeups for television as successful as those made for film, Vulich smiled and said, "Simply by racking my brains more than the others! I'm lucky to have a team that's incredibly talented, and can make in three days of work what other people would take

John Vulich with the facial prosthetic for the Narn ambassador and the thermoformed plastic matte that made it possible to paint the designs on the prosthetic quickly, using an airbrush

three weeks to accomplish. We've found ways to simplify the work without it appearing on the image, like how we make the molds. So we can concentrate on the sculptures and the details of the characters."

Makeup on *Buffy* and *Angel*

Debuting in 1997, the series *Buffy the Vampire Slayer* became a standard for the makeup of monsters. John Vulich established an efficient procedure for creating prosthetics in record time. The first stage in the crafting of makeup entails taking a mold of the actor's face, using alginate and plaster strips. This process would be sufficient if the actor were to appear in only two or three episodes, but if he played a more regular character, the imprint of his face would then made using a special silicone, from which a series of plaster casts could be taken. If he appeared in every episode, like David Boreanaz, who played the title role in the spin-off series *Angel,* the casts were made out of resin and fiberglass so they could be reused indefinitely. Boreanaz was often shot in close-up while he was transforming into a vampire. His forehead, nose, and cheekbones were covered with rubber foam, his eyes concealed behind contact lenses, and his canine teeth elongated with dental prosthetics. Vulich's team carefully prepared Angel's

makeup, crafting a prosthetic with edges as thin as cigarette paper. The prosthetic was glued to the actor's face with a very strong surgical adhesive and then, using a quick-drying paste, thinned with water, and the seams were smoothed onto his skin until they became invisible. Various shades of foundation makeup were applied to both the prosthetic and the actor's skin, perfecting the blend.

Here is how makeup was crafted for another vampire on *Buffy* (as shown in the sequence of photos at right and on the next page). After having first glued a latex bald cap on actor Jerry Gingerly's head, Gary Yee traced a line to indicate where the hair implantation on Gingerly's forehead would start. This line, traced with a grease pencil, imprints itself like a decal onto the materials used during the molding. Yee then applied the alginate. This supple material was then covered over with a rigid coating made of plaster strips. This negative mold was then used to obtain a positive mold cast in plaster. John Wheaton sculpted a vampire face on another casting of the face. Plaster was then applied over its entirety to obtain a mold for the prosthetic. Graig McIntyre mixed the different components of the foam rubber in a beater: very thick liquid latex, a foaming agent, and a cooking agent. When tiny bubbles formed in the material, a gelling agent was

added. The mixture was then transferred into a large plastic syringe and injected into the mold in two pieces. The mold was placed in an oven set to 212°F (100°C) and baked for two hours. Once the foam rubber was cooked, it was removed from the mold, and this rough prosthetic was applied onto an actor by Todd McIntosh.

The Hellish Tempo of Television

When John Vulich's collaborators analyzed a new *Buffy* script, they listed the new characters that had to be produced, which molds could be reused, and other effects relevant to "special makeups" such as wounds, scars, aging, etc. There were four main categories of vampire makeup: those very sophisti-cated ones used for regular char-acters, those for characters who appeared in only a few episodes, those for characters who appeared only in the back-ground, and those for the extras or stunt artists, seen from afar and very briefly. In this last case, Vulich and his team used masks that slipped on like hoods or prosthetics taken from the stock of already existing ones. There were about twenty different kinds of vampire prosthetics. When time was lacking, they would dig into this stock and choose one that could best be adapted to the face of the extra. In order to be dominant in the

Drawing of the demon in "The Wish," sent by fax to the production for its approval
Photo courtesy of Optic Nerve

The final makeup Photo courtesy of Optic Nerve

field, Optic Nerve bit by bit developed a reserve of thou-sands of prosthetics, contact lenses, wigs, and foam rubber costumes. Paradoxically, those makeups that appeared to be the simplest were the ones that required the most preparation time, because they had no

Previous page and above: Photos courtesy of Optic Nerve

Stages in the creation of the monster in "The Kindestod," interpreted by James Courtney   Photo courtesy of Optic Nerve

Two creatures from the series The X-Files: *the demon of "Terms of Endearment" and the extraterrestrial of "The Unnatural"*
Photos courtesy of Optic Nerve

sculptors sometimes modeled new elements on a preexistent character to create new molds and new monsters quickly. The average budget for vampire makeup on *Buffy* was approximately three thousand dollars. This included the fabrication of contact lenses, foam rubber makeup appliances, and false teeth. A complete monster costume that covered the entire body cost about thirty thousand dollars.

Farscape: Henson Productions' Leading Series

Having become the creative head of Jim Henson Productions upon his father's death, Brian Henson initiated the launch of the series *Farscape* (1999–2003), in which each episode was bursting with special effects. The Creature Shop conceived and fabricated the extraterrestrials on the series, such as Pilot, whose tentacles interwove with the spaceship *Moya*'s nervous system in order to steer it. Pilot was a giant puppet whose foam rubber skin covered an articulated structure made of resin and fiberglass. Two handlers hidden inside the character animated its body and head. Two or three others activated the arms and the remote radio controls that initiated the frowns and the movements of the eyes and eyelids. The little monarch Rygel XVI was also a puppet. A handler slid his right hand inside the head, and the

wrinkles or facial imperfections to hide the seams between the skin and the prosthetic. The time it took to apply these ranged from one and a half hours to two and a half hours, depending on their complexity. Because of time constraints,

tips of his left hand, with the little finger bent, went into a small four-fingered glove made from a Lycra base covered over with foam rubber. The team at the Creature Shop sometimes also slid articulated mechanisms inside Rygel's hands to shoot some scenes in which his arms were more visible. Paradoxically, one of the most spectacular makeups of the series was created with few prosthetics. This was the one for the priestess Zhaan. The hair of the actress was concealed under a latex bald cap, and prosthetics were attached to her earlobes. An airbrush was used to paint the various shades of blue on the skin of her face and body, and stencils helped to create the different texture effects. The warrior Ka D'Argo's makeup comprised a set of facial prosthetics, as well as a sort of dickey made of foam rubber that was glued on his throat and the tops of his shoulders. The makeups for Jool and the fearsome Scorpius also used foam rubber prosthetics. The space scenes and the wide shots of planets were created by two Australian companies, GMD during the first season and then Animal Logic. Twenty-five computer artists made forty to fifty effects shots for each episode. They had only seven days to create the visual effects for each adventure, at a rate of twenty-two episodes per year. This was no mean feat, as often two or three episodes were shot at the same

The very elaborate makeup of Zhaan and other characters from Farscape: *Pilot, Rygel, and Ka D'Argo (holding weapon)*

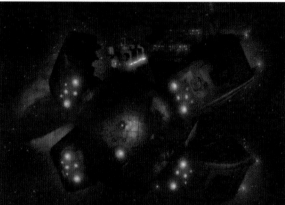

The organic oval-shaped vessel Moya *was often confronted by much larger spaceships. These superb computer-generated images were made for* Farscape *by the Australian firm Animal Logic.*

Jamie Kennedy in real life
Special makeup by Ed French

time. The third season alone required 1,109 different digital effects, which included battles between spaceships, the creation of landscapes, and the animation of such creatures as a giant snake. *Farscape* ended in 2003, after four seasons.

The Jamie Kennedy Experiment

In 2000, makeup artist Ed French accomplished a feat worthy of *Mission: Impossible:* he created makeup, undetectable to the naked eye, for Jamie Kennedy so that the comic could produce his candid camera skits.

"The challenge was very interesting, because the makeup had to look realistic to the naked eye in natural light," explained French. "I wouldn't have been able to do this work if I didn't have twenty years of experience behind me. I created two or three new characters every week, with no preparation time. I used translucent materials like gelatin and silicone to make extremely realistic prosthetics. If I'd used foam rubber, which is opaque, people would have noticed." French also made remarkable parodic makeups for the comedy show *Mad TV.* With these prosthetics, the actors could transform themselves into

Metamorphoses of comic actor Jamie Kennedy by Ed French to trap unsuspecting people as they were filmed. These makeups were undetectable, even when viewed close up, by the naked eye. Special makeup by Ed French

Actress Linda Gehringer transformed into Janet Reno, Bill Clinton's attorney general. A superb makeup job by Brian Penikas for the series Ally McBeal. Special makeup by Brian Penikas

celebrities. He developed techniques that enabled him to create makeups of the likenesses of Arnold Schwarzenegger or Robert De Niro, or a copy of Eddie Murphy's obese makeup in *The Nutty Professor,* in just two or three days.

Walking with Dinosaurs and *Walking with Prehistoric Beasts*: When Computer-Generated Images Resurrect Prehistoric Animals

When producer Tim Haines undertook to create the TV movie *The Lost World* for the BBC in 1993, he was far from imagining just where this adventure would lead him. In order to distinguish it from previous adaptations of the novel by Arthur Conan Doyle, he chose to imitate the "handheld camera" method used in animal documentaries. Haines contacted ILM, which a year earlier had made a sensation with its virtual dinosaurs in *Jurassic Park*. But he became disillusioned when he was quoted excessive Hollywood prices—ten thousand dollars for each second of 3-D animation! Haines then consulted the English studio Framestore CFC, whose effects test was convincing.

But while the technical problems were being resolved, the rights to *The Lost World* were bought by other producers. So Haines put to use the technical procedures developed with Frame-store and conceived *Walking with Dinosaurs,* a six-part documentary series. Having managed to obtain the 10 million euros (12.5 million dollars) needed, and with the investment of three years of work, he brought this project to fruition. He spent one year working with a professor of paleontology fine-tuning his scripts before setting off to fabricate the mechanical likenesses of the animals and the creation of the 3-D images. Crawley Creatures conceived the animatronic dinosaurs that would be filmed in close-up. Three sculptors made the miniature dinosaurs, based on measurements taken from skeletons. Framestore scanned these models and created three-dimensional images of them. The computer artists then started working inside these 3-D silhouettes. They re-created the articulated skeletons of the animals, endowing them with muscular masses that would pack down when the limbs were made to move, covered them over with skin and scales, and gave them teeth and a multitude of subtly colored details. The "virtual puppets" of the dinosaurs were ready. All that remained was to animate them.

Real Landscapes and Virtual Animals

Within real shots of real landscapes, animatronic dinosaurs from the studios of Crawley Creatures pass through the scenes. Most of them consisted of a fiberglass structure covered with a foam rubber skin. They were animated using servomotors and cables attached to their joints. The heads of tyrannosaurus babies, with remote-controlled eyelids and nostrils, were used during the filming of a family dinner. The enormous head of the mother T. rex weighed some forty-five pounds (twenty kilograms), but she was manipulated with great delicacy when she grabbed pieces of meat in close-up shots. When they were not filming the mechanical characters, technicians would thrash about, simulating the physical presence of the animals that would be added to the real images later on. They sawed branches in half and then, off in the distance, broke them up with steel cables. They threw objects into the water and then, to leave dinosaur tracks in the wet ground, ran across it wearing enormous "rackets" on their feet. They exploded charges buried in the ground, spreading dust clouds and giving the impression that a gigantic brachiosaurus had pounded upon the ground as it walked by. Other dust clouds and flying debris were filmed in the studio, on a blue background, to be part of a composite image. And the animators at Framestore succeeded in their impressive efforts integrating their virtual dinosaurs into natural landscapes. "When the BBC consulted us, we immediately realized the enormous amount of

Resurrected dinosaurs in the outstanding BBC series Walking with Dinosaurs
Photos courtesy of the BBC

shots that would have to be produced," recalled Mike McGee. "We conceived the animation of the dinosaurs from a series of movement cycles: walking, running, a stationary position, observing the landscape, etc. So we were in a position to produce a great number of scenes by modifying these cycles of animation, as well as by changing the camera angles and the composi-

tion of the images. We had to perfectly duplicate the real lighting onto the synthesized dinosaurs, control the texture and skin folds at the joint levels, and properly animate the masses of flesh during movement. The greatest difficulty was to make the contact of the dinosaur's foot with the ground look realistic. And also to take care of the shadows, the dust clouds that rose up as they

moved, and the splashes in the puddles of water."

The camera would rest a long time on an animal as it tore off leaves from a tree for food, giving the viewers the chance to scrutinize the tiniest details. "After having shot the background for each image, we would place a large, graduated ruler with a white sphere attached to one end in the set, and would film it," continued McGee. "The graduations let us spot the exact scale of the shot, and the shadows that appeared on the white ball indicated the direct and indirect light sources. We created a 3-D model of this ruler. By aligning the 3-D model of the ruler on an image of the actual ruler, we were able to duplicate the scale, the perspective, and the light sources of the real images onto the images of the synthesized animals." It is already difficult enough to create the illusion of the mass of a dinosaur as it moves, but the task becomes that much more complicated when filming two animals in the midst of a fight. Each detail is treated as an independent entity: the drops of saliva that fall from the dinosaur's mouth, the impact of the blows, the masses of flesh as each makes contact with the other dinosaur, the scratches. The teams at Framestore spent an entire year fine-tuning their CGI effects, shot by shot. When the series was broadcast, it became the television event of 1996 and beat all audience records worldwide. This phenomenal success led to a second project: *Walking with Prehistoric Beasts.*

Reconstructing the First Mammals

Ever since their discovery in the early nineteenth century, dinosaurs have always been a huge draw at museums. But other less popular—and less lucrative—animals have been neglected. The BBC decided to redress this injustice by devoting *Walking with Prehistoric Beasts* to the first mammals. Paleontologist Paul Chambers supervised the scientific aspects of the series. He undertook some real detective work in order to furnish Crawley Creatures and Framestore with the information they needed to resurrect these forgotten beasts. "We rummaged in museums throughout the world looking for skeletons, fossilized traces of skin, and even bits of fur from some of the mammals," Chambers recalled. "We reconstructed their outer look by taking information derived from their skeletal shapes. One can deduce the placement and formation of the muscles and

A fight to the death between an entelodon and a hyenodon

Above and opposite, below: *Stages in the creation of the saber-toothed tiger in the series* Walking with Prehistoric Beasts, *and the final rendition, digitally inserted into a real landscape*

Close-up shot of a battle between two saber-toothed tigers filmed using animatronic heads

Handlers manipulating a mechanical head and a foot of a chalicothere

Filming a close-up of an indricothere's snout as it drinks from a river

fleshy parts, as well as the position and shape of the ears. The choice of color, that was more complicated, with the exception of the mammoth fur, of which there exist well-preserved specimens. But in nature, colors respect certain rules. For the most part, mammals adopt camouflage colors that enable them to surprise their prey during the hunt. Thus, animals that live in

Antarctica are often white to fade into the snowy landscape." Whenever possible, Chambers obtained the authority to use museum pieces. Giant prehistoric

ants stuck in an amber flow were scanned in order to re-create them in 3-D. Information drawn from the fossil impressions were used to reconstruct the walking and running gaits of some animals. The frozen bodies of mammoths and woolly rhinoceroses found in Siberia also contributed to the effort. The horn of a rhinoceros was molded and the length of a mammoth's hair was measured, in order to make their digital clones! For the first time in the history of science, special effects made the reconstruction of poorly known animals possible. The series also presented the opportunity to correct an error: during the preparation of the animation sequences of the entelodon, it became clear that paleontologists had always mispositioned the hind feet of the animal! The poor beast would not have been able to move. Thanks to the teams at Crawley Creatures and Framestore CFC, special effects, previously reserved for fiction, had now reconstructed reality.

A gastornis chasing its prey

The animatronic model of a leptictidium

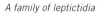

A family of leptictidia

The imposing machinery needed to animate the head of a mammoth

Opposite: *A mammoth attacked by a snow lion*
Photos courtesy of the BBC

The Hallmark Miniseries: Superproductions on TV

Starting in the 1990s, Hallmark produced prestigious miniseries that drew stars from both the small and big screens. Its first major success was *Gulliver's Travels* (1996), followed by *The Odyssey* (1997), *Merlin* (1998), *Alice in Wonderland* (1999), *Don Quixote* (2000), and *Arabian Nights* (2000). These three- to four-hour miniseries made great use of high-quality, often innovative special effects. For example, Framestore bestowed on Martin Short an enormous head for his interpretation of the Mad Hatter in *Alice in Wonderland*. Mike McGee divulged the secrets of this tour de force: "We filmed Martin Short's scenes normally, in front of a blue background. Then, once we had run the 35-millimeter negative through the telecine in order to get a video master, we made two sweeps: the first with the image framed normally, the second zooming in onto Martin's head. Since the enlargement was made directly from the 35-millimeter negative, we lost absolutely no definition. Then, frame by frame, we cut out his head at the level of his white shirt collar. And finally, we used a tracking computer program to align the perspectives of the big head onto the normal-sized cutoff body." Framestore also worked on the creatures in *Jason and the Argonauts* (2000), one of which was a gigantic metal bull.

The imposing sets and Cyclops from The Odyssey *(1997)*
Photos courtesy of Hallmark Home Entertainment

Above and left: *Seemingly more real than nature, animatronic animals constructed by Jim Henson's Creature Shop for the mini-series* Animal Farm
Photos courtesy of Hallmark Home Entertainment

Battling the white whale in Moby-Dick *(2001). Close-up shots were filmed in a pool with mechanized parts of the cetacean's body, while wide shots of the whale were made with synthesized images.*
Photo courtesy of Hallmark Home Entertainment

Dinotopia: Backstage at a Mega-Series

When American illustrator James Gurney conjured up the story of two sunken shipwrecks that discover an unknown continent inhabited by intelligent dinosaurs living in peace with humans, he did not foresee the success that awaited him. His books *Dinotopia: A Land Apart from Time* and *Dinotopia: The World Beneath* have sold two million copies, been translated into eighteen languages, and inspired producer Robert Halmi to create one of the most expensive television miniseries ever. Halmi can count many Hallmark productions to his name, but *Dinotopia* (2002) surpasses them all with its eighty-million-dollar budget. Straight off, he signed on Framestore to create the eighteen hundred visual effects for this enormous project.

Manufacturing a Giant City

On October 16, 2000, a team of four hundred people moved into Pinewood Studios in London. The complexity of the production and the size of the constructed sets surpassed even those built for the James Bond and Superman movies filmed at the same venue. At the height of activity during the *Dinotopia* filming, the series occupied nine stages. An army of 170 carpenters worked continuously constructing, modifying, and dismantling sets. Those of

One of the sentries of Waterfall City in Dinotopia   Image courtesy of Hallmark Home Entertainment

Waterfall City were the largest ever built in Europe. Its metal structures, if placed end to end, would cover a distance of 84.5 miles (136 kilometers). The city walls required 140 tons of plaster and 1,441 gallons (5,455 liters) of paint. In all, 275 extras populated the world of *Dinotopia,* along with herds of animatronic dinosaurs from the London studio of Jim Henson's Creature Shop: allosaurs, mososaurs (a kind of giant crocodile), and an adorable baby triceratops replete with servomotors that could be held by the actors, while two technicians animated it by remote control.

Framestore Feats

The teams at Framestore had already been working for several months by the time the filming of the real shots was completed in March 2001. Seventy-five computer artists and animators took great efforts to make the virtual humans and dinosaurs coexist in the same frames without having the 3-D characters vary from one shot to another. Eight Framestore animators worked full time on Zippo, the "stenosaurus" who accompanied and conversed with the human heroes. At this point, another team extended the real sets in accordance with the

virtual perspectives. The Waterfall City that is featured in the series was so big that 90 percent of it had to be created in highly detailed 3-D architecture, the gigantic size of the Pinewoods stages notwithstanding. After nineteen months of work, Framestore delivered a stunning effort that earned an Emmy Award for best visual effects.

This triceratops is one of the high dignitaries of Waterfall City.

Dinosaurs and humans living in harmony on the continent of Dinotopia
Images courtesy of Hallmark Home Entertainment

*The grand land-
scape of Waterfall
City*
Image courtesy of
Hallmark Home
Entertainment

INTERVIEW

MIKE MCGEE

Special effects supervisor on *Dinotopia* and cofounder of Framestore CFC, Mike McGee supervised the effects on mini-series such as *The Odyssey* and *Arabian Nights*, and the documentary series *Walking with Dinosaurs* and *Walking with Prehistoric Beasts*.

Mike McGee surrounded by the creatures and sets he created with the team at Framestore CFC
Photo courtesy of Framestore CFC

What are the differences between a television production and a film production, in terms of pre-production and postproduction organization?

Mike McGee: The preproduction organizational phases are identical. On *Dinotopia,* we created eighteen hundred visual effects, and most of the members of our team came from having collaborated on *Gladiator* and the *Harry Potter* movies. We worked on live-action shots filmed in 35 millimeter and on background frames onto which we had to add synthesized images. The effects scenes and the action scenes in *Dinotopia* were as complicated as those in film. The budgetary approach was identical: you are given X amount of money, with which you have to make as many shots as you can. The big difference is that the resolution of the TV image is obviously inferior to that of the film image. So compositing effects are created much faster, because the computers handle less data. For half the budget of film, you can produce three times as many effects shots.

Did you reuse some of the animal elements from "Walking with Dinosaurs" to create characters in "Dinotopia"?

Mike McGee: No. With experience, we learned how to produce characters more practical to animate. We constructed all the dinosaurs in *Dinotopia* from scratch. We even made new sculptures minus the scientific realities of the first series. The dinosaurs in *Dinotopia* are intelligent characters who can cross their legs and bend their tails in all directions. If a dinosaur tried to make these movements, he would dislocate his joints!

How did you transform the drawings of Waterfall City into a coherent 3-D universe in which a camera could move around?

Mike McGee: It was the fruit of a close collaboration with the creative director of the series, who wanted to delicately adapt James Gurney's creations. In his books, you only see a few waterfalls around Waterfall City. It was our idea to add a lot more. We started by looking for a natural site where we could get such images, and we chose the Iguaçu Falls, located near the border between Brazil and Argentina. We took a lot of reference photographs and filmed many shots from different angles, in such a way as to be able to combine them and mix them into the final composite image of the city. We extended the set constructed in the Pinewood studios in order to create the rest of the city in a wide shot. The architecture was also very complicated. The city is a mixture of European and Egyptian styles. We used the architectural textures and forms of old houses in Paris. The 3-D model is so specific that a person could walk through the streets and see all the details of the doors, the windows, the store signs, and the wrought iron balconies.

How did you extend the real sets with virtual architecture?

Mike McGee: We took down all the geometry of the Pinewood sets with a laser telemeter. This is a device used by architects and public works companies. The device is set in a precise spot, from which you aim at different points in the landscape or architecture. It measures the distance between the point of departure of the laser and the point of its impact on the surface of an object in the distance. By reproducing the readings, you can record complex architecture in three dimensions. We also took high-resolution photographs of all the textures of the sets. The first part of our 3-D model is thus an exact duplicate of the sets constructed at Pinewood. By aligning this referential set with the real set, it was then easy to make the composite shots. All that was necessary was to duplicate the distortions of the perspectives produced by the different objects used during the filming of the real shots. We also used a scanner to record the volumes of the giant statues of the pterodactyls, which were constructed at Pinewood and which we reconstructed in the virtual 3-D version of the set.

Harnessed brachiosauruses make long journeys possible.
Image courtesy of Hallmark Home Entertainment

Did you use real images of the Grand Canyon to create the set of Canyon City?

Mike McGee: Yes. We knew that we couldn't film the Grand Canyon, per se, for numerous reasons. First off, it isn't as deep as the one James Gurney conceived, and then it was impossible for us to bring our actors there and construct on-site the sets needed for the plot. But we took thousands of high-resolution photographs of its walls with a digital camera. The photographer was up in a helicopter. He took a shot of the summit of the canyon while the helicopter was stationary; then it descended about thirty-five feet, so he could take another picture; and they continued like that until they got to the bottom of the wall. We transferred these thousands of giant images of the walls of the Grand Canyon, which enabled us to assemble the entire Canyon City set. The dialogue scenes with actors were shot at Pinewood Studios with fake rock walls placed in front of a blue background.

How did you control the interactions between the dinosaurs and the actors?

Mike McGee: The most complicated scenes were those where you see the actors traveling in the baskets perched on the back of a brachiosaurus. The movements of the actors and the synthesized images of the animals had to be absolutely coordinated for the effect to work. Usually, to make this kind of scene, the actors are placed on a platform and a crew of stagehands rocks it as best they can, and then you try to animate the synthesized characters

The movements of the 3-D dinosaurs were used to program the animated platforms on which the actors were perched.
Images courtesy of Framestore CFC

One of the mechanical dinosaurs made by Jim Henson's Creature Shop that spring out of the water to snatch the heroes. Special effects that entail interaction with water are always complicated to make in CGI. This is why using animatronics is preferred.

in accordance with these movements. It's not the most satisfactory approach. We had the idea of reverse action, which is to say, using the animation of a computer-generated dinosaur to move the mount that the actors were standing on. To do this, we used a platform comparable to flight simulator platforms. It was animated by a series of computer-controlled hydraulic jacks and could rise, lower, and tilt in all directions. The gigantic saddle and part of the brachiosaurus's back were constructed and fixed to the platform, which was animated according to the walking pace of the brachiosaurus. Thanks to this device, the saddle with the eight actors and the synthesized image of the brachiosaurus were synchronized in the composite shot. We used the same procedure for the scenes where humans straddled pterodactyls and biped dinosaurs. Each time an actor had to straddle an animal, the support he was sitting on was shaped like the body of the synthesized animal.

How did you film the scenes where they interacted, and the dialogues between Zippo and the humans?

Mike McGee: We turned to a stand-in. He wore a costume with a fake head and a long tail. It was essential that the actors could look Zippo in the eye at the right level. The character needed a space of ten feet (three meters) in order to turn around. If we hadn't used a stand-in to regulate his movements, we would have had problems inserting the virtual character into the real shots. Each scene was rehearsed with the stand-in. We filmed a preliminary reference shot with him, and the subsequent scenes were filmed without him.

SOFTIMAGE|3D   Scene: demo-ZIPPO_A1.3-0   Model Motion Actor Matter Tools

The adorable baby triceratops made by Jim Henson's
Creature Shop   Images courtesy of Framestore CFC

Above and left: *Zippo,
the heroes' companion
in* Dinotopia, *was a
very expressive 3-D
character.*

Overleaf: *Pilots from the
school in Canyon City
astride pteranodons*
Image courtesy of Hallmark
Home Entertainment

Animals of the Future

In 2002, the documentary-style series *The Future Is Wild* superbly depicted a far distant future in which eight-ton octopuses stalk the forests of the earth. Here was a world in which the continents had merged into a single mega-continent inhabited by snails that could leap like kangaroos, fish that flew through the forests, and birds that were endowed with four wings. This future, which seems nutty, was conceived by scientists who worked out a scenario depicting the apparition of new animal species five million, one hundred million, and two hundred million years from now. Peter Bailey, the animation director, was in charge of breathing life into the fifty stunning beasts that appear in the series. For two years, he supervised the work of thirty computer artists at the 4:2:2 studios in Bristol who were in charge of this new genesis. He recalls the process of creating the carakilla, a seven-foot (two-meter) carnivorous bird that used its claws and sharp beak to hunt the babookari monkeys: "We drew the profile of this animal during meetings with specialists in biology, ecology, biomechanics, and physiology who were the scientific advisers of the series. This sketch was adapted in 2-D on Photoshop. After being approved by the scientists, the 2-D drawing was transposed into 3-D.

A cryptile spreads its sticky comb, and insects become entrapped as if it were flypaper, in The Future Is Wild. Image courtesy James Addams Productions

We constructed the skeleton of the carakilla in order to be able to animate it like a virtual puppet. Its body was covered with feathers painted with a graphics platform, and its feet were covered in scales." The computer artists referred to the bearings of real animals in order to create their virtual creatures, even if some of them, like the "squibbons," octopuses with long arms that swung from branch to branch like monkeys, were beyond all comparison!

Unlike the two series *Walking with Dinosaurs* and *Walking with Prehistoric Beasts,* all the close-ups with these animals were synthesized images. "We had to develop far more detailed models than had previously been shown on television," Bailey explained. The astoundingly realistic animations of *The Future Is Wild* proved once again that television special effects are in no way the second cousins of those in film.

A school of silver swimmers
Image courtesy James Addams Productions

An ocean flish: a fish whose fins gradually transform into wings
Image courtesy James Addams Productions

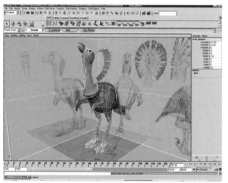

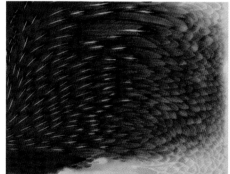

Different stages in the creation of the carakilla, a giant carnivorous bird
Images courtesy of 4:2:2

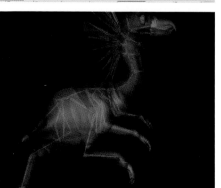

Peter Bailey, animation director on The Future Is Wild, *at work in the studios of 4:2:2, located in Bristol, England*
Photo courtesy of Peter Bailey

Theme Parks and Attractions

From the Carnival Show to the World's Fair

In the middle of the nineteenth century, itinerant entertainers latched onto the tricks of magicians, creating phenomena like the "Talking Head." Set on a four-legged square table, in a black stage set, the head of a woman would open her eyes and start talking with the dumbstruck audience. Her body was concealed behind a mirror that was placed on a diagonal under

A "Fijian Mermaid," created by taxidermist-artist Mark Frierson from a capuchin monkey and a fish. P. T. Barnum had exhibited a similar forgery at his circus and made a huge profit.
Photo by Ron Spellman. Courtesy of the American Dime Museum

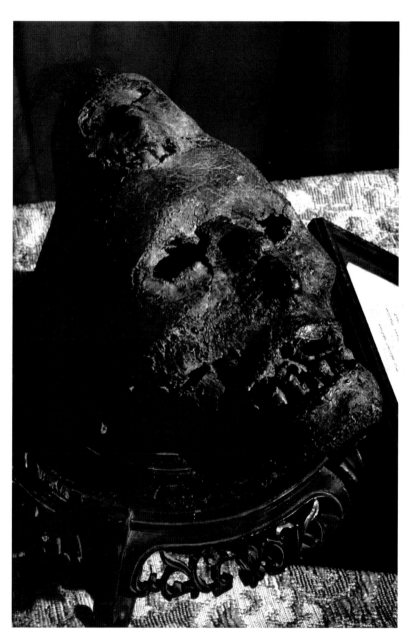

"The Two-Headed Enigma," a forgery of a skull made by the artist Dick Horne
Photo by Ron Spellman. Courtesy of the American Dime Museum

LE MARÉORAMA

Introductory subscription for the construction of Le Maréorama, *invented by Hugo d'Alesi*
Photo courtesy of the Laurence Botelle collection

the table, between the front left leg and the rear right leg of the table. The reflection of the front right leg appeared in the position of the rear left leg. The same mirror effects were used to create headless women, centaurs, or spider-women with their feet interlaced in an oversize web. Elsewhere, people got to gaze upon mermaids and chimera-like creatures created by taxidermists. The first attractions that employed brazen effects were conceived for world's fairs. In Paris in 1855, one could already visit an aquarium room that gave the impression of being in the depths of the sea. But at the Exposition Universelle there in 1900, four previously unseen effects were on display: the *Maréorama,* the *Cinéorama,* the *Transsibérian,* and the *Palais des Illusions.* The *Maréorama,* conceived by painter Hugo d'Alesi, simulated the voyage of a boat from Nice to Constantinople, passing through Venice on its way. D'Alesi spent one year traveling along the route in order to draw a series of the locales on dozens of sketch pads. An army of painters reproduced his work on two scrims measuring 46.5 feet (13 meters) tall and 2,706.6 feet (825 meters) wide. Each of these panoramas was wound around a "debtor" cylinder and a "receiver" cylinder. One of the cylinders was placed to the left of the set, a ship's gangway, where the audience was located, and the other to the right. When the voyage began, the giant cylinders started to turn slowly, unfurling the two panoramas, one on each side of the boat. The point of junction of the cylinders was concealed by masts and sails placed in front

Summary of the workings of the Cabinet des mirages

LE PALAIS DES MIRAGES AU MUSÉE GRÉVIN

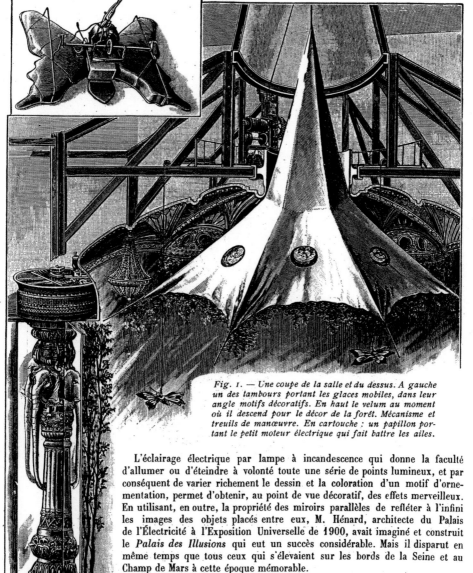

Fig. 1. — *Une coupe de la salle et du dessus. A gauche un des tambours portant les glaces mobiles, dans leur angle motifs décoratifs. En haut le velum au moment où il descend pour le décor de la forêt. Mécanisme et treuils de manœuvre. En cartouche : un papillon portant le petit moteur électrique qui fait battre les ailes.*

L'éclairage électrique par lampe à incandescence qui donne la faculté d'allumer ou d'éteindre à volonté toute une série de points lumineux, et par conséquent de varier richement le dessin et la coloration d'un motif d'ornementation, permet d'obtenir, au point de vue décoratif, des effets merveilleux. En utilisant, en outre, la propriété des miroirs parallèles de refléter à l'infini les images des objets placés entre eux, M. Hénard, architecte du Palais de l'Électricité à l'Exposition Universelle de 1900, avait imaginé et construit le *Palais des Illusions* qui eut un succès considérable. Mais il disparut en même temps que tous ceux qui s'élevaient sur les bords de la Seine et au Champ de Mars à cette époque mémorable.

L'Administration du Musée Grévin a voulu faire revivre ce spectacle, véritable réalisation d'un conte des Mille et une Nuits, et elle vient de faire construire le *Palais des Mirages* qui est la reproduction perfectionnée de ce que nous avions pu admirer en 1900.

Elle s'est adressée naturellement à M. Hénard dont le sens artistique si développé a dû se doubler cette fois du sens de la mécanique, car, véritable magicien, il a voulu donner au spectateur une série de transformations les plus surprenantes et les plus imprévues.

Il y est parvenu, mais on va voir, par la suite, quelle ingéniosité et quelle somme de travail il a dû fournir pour réaliser son rêve ; car lui seul a tout conçu et tout fait exécuter sous sa direction.

and behind. An additional realistic touch was achieved through hydraulic jacks that made the vessel pitch. Fans simulating sea breezes, lighting effects, and a cast of extras acting as the boat's crew all added to the illusion of a seagoing cruise. While the *Maréorama* was a hit, Raoul Grimoin-Sanson's *Cinéorama* was less fortunate. The audience boarded a giant basket that appeared to be suspended from a balloon. Ten movie projectors produced hand-colored images onto a large cylindrical screen. These shots of a real balloon ascent had been filmed by cameras placed in a circle. The takeoff sequence was simply projected in reverse to simulate the landing. The system worked perfectly, but the exhibition's directors could not bear the thought of ten flammable reels of film under the feet of the audience. The risk of fire was so great that the *Cinéorama* disappeared after three days.

The *Transsibérian,* like the *Maréorama,* used painted canvas but also developed another illusion. The audience was seated in three luxurious carriages facing windows, through which they could watch the landscape pass by from left to right. The panorama consisted of "slices" of landscapes that rolled at different speeds, in order to create the illusion of one perspective moving laterally. The closer images would go by very quickly, while the more distant ones were

The Cabinet des mirages *on display at the Musée Grévin*   Photo courtesy of Musée Grévin

much slower. The bushes and rocks that were supposed to be alongside the rail tracks were glued onto a loop that scrolled horizontally at a speed of 1,080 feet (330 meters) per minute. Behind this loop, a small vertical screen of shrubs scrolled at 433 feet (132 meters) per minute. A second screen-panorama set

farther back scrolled at 138 feet (42 meters) per minute, while the main screen—measuring 26 feet (8 meters) high and 377 feet (115 meters) wide—showed far-off landscapes at 16.5 feet (5 meters) per minute. Audiences got to travel from Moscow to the Great Wall of China and finally to Beijing—fourteen days of travel

Detail of the revolving columns Photo courtesy of Musée Grévin

The Futurama *attraction at the 1939 New York World's Fair*
Photo courtesy of General Motors

reduced to a forty-five-minute performance! Of all the attractions, the most magical was the *Palais des Illusions* (Palace of Illusions), created by Eugène Hénard. It consisted of a vast hexagonal room, the walls of which were covered with huge mirrors framed by columns covered with electric light bulbs. Set across from one another, these mirrors reflected to infinity in all directions. When the light bulbs were then illuminated, the bright motifs spread as far as the virtual horizon. The *Palais des Illusions* was so popular that visitors were willing to wait more than an hour for the experience. Dismantled at the end of the exposition, it would be resurrected in 1907 at the Musée Grévin, in a more perfected rendition called the *Cabinet des Mirages.* The vertical columns that framed each large mirror in the hall would turn around during a brief moment of darkness, to reveal three different decorations. The audience would first discover a Hindu temple with sculpted pillars, then the sparkling residence of Aladdin, and finally they would be transported to a dense jungle. A painted canvas would open up in the blackness, covering the cupola in foliage. When the lights came back on, the giant trees climbed beyond view and bright butterflies flitted just over the audience. (A century after its creation, this attraction continues to delight visitors to the Musée Grévin.)

Over time, attractions became more sophisticated. In 1902, at the Coney Island amusement park in New York, the *Trip to the Moon* show made its debut. Sixty visitors at a time took their places in a rocket and, through the use of a series of projections, discovered the different stages of their journey. In 1939, the General Motors Company unveiled its *Futurama*. The seated audience was moved around a miniature diorama that measured 35,738 square feet (3,320 square meters), in which designer Norman Bel Geddes had created futuristic landscapes. Seven-lane elevated highways passed over super-modern farms. Suburban houses were spread out around a megalopolis of the year 1960, spiked with skyscrapers. *Futurama* was bulldozed at the end of the New York World's Fair, but another entertainment concept, meant to endure, would soon see the light of day.

"Disney's Folly"

In the 1940s, Walt Disney often took his two daughters to a park in Los Angeles that had a merry-go-round. Forced to wait on the sidelines as they had fun, he had the idea of a place where the whole family could enjoy themselves together. He envisioned transforming the land around his studio into a Far West universe crisscrossed by a steam locomotive, but he abandoned the idea because he needed a far bigger

Walt Disney presents the first concepts of Disneyland. Photo © Disney Enterprises, Inc.

property to build his project on. While traveling in foreign countries, he took notice of what he liked in the zoos and attractions that he visited, such as Tivoli Gardens in Copenhagen. He would not, however, unveil his concept for Disneyland until the beginning of the 1950s. The media dubbed it "Disney's Folly" and predicted that it would bankrupt his studio. Determined, Walt and his brother Roy mortgaged their ranch to pay the team who were to develop the project within the WED (for Walter Elias Disney) company. Thanks to Walt, the Disney Studios were the first to associate themselves with television, then considered the sworn enemy of the film industry. The contract signed with ABC brought them five hundred thousand dollars in cash and four and a half million dollars in bank guarantees. He chose an orange grove in the town of Anaheim, near Los Angeles, to become the site of his park. Walt tied a green ribbon around the trees he wanted to integrate into future settings and a red one around those he wanted cut down. As luck would have it, the driver of the bulldozer was color-blind, and he destroyed some beautiful specimens before the mistake was discovered!

An Instant Jungle

The first broadcast of the television series *Disneyland,* on

The Jungle Cruise *attraction, created in 1955*   Photo © Disney Enterprises, Inc.

October 27, 1954, described the different areas of the park a year before it opened: Tomorrowland would project the visitors into the future, Fantasyland was to be dedicated to fairy tales, Frontierland would evoke the Far West, and Adventureland was to offer exotic excursions. This sector of Disneyland was quickly invaded by tropical vegetation. The designers recovered uprooted palm trees from the routes of the highways being constructed around Anaheim and replanted them along the banks of the *Jungle Cruise* attraction! In January 1955, the estimated construction costs of four and a

half million dollars had already reached seventeen million dollars. When Tomorrowland was in danger of going under, Walt Disney withdrew money from his personal accounts, found new sponsors, and set his own crew to work on the production of six new attractions, six months before the inauguration of the park. The first attraction, *Rocket to the Moon,* simulated a voyage to our planet's satellite. The visitors were seated on the periphery of an amphitheater with two circular screens in the center, one placed on the ceiling, the other on the floor. Using back projections, two facing angles of the

liftoff and then the landing on the moon were shown. As a final touch to the effect, the seats were made to vibrate. The second attraction, *Space Station X1,* let the audience observe Earth as if from an orbital space station. The third, *The World Beneath Us,* proclaimed new sources of energy. The Cinerama process (the showing of a movie with three films projected onto three screens set side by side) gave Disney the idea for a fourth attraction: the projection of a movie onto screens that formed a circle around the audience. Roger Broggie and Ub Iwerks assembled eleven 16-millimeter cameras with synchronized mechanisms onto a metal ring and invented the Circarama. With this strange apparatus fixed onto a van, director Peter Ellenshaw set out to film the most beautiful American landscapes in a 360-degree view. He soon discovered hideous buildings or electricity poles often located just across from famous landscapes. Forced to replace some images, Ellenshaw got the idea to drive along Wilshire Boulevard while the camera filmed the scene at eight frames per second. During projection at twenty-four frames per second, the images went by three times as fast, giving the viewer the impression of being in a racing car that bolted from intersection to intersection! Walt Disney then came up with a fifth attraction: a presentation of the giant octopus in the film sets from *20,000 Leagues Under the Sea*. He had forgotten that the monster had been hacked with a harpoon during the filming and therefore would require many repairs. Its tentacles—long sausages of rubber suspended from cables—had been animated by technicians, who would have to be replaced by motorized mechanisms. Despite an incredible race against the clock, the octopus was not up and running until three weeks after the opening of the park. Fortunately, the miniature racing cars on the *Autopia* circuit, the sixth and final attraction at Tomorrowland, were to be ready in time.

D-Day at Disney

On July 17, 1955, while the opening ceremonies were being broadcast live on ABC-TV, backstage one catastrophe after another was taking place. High heels were getting stuck in the fresh asphalt, attractions stopped working, and the park had to welcome thousands of unexpected visitors who had bought counterfeit tickets. The next day, one headline read: "Walt's Dream a Nightmare." Critics fell silent, however, after three weeks, with Disneyland already a great success. With his first profits, Walt Disney bought back the shares of the outsider investors, and he was free to conceive attractions that were even more audacious.

A New Show Technology

The first automatons at Disneyland were animated by cyclical electric motors or pneumatic actionators. The resin-and-fiberglass *Jungle Cruise* hippopotamuses shot up out of the water and then sank back down only a few seconds later. Disney hated these primitive animations. He wanted his mechanical characters to move as well as his animated characters. So he gathered together his "imagineers" and asked them to create an automaton that could do a soft-shoe dance routine. Actor Buddy Ebsen was filmed as he danced in front of two mirrors placed in a

The Dancing Man, an automaton constructed at Walt Disney's request to develop animation techniques for three-dimensional characters
Photo © Disney Enterprises, Inc.

"V" so as to capture full-face and profile shots of his movements. This sequence was studied, frame by frame, in order to define the movements of the automaton. They then built a figurine that measured eight and a half inches (twenty-two centimeters). Its joints were attached to rods that passed between the pleats in the curtain of the small theater set. They were animated by a series of disks cut in such a way as to activate each different movement as they turned on their own axes. After a lengthy period of development, *The Dancing Man* presented his routine to a thrilled Walt Disney—who was already preoccupied by another project, the creation of a little turn-of-the-century street band that could sing "Sweet Adeline"! He intended to make this mechanical headache profitable by a coin-payment system, but at twenty-five cents per song, it would have been impossible to maintain the upkeep. The project was abandoned, and the imagineers breathed a sigh of relief!

The Imitation of Life

Following on the heels of *The Dancing Man,* Roger Broggie presented Walt Disney with the idea of creating life-size characters with the mechanisms placed inside their bodies. Disney then thought of animating an ancient Chinese philosopher this way, who would answer questions from the audience by reciting proverbs. He wanted the character to give the impression that it was articulating the words, and he instructed the WED team to watch television with the sound turned off while observing the associated facial movements. WED made a skull out of resin and fiberglass and covered it with a latex skin. The mechanisms that animated the eyes and the eyelids were activated by solenoids and several electromagnetic coils. When electricity was sent through the wire cylinder, a small metal bar slid inside and pulled a mechanism. These handlers could control on/off basic actions (for example, the eyelids completely open or completely closed), but could not make proportional or progressive movements. The

This toucan from Walt Disney's Enchanted Tiki Room *was one of the first Audio-Animatronic characters.*
Photo © Disney Enterprises, Inc.

latex skin tore during the first animation tests, so the imagineers created a more resistant, urethane-based skin and named the material Duraflex. Once finished, the Chinese philosopher gave the unpleasant impression of a decapitated head speaking. Disney thus launched a new project that would entail the creation of a full character— and none other than Abraham Lincoln! To leave his technicians time to tackle this challenge, he assigned them a concurrent task: to create toucans and parrots that could act and sing songs.

The Birth of Audio-Animatronics

Once again, the problem of programming gestures synchronized with sound arose. At the time, the first computers were still prototypes, financially out of reach and available only to the government, including the U.S. Army and NASA. The

imagineers came up with the idea of recording different tones on magnetic audiotapes. When these magnetic tapes were played, each tonality caused a small metal reed to vibrate independently, which in turn closed the electrical circuit and triggered the relay action. The relay sent an electrical current to a pneumatic valve, which opened, pushed compressed air into a jack, and caused an animation, such as the opening of the toucan's beak. Each movement had a resting position, for example the closed beak, which let the automaton remain in a neutral position when not being activated. While the pneumatic animation was effective for controlling small movements, it could not lift heavy objects, such as the arms of a character. The imagineers then obtained new equipment that was used to activate the flaps on airplane wings; these were hydraulic jacks that through electro-valves controlled extremely precise

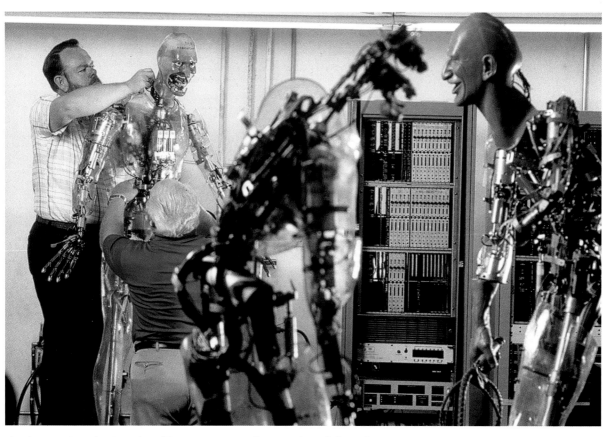

deployment and retraction. To set these in motion, many tonalities were employed. Take the example of the rotation of a character's head. If its rest position were placed on the left, a tonality would trigger an increase in the voltage of the electrical current in the hydraulic electro-valve, which would activate the rotation of the character's head to the right. Other tonalities would make it possible to vary the voltage of the current, to slow down the movement and hold the head facing the audience, or otherwise to extend the movement to continue to the extreme right. When the digital system (all or nothing) and the analog

system (proportional) functioned in parallel by a set of pneumatic and hydraulic actuators, natural animation could be achieved. The imagineers tested their discoveries on a toucan. The bird could open its beak, turn its head, blink its eyes, puff up its chest, lean forward and backward, spread its wings, and shake its tail feathers. The tonalities that controlled the character's movements were recorded on a 35-millimeter magnetic tape track. The programming of the gestures was made with a potentiometer, which regulated the intensity of the voltage. Each action was rehearsed for a long time and then recorded independently. By

Stripped of their clothing, these Audio-Animatronic pirates reveal the sophisticated technology developed by Disney to imitate human gestures. The latest models of these characters function with such speed and subtlety that they could be confused with flesh-and-blood actors. They cost one million dollars apiece.
Photo © Disney Enterprises, Inc.

playing the tape, the accuracy of the movements could be verified. Once each action had been recorded correctly on separate tapes, the recordings of ten actions were then mixed on single ten-track tape, and the global animation of the character was studied. To correct an animation, either the entire magnetic tape would be re-recorded or just one track would be shifted by a few seconds.

NASA to the Robot Rescue

The imagineers did resolve the problem of programming the toucan, but it remained for them to discover how to animate dozens of birds simultaneously, along with the lighting for the show and the triggering of the special effects. Their state-of-the-art tape recorder could record only thirty-two tracks on one tape, while the animation of a single bird monopolized twenty. WED managed to unearth a NASA invention that at the time of the space race had been classified as top secret. The IRIG (Inertial Reference Integrating Gyro) System employed six tones, from high pitch to low pitch, that could be recorded together on a single track without interfering with one another. Using this system, the imagineers could record 320 actions on a single thirty-two-track tape. WED possessed a revolutionary animation technology, which Walt Disney would name Audio-Animatronics. Its first use was for *Walt Disney's Enchanted Tiki Room,* which opened in June 1963. In the setting of a Polynesian hut, dozens of birds, flowers, and wooden totems talked and sang for a quarter of an hour. Walt Disney appeared to be a magician for whom nothing was impossible. The organizers of the New York World's Fair that was to take place in 1964 asked him to

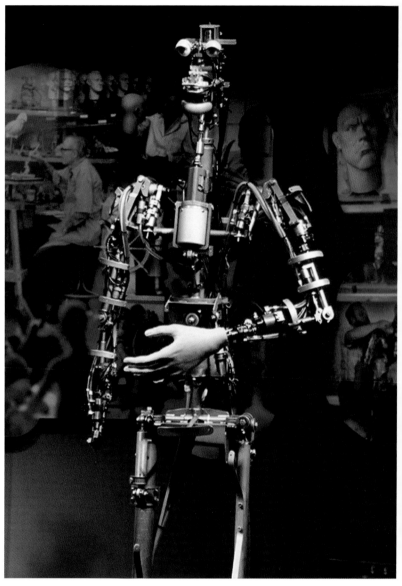

The hydraulic and pneumatic mechanisms of an Audio-Animatronic character
Photo © Disney Enterprises, Inc.

conceive four attractions. He accepted, on the condition that he could repatriate them to Disneyland. With the budget he received, he perfected the uses of Audio-Animatronics. In *It's a Small World,* hundreds of small dolls sang the same song in all the languages of the world.

Magic Skyway, sponsored by Ford Motors, presented time travel in a car, beginning with the discovery of (animated) animals and ending at a futuristic space station. But the third attraction was Disney's masterpiece: *Great Moments With Lincoln.*

Lincoln's Foibles

The President Lincoln robot finally was ready. Pushing against the armrests, it was able to rise up from its chair. The programming of the movement was quite problematic, and the android crushed the chair beneath him during test runs! Folding chairs were made to finish the recording of the animation. The robot worked well in California, but its movements became chaotic when it was set up in New York. On opening night, when the room was filled with celebrities, Walt Disney walked onstage and announced that the robot would not appear until it functioned properly. Bob Gurr, the engineer who had conceived of Lincoln's mechanisms, recalled the event: "Lincoln's movements were controlled by information recorded on magnetic tracks. Many animations were recorded under different frequencies on one single track, so that you could manage to control a great number of simultaneous movements. The electronic device that separated these frequencies was disrupted by electric interference produced by the room's lighting system. As soon as we had isolated the animation monitor room, Lincoln worked like a dream." A few days later, Lincoln nimbly rose, presented his speech, and became the sensation of the New York World's Fair.

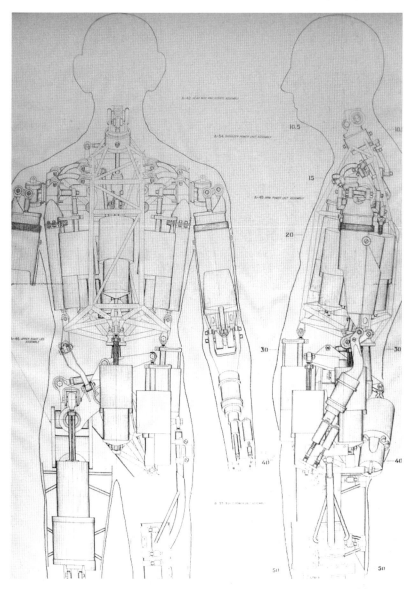

The blueprint for the mechanisms of the Lincoln robot designed by Bob Gurr in 1964
Photo courtesy of Bob Gurr

The Carousel of Progress

Walt Disney himself conceived the fourth attraction, *The Carousel of Progress,* which described the evolution of equipment in the American home in 1880, 1920, 1950, and 1964. The audience was seated in a ring that revolved around a circular stage. With each rotation, it discovered a new "slice" of the set and a new group of Audio-Animatronic characters. Wathel Rogers used a "control harness" to record the movements of the narrator, the father of the family. This gear consisted of jointed pieces attached to the technician's hands, arms, and head. When Rogers moved an arm, potentiometers attached to his joints would record many actions at the same time: the extension of the arm, the rotation of the forearm and the wrist, and the opening of the hand. The process was limited, but it made it possible to program the basic movements of the character quickly. The media, won over, crowned Walt Disney "King of the New York World's Fair."

Disneyland: Phase 2

Upon returning to California, Walt Disney described a project for a wax museum dedicated to pirates, an idea he presented Marc Davis, the creator of *Peter Pan*'s Tinkerbell and Cruella De Vil of *One Hundred and One Dalmatians,* as well as the outstanding graphic design

of *Sleeping Beauty.* Davis immersed himself in research about pirates and drew irresistible villains. Disney, enthusiastic, decided to animate them using Audio-Animatronics. Visitors passed through the attraction in the flat-bottom boats created for *It's a Small World.* Propelled by jets of water that were distributed all along the route, these boats became integrated into the fantasy scene of the pirates and could even glide on flooded overpasses, to the surprise of the visitors. Designer Claude Coates placed the models on trestles set at eye level. By doing this, he could see the sets just as future visitors would. He used this viewing angle to establish which areas still lacked props and set details, and where he could install hollow props to conceal the light sources.

Three-Dimensional Animation

Marc Davis deconstructed the animation of the pirates into many drawings. Blaine Gibson transposed them into statuettes that were then approved by Davis, before serving as models for life-size figures. Molds of these sculptures were used to make transparent plastic bodies and soft urethane faces. According to their animation, the bodies were cut open and equipped with hydraulic mechanisms. By merely removing the character's clothing, technicians could examine the mechanisms through the plastic

without dismantling anything. This gained precious time, as more than twenty robots often had to be thoroughly examined to locate the source of a single oil

leak. To animate a pirate, a technician started by programming the movements of the character's mouth, then those of the head, followed by the arms and finally the rest of the body. In all, 119 Audio-Animatronics—64 humans and 55 animals—brought to life the grand fresco of the *Pirates of the Caribbean.*

Forty years after its creation, the Pirates of the Caribbean *attraction remains one of the most beautiful in the world.*
Photo © Disney Enterprises, Inc.

A Surprising Wardrobe

With the constant repetition of their motion cycles, the robots quickly wore out their costumes. Mark Davis's wife, Alice, fashioned clothes with very sturdy linings that enabled the outfits, which had openings that corresponded to the poses of the robots, to be slipped over the plastic without catching at the joints. When a pirate had his hands on the stock of a cannon, his sleeves and shirt were equipped with a zipper that ran the length of his arm and all the way to his waist. Each outfit was made in duplicate.

Innocuous Flames

The fire in the fortified city was one of the major scenes in the pirate attraction. The imagineers cut pieces of silvery cloth in the shape of flames, placed them over bellows powerful enough to make them stand erect, and then illuminated them with orange projectors. The fiery effect was so successful that the Los Angeles Fire Department required the installation of an emergency cut-off system for the fake flames, because they were afraid firefighters would not be able to differentiate them from the real thing in the case of a fire! During the completion of the attraction, Walt Disney began preparing another project: an amusement resort even bigger than Disneyland, in which he was already feeling

cramped. He traveled to Florida incognito and, for five million dollars, bought plots of land one by one totaling 32,125 acres (13,000 hectares), an expanse equivalent to the size of San Francisco. But he would not see the completion of the detailed Disney World that he had conceived. After years of battling lung cancer, he died on December 15, 1966, three months before the triumphant inauguration of the *Pirates of the Caribbean*.

999 Ghosts, 0 Holograms

Thanks to the success of Disneyland, the small entity of WED was transformed into Walt Disney Imagineering (WDI). In 1969, after the *Pirates of the Caribbean*, WDI brought to fruition a project initiated by Walt twelve years earlier: *The Haunted Mansion*. The ghosts that vanished before the eyes of the visitors were not holograms, as was often reported, but reflections that appeared on the glass panes in front of the sets. Real Audio-Animatronic characters, dressed in white, were situated out of the audience's view in a darkened area. Their reflections on the glass were perceptible only when they were brightly lit. The trick consisted of positioning them in such a way that their reflections seemed to "hang out" in the set. This effect worked like a charm in the banquet hall. Visitors seated in buggies traveled along with the impression that the ghosts were seated on chairs

down below, or hanging from the chandeliers, or playing the organ. It was all a matter of positioning. The large panes of glass placed between the room's metal girders were plotted on a straight line that separated the visible set from its symmetrical invisible part and were hidden beneath the route of the buggies. The ghosts sitting behind the large table were characters whose bottom halves were hidden by a black cloth. They were placed equally far from the glass as the chairs in the visible set. So when each ghost was illuminated, its reflection was perfectly aligned with its corresponding chair, regardless of the angle of observation. The other amazing effect in this haunted house was the apparition of Madame Leota's head inside a crystal ball perched on a pedestal. The ball contained a frosted glass screen in the shape of a face. The screen-face was surrounded by a white wig that hid a mirror set at a forty-five-degree angle inside the head. A movie projector placed under the ball projected images of an actress's face, her eyes and mouth heavily made up, onto the mirror. Because of the tilted mirror, this projection was reflected toward the screen in the form of a face, fitting its contours. In recent years, a video rear projection has been substituted for the original film system.

The superb illusions of Phantom Manor *at Disneyland Paris*
Photo © Disney Enterprises, Inc.

Post-Walt

Walt Disney's brother Roy died in 1971, after having successfully launched Walt Disney World. The first theme park realized without the input of Walt Disney would be a liberal adaptation of his last ideas: the World Showcase, a lake surrounded by sets depicting countries all around the world, and EPCOT (Experimental Proto-type Community of Tomorrow), a veritable proto-city. Inaugurated in 1982, EPCOT Center comprises Futureworld and the World Showcase. In *Ellen's Energy Adventure* (renamed and reconceived in 1996 from the original *Universe of Energy*), visitors sit in three train cars, each with a 150-person capacity, that automatically detect and follow metal guidelines embedded in the floor and enter a landscape populated with dinosaurs. Odor generators are dispersed along the route, and visitors breathe in the fetid smells of a swamp, the sulfur fumes of a volcano, and the iodine scent of a cave, home to a sea monster. *Mission: Space,* inaugurated in 2003, lets visitors experience a journey on a space shuttle. Installed in booths set along the axle of an enormous centrifuge, they get to feel sensations similar to those of acceleration at liftoff. The different positions the booths can take during their rotations also give a brief feeling of weightlessness. At the American pavilion of the World Showcase, *The American Adventure* compresses two hundred years of the history of the United States into a half-hour show that uses thirty-five robots placed in front of the world's largest back projection screen (one hundred feet, or thirty meters, at its base). Miniature landscapes are projected onto the screen, while characters and set elements emerge from a stage without any floorboards, which would look like a huge rectangular trench if the audience could see it from above. During the show, an animated likeness of Benjamin Franklin limps up a staircase. The support attached to the stiff leg, which lifts up and moves the robot as he walks, is concealed through a slit in the steps. This character benefits from the many advances made in Audio-Animatronics since 1969, when WDI abandoned the technique of recording movements on different magnetic tapes in favor of using DACS (Digital Animation Control System) computers. This makes it possible to record a character's movements, analyze them, and then manipulate the data in order to insert changes. An entire day of programming will yield only one second of animation for a complicated character.

George Lucas Lends a Strong Hand to Disney

At the request of Michael Eisner, the new CEO of Disney, George Lucas produced *Captain Eo,* a mini-musical comedy that ran for seventeen minutes, was shot in 70 millimeter, and was shown in 3-D. It was directed by Francis Ford Coppola and starred Michael Jackson. During the screening, the ceiling and screen were lit up with fiber optic stars. Smoke and beams of light and laser rays were synchronized with the effects in the film. Pleased with their collaboration, Lucas and Eisner decided to create an attraction based on *Star Wars,* called *Star Tours.* ILM produced a long sequence shot from a subjective point of view that re-created space battles, the chase sequence in the trench of the Death Star, and the final explosion in *Star Wars.* Seated in a spaceship that is moved by hydraulic jacks, visitors feel the maneuvers of the trip as they survey space outside the cockpit. The third Lucas-Eisner collaboration was a teleportation experience entitled *Extraterrestrial Alien Encounter.* A restraint comes crashing down onto the shoulders of visitors, immobilizing them in their seats, which surround a large glass cylinder. A monster is teleported by accident. It pulverizes the cylinder and hurls itself into the room, diving into the darkness. Special sound effects make the audience believe that the creature is right up close to them. The sound effects were recorded using four microphones inserted into a reproduction of a human head replete with ears. The sounds are so precise that the audience can locate the grunts of the creature as it approaches, while a hot exhalation breathes down their backs! In 2004, the ugly monster made way for a cuter one: *Stitch's Great Escape,* based on the *Lilo and Stitch* animated feature film, replaced Lucas's scary concept.

Backstage at the Movies

In 1989, Walt Disney World opened a third park, Disney-MGM Studios, dedicated to the film world of Hollywood. The witch who springs out of the *Wizard of Oz* scenery in the *Great Movie Ride* attraction was the first robot equipped with the Compliance System, which generates perfectly natural movements. Its great innovation consisted of placing digital decoders in the axes of a character's joints. The computer system that controlled the animation received a "report" twenty-four times per second on the position of each joint, enabling it to correct the robot's stance to correspond with the initial programming. The animation was supple, rapid, and so precise that the witch could grasp two ends of a rope to make a knot.

Jules Verne at Disneyland Paris

Since opening in 1992, Disneyland Paris has paid homage to Jules Verne in its Discoveryland. Introduced by the robot Time-keeper, the *Visionarium* space voyage is depicted with a ten-minute movie in Circlevision that cost eighteen million dollars. It ends with a spectacular flyover of a future Paris created with synthesized images. *Space Mountain* evokes the novel *De la terre à la lune* (*From Earth to the Moon*) with its cannon that projects visitors toward our satellite. The submarine attraction, the *Nautilus,* anchored next door, lets visitors looking through the portholes in Captain Nemo's cabin witness an attack by a giant octopus.

Indiana Jones and the Temple of the Forbidden Eye

In 1995, WDI celebrated the fortieth anniversary of Disneyland by unveiling one of its most beautiful attractions: *Indiana Jones and the Temple of the Forbidden Eye.* After walking through the corridors of an archaeological site, visitors got into jeeps to explore an underground temple. They discovered an immense room flooded with lava but escaped thanks to the warnings from a robotic Indiana Jones. The fifteen twelve-seat jeeps in which visitors traveled were "Enhanced Motion Vehicles" that weighed six tons and cost a million dollars apiece. While moving on flat land, each vehicle would rock the platform/chassis in which the passengers were seated. It would also simulate accidents, amplify the effects of acceleration by pitching the platform backward, and accentuate the braking by brutally tilting it toward the front. Its six axes of motion were animated by hydraulic jacks equipped with electric servo-valves. The jeep seemed to tear along at top speed, while in truth it never went more than twelve and a half miles (twenty kilometers) per hour. The random programming, sent by a radio modem link, triggered novel surprises on each journey. These vehicles were also equipped with a stereo system that generated atmospheric music and sound effects such as the screeching of tires and the humming of the engine.

An Asian Forest in Flames

Disney's Animal Kingdom, inaugurated in Florida in 1998,

At the Dinosaur attraction in Animal Kingdom, visitors travel aboard all-terrain vehicles to come face-to-face with the carnotaurs and mastodonts that spring out from the shadows. The seats of the jeep are set on an animated platform that magnifies the action of the brakes, the turns, and the acceleration as the vehicle moves.
Photo © Disney Enterprises, Inc.

exhibits not only real animals in their natural habitat, but also mythological and prehistoric creatures. The symbol of the park is a tree the height of a fourteen-story building, which is composed of a tubular steel structure with a cement bark covered by the sculpted images of three hundred animals. In the Asian zone, the *Tiger Rapids Run* presents an exciting river raft journey. The rapids cross through a tropical forest impregnated with the smell of burning wood. A fire spreads through the hewn trees spread out on the ground. An enormous flaming trunk has crashed down into the river. Designer Rex Harris was assigned the task of creating these trees that burn 365 days a year: "We chose a material that was resistant to both flames and the torrential rains that hit Florida. It's a heat-resistant cement that's used to build furnaces. We cast it onto metal structures covered with wire fencing. While the cement was drying, sculptors gave them the appearance and texture of wood. We applied many coats of paint on the material when it was still fresh, following the technique of frescoes, and then the final coat."

The Attractions of the Virtual World

Battle for the Buccaneer's Gold is the virtual version of the *Pirates of the Caribbean* that is the focal point of DisneyQuest at Walt Disney World. Wearing special

glasses, the players seated on the bridge of a ship shoot cannonballs at the pirate ships appearing in 3-D. The computer-generated images projected onto the screens are produced in real time so as to present two points of view—one from the right eye, and one from the left. The video is projected at a rate of fifty frames per second. The glasses worn by the players are equipped with liquid crystal shutters that alternately blind the right and left eyes, fifty times per second. Each eye perceives only the twenty-five images intended for it, and it is the mix of these two sources that creates the 3-D projection. Joe Garlington, the producer of attractions at DisneyQuest, has other innovations in mind for upcoming years. "Some of the technologies that we test stimulate the sense of smell. It's more complicated than you'd think, because the nose quickly adapts to an odor and stops smelling it. We also test sensory perception generators—hot, cold, pressure, detection of textures. We are looking forward to using the skin as a sensor, as well as an emitter. Our body is an electrical field crossed by impulses. By attaching a system to your hands that measures their electrical conductivity, you can transform them into controls for the game, into 'organic joysticks.'"

The attraction Battle for the Buccaneer's Gold *at DisneyQuest*
Photo © Disney Enterprises, Inc.

Tokyo DisneySea

Inaugurated in 2001, the Tokyo DisneySea park was the most expensive ever built, costing two and a half billion dollars. It was the result of a collaboration between Disney and the Japanese firm Oriental Land Company (OLC). Since 1983, Tokyo Disneyland has had the highest attendance record of all the Disney parks—seventeen million visitors per year. Encouraged by this success, OLC invested a colossal budget into the creation of a second park, this one dedicated to the universe of the sea. The Hotel MiraCosta, located at the entry of the park, is a reconstruction of a small Italian coastal city. After passing through its archways, you discover an enormous volcano, at the foot of which is a Renaissance fortress. Walking around the volcano, you come upon the retro-futuristic building housing the *StormRider* attraction. The audience gathers in the cockpit of a giant airplane—a platform with a 120-person capacity—and descends into the eye of a cyclone. Despite its fifty-eight-ton weight, the platform moves and tilts up and down very smoothly to match the images of the aerial maneuvers of the plane. The flight sequence depicting the audience's point of view "from the cockpit" was produced by Digital Domain. The superb computer-generated effects are rear-projected on a giant screen. The most beautiful achievement at Tokyo DisneySea is Captain Nemo's Mysterious Island, in a set of a gigantic

The Mount Prometheus volcano at Tokyo DisneySea, and the crater in the set of Captain Nemo's Mysterious Island. The visitors walking along the bridge give an idea of the scale of the set.
Photo © Disney Enterprises, Inc.

crater. There, you get to see a drill hoisted up, ready to bore through one of the level's walls. Just across from it, near the moored *Nautilus,* an enormous, bubbling mass of water sporadically shoots up from the crater lake, to the great astonishment of the spectators. A metal spiral leads to Captain Nemo's bathyscaphe and *20,000 Leagues Under the Sea.* Inside the riveted capsule, spectators get to discover wrecks of gold-filled Spanish galleons, the realm of a giant octopus, and the ruins of Atlantis. Different levels of the crater give access to Nemo's underground laboratory and to the vehicles created for the *Journey to the Center of the Earth,* through caverns covered in bright crystals and a forest of giant mushrooms populated with strange creatures. When a monster emerges from a lava lake, the exploration vehicle shoots up to the surface from

The superb computer-generated images of the StormRider *attraction at Tokyo DisneySea*
Photo © Disney Enterprises, Inc.

one of the fuming openings of the volcano and hurtles down a dizzying slope. The quality of the sets and effects presented at Tokyo DisneySea are unequivocally stupendous.

Walt Disney Studios Park

Ever since 2002, Walt Disney Studios Park, the second Disney

Visitors embarking on a discovery of the subterranean world of Journey to the Center of the Earth *at Tokyo DisneySea*

installation in France, has presented a glimpse into the secrets of special effects. Aboard the *Studio Tram Tour,* visitors get to discover the rock formations of Catastrophe Canyon as the tram stops next to a tanker truck filled with fuel. Enormous hydraulic jacks then shake the tram cars, simulating an earthquake. Sparks fly from the electricity poles installed throughout the set, while jacks concealed at their bases make them sway and come crashing down just millimeters from the truck, which then catches fire. Thanks to gas pipes hidden in the slits of the reinforced cement rocks, flames spread across the area. Aftershocks then generate the deluge of 70,000 gallons (265,000 liters) of water over the set, flowing

The spectacular demonstration of special effects at Catastrophe Canyon, presented at the Walt Disney Studios theme park near Paris
Photo © Disney Enterprises, Inc.

from three vast reservoirs. The water is recycled, and all the elements automatically reposition themselves after each show.

Overleaf: *The spectacular* Moteur, Action! *show devised by Rémy Julienne, one of the best car stunt experts in the world, for the Walt Disney Studios theme park*
Photo © Disney Enterprises, Inc.

A High-Tech Roller Coaster

Not far away, you come upon the *Rock 'n' Roller Coaster*, whose limousines take off horizontally at 57 miles (90 kilometers) per hour. The propulsion system is modeled on the catapults that are used to help jets take off from an aircraft carrier. The takeoff runway houses an enormous electric motor that

tows a four-ton "pusher" vehicle installed on tracks. As soon as one of the four twenty-four-seat cars is in position, the pusher vehicle takes it from 0 to 57 miles per hour in 2.8 seconds. The technology of this pusher vehicle is the same as the one that activates the dizzying fall of the elevator in the *Tower of Terror* attraction presented in California and Florida.

INTERVIEW

Roy E. Disney

For millions of people, Walt Disney was a legendary creator. What memories do you have of your uncle?

Roy E. Disney: He was an extraordinary storyteller. I remember coming down with a terrible case of flu when I was nine years old. Walt sat on my bed and told me the story of his next movie, *Pinocchio*. He took on the voices of all the characters, mimicked their moves, and made all the sound effects with his mouth! I worked with him during the last five years of his life, once the disease had already taken hold. He was tired, but he worked every day as much as his strength allowed, because he was incapable of delegating the smallest detail. He was so exhausted that he sometimes was in a bad mood. It was not easy to talk with him then. Notes sent to him could go unanswered. If he deemed them insignificant, he'd throw them in the wastebasket! People have complained about his nastiness toward them, but the truth is that he was uncompromising about the quality of the work. You might get a smile or a pat on the back if he were satisfied,

but if you let him down, you'd see one of his eyebrows rise up in incomprehension, and then the best thing to do was to hide in a mouse hole! He couldn't stand it if you didn't immediately understand what he wanted or took the liberty of changing something he'd asked for. He had a phenomenal memory!

The greater public is not aware that your father, Roy Disney, found the financial backing for Walt's technical innovations.

Roy E. Disney: I think in his realm—the financing and marketing of the projects—Dad was as amazing as Walt. He was born eight years before him, in 1893. My father was the third of the Disney brothers, and Walt was the fourth and last. Dad

always took care of Walt when he was small. And God knows, Walt was a handful. He was a little devil bursting with ideas, a practical joker, and mischievous. During his whole life, Dad always took care of his "little brother," even when they were both over sixty!

How did Roy react when Walt came up with a project as unheard-of as the first full-length animated cartoon or the first theme park?

Roy E. Disney: Dad understood from the start that Walt's ideas were fantastic, even when the whole world considered them crazy and unrealistic. They both invested their last penny in *Snow White* before managing to finish the movie. They went to see Joe Rosenberg, who headed the film division at Bank of America. Dad explained some sequences to him, and Mr. Rosenberg said to him, "Tell me how much money you need. This movie is going to be a huge success." Without this wonderful banker, the studio would have gone bankrupt. And the same thing happened during the construction of Disneyland. The estimates were far exceeded. Dad and Walt had financial problems their entire lives. You take risks when all you build are prototypes, like Disneyland and its revolutionary attractions.

Disney Studios has produced many special effects movies. Which is your favorite?

Roy E. Disney: *Mary Poppins.* It was the first time anyone mixed real actors with animated cartoon characters in such a complicated way. A production of this kind is the equivalent of making a full-length feature with real shots, and then a cartoon. It was twice as much work. Our technical crews took a lot of time perfecting the effects that made it possible to insert the actors into drawn sets. We knew that this movie was unique, but on the opening night the entire crew was moved to tears by the ecstatic response of the audience.

Do you remember a day when your father seemed particularly happy with the success of one of his projects?

Roy E. Disney: Yes. Opening day of Walt Disney World in Florida, in 1971. Walt died in December 1966, and during the following five years, Dad exerted an insane energy to bring his project to fruition. The land had been dotted with swamps. Everything was drained and cleaned up. Roads, gardens, lighting, golf courses, and hotels were built all around our first park in Florida, the Magic Kingdom. On inauguration day, when Dad declared the park open, a band of 76 trombones and a 101 cornets marched in front of us. The sound was so powerful that the ground vibrated. Afterward, everyone came over to offer their congratulations to this private man who had chosen to stay in the shadows. He was so radiant that the day remains etched in my memory. Three months later, when my parents and I were going to take the children to Disneyland so my wife could get a break, Dad called me to say he wasn't feeling well. We went without him. I don't know why, but during that day I couldn't think about anything but him. And when we got back to the house, we found him motionless on the floor. He had had a violent attack.

(Roy E. Disney is silent for a moment.) He devoted his last efforts to this project. We told ourselves in consolation that he died quickly, without having spent time suffering.

The work your father accomplished was that much more important because Disneyland and Walt Disney World saved the Disney Corporation when it underwent setbacks in the film world.

Roy E. Disney: Thank you for mentioning that. It's true that a genius like Walt always needed the backing of an equal.

INTERVIEW

STEVE KIRK

Executive Producer of Tokyo DisneySea

Steve Kirk worked for Walt Disney Imagineering for twenty-five years. Responsible for the design of Tokyo DisneySea, he oversaw the work of the entire conception team for the ten years of preparation that preceded the opening of the park.

How does the "20,000 Leagues Under the Sea" attraction work?

Steve Kirk: The bathyscaphes hold six people. They are suspended from the top and progress down the length of an invisible track. The sets are illuminated by fluorescent "black light" and moiré light patterns. The diving effect is produced "dry," using a double-walled porthole in which we make bubbles rise. We use hundreds of hydraulic and pneumatic

mechanisms to slowly animate the algae and the props so it seems that they're being moved by the sea current.

What's the size of the volcano, the icon of the park, and how was it conceived?

Steve Kirk: Mount Prometheus is 168 feet (51 meters) tall. The interior crater, Vulcan's Cauldron, ranges in diameter from 360 to 460 feet (110 to 140 meters). It's the largest sculpture ever made for an attraction park—an area of 754,000 square feet (70,047 square meters), adorned with 128,000 artificial plants, with 2,000 pieces of rock to simulate rock falls, four waterfalls, and some twenty beds of bushes equipped with a watering system. We started by constructing a very big model on a 100th scale, which we scanned to get a 3-D representation. This computer-generated image

Above and overleaf: Mission: Space's magnificent building and cabin, presented at EPCOT in Florida. Visitors are seated in capsules attached to a centrifuge and get to experience the sensation of takeoff in a space shuttle, which is approximately twice the force of gravity. This technical feat required the participation of 650 imagineers and more than 400,000 work-hours.

was cut into sections that were used to create the plans for the crater's metal armatures. It was a gigantic puzzle, each element of which was composed of a set of steel bars adjusted to the millimeter. The shapes of the rocks were also obtained by twisting steel bars that were then encased in metal fencing and covered over with cement. Such a complicated construction process could only have been done with a computer. The geyser that shoots up in the center of the crater works by a very large reservoir beneath the surface that slowly refills. The air pressure mounts in a second part of the reservoir, just below, and when the pressure is sufficient, the valve opens and 32,000 gallons (121,000 liters) of water are projected 65 feet (20 meters) into the air. The system program varies the rhythm of the eruptions and the amount of water projected to replicate a natural phenomenon.

How did you create the "Journey to the Center of the Earth" attraction?

Steve Kirk: We used electric vehicles, self-propelled by a 322-horsepower Mitsubishi engine controlled by an onboard computer. Differing from roller

coaster cars, these vehicles can accelerate on the incline, which gives a completely new sensation! They start off at 4.6 feet (1.4 meters) per second and then, in a flash, exceed 70 feet (21 meters) per second. The giant crystals that come out of the walls are sculptures out of which we made silicone molds. We made casts of them in transparent resin and inserted fiber optics that allow us to program subtle color changes. The fauna and flora of the subterranean world are composed of some twenty species, on which we spent a long time testing the effects of transparency and translucence. The giant creature that appears at the end of the attraction is animated by special hydraulic valves. The oil that activates the hydraulic pistons can be sent faster, in greater quantities, and under greater pressure with the above systems. The creature can move very quickly despite his ten tons.

Universal Studios: When the Audience Is Projected into the Movies

In 1884, a German immigrant named Carl Laemmle landed on American soil. After a variety of other jobs, he opened a small movie house in a Chicago neighborhood in 1906. Soon he was heading a network of several dozen theaters. He founded a film distribution company, entered the production side of the industry in 1909, and then, in 1912, joined with other companies to form the Universal Film Manufacturing Company. His movie about slavery, *Traffic in Souls,* had a huge success in 1913. Laemmle invested $165,000 of the total $450,000 of receipts in the purchase of Taylor Ranch, located just north of Hollywood. Construction work began on Universal Studios in June 1914, and by September, film production was in full swing.

Carl Laemmle, the founder of Universal Studios
Photo courtesy of Universal Studios Hollywood

The Discovery of the Mysterious World of Film

Laemmle was aware that the public was fascinated by the backstage workings of film. He opened the doors of his studios to them for the nominal fee of twenty-five cents. On March 15, 1915, the first visitors attended the filming of a movie and ate a meal served on-site. Universal Studios continued to welcome hundreds of thousands of guests until 1930. Visits were discontinued with the advent of talking pictures, in order to maintain silence on the sets. In 1931, with such great successes as *Dracula* and *Frankenstein,* Universal became one of the major companies in the American film world. In the following thirty years, it would specialize in horror movies and thrillers, would join forces with Alfred Hitchcock, and would become one of the main producers of television series. In 1958, MCA (Music Corporation of America) offered to buy the land from Laemmle's heirs for one million dollars and rent the studio space for an additional one million dollars a year. The success Disneyland had experienced ever since 1955 gave the company the idea of once again organizing visits to the sets at Universal Studios. In 1961, the Grey Line Bus Company, in association with the project, created a small tour of the movie sets. The visit ended with a meal at the studio canteen, where visitors

Beginning in 1917, visitors could attend the filming of a western.
Photo courtesy of Universal Studios Hollywood

Visitors meet John Wayne during the filming of one of his movies.
Photo courtesy of Universal Studios Hollywood

Discovering a painted trompe l'oeil panorama backstage on a film set Photo courtesy of Universal Studios Hollywood

Resin-and-fiberglass boulders at the Avalanche! *attraction roll down toward the tram without causing the least damage.*
Photo courtesy of Universal Studios Hollywood

Charlton Heston with his staff of Moses . . . and once again, the Red Sea parts.
Photo courtesy of Universal Studios Hollywood

Visitors arrive on the other side perfectly dry.
Photo courtesy of Universal Studios Hollywood

could catch a glimpse of the stars as they went by. The public came streaming in, but the roar of the bus engines was a nightmare for the sound engineers. Silent trams were introduced in 1964. Two years later, the visitors' entrance was relocated to an upper area of

the land that led directly into the studios, where visitors continued down into the back lot to find themselves in the streets of European cities and the ruins of Roman temples. The first show was a demonstration of stunts from westerns. The special

effects attractions would not debut until the 1970s.

In 1973, the "Red Sea" would begin to part before each tram, but instead of Moses' efforts, a system of locks hidden along the route made it possible to cross the sea while remaining dry. In

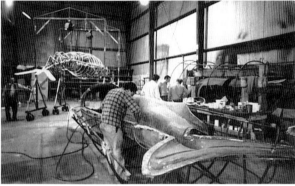

1975, *The Jaws Experience* let
visitors have a brief close
encounter with the infamous
shark. The robotic shark would
swim alongside the tram and leap
out of the water, gnashing its
teeth to terrorize the visitors.
When they were scarcely out of
the tram, the Frankenstein monster would appear and escort
them to the *Dracula* show. The
confrontation between the vampire and humans armed with
crosses and flasks of holy water
was punctuated with stunts and
pyrotechnical effects. One of the
most fantastic effects appeared
at the end of the show, when
Dracula freed his vampire bats.
Emerging from the scenery, hundreds of flapping wings skimmed
past the heads of the frightened

*Construction of the
set and the
mechanical shark
in* Jaws
Photos courtesy of
Universal Studios
Hollywood

The shark in action

Alfred Hitchcock visits the studio with a friend. Photo courtesy of Universal Studios Hollywood

The set of the Dracula show Photo courtesy of AVG & Universal Studios Hollywood

A robotic mannequin of the Phantom of the Opera—created by AVG—welcomes the audience to the opening of Dracula.
Photo courtesy of AVG & Universal Studios Hollywood

audience. The terrifying bats, however, were merely pigeons illuminated by a strobe light! The *Dracula* show closed in 1984 to make room for *The Adventures of Conan: Sword and Sorcery Spectacular*. Onstage, an Arnold Schwarzenegger impersonator battled a horde of brigands in the set of a temple. A sorcerer grabbed the magic jewel embedded in a bas-relief and hurled lightning bolts at the Barbarian. When Conan attacked him with a crash of his sword, his enemy turned into a twenty-six-foot-tall (eight-meter), fire-breathing dragon whose eyes shot lethal rays. The dragon, Universal's first giant robot, was the conception of Bob Gurr, an expert in hydraulic animations ever since his collaboration with Disney on the character representation of Lincoln. The monster was piloted by computer. A number of photoelectric cells were placed throughout the set to make certain the actors and stuntmen were not at risk of being hurt by the flames or lasers. If the surveillance system

detected a malpositioning, the pyrotechnical effects would be momentarily interrupted. The *Conan* show was such a success that it continued for ten years. Still banking on Gurr's monsters and expertise, Universal Studios inaugurated its *King Kong* attraction in 1988. The tram crossed over a New York bridge as it was being shaken by the giant gorilla, whose exhalation smelled of bananas! The *Earthquake* attraction, which debuted in 1989, was even more spectacular. The tram traveled through the set of a subway station devastated by an earthquake. The cement floor caved in, flames shot up from all sides, and a life-size subway car crashed into the fallen rocks. Tens of thousands of gallons of water flooded into the set. Once the enactment was over, all the elements automatically returned to their original places. The set would remain intact just until the next tram arrived.

The destructive gaze of the dragon created by Bob Gurr

The dragon exhaling fire

Kong's enormous mechanical structure
Photos courtesy of Bob Gurr & Universal Studios Hollywood

King Kong shakes the bridge over which the visi- tors' tram crosses.
Photo courtesy of Bob Gurr & Universal Studios Hollywood

The Earthquake *attraction*
Photo courtesy of Universal Studios Hollywood

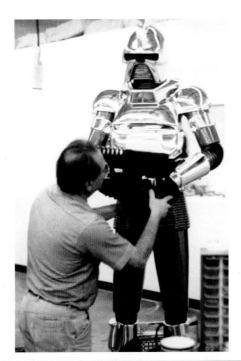

Constructing the Cylon robots at the AVG studios
Photo courtesy of AVG

The Battle of Galactica *attraction: a laser gun battle between actors and computer-controlled robots*
Photo courtesy of Universal Studios Hollywood

Spielberg's World

In 1964, a seventeen-year-old boy jumped off the tram to walk around where he wanted. He wandered into the production offices looking for a low-level job and then, passing for an employee, managed to get past the studio guards, who let him come back every day. The adolescent lent a hand to whomever he met and, during the course of his summer vacation, took in the atmosphere of the studio. The boy's name was Steven Spielberg. Five years later, after having made two promising student films, he was hired by Universal Studios to direct one of the segments of the pilot for the television series *Night Gallery*. The collaboration between Spielberg and Universal Studios moved on to film production with *Jaws* and *E.T.*, two of Universal's biggest

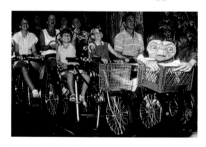

Visitors take off with E.T.
Photo courtesy of Universal Studios Florida

hits. Spielberg became a creative consultant for Universal and oversaw the adaptations of his movies into attractions and spin-off merchandise. In 1992, he created the screenplay for

E.T. Adventure. Visitors hop aboard bicycles on a platform suspended along a track. They fly over a forest invaded by scientists, who try to capture the little extraterrestrial, and then soar into the stars to discover the rich plant life on E.T.'s planet. On entering, each visitor enters his or her first name into a computer, allowing the extraterrestrial to bid a personal farewell to his guests.

The Florida Studios

In 1990, Spielberg inaugurated a new theme park costing $630 million: Universal Studios Florida. This is where you can discover *Back to the Future: The Ride,* based on the trilogy of movies. Visitors take their seats in a car/time machine to intercept the evil Biff before he creates a time paradox, as well as

Images from the Omnimax movie at the Back to the Future attraction, which was made with miniatures and superbly filmed by Douglas Trumbull
Photo courtesy of Universal Studios Florida

Seated aboard the famous DeLorean from Back to the Future, the audience is projected inside a giant image.
Photo courtesy of Universal Studios Florida

fly over a futuristic city and a landscape from the Ice Age, and then just miss getting swallowed by a dinosaur at the edges of an erupting volcano. During the four-minute ride, the eight passengers in each car—a cleverly

Events along the journey of
Back to the Future
Photo courtesy of Universal
Studios Florida

decorated flight simulator—are plunged into the 70-millimeter movie projected onto a hemispherical screen. The Omnimax image fills the field of vision. Douglas Trumbull used a computer-assisted camera to film the miniature sets of this mind-boggling sequence, which cost a mere $15 million.

The Return of the Giant Shark

When Spielberg created a new adaptation of *Jaws* for the Florida park, he was given forty-five million dollars—twice the budget of his original 1975 movie! This time, visitors board a tour boat and discover that the boat preceding theirs has been reduced to shreds. An enormous fin tears through the surface of the water and heads straight toward them. The shark will follow the visitors

into the floating hangar where they have taken refuge, and then reemerge when least expected. Three cybernetic sharks, each weighing three tons, attack the boat in turn. A submerged hydraulic system propels them along tracks at a speed of twenty-three feet (seven meters) per second, reaching a force equivalent to that of a 747 jet engine. Their steel structure is encased in a fiberglass-and-resin shell that is covered by a latex skin.

The Biggest Robot in the World

When Spielberg was not working on attractions, he was drawing inspiration from them. He was especially impressed by the new *Kongfrontation,* in which King Kong embarks on a destructive frenzy through the streets of New York. The giant gorilla

extends his arm as if to shake the cable car carrying the visitors. Bob Gurr was the animator of this, the world's biggest robot, whose arms alone weigh several tons: "A giant creature is easier to animate than a human-sized character because you have all the space you need to put the mechanisms inside the body. The animation of King Kong's arms was built on a very basic pendulum principle. Jacks would push the arms downward toward the basket where the audience was. The jacks were assisted by a mass placed on the other side of the character's shoulder joint. As soon as the jacks were disengaged, the arms would automatically rise up again to a position that guaranteed perfect safety. It was one of the easiest jobs I'd ever done!" Won over by this effort, Spielberg asked Gurr to collaborate with Stan Winston on

the animation for the life-size tyrannosaurus that was to appear in his next movie, *Jurassic Park.* "I met Stan Winston in his studio with Steven," recalled Gurr. "Stan had already created the mechanical puppets, but they'd never been animated by powerful hydraulic systems. I offered my advice to Stan and suggested he hire two of my collaborators who'd worked on King Kong. They brought him top-notch knowledge in the field." The giant gorilla left in 2004 to make way for *Revenge of the Mummy,* an innovative attraction featuring a wild rollercoaster ride, a superb robotic Imhotep mummy created by Walt Conti, and scary effects based on the *Mummy* blockbuster films directed by Stephen Sommers.

Jurassic Park

In 1994, one year after the release of *Jurassic Park,* technology came full circle when Spielberg transposed his movie to Universal Studios Hollywood. Visitors seated aboard pneumatic boats first came upon an ultrasaurus and some stegosauruses grazing on leaves. Robotic mastodonts would shoot up to the surface of the river. Their electric and electronic instruments were carefully insulated from the water. Several systems designed to detect any

The ultrasaurus that welcomes visitors to the Jurassic Park *attraction*
Photo courtesy of Universal Studios Florida

leakage of the hydraulic liquid (a biodegradable oil) made it possible to interrupt the animation of a character should a problem arise. At the entry to the "Jurassic Park" research complex, the boats are hoisted up by a moving pathway onto a large ramp.

During the climb, large velociraptors spring from the scenery. To control the element of surprise, the dinosaurs are linked to a battery of detectors that activate them to move just as each boat passes by. Next, the passengers are beset by a life-size

A parasaurolophus shoots up
from the depths.

Velociraptors on the attack in
the desert region

Re-creation of the spinosaur in
Jurassic Park III

Opposite: *The enormous T-Rex
leans toward the spectators,
ready to grab one.*

Photos courtesy of Universal Studios
Florida

A baby raptor hatches in the nursery on "Jurassic Park" island at Universal's Islands of Adventure.

Steven Spielberg pets the sick triceratops at the "Jurassic Park" island infirmary.

T. rex that bends down toward them, ready to take a bite. They escape by plunging down a slide eighty-four feet (twenty meters) high that leads to a pool. The T. rex is animated by enormous hydraulic jacks, using a feedback system to verify that the movements produced correspond precisely to those programmed. It is an indispensable precaution, as this robot is so powerful that should it deviate from the planned movements, it could destroy the surrounding building. In 1999, Universal's new theme park, Islands of Adventure in Florida, dedicated one of its five islands to the theme of "Jurassic Park." In addition to the *River Adventure*

attraction, which surpasses Universal Studios Hollywood's original version, visitors get to discover a dinosaur nursery and attend the hatching of a velociraptor egg, an effect developed by the California company Animal Makers. The baby dinosaur is animated by servomotors linked to a series of microprocessors, in which its remote-controlled programmed movements have been entered. Once activated, the baby raises its head and breaks apart the precut pieces of its eggshell. In the island's infirmary, a female triceratops interacts with the visitors and her veterinarians. The dinosaur's behavior is adapted to the audience by

The Ghostbusters *show, created in 1990, was replaced by the attraction* Twister *in 1998. The famous ghost hunters confronted supernatural creatures at the peak of a skyscraper. The animatronic "ghosts" hidden above the audience were reflected on the arced glass panes that separated the stage from the hall. As soon as they were brightly lit, they appeared to be superimposed on the sets. Twisting neon floodlights were also set in the wings in such a way that their reflections would correspond with the actors' weapons. When the neon lights were momentarily illuminated, the rays appeared to shoot from the Ghostbusters' plasma guns and strike the ectoplasm.*

alternating different program sequences. It can be made to appear calm or agitated or even to sneeze when a child asks to pet it. This superb robot executes thirty-four simultaneous movements.

One of the Worm Guys of the Men in Black: Alien Attack *attraction banters with the audience in a sarcastic tone.*
Photo courtesy of Universal Studios Florida

Men in Black: Alien Attack

In the year 2000, Spielberg transposed the universe of *Men in Black* (he was the producer of the movie) into an interactive attraction. The audience enters replicas of buildings from the 1964 World's Fair, as seen in the first movie, and discover the secret headquarters of the MIB. Agent J, played by Will Smith, warns them that criminal extraterrestrials have escaped into the streets of New York City. The new recruits are divided into groups of six and put in special vehicles. Armed with laser guns, they are sent off to chase down the fugitives. Aliens spring up on all sides for the audience to shoot them down. If they touch the players' vehicle, it starts to spin like a top. Individual scores and cumulative points are displayed on the dashboard. At the end of the journey, Will Smith castigates the hapless players, congratulates the sharpshooters, and, as a bonus, lets them see a hidden alien MIB agent.

The extraterrestrials at the Men in Black *headquarters do their work on the tips of their tentacles.*
Photo courtesy of Universal Studios Florida

A Life-Size Video Game

"*Men in Black* is one of the biggest attractions ever built," says Dave Cobb, who supervised the design. "The total budget of one hundred million dollars surpasses that of the first movie. We had to construct a gigantic building to house the headquarters and the New York street, and there was a huge amount of effects to invent and test. The guns are equipped with a laser sight so players can aim their shots, as well as an infrared sight. The infrared rays are detected by sensors inserted into the characters, and they activate the animation that

Above and top: *Visitors win points by shooting the extraterrestrials that pop up.*
Photos courtesy of Universal Studios Florida

The Backdraft Experience (1992). Director Ron Howard (Apollo 13, A Beautiful Mind) conceived an attraction at Universal Studios Hollywood based on his movie Backdraft. The show re-creates a fire in an enormous hangar. Computer-controlled gas nozzles regulate the intensity, movement, and height of the flames that spread through the fireproof set. As in the movie, barrels of fuel explode and are hurled into the air. The audience is surrounded by the blaze while, at the same time, the balcony they're sitting on seems to start to collapse. After the show, the set is washed down and all the destroyed elements return to their original places within two minutes.
Photo courtesy of Universal Studios Florida

The set is replete with weird characters.
Photos courtesy of Universal Studios Florida

indicates when they have been hit. The sensor on the gun then receives the information that the shot was good and adds points to the counter. The data are stored in the vehicle's computer, which also can trigger the projection of the Will Smith sequence that corresponds with the final score." The animatronic characters are animated with computer-controlled hydraulic and pneumatic jacks. Their skins are made of colored silicone, detailed and repainted on the surface. Other, simpler aliens were made using a new procedure: "We made eight-inch (twenty-centimeter) statuettes. These models were scanned from all angles in order to program a computer-controlled drill. The machine cut large blocks of polyurethane foam to enlarge the characters to the scale we'd chosen, and the sculptors only had to refine the details of the textures. The aliens were covered with fiber-glass and resin and then cut open to be equipped with the mechanisms. Because of the direction suggested by Steven Spielberg, you don't have the time to realize that some of the aliens are very simple, but you do clearly see the robots that are the most complex. When you have the chance to develop an attraction with such a wonderful creator, who is at the same time a specialist in theme parks and an expert in video games, you take into account all his suggestions."

Terminator 2: 3-D: James Cameron's Shock Attraction

In 1996, James Cameron created a major attraction for Universal: *Terminator 2: 3-D*. His brilliant direction hooks the audience within the first few seconds and then never lets go. It all starts at the reception hall of Cyberdyne Systems, the company depicted in *Terminator 2* as the manufacturer of a network of satellites and cyborgs who one day will declare war on humans. As Cyberdyne's video pronounces a radiant future, the presentation is interrupted by Sarah and John Connor (Linda Hamilton and Edward Furlong, re-creating their *Terminator 2* roles), who encourage the audience not to believe these lies. The visit continues with a demonstration of the shooting capabilities of the six T-70s, the ten-foot (three-meter) robots. The two rebels then burst into the room. They are being played by doubles who talk by playback and move in synchronization with the close-ups of Linda Hamilton and Edward Furlong, which are projected on video screens throughout the room. They are interrupted by the arrival of T-1000, the liquid metal killer. The Terminator arrives perched on his Harley-Davidson and grabs John Connor in order to save his life. The cyborg and his young cohort

then cross the time portal and break through the screen on which it is projected. They reappear in 3-D, played by the real Arnold Schwarzenegger and Edward Furlong, and confront flying sentry robots equipped with submachine guns. Our heroes penetrate the headquarters of Skynet to destroy the

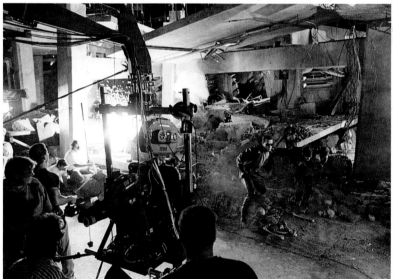

Top: *James Cameron conceived and directed* Terminator 2: 3-D. *He used computer-generated effects from Digital Domain and robots by makeup artist Stan Winston to produce 3-D effects that take your breath away.*

Above: *Filming the 3-D sequences of* Terminator 2: 3-D. *The two cartridges can be seen on top of the 3-D camera.*
Photos courtesy of Universal Studios Florida

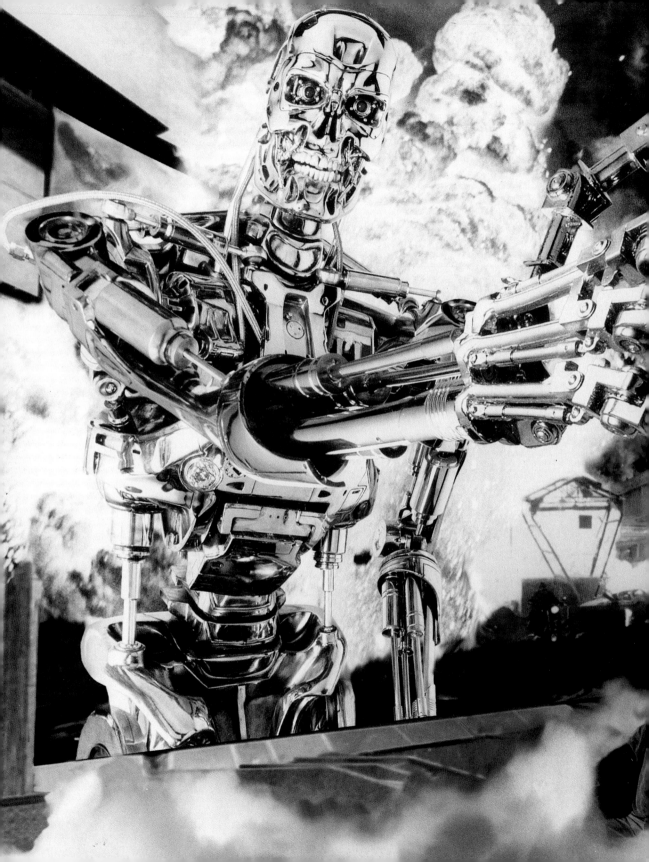

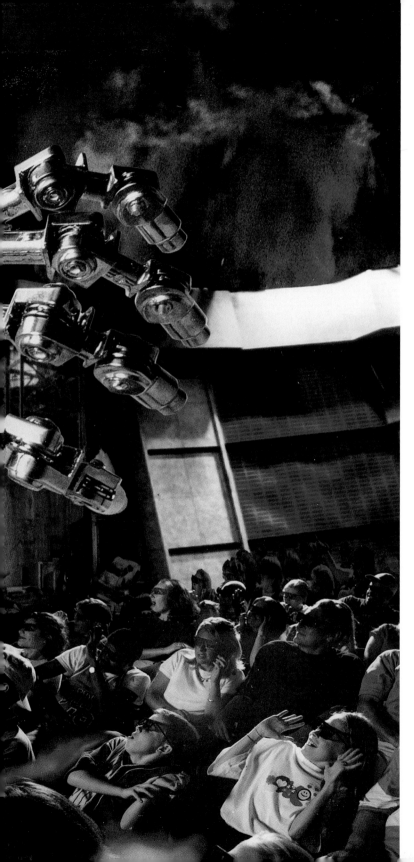

control systems responsible for the apocalypse. At this point, T-Meg, a colossal metal spider that unfurls its full size across three screens, joins the fray. The battle between the 3-D monster and the actors present in the room is the highlight of this fabulous show. The spider was created by Daniel Robichaud at Digital Domain: "The appearance of T-Meg is spread across the giant curved screens. This 180-degree panorama plunges the audience into the heart of the action. The simultaneous projection of six 65-millimeter movies was required to get three giant 3-D images, and animating this sequence on three different axes also meant taking into consideration the perspective of the set. The T-Meg sequence is a continuous shot, which prevented us from correcting errors using editing tricks. The three-part shot, composed of twenty

The Terminator 2: 3-D *attraction is a formidable mixture of 3-D projections, robotics, special effects, and stunts performed live by actors.*
Photo courtesy of Universal Studios Florida

The creation of the synthesized images for T-Meg, an enormous liquid metal creature that spreads itself out in 3-D over three screens
Photo courtesy of Digital Domain & Universal Studios Florida

element layers calculated by several programs, had to be absolutely perfect. As each of the three images was doubled, with a 'left-eye' version and a 'right-eye' version, this scene required six times more work than a normal movie. Also, the movie is projected at thirty frames per second instead of twenty-four, to eliminate certain stroboscopic effects. Thus, there are six additional animations of T-Meg per second. I used the 'bi-spinal' technique to constitute the creature's body. This entails bending a surface that resembles a sheet of rubber in order to get volume. I constructed a sort of starfish whose two symmetrical hollow parts I folded onto themselves to make a 'full' form. The classic 'block-by-block' construction system would not have permitted getting this aspect. Using the bi-spinal construction, I could animate the T-Meg's internal skeleton by playing with the curves of its legs." The seventy million dollars invested in *Terminator 2: 3-D* has paid off. The attraction was such a success that it has been duplicated in California and in the Universal Studios theme park in Osaka, Japan.

The entrance to Universal's wonderful Islands of Adventure theme park in Florida; the gigantic facade of the Poseidon's Fury *attraction*
Photo courtesy of Universal Studios Florida

The Islands of Adventure

A tunnel of swirling water leads to Atlantis at Poseidon's Fury.
Photo courtesy of Universal Studios Florida

In 1999, Spielberg, always true to his allegiance, inaugurated the second Florida park, Universal's Islands of Adventure, a superb project costing a billion dollars. The park is composed of five thematically different islands: "Jurassic Park" (described earlier); "Seuss Landing," devoted to the characters in the Dr. Seuss books; "The Lost Continent," which evokes *A Thousand and One Nights,* medieval legends, and ancient mythology; "Toon Lagoon," a universe filled with the most popular comic book characters, from Popeye to Flash Gordon; and "Marvel Superhero Island," a magnificent homage to Stan Lee's superheroes. And it is here that you will find the most

sophisticated attraction in the
world: *The Amazing Adventures
of Spider-Man*. This two-
hundred-million-dollar show
leads the audience inside the
Spider-Man comics. While
waiting on line, visitors pass by
the offices of the *Daily Bugle,*
J. Jonah Jameson's newspaper.
Jameson, the superhero's sworn
enemy, asks visitors to take
their places in the remote-
controlled vehicle that he has
designed to capture Spider-
Man. They then travel through
sets of deserted New York City
streets. Emerging in front of a
building, the visitors catch sight
of Spider-Man perched on a
balcony. He throws his web
and, hurling himself, lands on
the moving vehicle, which
shakes at the moment of
impact! The effect is sensational. The superhero is
depicted with a 3-D computer-
generated image, but he truly
seems to be there. Pointing his
right index finger at the passengers, he demands their help in
finding the gang of criminals
led by Dr. Octopus. What follows is a mind-boggling series

The stunning attraction The Amazing
Adventures of Spider-Man *hurls the
audience into the heart of the battle
between Spider-Man and a gang of
super-criminals. Spider-Man appears
in 3-D digital images.*
Photo courtesy of Universal Studios Florida

of fights with each of the adversaries. Electro pulls down a high-tension cable in order to fry the audience. Dr. Octopus suddenly appears, smashing a wall of bricks, and chases after the vehicle, trying to grab it with his steel tentacles. The highlight of the attraction is the battle between Spider-Man and the whole group of enemies. The visitors' vehicle seems to be lifted off the earth by one of Octopus's antigravitational rays. It soars higher than the tallest New York skyscraper and then plunges in a free fall before, in extremis, being caught in the spider's web a few inches from the ground! This extraordinary feat combines several effects—the back projection of 3-D images, movements generated by the vehicle (a flight simulator on wheels), and special sets, placed on their sides and then inverted. This prodigious display of technology marks a new stage in the history of the special effects at theme parks.

Electro threatens the audience with a high-tension cable. Differences in perspective are evident in these two images composing the 3-D aspect of the scene.

Dr. Octopus springs from a wall to grab at visitors.

INTERVIEW

Mark A. Woodbury

Vice President of Design and Creative Development for Universal Studios Florida

Preparatory drawing of the waiting line at the Dueling Dragons *attraction*
Photo courtesy of Universal Studios Florida

How did you collaborate with Steven Spielberg on the adaptation of his movies?

Mark A. Woodbury: Steven first described to us his vision of the attraction. We chose the most memorable sequences and then the best way to reproduce them—a show with actors, a show with special effects, inter-active projections, etc. *Back to the Future,* for example, involved a quick succession of

scenes that took place during different times. The use of high-definition film and flight simulators was a natural choice. The final stage consisted of drawing a detailed storyboard, which was submitted to Steven and the studio directors.

Were the flight simulators used in "Back to the Future" programmed according to the film, or was it the other way around?

Mark A. Woodbury: The process went back and forth. We explained to the film crew what our equipment would be able to do. Our computer programmers spent seven months program-

ming the hydraulic jacks on the simulators to accentuate the slightest movement suggested on the screen.

How do you take care of the main-tenance of the robotic dinosaurs in "Jurassic Park"? Does the gigantic ultrasaurus have a zipper installed from its head extending down to the base of its long neck to give easy access to the mechanisms?

Mark A. Woodbury: Yes. There's an entire crew whose job is to hide these technical accesses from the audience. They're the only ones who know where to find the openings. They make a small scalpel cut in the surface

The robots and the motorcycle, which is guided along tracks, in the theater of the Terminator 2: 3-D *attraction*
Photo courtesy of Universal Studios Florida

of the skin to free the zipper, open it up to make the repairs, reclose it, and then use a little silicone to camouflage any trace of their surgery. We fight the impact of ultraviolet rays, which make the colors fade, by adding a product that combats their effects in the material and on the surface. We replace the exterior layer of skin on the animals once a year. Our production studio can change all the dinosaurs' skin in less than three days. The heat causes cracks in the silicone. The inside temperature of the char-

acters exposed to the sun rises to 175°F (80°C), since their hydraulic circuits generate additional heat.

How did you develop the 3-D triple projection of the "Terminator 2: 3-D" attraction?

Mark A. Woodbury: We re-created the attraction hall in a hangar in Los Angeles. Three semicylindrical screens and three 65-millimeter projectors were permanently installed to

view the 3-D synthesized images from the point of view of future audiences. We also had to make sure, with a tape measure in hand, that the scale of the characters in the film would correctly correspond with that of the actors who'd be playing on the stage in front of the audience. We spent a lot of time adjusting the "intraocular distance," which is to say, a respect for the distance between the two eyes that ensures a realistic aspect to the 3-D. If you change this distance from one shot to the next to

The show Waterworld: A Live Sea War Spectacular *(1994)*   Photo courtesy of Universal Studios Hollywood

magnify the effects, the eyes can't converge correctly on the subject, which is annoying.

Can you explain the new 3-D projection techniques used in the "Spider-Man" attraction?

Mark A. Woodbury: We back-projected 3-D synthesized images in 35 millimeter and 70 millimeter onto giant screens. These projections were integrated into the sets of streets and into the hangars where the action took place. The innovation was that we managed to coordinate the perspective of the 3-D images so that they coincided with the movement of the vehicles, which were equipped with motion simulation bases. The 3-D feeling and the "penetration into a 3-D scene" were greatly amplified. This made it possible for us to create the illusion of Spider-Man landing on the hood of the vehicle. The 3-D perspectives change as the vehicle moves laterally, and the impact is simulated by integrated hydraulic jacks. This technology was invented specifically for this attraction and is registered under the name of "squinching." It let us move the point of convergence of the 3-D and the perspectives of the set in relation to the movement of the vehicle in front of the back projection screen. First we defined the composition of the sets, the animations of the characters,

Overleaf: *The wind tunnel at the* Twister *attraction simulates the disastrous effects of a tornado.*
Photo courtesy of Universal Studios Florida

the special effects, and then we programmed the movements of the vehicles to conceive the computer-generated images.

How do the vehicles work, and how are they synchronized with the computer-generated images?

Mark A. Woodbury: They're equipped with six axes of motion and are capable of moving at the same time very quickly and very precisely, while being resistant to rapid accelerations. The vehicle knows exactly where it is, to the millimeter, every second. Its preprogrammed animation sequences, synchronized with each frame of the movie, are triggered in sections as it advances along the circuit. It was the Kleiser-Walczak Construction Company that made the remarkable computer-generated attraction images. We first made animation tests with a motion capture system and actors, but this technique was too limited. It required our superheroes to move in a theatrical, almost unreal manner, as in the *Spider-Man* comics. We spent more than a year and a half working on these sequences. At the beginning, it was a classic animation process with a rough body animation. We then made a more sophisticated facial animation with more subtle pronunciation movements and

gestures. We adjusted the lighting, fine-tuned the sets, etc. The rough animation was tested with a prototype vehicle. We passed on our observations to the animators, who could then refine their work even more. And here is one of the major difficulties in the conception of an attraction: you have to piece it together before it's been built, to make sure that all the elements that make it up work perfectly together.

Models of extraterrestrials from Men in Black: Alien Attack, *conceived by AVG*
Photo courtesy of AVG & Universal Studios Florida

Special Effects Hotels

The extension of the Florida site prompted Universal to outfit new hotels thematically, using special effects experts from the studios. Steven Spielberg suggested re-creating the small Italian village of Portofino in the form of the luxurious Portofino Bay Hotel, which opened in 1999. The structures of the hotel were spread out around the port, forming the giant set of the village. Transportation between the hotel and the park is by boat.

After opening the Hard Rock Hotel, which is decorated with collectibles from the pop/rock world, Universal re-created the atmosphere of the Pacific Islands and, in 2002, opened the Royal Pacific Resort. A seaplane made of resin and fiberglass is moored near a landing pier surrounded by white sand beaches and palm trees.

Las Vegas: The Gaming Capital Becomes the Attractions Capital

Las Vegas has changed its spots in order to become more attractive to families. Its hotel-casinos, colossal structures of two thousand to five thousand guest rooms that cost as much as one billion dollars, offer many attractions regaling magic, fantasy, and science fiction. From 1989 to October 2003, thanks to Siegfried & Roy, the Mirage had a packed house every night. In their show, the magicians would elude an elephant and then levitate above the stage, only to disintegrate and reappear with one of their famous white tigers. The Mirage was the first hotel to offer an attraction to passersby walking on the Strip. The facade is adorned with a volcano that erupts every twenty minutes. The water bubbling in the crater is lit in red and orange to simulate lava, while gas burners (replete with coconut perfume, so as not to offend anyone) spread flames and shoot balls of fire. A little farther down the Strip, you come upon a pirate village, adorning the Treasure Island Hotel, that seems to be straight out of a Technicolor movie. Bob Gurr, the magician of hydraulic animation, devised the technical aspects of the spectacular sea battle that took place there. Coming around the cliff of the hotel, advancing along submerged tracks, a life-size English

The famous Las Vegas Strip, along which you find the craziest hotels on the planet
Photo courtesy of Las Vegas News Bureau

The facade of the Paris-Las Vegas Hotel is an amalgam of Parisian monuments.

three-master approached the moored pirate ship to force it to surrender. The cannons thundered; the pirates drew their swords and launched their attack. His Gracious Majesty's ship blew up in no time and sank, thanks to impressive machinery hidden in the dock. The most recent version of the pirate show is titled *Sirens of TI*.

The facade of New York, New York Hotel re-creates in miniature New York sky-scrapers and venues. This gigantic model serves as a support for the roller coaster that zigzags between the buildings.

A re-creation of the city of the Doges inside the Venetian Hotel. Beneath a trompe l'oeil sky, gondoliers navigate on the canals of the vast set.

The sea battle presented by the Treasure Island Hotel
Photo courtesy of the Treasure Island Hotel

A magnificent animatronic Indian goddess created by the Sally Corporation to bring good luck to the gamers at the MGM Grand Hotel
Photo courtesy of Sally Corporation

Its creators dumped the Hollywood-style approach in favor of a sexy MTV video look.

The Most Expensive Show in the World

In 1995, the MGM Grand Hotel created a seventeen-hundred-seat theater expressly for presenting *EFX,* a show with exceptional scenic effects. The theater cost sixty-five million dollars, and the show forty-five million more. The hero of *EFX* went from being Merlin the Sorcerer's assistant, to P. T. Barnum in a futuristic circus, to the magician Houdini, and then to the inventor of H. G. Wells's time machine. When Merlin and his assistant confronted the sorceress Morgane, she changed into a dragon 20 feet (6 meters) tall. Merlin then transformed into a 40-foot-tall (12-meter) dragon, and the two creatures battled while spitting flames. The two robots were animated by some twenty pneumatic and hydraulic jacks. A security system interrupted the projection of the flaming gas if an actor crossed the "security perimeter." The arrival of Barnum's spaceship was shot with models using 70-millimeter film, so as to obtain the best clarity possible. At the end of the filmed sequence, thirty electric engines were used to deploy three enormous pieces of the spaceship from the flies to simulate its touchdown on the stage. The scene dedicated to Houdini began with a séance, in which

The host and characters from EFX
Photo courtesy of the MGM Grand Hotel

Opposite: *Merlin and the sorceress Morgane turn into dragons when they confront each other in* EFX.
Photo courtesy of the MGM Grand Hotel

people sitting around a table suddenly took flight and disappeared. The four actors in this scene were wearing harnesses attached by cables to four motorized winches that glided independently on tracks. The process was entirely controlled by computer, to eliminate any risk of human error.

But the true highlight of the show was the evocation of the time machine. The space traveler took his place in his machine, asking the audience to put on their protection goggles. A screen concealed the set and the audience joined the journey, via a 3-D movie featuring computer-generated effects. When the machine returned to the stage, as if by magic, the enormous set of the city of the Morlocks appeared. The theater was constructed specifically for this show. Even the visible opening onto the set was 33 feet (10 meters) high by 82 feet (25

meters) wide, and the actual size of the theater, including the backstage areas, was 194 feet (59 meters) wide and 112 feet (34 meters) high. A basement of an equivalent surface area was situated directly below, making it possible for the crew of thirty stagehands to transport the sets using two elevators and to execute incredibly fast scene changes. The colossal city of the Morlocks set materialized in less than four minutes. The two elevators situated under the stage were first loaded up with the 36-foot (11-meter) mountain that sheltered the central sector of the city, which was installed in its proper place. The crew then positioned the four 43-foot (13-meter) towers on the sides of the stage. As they were taller than the central sector, they created an effect of false perspective. A little fog and light were added, and then the set was revealed to the audience. *EFX* also employed

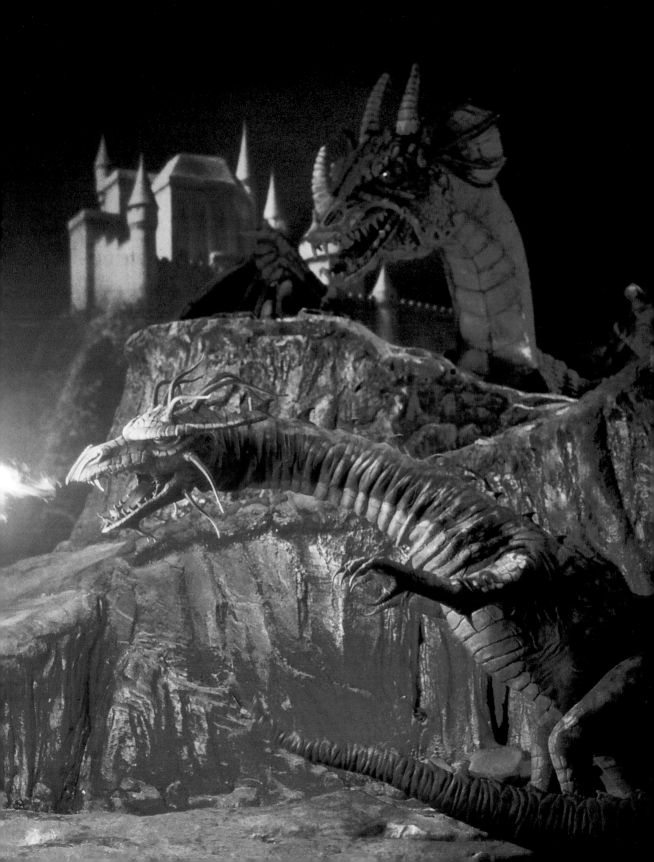

Three-dimensional computer-generated animation created by Kleiser-Walczak for In Search of the Obelisk, *the second section of the Luxor attraction. A new production by the Trumbull Company for Circus Circus Enterprises, Inc.* Photo courtesy of Kleiser-Walczak

a number of rear-projected still images to make different backgrounds appear on the set. To obtain an image large enough from a single source, the enormous stage would have had to be retracted. Instead, the shots were divided among eight 6,000-watt Pani projectors, each of which projected a part of the whole image in order to give it an exceptional brightness. *EFX*'s final performance occurred on December 31, 2002.

The Secrets of the Great Pyramid . . . in Las Vegas

The black pyramid of the Luxor hotel houses the attraction *Secrets of the Luxor Pyramid,* created by Douglas Trumbull. Initially presented in three sections, this attraction started with a visit to an archaeological site where the visitor discovered the pyramid, followed by a flying journey in a luge (a flight simulator placed in front of an arced

screen) inside a vast underground temple. The second part, a confrontation on a talk show between historical protagonists, was a bit on the long side, but technically clever. The actors, who appeared to be arguing directly in front of the audience in the re-created TV studio, were not really there. They were filmed at a rate of sixty frames per second on 70-millimeter film, using the Showscan Film Process invented by Trumbull.

Computer-generated images from the ReBoot: The Ride *attraction, presented in the Adventuredome Park at the Circus Circus Hotel*
Photos courtesy of the Circus Circus Hotel

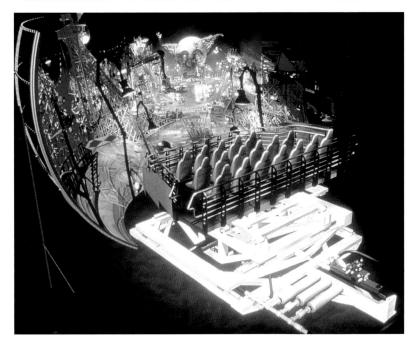

The third part of the adventure led the spectators to the discovery of an apocalyptic future created for the evildoers, and then a radiant one reserved for the heroes. The models of the futuristic buildings in this third part were conceived by computers and pre-visualized in CGI so that Trumbull could fine-tune the architectural composition of the city. The structures of the different buildings had been carved in plastic by lasers before being assembled. Trumbull secured a special dolly track on a structure placed above the models. His computer-controlled camera could thus fly over the miniature countryside, which was fabricated on a one-fiftieth scale. The scenes were shot in stop-motion with the shutter left open for a very extended time, while the diaphragm was practically shut. This made it possible to obtain an enormous depth of field—everything was sharp, and the final images were superb. Unfortunately, two of the three parts that made up the attraction's story were ultimately suppressed. The end of the adventure was the first one to vanish—a strange scheme that left many in the audience puzzled!

The short feature Funhouse Express *is the only three-dimensional animation movie ever made for theaters equipped with motion simulation platforms.*
Photos courtesy of the Circus Circus Hotel

Sets and extravagant characters from Funhouse Express   Photos courtesy of the Circus Circus Hotel

An image from the Race for Atlantis *attraction that was presented at Caesars Palace*   Photo courtesy of Caesars Palace

The Biggest Screen in the World

Located away from the Strip, the venerable artery that is Fremont Street is completely covered over by the world's largest electronic screen. Six times a day, the Fremont Street Experience is displayed on it. Not far from there, the Las Vegas Hilton Hotel invested seventy million dollars in its attraction, *Star Trek: The Experience*. The universes of the different *Star Trek* series have been re-created down to the minutest details. Visitors first discover the props, clothing, and models from *Star Trek* in the "History of the Future" museum. Then, in small groups, they penetrate into the room that leads to the attraction and, through a clever special effect, are "tele-ported" aboard the spaceship *Enterprise*. A flash of light violently illuminates the walls of the small room in which they wait. The walls around them are then quickly lifted up in total darkness, while the flash effect is prolonged by persistence of vision. When the sets of *Star Trek,* previously hidden behind the room's false walls, become progressively brighter around them, visitors get the impression that they have materialized in a different place. They are then escorted to the *Enterprise* bridge, a faithful reconstruction of *Star Trek: The Next*

Above: *The Fremont Street Experience, presented six times a day on the world's largest electronic screen* Photo courtesy of Las Vegas News Bureau

Generation's iconic set. The heroes from the series appear on screens to explain to them that they have been accidentally transported into the twenty-fourth century! The visitors return to their time and their planet in a space shuttle, which in fact is a flight simulator equipped with six axes of

motion. A space battle precedes the return to Earth, to the heart of a city that itself has become a gigantic special effect—Las Vegas!

Opposite below, this page, and overleaf: *The Las Vegas Hilton has become the "Star Trek Hotel." Fans of the celebrated series can eat the cuisine of extraterrestrials and get teleported aboard the legendary spaceship* Enterprise.

Photos courtesy of Paramount Parks and Las Vegas Hilton

At the far end of the Strip, the stunning "Blue Man Group" production mixes music with sound and visual effects to create an irresistible show of nonsensical humor. The members of the group are mute characters with blue skin who look out onto the world with their round eyes, marvelously playing their instruments made of PVC piping, and tossing mountains of recycled paper onto the audience.
Photo courtesy of the Blue Man Group & the Luxor Hotel

Special Effects Attractions Throughout the World

The growing popularity of theme parks proves the public's enjoyment of special-effects-laden shows. Curators of museums have recognized this evolution in taste. Stiff presentations of times past have given way to ever more sophisticated interactive exhibits.

Seattle's Rock Museum and James Brown's Clone

A James Brown rejuvenated by thirty years appears in the movie *The Artist's Journey,* presented by the Experience Music Project, Seattle's rock museum. When the Father of Soul sings "Sex Machine" while performing his famous dance steps, the audience can hardly believe that it is not the real James Brown, but rather a technical feat from the Digital Domain team directed by André Bustanoby: "We worked eight months on this movie. In it, you see two young fans leap back thirty years into Seattle's past. James Brown suddenly leaps from one of his posters to sing 'Sex Machine,' surrounded by hundreds of dancers." Because of the very short shooting schedule, Bustanoby did not have time to create a complete computer-generated clone of the singer. He filmed a dancer who was quite adept at James Brown's choreography, onto

which he added a digital recreation of the singer's face, made younger by thirty years. "We cyber-scanned James Brown in his house in Augusta. We filmed it in 35 millimeter, photographed in close-up, and we molded his face to have a plaster bust. We glued fifty-two motion capture points on his face to animate the thirty 'muscles' of the 3-D face. The mouth and the eyes of the clone were made using 'NURBS,' thousands of small spheres that compose the organic shapes."

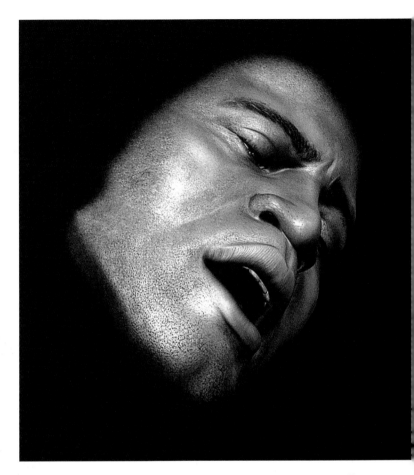

James Brown's face, scanned in 3-D
Photo courtesy of EMP & Digital Domain

Opposite: *Images from* The Artist's Journey, *before and after the insertion of the computer-generated rendering of James Brown's face.*
Photos courtesy of EMP & Digital Domain

Re-created Historical Figures

The American firm Sally Corporation, founded in 1977, has created attractions for theme parks around the world. Its robotics studio has produced superb re-creations of historical figures such as the Charles Darwin who appears in the "Living World" exhibition at the Saint Louis Zoo. His face is made of translucent silicone and endowed with a white beard, each hair of which was implanted individually. Darwin rises up from his stool to greet the visitors and then introduces them to the basics of the evolution of the species.

Photos courtesy of Sally Corporation

Ol' Billy narrates for visitors to the Fire Museum of Memphis a heroic epic in which firemen battle fires using vehicles drawn by his forefathers.

Photo courtesy of Sally Corporation

The CAVE System

Imagine an open space in the shape of a cube, in which each wall is a screen. Wearing liquid crystal glasses that alternately block the vision of your right and then your left eye twenty-five times per second, you enter, a motion sensor affixed to the top of your head. Suddenly the walls retract and you find yourself *inside* a 3-D image, totally immersed in a virtual world. Such is the power of the CAVE system, invented in 1995 by Caroline Cruz-Neira at the University of Illinois at Chicago. The video projections on each side of the cube are in 3-D, and the sensor on the viewers' head makes it possible for them to make a new reckoning in real time and compensate for the distortion of the perspectives on the walls. The

"Caves" gradually escaped the confines of laboratories, where they were used to visualize what could not be seen in the real world, such as galaxies or complex molecules. Julien Berta, of the American firm Fakespace, the current owner of this invention, elucidates: "Right now, the optimal 3-D vision is only intended for a single spectator at a time, as the projection is calculated based on the movements of his head. The system will evolve to be able to be used in theme park attractions and work with a group of spectators." In the coming years, larger cubes will be developed, equipped with high-definition digital projectors, even more powerful Silicon Graphics computers, and 3-D systems that will enable two or three spectators to travel together into the heart of the 3-D.

Using the CAVE system, a spectator outfitted with sensors and wearing liquid crystal glasses becomes surrounded by a 3-D universe. The computer-generated projections onto the sides of the cube are distorted to produce a perfectly coherent 3-D image, regardless of where the spectator moves, giving entry into the virtual image.
Photo courtesy of Fakespace

Le Défi d'Atlantis, *presented in the dynamic Imax format at Futuroscope in Poitiers, France* Photo courtesy of Planète Futuroscope

Attractions in Europe and Asia

While the United States had for a long time been the leader in the realm of high-tech attractions, theme parks throughout the rest of the world caught up during the 1990s. The European parks (too numerous to be definitively cited

in this work) had for a long time favored thrill rides and roller coasters. But now, high-tech attractions are everywhere. The Futuroscope in Poitiers, France, presents a great selection of the most beautiful short-length special effects movies in the world, in many formats. *Le Défi d'Atlantis* (*Ride for Atlantis*) is a

dizzying race in Imax 3-D through the legendary sunken kingdom. *T-Rex: Retour au crétacé* (*T-Rex: Back to the Cretaceous*) and *CyberWorld* use the same 3-D system to present startling computer-generated sequences. At the *Images Studio*, visitors get to learn some of the secrets used by special effects wizards.

The audience at Futuroscope dives into the 3-D of the movie T. rex: Retour au crétacé.

Discovery of the Lost Temple

Photos courtesy of Planète Futuroscope

Imax: Great Thrills on a Giant Screen

It was in 1970 that the Canadian process Imax was used in a theater for the first time. Since then, more than five hundred million people have seen one of these films from a catalog rich with hundreds of titles. An Imax camera threads 70-millimeter film horizontally. Each frame has a surface area equivalent to three 70-millimeter frames threaded normally. The definition is such that the film can be projected onto a giant screen eighty-two feet (twenty-five meters) tall. Omnimax cameras are fitted with a fish-eye-like lens, which produces a distorted hemispherical image. A projector equipped with an identical lens reestablishes the perspectives as long as the image is projected onto a hemispherical screen. The Omnimax process thus encompasses the viewer's peripheral vision. With its Imax 3-D, the company also developed the best 3-D system in the world. The film is projected

In order to see the 3-D effect of the Imax movie Rencontre dans la 3-D, *viewers must wear two-colored red-and-blue glasses.* Photo courtesy of Planète Futuroscope

at fifty frames per second. The liquid crystal glasses worn by viewers effectively blind the right eye, while the left eye sees the image intended for it, and then the process is reversed. The alternation of the right-left images on the film occurs fifty times per second, enabling the viewer to perceive the 3-D image at twenty-five frames per second. The result is astoundingly sharp.

The liquid crystal glasses used by the Imax 3-D system are also equipped with speakers that add a complementary audio effect. Photo courtesy of Planète Futuroscope

In his movie Special Effects: Anything Can Happen, *Ben Burtt re-created key scenes from* Star Wars *and* King Kong *in the large Imax format.* Photo courtesy of *Special Effects: Anything Can Happen*

Showscan: High-Fidelity Film

Unfortunately not well known, the Showscan Film Process invented by Douglas Trumbull in 1976 remains the most realistic film projection system. Trumbull's invention gives the impression that the screen disappears to become an open window on the world. Showscan movies are filmed and projected in 70 millimeter, on film twice as wide as the normal 35 millimeter and at a rate of sixty frames per second. The fluidity of the restored motion is exceptional, and at this speed, the grain of the image is no longer perceptible— a performance that the most advanced digital projectors still cannot equal and that can be enjoyed at Futuroscope.

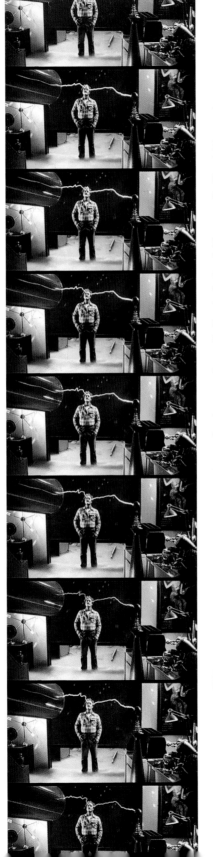

A strip of 70-millimeter film from Douglas Trumbull's 1983 Showscan demonstration short, New Magic
Photo courtesy of Showscan Film Corporation

Terra Mitica

Located in Benidorm, Spain, Terra Mitica offers multiple attractions dedicated to mythology. The most popular of them is *El Laberinto del Minotaur* (*The Minotaur's Labyrinth*). Visitors ride in their own chariots and, traveling through the labyrinth, use their crossbows (equipped with infrared sights) to fend off the various creatures that spring up around them, like the seven-headed Hydra, Cerberus, Harpies, the fire-breathing dragon, and finally the ten-foot Minotaur brandishing an enormous club. Some 333 "reactive" targets and 76 animatronic characters are hidden along the route. When visitors aim well and score high, their chariots are led into the "Treasure Room" as if to be rewarded.

Model of the Hydra in El Laberinto del Minotaur *at the Spanish theme park Terra Mitica*
Photo courtesy of Sally Corporation

Players shooting at Cerberus Photo courtesy of Terra Mitica

The final airbrush touches on the animatronic Minotaur Photo courtesy of Sally Corporation

The extraordinary facade of the WonderWorks entertainment center in Orlando, Florida. Many activities revolving around the phenomena of static electricity, optical illusions, and virtual games are on offer.

The Six Flags theme park in Belgium also has an interactive attraction: Le Défi de Tutankhamon (Challenge of Tutankhamen). Visitors try to escape the evil spells cast by Seth, the Egyptian god of evil. Upon entering, Nazeer advises visitors not to go into the tomb of Tutankhamen. This superrealistic animatronic character is endowed with a translucent silicone skin.

The giant scorpion

The god Seth

Photos courtesy of Sally Corporation

The Batman Thrills
Spectacular, *a stunt show
presented at the Warner
Bros. Movie World
theme park in Bottrop-
Kirchhellen, Germany*
Photo courtesy of Warner Bros.
Movie World

Movie Magic *explains to visitors to Warner
Bros. Movie World how a gimbal is used. This
platform mounted on jacks makes it possible
to move a set of a submarine in all directions, as would be needed during a descent,
for example.*
Photo courtesy of Warner Bros. Movie World

Programming The Orchid Show *at the offices of AVG*
Photo courtesy of AVG

The Legend of the Nine Dragon Princes and the Dragon King *attraction in Beijing, China*
Photo courtesy of AVG

Final touches on a dragon at the Sultan's Adventure *attraction, presented in Taiwan*
Photo courtesy of AVG

The entry hall to Space Park Bremen, *dedicated to the exploration of real and imaginary space*
Photo courtesy of Space Park Bremen

Passengers in Tomb Raider:
The Ride *prepare for a dizzying
descent into an abyss.*
Photo courtesy of Paramount Parks

Preparatory drawing for
Tomb Raider: The Ride
Image courtesy of Paramount Parks

The 3-D attraction Corkscrew Hill *was conceived and produced by Jeff Kleiser and Diana Walczak. Visitors enter onto an animated platform and are projected into a universe of traditional Irish folklore. Victims of a magic spell, they are "miniaturized" and then placed inside a wooden box, where they feel the movement. The computer programs SensAble and Paraform were used to model characters and link their joints, respectively. Computer artists then used the Maya program in order to execute the animations and renderings of the scenes, which were digitally projected in a large format using Electrosonic technology.*

These images are from the 3-D movie Santa Lights Up New York, *conceived and produced by Jeff Kleiser and Diana Walczak for the Christmas show at Radio City Music Hall in New York*

Special Effects at the Table

Ever since the 1990s, themed restaurants have been trying hard to captivate families as much by the quality of their cuisine as by the imaginary worlds that they create using special effects.

Rainforest Cafés

In 1989, Steven Schussler got the strange idea of re-creating a tropical jungle in his house in Minneapolis. He installed tree trunks, vines, flowers, and leaves to hide the ceiling. He then made his own special effects to simulate rain, lightning, the roar of thunder, and the cries of the animals, and then, to add a realistic touch, he populated his scene with robot gorillas and birds. A financier liked it, and Schussler was able to achieve his goals. Today, some forty Rainforest Cafés around the world, all populated with animatronic animals, draw those longing for a change of scenery.

The twenty-foot (six-meter) shooting flame at Caesars Magical Empire, the fabulous dinner-show that was presented at Caesars Palace in Las Vegas, but has unfortunately been closed down
Photo courtesy of Caesars Palace

The tropical forest and animatronic fauna at the Rainforest Café
Photo courtesy of Rainforest Café

Mars 2112

Mars 2112 is located in the heart of New York City, about halfway between Times Square and Central Park. On entering, you are handed a ticket for your trip to Mars. A flight simulator creates the impression of soaring over Manhattan and crossing the cosmos. The flight comes to an end next to a gigantic volcano on Mars. Passengers enter the set of a Martian colony. A glass tree, three stories tall, stands grandly in the central room. After giving their orders to a friendly creature, diners then wait for their meals while watching Martian TV programs, presented by an extra-terrestrial announcer.

Martians aboard a space shuttle at Mars 2112
Photo courtesy of Mars 2112

The main dining room
Photo courtesy of Mars 2112

Jekyll and Hyde Club

New York's Jekyll and Hyde Club takes the guise of an old mansion, filled with eccentric characters and creatures who, in turn, act out their roles. The different levels of the restaurant are occupied by robotic characters, animated "live" by actors who lend their voices and hurl jokes at the visitors. And with the crack of a storm, Dr. Frankenstein tries to grab the bolt of lightning and animate his monster! The actors present in the room and the monsters hidden in the scenery launch into a good-natured conversation. There are two other Jekyll and Hyde clubs under the name Eerie World Café, one in Chicago and the other in Grapevine, near Dallas.

Awakened by a skeleton organist, the Frankenstein monster comes to life before the diners at the Jekyll and Hyde Club in New York.

Opposite: *The Monsters Café restaurant at Universal Studios in Florida serves up an ideal assortment of Halloween dishes, along with a decor of the studio's famous monsters—the Mummy, the Creature from the Black Lagoon, Dracula, and the inescapable Frankenstein monster.*
Photo courtesy of Universal Studios Florida

DVDs—Required Viewing

Television

Alice in Wonderland / Hallmark / 1999
A faithful adaptation of the Lewis Carroll work. The enlargement of the Mad Hatter's head (played by Martin Short) is a stunning effect by Mike McGee of the Framestore studios.

Arabian Nights / Hallmark / 2000
The tales of *1,001 Nights* cleverly revisited. Mark Coulier's makeups and the digital effects by Framestore are particularly successful.

The Avengers / A&E Entertainment / 1961–1969
This legendary series frequently relied on smart effects such as those in "The Flying Avenger" episode, in which a comic book character comes to life—the cartoons transform into animated images—and those in "Mission . . . Highly Improbable," in which John Steed and Emma Peel appear miniaturized, thanks to oversize sets and props.

Babylon 5 / Warner Bros. / 1993–2002
The first 3-D spaceships on TV, created by Ron Thornton. The extraordinary makeups of the extraterrestrials were by John Vulich. A top science fiction series.

Band of Brothers / Warner Bros. / 2002
A stunning evocation of the journey of the "Easy Company" group of American soldiers, starting with the Normandy landing and continuing through the fall of the Nazi regime. The special effects by Cinesite make the pain of battle palpable.

Buffy the Vampire Slayer / Fox / 1997–2003
This amusing and dynamic series introduces a horde of vampires, werewolves, demons, and other wild creatures conceived by John Vulich.

Battlestar Galactica / Universal / 1978–1980
The movie version of the pilot for the series *Battlestar Galactica*. With beautiful space battles orchestrated by John Dykstra.

Captain Scarlet / Carlton (U.S.: A&E Home Video) / 1967
The Spectrum organization battles the Mysterons from the planet Mars. The marionettes appearing in this series, created by Gerry and Sylvia Anderson, were endowed with realistic proportions. Extras: commentary by Gerry Anderson and a photo gallery.

Cosmos / Cosmos Studios / 1980s
Made in the 1980s, Cosmos remains *the* greatest scientific series ever produced. Carl Sagan clearly explained complex

phenomena with the aid of excellent special effects.

Creature Features / Columbia-TriStar / 2001–2002
Makeup maestro Stan Winston produced this series of remakes of the Samuel Z. Arkoff science fiction B movies

from the 1950s. The monsters are especially delightful.

Dinotopia / Hallmark / 2002
The most sumptuous of all miniseries. The special effects produced by Framestore are of a beauty to take one's breath away. Extras: backstage visit during filming, explanations of how the giant sets were built at Pinewood Studios and

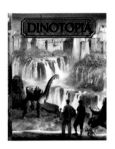

creation of the 3-D dinosaurs.

Dinosaur! / Family Home Entertainment / 1985
A very nice documentary with dinosaurs

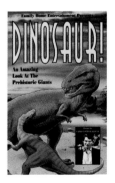

animated by stop-motion master Phil Tippett.

Flash / **Warner Bros.** / **1990–1991**
Flash sports a beautiful costume designed by Robert Short, and his lightning-speed movements are the product of spectacular special effects.

From the Earth to the Moon / **HBO Studios** / **1998**
This superb miniseries describes the great steps taken during the race to the moon. "Astronauts" were suspended by cables from helium balloons so they could make leaps as high as ten feet (three meters) in the set of the moon's surface, constructed in an enormous hangar.

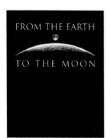

Farscape / **Henson** / **1999–2003**
The great science fiction series from Jim Henson Productions. A lavish visual universe, with special effects that never cease to amaze.

Futurama / **Fox Home Entertainment** / **1999–2003**
The second animated series by Matt Groening (*The Simpsons*) parodies the science fiction genre. Effects in 3-D are used for the spaceships, futuristic cities, and occasionally to

depict Bender, the irascible robot.

The Future is Wild / **Direct Video Distribution** / **2002**
A team of scientists has imagined various species of animals that might be found on earth in five million, one hundred million, and two hundred million years. The computer-generated images of these incredible creatures in this

documentary-style film were created by the 4:2:2 studios in Bristol, England. A DVD not to be missed.

IT / **Warner Bros.** / **1990**

The best adaptation of a Stephen King novel ever made for television. The special effects of this miniseries will give you goose bumps.

Joe 90 / **Carlton (U.S.: A&E Home Video)** / **1968**
Using a machine conceived by his father, young Joe can learn in a few minutes how to be a jet pilot, an astronaut, or a specialist in nuclear fission. And so he becomes a secret agent above suspicion. A series with mari-

onettes by Gerry and Sylvia Anderson. Extras: scenes not previously shown, photos, and production drawings.

Mission: Impossible / **Paramount** / **1966–1973**
A cult series par excellence, *Mission: Impossible* made great use of special effects and makeup in every episode, relying on the talents of John Chambers, Dan Striepeke, Bob Dawn, and Jonnie Burke. A great moment in television history.

The Outer Limits / **MGM** / **1963–1965**
Many episodes in this series are small masterpieces, even if their special effects are now dated. In "Demon with a Glass Hand," the last man on earth tries to escape from the extraterrestrials chasing him, guided by the computer-controlled compass embedded in his glass hand. The presidential candidate who appears in "The One Hundred Days of the Dragon" is replaced by a spy who has been injected with a substance that makes his face as malleable as clay. Captivating tales, well directed.

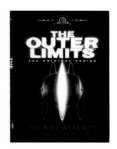

Police Squad / **Paramount** / **1982**
Frank Drebin's first blunders in the six-episode series that would give birth to the movie trilogy *The Naked Gun*. Special effects used to humorous effect.

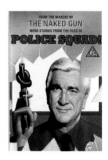

Red Dwarf / **BBC** / **1988–1999**
A great science fiction sitcom from the special effects department at the BBC, which unfortunately closed its doors in 2003.

Space: 1999 / Carlton (U.S.: A&E Home Video) / 1975–1977
The two seasons of this series have been collected in this single boxed set. Among the extras: "behind the scenes" footage, photo galleries, production drawings, storyboards, interviews with the actors and Brian Johnson, the special effects supervisor, and outtakes. Many episodes from the first season benefited from interesting story lines, for example, "The Infernal Machine,"

"War Games," and "Mission of the Darians."

Roughnecks—The Starship Troopers Chronicles—The Pluto Operation / Columbia / 1999
The *Pluto Operation* is a compilation of six of the best episodes from this television adaptation of the Paul Verhoeven movie *Starship Troopers*. The director coproduced the series, which used computer-generated images. Thanks to Ron Thornton's expertise, the 3-D characters are both expressive and

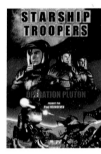

well animated, and the action scenes are as exciting as the visual universe depicted here.

Star Trek Classic / Paramount / 1966–1969
Captain Kirk and Mr. Spock have become science fiction icons. While the sets of the planets they explore may look a bit cheesy by today's standards, their adventures are filled with a spirit of great tolerance and are peppered with original special effects.

Star Trek: The Next Generation / Paramount / 1987–1994
The saga of the new crew of the *Enterprise* was replete with realistic sets and spectacular special effects. The boxed sets, each a collection of a season's episodes, are loaded with extras. You get to learn how Michael Westmore made the makeups for the extraterrestrials and also

how the space scenes were shot.

Stingray / Carlton (U.S.: A&E Home Video) / 1964
A "Supermarionation" series from Gerry and Sylvia Anderson produced before *Thunderbirds*. Troy Tempest explores the oceans aboard his submarine *Stingray* and eludes Titan, the lord of the abyss, and his traps. Extras: commen-

tary by Gerry Anderson, never-before-shown scenes, and a commercial with characters from the series.

The Storyteller / Henson / 1987, 1990
This magnificent series produced by Jim Henson presents original versions of European fairy tales and Greek myths. The makeup, the animatronic creatures, and the sets are all marvelous. A visual treat.

Thunderbirds / Carlton (U.S.: A&E Home Video) / 1966
The *Thunderbirds Mega Set* contains thirty-two digitally remastered episodes, behind-the-scenes documentaries, TV commercials with Lady Penelope, etc. Thanks to Derek Meddings, a genius of model making, each episode of the *Thunderbirds* is also a spectacular super-production. Stanley Kubrick contacted Sylvia Anderson asking (in vain) if she could lend him her technicians during the production of *2001: A Space Odyssey*! A television masterpiece.

The Twilight Zone / V3 Media (U.S.: Image Entertainment) / 1959–1964
One of the best anthology series ever. Marvelous short tales—often written by Rod Serling—with twist endings that make you smile . . . or shiver. All 156 episodes are available in a series of boxed sets.

UFO / Carlton (U.S.: A&E Home Video) / 1970–1973
UFO follows the intrigues of SHADO, a secret organization battling against mysterious extraterrestrials. Special effects by Derek Meddings. The UFO Megaset presents the entire series, along

with many extras, including a documentary of the filming.

V / Warner Bros. / 1983–1985
First a miniseries, then a series describing the invasion of Earth by seemingly well-intentioned visitors. Quality makeup (human masks concealing the lizard heads of the extraterrestrials) and the

arrival of saucers reminiscent of those in *Independence Day.*

Walking with Dinosaurs and *Walking with Prehistoric Beasts* / BBC / 1999 and 2001
Walking with Dinosaurs lets the viewer discover the daily life of the giant reptiles in the tradition of a nature documentary. A look "behind the scenes" reveals the technical exploits of the filmmakers. *Walking with Prehistoric Beasts,* produced by the same team, recounts the appearance of the first mammals on earth and describes other, lesser-known creatures. These animals were

re-created using computer-generated images by Framestore CFC in London.

Weird Al Yankovic: The Videos / Image Entertainment / 1986–1996
Al Yankovic is both an excellent musician and a genius of parody. This DVD is a collection of his funniest videos, many of which use sophisticated special effects like the obese makeup applications in "Fat," the spoof of Michael Jackson's "Bad," and even stop-motion clay

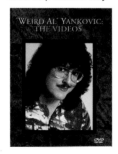

animations for the song "Jurassic Park," made with the blessings of Steven Spielberg, a great Yankovic fan!

Animation

Winsor McCay: Animation Legend / Lumivision (U.S.: E-Realbiz.Com)
An exceptional DVD that collects all of Winsor McCay's animated movies, including some unfinished works. Especially stunning are *Little Nemo* (1911) and *The Sinking of the Lusitania* (1918), one of the first dramatic applications of the cartoon format.

Akira / Twentieth Century-Fox / 1988
One of the most important Japanese animated feature films.

Extra: a documentary on the making of the movie and the mixing of 2-D and 3-D.

Behind the Scenes at the Walt Disney Studios / Disney
An exceptional DVD that reveals the workings of the Disney Studios, the functioning of the multiplane, the study of lifelike character animation, and the special effects used in the cartoons. Contains numerous documentaries, including *The*

Reluctant Dragon (1941). *DVD cover* © Disney Enterprises, Inc.

A Bug's Life / Disney & Pixar / 1998
The insect world reexamined and corrected by Pixar. Endearing characters and wonderful sets. Extras: the Oscar-winning short *Geri's Game* and two hilarious sets of animated characters' bloopers. *DVD cover* © Disney Enterprises, Inc.

Chicken Run / DreamWorks & Pathé / 2000
After the short adventures of *Wallace and Gromit,* Peter Lord and Nick Park produced a full-length feature in modeling clay. Many highlights, one of which is the extraordinary rescue scene from the chicken-pie factory. Extras: "making of" and excerpts from other Aardman Studio shorts.

Claymation Comedy of Horrors / Family Home Entertainment / 1991
A brilliant parody of horror movies, made with modeling clay characters by Will Vinton.

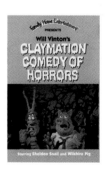

***Dinosaur* / Disney / 2000**
A superb prehistoric fable. A new studio had to be constructed (the Secret Lab, which has since been closed down) to create the 3-D dinosaurs, which were then inserted into real landscapes. Extra: a very extensive "mak-

ing of." *DVD cover © Disney Enterprises, Inc.*

The Road to El Dorado / DreamWorks / 2000

A great animated adventure and perfect mix of 2-D characters with 3-D sets.

***Fantasia* / Disney / 1940**
One of the most important animated movies in the history of film. The musical segments of this masterpiece are testimony to the prodigious expertise Disney artists acquired since 1939. *DVD cover © Disney Enterprises, Inc.*

Final Fantasy: The Spirits Within / Columbia-TriStar / 2001
A DVD on a par with the technical feats of the movie. Surprising extras, like a remake of the Michael Jackson video "Thriller" with characters from the movie.

***Ghost in the Shell* / Twentieth Century-Fox / 1996**
A fascinating animated movie that mixes 2-D and 3-D. Director Mamoru Oshii presents his dominant themes: political terrorist plots, internal power struggles, and people's growing dependence on technology. Extra: a

very well presented "making of."

***Hoppity Goes to Town* / Republic Pictures / 1941**
Unfortunately forgotten, a cartoon by Max Fleischer (originally

titled *Mr. Bug Goes to Town*) that quite amusingly describes the insect world fifty years before *A Bug's Life*.

The Iron Giant / Warner Bros. / 1999
A wonderful animated movie by Brad Bird, who later directed *The Incredibles* for Pixar. The giant robot was made in 3-D and mixed into a stylized 2-D environment to evoke the graphic look of the 1950s and

1960s. Extra: a good "making of."

***Jimmy Neutron* / Paramount / 2001**
Jimmy Neutron is great CGI animated fun with its "retro-futuristic" style, bouncy rhythm,

and clever gags. Extra: "making of."

The Incredible Adventures of Wallace & Gromit / BBC / 1989, 1993, and 1995
The three fabulous Wallace and Gromit shorts. Extras: a documentary, commentary by Nick Park, and excerpts from his early works.

The Little Prince & Martin the Cobbler / Braveworld / 1976, 1987
Two remarkable modeling clay animations by Will Vinton—an adaptation of *The Little Prince* and *Martin the Cobbler,* inspired by Tolstoy.

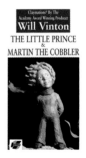

Metropolis / Columbia-TriStar / 2001
This adaptation of Osamu Tezuka's comic strip, itself inspired by the Fritz Lang silent movie, was shot with lavish 2-D and 3-D sets. A landmark of Japanese animation movies. Extras: a "making of" and very extensive documentaries.

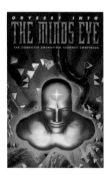

Odyssey Series: Into the Mind's Eye / Sony / 1996
An attractive compilation of CGI sequences created for commercials, short features, and attractions. The dreamlike world typical of 1990s 3-D images on display.

Le Monde magique de Ladislas Starewitch / Doriane Films / 2002
A collection of four wonderful movies by Ladislaw Starewicz: Le Rat de ville et le rat des champs (1926), Le Lion devenu vieux (1932), Fétiche mascotte (1933), and Fleur de fougère (1949).

Extra: commentary by his granddaughter. (In French.)

Monsters, Inc. / Disney & Pixar / 2002
Pixar magic reigns supreme: characters bubbling with life, sumptuous 3-D images, tasteful jokes, and emotionally moving scenes. Extras: the exclusive short Mike's New Car, the Oscar-winning short For the Birds, animation gags and outtakes.
DVD cover © Disney Enterprises, Inc. / Pixar Animation Studios

The Nightmare Before Christmas / Disney / 1993
A masterpiece conceived by Tim Burton and directed by Henry Selick. The animation of the puppets is a work of perfection, and the sets are marvelous. Extras: Tim Burton's first two shorts, Vincent and Frankenweenie, outtakes, an excellent "making of," and a gallery of concept art.
DVD cover © Disney Enterprises, Inc.

Peter Pan / Disney / 1953
A wonderful animated film and a particularly spectacular use of the multiplane in the sequence "You Can Fly."
DVD cover © Disney Enterprises, Inc.

Pinocchio / Disney / 1940
A masterpiece that also has the distinction of containing the most complicated and most expensive shot ever produced with the multiplane camera.

DVD cover © Disney Enterprises, Inc.

Princess Mononoke / Miramax & Studio Ghibli / 1997
A depiction of a mythical Japan where magic and spirits inhabit all the people, animals and plants. Hayao Miyazaki's drawings are

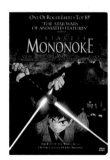

exceptionally beautiful. Extra: a "making of."

The Puppet Films of Jiri Trnka / Image Entertainment / 1945, 1951, and 1960
An impressive collection of movies by the Czech Jiri Trnka, one of the greatest animators of puppets. Among those included are The Emperor's Nightingale, The Song of the Prairie, and The Hand, a sublime allegory on oppression.

The Puppetoon Movie / International Video Entertainment / 1987
A fine homage to the animated movies directed and produced by George Pal. The novel technique consisted of making a series of different heads of the same character that were then placed in succession, using stop-motion, on the puppet in order to obtain vivid facial expressions.

Le Roman de Renard / Doriane Films / 1930

Starewicz's masterpiece. A rereading of classic works from the French Middle Ages, along with the more familiar fables of La

Fontaine. An absolute must-see. (In French.)

Shrek / DreamWorks / 2001

Shrek is not only an amusing parody of the world of fairy tales, but also one of the most accomplished movies produced with CGI in recent years. Includes many extras describing the making of the movie and its innovative techniques, notably in the field of fluid simulation.

Spirited Away / Miramax & Studio Ghibli / 2001

A new masterpiece by Hayao Miyazaki that falls somewhere between *Alice in Wonderland* and Japanese mythology. A very refined use of 3-D that wonderfully draws upon digital compositing.

Tarzan / Disney / 1999

A fine adaptation of the Edgar Rice Burroughs novel and the first use of the Deep Canvas system that enabled Tarzan to leap from branch to branch through 3-D jungles.

Titan A.E. / Twentieth Century-Fox / 2000

Directed by Don Bluth and Gary Goldman, *Titan A.E.* is a space opera that deserves to be rediscovered on video. The mix of 2-D and 3-D animation is very beautiful. Extras: photo gallery, outtakes, and a documentary on the making of the movie.

Toy Story and Toy Story 2 / Disney & Pixar / 1995, 1999

The first movie made entirely in CGI, with characters both appealing and brimming with flaws—in a word, lifelike! While *Toy Story 2* is even more successful, these two gems deserve their spot in the upper echelons. Extras: Oscar-winning short *Luxo Jr.*, outtakes, and in-depth documentaries.

DVD cover © Disney Enterprises, Inc.

Film

Abbott & Costello Meet Frankenstein / Universal / 1948

A famous comedy in which the monsters of Universal Studios play foils to the comic duo. With Jack Pierce's winning monster makeups.

The Abyss / Twentieth Century-Fox / 1989

More of James Cameron's unique talent: incredible underwater scenes, filmed partly at an unfinished nuclear plant. ILM's first computer-generated simulation of liquids.

Addams Family Values / Paramount / 1993

Inspired by the drawings of Charles Addams, the sequel *Addams Family Values* is even more striking than the first movie, which was excellent. The special effects bring off very funny gags.

Alien / Twentieth Century-Fox / 1979

A timeless horror classic, crafted by director

Ridley Scott, with unforgettable images and shocking special effects. Extras: outtakes from the famous "cocoon" sequence, commentary by Ridley Scott, and a photo gallery.

Aliens (Collector's Edition) / Twentieth

Century-Fox / 1986

Another masterpiece! Whereas the first movie played on suspense, the second one (written and directed by James Cameron) is a phenomenal action movie with heart-stopping scenes. This extended version is even better than the theatrical release. Extras: an excellent "making of" that shows the creation of the Alien queen.

A.I.: Artificial Intelligence / Warner & DreamWorks / 2001

Originally a Stanley Kubrick project, nicely brought to the screen by Steven Spielberg. With beautiful special effects by ILM and robots by Stan Winston, which are true works of art in motion. Extras: explanations of ILM special effects and interview with Stan Winston.

Amadeus / Warner Bros. / 1984
A masterpiece from Milos Forman. Antonio Salieri's old-age

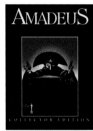

makeup is the feat of Dick Smith.

An American Werewolf in London / Universal / 1981
With memorable transformation scenes orchestrated by Rick Baker.

Apollo 13 / Universal / 1995
The re-creation of the real Apollo 13 mission, brilliantly directed by Ron Howard. Superb special effects from Digital Domain.

Star Wars: Episode 2— Attack of the Clones / Twentieth Century-Fox / 2002
After the first disappointing episode of the new *Star Wars* saga, George Lucas refinds his footing. The fine digital special effects by ILM prop up a more captivating story line.

Austin Powers: International Man of Mystery and Austin Powers: The Spy Who Shagged Me / New Line / 1997, 1999
Two funny parodies of 1960s spy movies. Mike Myers is cleverly made up to play three characters: Austin Powers, Dr. Evil, and Fat Bastard.

Le Boulet (Dead Weight) / Warner Bros. / 2002
The special effects sequence of the Ferris wheel is the most complex and expensive ever made in France. Extra: documentaries on the effects by Mikros Image. (In French.)

Babe: Pig in the City / Universal / 1998
The second adventure of the brave little pig. The perfect special effects by Rhythm and Hues, Mill Film, Animal Logic, and Jim Henson's Creature Shop are complemented by

George Miller's narration of one of film's nicest fables.

Back to the Future: The Trilogy / Universal / 1985, 1989, 1990
The *Back to the Future* saga has not aged; it is still as entertaining and funny as it was in the late 1980s. Multiplied by ILM, the actors play several versions of the same characters. Extras: ten hours of bonuses, featuring outtakes and bloopers, behind-the-scenes footage, and makeup tests.

Batman—The Movie / Twentieth Century-Fox / 1966
This likable full-length feature was made at the same time as the 1960s TV spoof series. George Barris, the creator of the famous Batmobile, is the great specialist of special effects cars for the American film industry.

Batman and Batman Returns / Warner Bros. / 1989, 1992
Two wonderful adaptations of the comic strip, directed by Tim Burton at the apogee of his gothic inspiration. With superb miniatures by Derek Meddings in the first episode and Stan Winston's incredible makeup of the Penguin in the second.

Blade and Blade II / New Line / 1988, 2002
A man contaminated by vampires mercilessly tracks them down to wipe them out. The first of these adaptations from the Marvel Comic was directed with great panache by Stephen Norrington, ex-prodigy in mechanical special effects. Extras: outtakes and many documentaries on the making of the special effects. The sequel, directed by Guillermo Del Toro, is even more accomplished. Digital special effects supervised by

Phil Tippett were used to create spectacular

fight scenes between the superhumans.

Blade Runner / Warner Bros. / 1982
Directed by Ridley Scott, special effects by Douglas Trumbull, music by Vangelis— the elements coalesce to evoke the most amazing vision of a futuristic city since Fritz Lang's *Metropolis*.

La Belle et la Bête / Canal + and René Château Vidéo (U.S.: Criterion) / 1946
Sublime direction by Jean Cocteau. Jean Marais's makeup is legendary. (New English subtitles.)

Bicentennial Man / Columbia-TriStar / 1999
An underappreciated story by Chris Columbus. The "making of" extra explains how Steve Johnson transformed Robin

Williams into a robot and how Greg Cannom created the best old-age make-ups ever made.

The Birds / Universal / 1963
Alfred Hitchcock's extraordinary work, enhanced by the matte paintings of Albert Whitlock, the genius of his art. The scenes with the attacking birds are particularly terrifying. Extra: an alternative ending.

Brazil / Universal / 1985
Flawless special effects from the brimming imagination of Terry Gilliam, of Monty Python fame.

Bride of Frankenstein / Universal / 1935
The most beautiful and most moving of all the

Frankenstein movies. A masterpiece. Extra: an excellent documentary.

Citizen Kane / Warner Bros. / 1942
Orson Welles's masterpiece is also a landmark in the history of special effects. The aging makeup of Kane, created by Maurice Seiderman, was one of the most advanced of its time. Gregg Toland, the director of photog-

raphy, used the most sensitive film available at the end of the 1930s and new lenses to create images in which the objects in the foreground and the sets in the background were both perfectly sharp.

Clash of the Titans / MGM / 1981
In his last movie, Ray Harryhausen once again delved into Greek mythology. Pegasus the winged horse, Cerberus, and the Kraken all are spectacularly present, but best of all is the battle between Perseus and the Gorgon.

Close Encounters of the Third Kind (Collector's Edition) / Columbia-TriStar / 1977
Spielberg's talent is on grand display in the scenes in which the UFOs arrive and the extraordinary sequence of the landing of the mother ship. A remarkable documentary reveals how primitive computer-generated effects—the very first of their kind—were almost used to depict the probes sent by the UFOs.

Coneheads / Paramount / 1993
Beldar and Prymaat, extraterrestrials with cone-shaped heads, are sent to Earth to prepare for its invasion. But they fit in too well with the locals. A successful comedy with special effects by Phil Tippett.

Creature from the Black Lagoon / Universal / 1954
A poetic fantasy movie like they don't make anymore. The underwater sequences with the creature lurking alongside the explorers' boat are extremely well done.

Cube / Trimark / 1997
A group of people work their way through a maze in which each square room might be hiding a lethal trap. Vincenzo Natali directed this highly original movie of suspense and drama, brilliantly making the most of his limited budget. The special effects are perfect.

Dante's Peak / Universal / 1997
Digital Domain's vast expertise helped make Dante's Peak one of the best

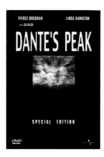

disaster movies in recent years.

Daredevil / Twentieth Century-Fox / 2003
A nice adaptation of the comic strip with an especially poetic effects sequence—drops of water whose

impact lets the blind superhero perceive the landscape around him and "see" the face of the woman he loves.

Dark City / New Line / 1998
This superb movie by Alex Proyas, somewhat unnoticed, is a stunning success on all fronts: the story is fascinating, and the sets and special effects conceived by Patrick Tatopoulos are impressive. Extra: concept art of set designs.

Darkman / Universal / 1990
A powerful superhero movie directed by Sam Raimi long before he made Spider-Man. After being horribly disfigured in an attack, a scientist uses his own invention of a synthetic skin to usurp the identities of those criminals to get back at them.

Die Another Day / MGM / 2003
One of the best James Bond movies ever. Pierce Brosnan is perfect, and the special effects are mind-boggling from the opening credits, conceived by Framestore.

Die Hard (Five Star Collection) / Twentieth Century-Fox / 1988
A masterpiece of the action genre, *Die Hard* contains spectacular scenes that are always believable, a rule horribly trampled on in the two next installments. John McTiernan's direction is exemplary. Extra: a "making of" revealing how Richard Edlund created the movie's stunning visual effects.

Dragonslayer / Disney / 1981
A beautiful movie that went somewhat unnoticed. The dragon Vermithrax was animated using the revolutionary Go-Motion system created by ILM.

Dragonheart / Universal / 1996
A new stage in 3-D animation from ILM—the creation of an expressive dragon capable of articulating each word.

Dune / Universal / 1984
While this adaptation of the Frank Herbert novel may skip over its most important passages, it remains a

beautiful science fiction feature with astonishing special effects.

E.T.: The Extraterrestrial (Collector's Edition) / Universal / 1982
Spielberg's most personal movie. In this new edition, an unreleased bathing scene was finished using an E.T. modeled in 3-D by ILM. Extras: making of the movie, reunion of

the team twenty years later, and many other interesting features.

Evolution / Columbia-TriStar / 2001
A very likable science fiction comedy. The extras reveal how Phil Tippett's team created the many monsters.

The Exorcist / Warner Bros. / 1973
A terrifying movie from director William Friedkin, with incredible makeup effects by Dick Smith.

Earthquake / Universal / 1974
One of the best disaster movies. It makes you tremble as you watch the catastrophes that beset the engaging characters. The special effects, largely reliant on Albert Whitlock's sublime matte paintings, were awarded an Oscar.

Enemy Mine / Twentieth Century-Fox / 1985
A science fiction adventure directed by Wolfgang Petersen and produced in Bavaria. A fine example of German technical expertise. The space battles were created by ILM. Extra: unreleased scenes.

Fantastic Voyage / Twentieth Century-Fox / 1966
An unbelievable adventure through the human body.

Spectacular and often beautiful visual effects.

The Fifth Element / Columbia-TriStar / 1997
This science fiction adventure created by Luc Bresson also benefits from the magnificent visual effects work by Digital Domain.

The Flintstones / Universal / 1994
Kitty the saber-toothed tiger, the Flintstones' pet, was the first 3-D character to be covered in simulated fur.

Forbidden Planet / Warner Bros. / 1956
The appearance of Robby the Robot, the discovery of the gigantic subterranean city of the Krell, and the nighttime attacks of an invisible monster make up some of the unforgettable moments in this science fiction classic. With impeccable special effects.

Forrest Gump / Paramount / 1994
The unusual story of a dim-witted man played by Tom Hanks whose path crosses great moments in American history from the 1950s to the 1990s. ILM inserted the actor into many real-life scenes, not least of which is when Gump shakes President Kennedy's hand. Extras: documentaries on the makeups and the visual effects.

Frankenstein / Universal / 1931
The inspired direction of James Whale, the expressionistic laboratory scenery, the fabulous makeup conceived by Jack Pierce, and the monster so wondrously played by Boris Karloff make this movie immortal.

Galaxy Quest / DreamWorks / 1999

A terrific science fiction comedy, as funny as *Men in Black,* that deserves to be discovered in DVD. Makeups by Stan Winston and special effects by ILM.

Godzilla / Toho / 1954

Since his debut in 1954, Godzilla has tirelessly destroyed large Japanese cities and has confronted enemies at his level: Ghidrah, Mothra, and so many others. This first movie is one of the best, but good Godzillas, like *Godzilla versus Monster Zero.* directed by Inoshiro Honda in 1966, have been produced all along. Eiji Tsuburaya, a great special effects artist, orchestrated the most famous instances

of the monster's destructiveness.

Godzilla / Columbia-TriStar / 1998

Whatever fans of the original Godzilla may think, Roland Emmerich's version is an enjoyable "popcorn movie," thanks to the special effects orchestrated by Volker Engel, Patrick Tatopoulos, and Centropolis Effects. Extras: several documentaries, commentary

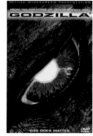

by Tatopoulos, and before-and-after shots of the effects.

Goldeneye / MGM / 1995

This James Bond movie was the first to use digital special effects in its opening credits. These surrealistic images are worth the trip. Also worth noting is the sequence in which the magician of models, Derek Meddings, drains a lake to reveal a

satellite antenna hidden in the depths of the jungle. This was his final work prior to his death.

The Golden Voyage of Sinbad / Columbia-TriStar / 1974

This second Sinbad adventure has some very beautiful scenes: a figurehead on a bowsprit comes to life, a statue of the goddess Kali arms itself with six swords to fight with Sinbad, and a centaur confronts a griffin (a beast that's part lion, part eagle). More wonderful creations from Ray Harryhausen's unique wizardry.

Golden Child / Paramount / 1986

The visual effects by ILM are quite accomplished, in particular the stop-motion confrontation between Eddie Murphy and a winged demon.

Gladiator / DreamWorks / 2000

A wonderful resurrection of the gladiator movies of the 1950s and 1960s, orchestrated by a visual aesthete—Ridley Scott. The many extras on the DVD describe the work of the set designers, the costume artists, and the stuntmen, as well as how the computer artists at

Mill Film re-created Roman antiquity.

Gremlins / Warner Bros. / 1984

A fantasy comedy steeped in the sarcastic humor of Joe Dante. The animatronic creatures by Chris Walas are irresistible.

Harry and the Hendersons / Universal / 1987

The Bigfoot created by Rick Baker is so endearing that he carries the whole movie on his (rather large) shoulders.

Harry Potter and the Sorcerer's Stone and Harry Potter and the Chamber of Secrets / Warner Bros. / 2001, 2002

Faithful and accomplished adaptations of novels from the *Harry Potter* series. The synthesized images were

created at Jim Henson's Creature Shop, and later by ILM.

Hollow Man / Columbia-TriStar / 2000

The DVD lets you deconstruct, frame by frame, the incredible sequences in which the scientist injects himself with the invisible serum—when his skin, tendons, veins, and muscles disappear one by one. The "making of" explains how Sony Imageworks re-created Kevin Bacon's internal

and external anatomy in CGI!

Hot Shots and Hots Shots Part Deux / Twentieth Century-Fox / 1991, 1993
The two *Hots Shots* are hilarious. The direction is amazing, and the quality of the special effects take the visual gags, which fly by every few

seconds, to the heights.

Hulk / Universal / 2003
Despite its confusing screenplay, Ang Lee's movie often re-creates the frames in the Stan Lee and Jack Kirby comic book. The 3-D likeness created by

ILM is superbly animated. The excellent extras detail the creation of the movie.

The Incredible Shrinking Man / Universal / 1957
A man exposed to a nuclear cloud becomes progressively smaller. Reduced to the size of a mouse, he is attacked by his own cat and escapes into the cellar of his house. The very clever giant sets, rear projections, and traveling matte shots are used to depict his exploration through this hostile environment, in which he must battle a spider twenty times his size in order to survive. A powerful movie by Jack Arnold.

Independence Day / Twentieth Century-Fox / 1995
Even if its cliché-ridden script verges on parody, *Independence Day* is an entertaining

science fiction/action movie, with superb effects supervised by Volker Engel and Patrick Tatopoulos.

Innerspace / Warner Bros. / 1987
A great comedy from Joe Dante, the director of *Gremlins,* with superb effects by ILM that depict a journey through the human body.

The Invisible Man / Universal / 1933
The invisible man is able to show himself by way of John P. Fulton's ingenious visual effects. The movie cleverly mixes suspense, action, and horror, most particularly in the scene where the hero puts into action his promise to kill the one who betrayed him to the

police—at the specified day and hour!

The Indiana Jones Trilogy (Raiders of the Lost Ark, Indiana Jones and the Temple of Doom, and Indiana Jones and the Last Crusade) / Paramount / 1981, 1984, and 1989
The first Indiana Jones installment is one of the best action movies of all time. The two other adventures are quite entertaining, but not as perfect. ILM created some of the wonderful effects for this trilogy by Spielberg.

Jaws / Universal / 1975
A terror classic directed by a very young Spielberg, who was already at the top of his art. Despite its famous unreliability during the filming, the mechanical shark created by Joe Alves made millions of viewers throughout the world tremble in fear.

Jeepers Creepers / Universal & Studio Canal / 2002
One of the best horror movies in recent years. The Creeper, conceived by Brian Penikas, is a new and very disturbing character. Extras: an hour-long "making of," a documentary on fantasy movies, nine cut scenes, and an alternative ending.

Jason and the Argonauts / Columbia-TriStar / 1963
Ray Harryhausen's masterpiece. The movie overflows with gems such as the scene in which Talos the bronze giant appears and the battle with a horde of skeletons. Extras: a recent interview and the fifty-two-minute documentary *The Harryhausen Chronicles* give great insight into the career of this genius of animation.

Journey to the Center of the Earth / Twentieth Century-Fox / 1959
One of the two most beautiful adaptations of a Jules Verne work (along with *20,000 Leagues Under the Sea*). With its sets and impressive special effects, this movie remains a must-see.

Jumanji (Collectors' Edition) / Columbia-TriStar / 1995
With its stunning visual effects by ILM, *Jumanji* is a movie that constantly surprises. The DVD contains a host of fascinating documentaries: a "making of," a new documentary on the special effects, photo galleries, storyboards, and much more.

Jurassic Park / Universal / 1993
The dinosaurs in *Jurassic Park* are the first realistic computer-generated creatures ever created for a film. The "making of" narrates this revolution in special effects and reveals Phil Tippett's preparatory animations, which he made with puppets in miniature sets.

Jurassic Park III / Universal / 2001
Stan Winston's animatronic dinosaurs and their digital clones made by ILM achieve perfection. The spinosaur is the largest mechanical character ever constructed for a movie.

Koyaanisqatsi / MGM / 1983
Director Godfrey Reggio collected striking images from around the world—flyovers of virgin landscapes directly follow descriptions of urban life in the biggest cities. The dissolve and time-lapse effects (an acceleration obtained by taking a single image every second or minute) produce hallucinatory images, which inspired John Gaeta, the creator of the special effects for the *Matrix* trilogy.

Labyrinth / Columbia-TriStar / 1986
This superb fairy tale was produced by George Lucas, directed by Jim Henson, and written by Terry Jones of Monty Python. Brian Froud drew the creatures in the movie, which were then crafted by Jim Henson's Creature Shop.

King Kong and The Son of Kong / Warner Bros. / 1933
King Kong is an immortal masterpiece. The exploration of a jungle infested with prehistoric monsters on Skull Island, and the havoc on the streets of New York wrought by King Kong on the loose, count among the many memorable scenes of this great movie. *The Son of Kong* was a comedy produced on a modest budget, but its effects are as accomplished as those of *King Kong*.

Lake Placid / Twentieth Century-Fox / 1999
Lake Placid is a delightful B movie that mixes action, horror, comedy, and romance. The "making of" explains how the animatronic crocodile conceived by Stan Winston was animated and describes the creation of the computer-generated croc by Digital Domain.

Legend / Twentieth Century-Fox / 1985
The magnificent devil conceived by Rob Bottin and Ridley Scott's sublime images

compensate for the almost complete absence of a story.

Licence to Kill / MGM / 1989
Licence to Kill is one of the best recent 007 adventures, in a large part due to the breathtaking car stunts developed by Rémy Julienne. A behind-the-scenes documentary reveals how the spectacular oil-tanker chase scene was conceived. A series of retractable supports is what made it possible for the monster truck to drive steadily on only its left wheels.

The Lord of the Rings: The Fellowship of the Rings, The Two Towers, and The Return of the King / New Line / 2001, 2002, and 2003
Peter Jackson's highly successful adaptation of this trilogy, a contemporary masterpiece that has already become a classic. The acting is wonderful, the sets sublime, the visual effects stunning, and the music enchanting. Extras: scene outtakes, several remarkable "making of" documentaries, photo galleries, and commentaries by the director. The Collectors' Edition of each installment presents extended versions especially prepared by Jackson for the DVDs.

Mary Poppins / Disney / 1964
A delightful fairy tale that incorporates real actors into animated cartoon scenes, to the height of perfection.

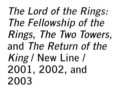

The Mask / New Line / 1994
ILM used CGI to produce amazing effects based on the Tex Avery cartoons.

The Matrix Trilogy / Warner Bros. / 1999, 2003
Matrix, Matrix Reloaded, and *Matrix Revolutions* are among those very few movies in which you can watch some sequences over and over again. The Wachowski brothers, in collaboration with conceptual designer Geoff Darrow and visual effects supervisor John Gaeta, have transposed the world of Japanese animation into live action. Keanu Reeves escaping bullets in slow motion, Carrie-Ann Moss's leap suspended in midair, the freeway chase sequence, the scenes in which hundreds of clones of Neo and agent Smith fight, and the final battle defending Zion are thoroughly unforgettable moments contingent on Gaeta's revolutionary special effects. Besides Bullet-Time Photography, his Universal Capture system, which enables the

virtual recording of the performances of

actors, represents a new technical feat.

Men in Black (Deluxe Edition) and Men in Black II (Special Edition) / Columbia / 1999, 2003
The deluxe and special editions present filmed scenes that were never used, the step-by-step deconstruction of many sequences (from storyboard, to real shots, to effects and final scenes), conceptual art for the extraterrestrials, Rick Baker's makeups, and several documen-

taries including the excellent *The Metamorphosis of Men in Black.*

Mighty Joe Young / RKO / 1949
A giant gorilla raised in Africa by a young girl is exhibited in America. With wonderful effects conceived by Willis O'Brien, who collaborated here for the first time with Ray Harryhausen.

Moulin Rouge / Twentieth Century-Fox / 2001
A musical fairy tale by Baz Luhrmann. Visual

effects are mixed in with lusciously rich images.

Mouse Hunt / DreamWorks / 1997
Two brothers want to get rid of a very clever mouse that has decided to live with them. A true live-action cartoon, with quite spectacular destruction special effects. A movie by Gore Verbinski (*Pirates*

of the Caribbean) that, although not well known, is very enjoyable.

The Mummy / Universal / 1933
The original version of *The Mummy* is a beautiful and timeless love story. Boris Karloff only briefly appears in the guise of the mummy—makeup by Jack Pierce—but the scene

of his awakening is unforgettable.

The Mummy / Universal / 1999
The special effects in this version of *The Mummy* are more successful than the jokes. The "making of" shows how the computer artists at ILM created the 3-D mummy and how they rigged out Arnold Vosloo with "3-D prosthetics," giving the impression that his bones and muscles are visible through his skin.

The Mummy Returns / Universal / 2001
The Mummy Returns interweaves action sequences and special effects by ILM with

infectious fun. The DVD presents a step-by-step explanation of the visual effects.

Mysterious Island / Columbia-TriStar / 1961
Ray Harryhausen's very free adaptation of the continuing adventures of Captain Nemo. The shipwrecked crew have the great surprise of being attacked by a gigantic crab, an enormous bumblebee, and some sort of prehistoric ostrich! There are lots of special effects (the eruption of a miniature volcano, matte paintings, models of Nemo's submarine), along with the remarkable animated scenes.

The Naked Gun, The Naked Gun 2 1/2, and The Naked Gun 33 1/3 / Paramount / 1988, 1991, and 1994
The hilarious Leslie Nielsen, who is a special effect unto himself, plays Lieutenant Frank Drebin in this comedy trilogy from the ZAZ trio (two Zucker brothers and Jim Abrahams). These three movies are chock-full of sight gags that make use of an arsenal of special and visual effects.

_1941_ / Universal / 1979
A somewhat misguided comedy-disaster movie with superb miniature effects. A forgotten Spielberg worth seeing on DVD.

The Neverending Story / Warner Bros. / 1984
A wonderful fairy tale directed by Wolfgang Petersen in Bavaria, Germany.

The Nutty Professor / Universal / 1996
While Eddie Murphy's jokes are painfully gross, Rick Baker's makeups are the true miracles of this heavy-handed remake of the Jerry Lewis 1960s classic. The transformation of the comedian into an obese man is exceptional.

One Million Years B.C. / Warner Bros. / 1967
Cavemen confront the superb dinosaurs created by Ray Harryhausen. The attack by a giant turtle, the sudden appearance of a young tyrannosaurus in the homestead, and Raquel Welch being carried off by a pterodactyl are just a few of the best sequences in the movie.

The One / Columbia-TriStar / 2001
Kleiser-Walczak created a double of actor Jet Li so he could enact both the role of the policeman and his evil double who's determined to kill him. Extras: several documentaries describing the digital makeup process that made it possible to graft Jet Li's face onto a stuntman.

Phantom of the Opera / Universal / 1925
One of Lon Chaney's most startling creations.

Planet of the Apes / Twentieth Century-Fox / 1968
Surprising, spectacular, thoroughly modern, the movie that Franklin J. Schaffner directed in 1968 remains superior to Tim Burton's

version. The ape makeups created by John Chambers are as expressive as they are charming. The final shot of this first adventure is one of the most famous matte paintings in the history of film.

Planet of the Apes / Twentieth Century-Fox / 2001
This new version of the _Planet of the Apes_ benefits from some new interesting characters and Rick Baker's wonderful makeups. The DVD documentaries describe how the actors were trained to play apes, the creation of the makeups, and building the set of the city of the apes.

The Poseidon Adventure / Twentieth Century-Fox / 1972
The fight for survival on a cruise ship turned upside down by an enormous wave. An original and spectacular disaster movie.

Predator (Collector Edition) / Twentieth Century-Fox / 1987
Predator was superbly directed by John McTiernan. The confrontation between Schwarzenegger and the creature imagined by Stan Winston is destined to become a classic. Extras: an excellent "making of"

and a photo gallery that delineates the evolution of the monster.

Reign of Fire / Touchstone / 2002
While dragons ravage the earth, a small group of humans organize themselves in defense. Excellent special effects from the Secret Lab, which has since folded. Extra: a

good "making of" about creating the dragons. _DVD cover © Disney Enterprises, Inc._

RoboCop / MGM / 1987
An spectacular and emotional dramatic action movie. Terrific makeups by Rob Bottin

and superb animations by Phil Tippett.

The Spy Who Loved Me / MGM / 1977
The best of the James Bond movies starring Roger Moore. Two fascinating documentaries: _Inside The Spy Who Loved Me_ and _Designing Bond,_ an homage to set designer Ken Adam, creator of stunning visual concepts and master of false perspective, without whom the James Bond series would never have been what it is.

The Seventh Voyage of Sinbad / Columbia-TriStar / 1958
A lavish fairy tale by Ray Harryhausen in which every scene is a treat: the apparition of a Cyclops with forked feet, Sinbad fighting with a skeleton armed with a sword, the giant crossbow used to slay the dragon, etc. A masterpiece of fantasy movies.

**The Shadow /
Universal / 1994**
Russell Mulcahy has
carried off a beautiful
account of the adven-
tures of a mysterious
avenger who knew his
finest hours in the
1930s and 1940s. A
movie little known, yet
with very fine
special effects.

**Small Soldiers /
DreamWorks &
Universal / 1998**
The winning duo of
Joe Dante and his
producer, Steven
Spielberg, once again
joined forces to
recount this tale of
toys that destroy. The
"making of" details

Stan Winston's anima-
tronic animations and
ILM's digital effects.

Species / MGM / 1995
An excellent science
fiction suspense film
with very accomplished
special effects by

Richard Edlund and an
extraterrestrial creature
conceived by H. R.
Giger (*Alien*).

**Spider-Man /
Columbia-TriStar /
2002**
A perfect adaptation of
the comic book. A
moment of pure pleas-
ure for all fans of this

arachnid–homo sapien.
Extras: documentaries
on all aspects of the
making of the movie
and the first tests of
the 3-D animation.

**Star Trek: The Motion
Picture (the Director's
Edition) / Paramount /
1979**
This new special edi-
tion, especially made
for DVD by Robert
Wise, is more dynamic
and an unmitigated
success. The director
added some special
effects that had been

missing for twenty-
three years. A fine
excuse to look again at
the exceptional visual
effects conceived by
John Dykstra and
Douglas Trumbull.

**Starship Troopers /
Warner Bros. / 1978**
Hordes of giant insects
let loose by Phil
Tippett and his team of
unparalleled anima-
tors. With terrific
space battles created
by ILM.

**The Star Wars Trilogy
Star Wars, The Empire
Strikes Back, and
Return of the Jedi /
Twentieth Century-Fox
/ 1977, 1980, and
1983**
The saga that con-
tributed to making
special effects the
be-all and end-all of
American filmmaking.
A fabulous space opera
by George Lucas, the
first two installments of
which were produced
by Gary Kurtz and are
sublime.

**Stuart Little and Stuart
Little 2 / Columbia-
TriStar / 1999, 2002**

The computer artists at
Sony Imageworks have
demonstrated quite
beautifully their talent
by creating the adorable
Stuart Little. With sev-

eral excellent "making
of" documentaries.

**Superman / Warner
Bros. / 1978**
Superman remains one
of the best adaptations
of a comic book. Extras:
three documentaries
revealing the makings of
the movie, starting with
the first disastrous
screen tests for
Superman (hilarious)
and continuing through
to the filming of the
special effects at the

English Pinewood
Studios. You get to learn
all the tricks used to
make Superman fly.

**Superman II / Warner
Bros. / 1981**
With its first half
directed by Richard
Donner and the second
half by Richard Lester,
Superman II is both a
funny and spectacular
sequel. The fight
between Superman and
three other Kryptonians
in the heart of New

York is a gem conceived
by Derek Meddings and
Roy Field.

**The Ten
Commandments /
Paramount / 1956**
The incredible
sequence of the part-
ing of the Red Sea,
conceived of by John
P. Fulton, is the crown-
ing jewel in what would
be Cecil B. De Mille's
last movie.

**Terminator (Special
Edition) / MGM / 1984**
The many fascinating
anecdotes that fill the
documentary produced
especially for this edi-
tion are enlightening.
Also included are ten
originally deleted
scenes.

**Terminator 2:
Judgment Day (The
Ultimate Edition) /
Universal / 1991**
Terminator 2 is a mas-
terpiece of an action
film. This terrific DVD
edition lets you read
the entire screenplay
page by page, view
dozens of documen-
taries, discover never-
released scenes, and
sit in on the filming of
the attraction

Terminator 2: 3-D. A
true continuation of the
original directed by
James Cameron for
Universal Studios.

Them! / Warner Bros. / 1954
A classic from the 1950s. Nuclear radiation has created a colony of gigantic ants that attack humans. The clever effects were

done using giant mechanical ants.

Tora! Tora! Tora! / Twentieth Century-Fox / 1970
The attack on Pearl Harbor re-created, using extremely well-crafted models. The fine work

by A. D. Flowers and L. B. Abbott earned them an Oscar.

The Thing / Universal / 1982
The metamorphoses conceived by Rob Bottin constitute some of the most nightmarish images in the history of fantasy film. An exceptional example of special makeup effects.

The 3 Worlds of Gulliver / Columbia-TriStar / 1960
With beautiful animations by Ray Harryhausen, such as the fight scene depicting the tiny Gulliver battling a squirrel and a crocodile in the land of the giants. But also delightful effects when the hero himself turns into a giant and is surrounded by tiny beings.

Titanic / Twentieth Century-Fox / 1997
The shipwreck directed by James Cameron is a triumph of special effects, an extraordinary mix of scenes filmed in the world's largest tank and shots of models and computer-generated effects conceived by Digital Domain.

The Time Machine / Warner Bros. / 1960
Produced and directed by George Pal, this movie remains a classic of the science fiction genre. The superb design of the machine and the effects used to accelerate time coalesce to make this one of the great moments in the history of film. Extras: a documentary on the production of the movie, another on the repairs of the time machine used during filming, and an endearing short in which Rod Taylor and Alan Young once again assume their roles forty years later!

Top Secret / Paramount / 1984
One of the best from the ZAZ team. A plethora of one-liners and visual gags made

with hilarious special effects.

The Towering Inferno / Twentieth Century-Fox & Warner Bros. / 1974
The paragon of disaster movies, hair-raising from start to finish. The special effects are terrifyingly realistic.

Tremors / Universal / 1990
An excellent adventure movie, full of humor and suspense. The surface attacks of the underground creature created by Tom Woodruff and Alec Gillis are as frightening as can be.

True Lies / Twentieth Century-Fox / 1994
Action scenes to take your breath away, brilliantly conceived by James Cameron. The destruction of a bridge in the Florida Keys and the final battle with a Harrier army jet are two of the technical feats orchestrated by

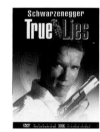

Mark Stetson, Joe Viskocil, and Digital Domain.

Tron / Disney / 1982
The introduction of the first computer-generated images into a full-length feature. A virtual world as surprising today as when the movie was first released, thanks to the production design by Syd Mead and Moebius, and the stunning special effects.
DVD cover © Disney Enterprises, Inc.

Twister / Universal / 1996
Impressive scenes of destruction, produced with a mix of real shots and computer-generated

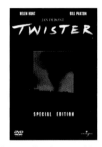

images by the capable computer artists at ILM.

20,000 Leagues Under the Sea / Disney / 1954
A fabulous adaptation of the Jules Verne novel. James Mason shines in his interpretation of Captain Nemo, and the attack by the giant octopus is incredible.

2001: A Space Odyssey / Warner Bros. / 1968
A monumental work in the history of film. *2001* has achieved the feat of remaining contemporary. The viewer relinquishes himself to Stanley Kubrick's dizzying vision and his desire to show the unimaginable. The special effects conceived by Douglas

Trumbull are still astonishing.

Vidocq / **TF1 Video** / **2001**

The very first movie shot in high definition. Also the first (and stunning) direction by Pitof, a master of special

effects, which was to be followed by *Catwoman*. (In French.)

What Dreams May Come / **Universal** / **1998**

Superb sets by Eugenio Zanetti and astounding computer-generated images used to represent the hereafter.

When Worlds Collide / **Paramount** / **1951**

The planet Zyra is heading straight toward Earth, threatening the annihilation of humankind. A billionaire has constructed a gigantic rocket so he can escape the apocalypse. Produced by George Pal, *When Worlds Collide* is still fun to discover today, primarily because of the quality of the direction and the special

effects, which were awarded an Oscar.

Willow / **Paramount** / **1988**

The very first usage of morphing appears in a scene where a witch, who had been transformed into an opossum, slowly regains her human appearance but first passes through numerous animal forms.

The Wizard of Oz / **MGM** / **1939**

A masterpiece. Eternally fresh and scintillating. One of the most beautiful fairy tales ever brought to the screen. And the first foam rubber prosthetics in the history of film!

X-Men and *X2: X-Men United* / **Twentieth Century-Fox** / **2000, 2003**

Excellent adaptations from Marvel Comics, these two movies by Bryan Singer can be rediscovered here with the addition of previously unshown scenes. The DVDs also show some "animatic" sequences for the first time. These are simplified computer-generated images created to pre-visualize the camera moves, speed, and angle of shots in the action scenes long before they were filmed. Several

documentaries reveal the preparation of the special effects, from Wolverine's claws to Nightcrawler's makeup.

You Only Live Twice / **Twentieth Century-Fox** / **1967**

The best James Bond movie with Sean Connery. A fabulous set of the secret base, imagined by Ken Adam, and nonstop action.

Young Frankenstein / **Twentieth Century-Fox** / **1974**

A Frankenstein parody and a work of genius by the comic duo of Mel Brooks and Gene Wilder. A masterpiece made with an incredible attention to detail. The electrical equipment used in the laboratory is the paraphernalia created by Kenneth Strickfaden for the original movie!

Young Sherlock Holmes / **Paramount** / **1985**

A meeting between Holmes and Watson when they are both still teenagers. The first character made with synthesized images, animated by John Lasseter, appeared in this movie; it is the knight who emerges from a stained-glass window.

Zelig / **Warner Bros.** / **1983**

A marvelous fictitious documentary by Woody Allen, who plays Leonard Zelig, a human chameleon with such a weak personality that he absorbs both the ideas and the physical appearance of every person he encounters! The stunning makeups and very good optical effects prefigure the digital effects later seen in *Forrest Gump*—for example, Zelig appears in newsreels next to William Randolph Hearst and Adolf Hitler!

Theme Parks

Disneyland USA / **Disney**

An exceptional DVD that offers a new look

at the inauguration of Disneyland, originally broadcast live in 1955. In addition, the viewer gets to discover the behind-the-scenes workings at the parks via television specials broadcast through 1970. Extra: a gallery of wonderful advertising posters.

DVD cover © Disney Enterprises, Inc.

The Haunted Castle / **Slingshot & IMAX** / **2001**

This movie in CGI and 3-D was expressly conceived for an Imax large screen. Both the 2-D and 3-D versions are presented on this DVD, but to view the movie in three dimensions, you must purchase the special equipment (H3D Stereoscopic Video System, which makes the liquid crystal glasses function). Extras: a "making of" and a commentary by director Ben Stassen.

Taking the Trip—Getting There

Museums

La Maison de la Magie, located in Blois, pays homage to the father of modern magic, Robert-Houdin. With exhibits of magic objects found nowhere else in the world, and shows and attractions that make the visit fun and entertaining. Accessible by car on the A10 Autoroute, approximately one and a half hours from Paris. http://www.maisondelamagie.fr (In French.)

The **American Dime Museum**, located at 1808 Maryland Avenue in Baltimore, Maryland, presents a wonderful exhibition on the art in sideshows and the magic and phenomena of yesteryear. http://www.dimemuseum.com

The **Musée Grévin** in Paris not only displays wax figures of famous people, but also has been presenting the superb attraction *Cabinet des Mirages* ever since 1907. Near the Grands Boulevards Métro stop. http://www.grevin.com

Theme Parks

The **Disneyland Resort** in Anaheim, California, is the site of the original Disney park, inaugurated by Walt Disney in 1955. Next to it you'll find **Disney's California Adventure**, dedicated to the charms of California. http://www.disneyland.disney.go.com

The **Walt Disney World Resort** in Florida, inaugurated in 1971 by Roy Disney, offers four theme parks: **The Magic Kingdom** (comparable to Disneyland); **Epcot**, dedicated to the future and showcasing many foreign countries; the **Disney-MGM Studios**, which lets visitors glimpse the behind-the-scenes of filmmaking; and **Disney's Animal Kingdom,** with its attractions of real and imagined beasts. A dream destination. http://www.disneyworld.disney.go.com

Disneyland Paris and the **Walt Disney Studios** park are open year-round. The two parks are accessible by the A4 Autoroute, the RER A Paris suburban rail system (Marne-la-Vallée-Chessy station) and the TGV high-speed train. There is also a direct shuttle service from both Roissy Charles-de-Gaulle Airport and Orly Airport. Further information can be found on their Web site. http://www.disneylandparis.com

The sublime **Tokyo DisneySea** park, located in the **Tokyo Disneyland Resort**, is unique in the world. The richness of its decorations and the quality of its attractions are indescribable. A direct bus service from the Tokyo Narita airport makes the park, surrounded by its hotels, easily accessible at a minimal price. http://www.tokyodisneyresort.co.jp

Universal Studios Hollywood and **Universal Studios Florida & Universal's Islands of Adventure:** The two Universal Studios parks transpose some of the greatest success in film into spectacular attractions, while the Islands of Adventure in Florida brilliantly evokes mythology, superheroes from the Marvel comic books, and the fairy-tale world of Dr. Seuss. Universal's Web site presents excerpts on all the fabulous attractions in California and Florida. The Florida venue offers the advantage of two superb parks side by side, which can be visited without waiting on line if you are a guest at one of Universal's hotels. Your room key serves as your passport to directly enter the attractions. *The Amazing Adventures of Spider-Man*—perhaps the most perfect attraction in the world—is found here in Universal's Islands of Adventure. http://themeparks.universalstudios.com

The new **Universal Mediterranea Resort** is a complete vacation destination on the Spanish Mediterranean. Located in the heart of Costa Dorada between the coastal towns of Salou and Vila-seca, some sixty miles (ninety-five kilometers) from Barcelona, it offers two parks: **Port Aventura** theme park and **Costa Caribe** water park. The superb Port Aventura theme park makes the most of the year-round exceptionally warm climate. Divided into five themed areas, all with lush gardens and beautifully detailed sets, the visitor gets to meander through Mediterranea, Polynesia, China, Mexico, and the American Far West. Among the thirty attractions and one hundred shows, several present top-rate special effects that should not be missed. *El Templo del Fuego* (*Temple of Fire*) might well be the best pyrotechnics show ever produced for a theme park. *Sea Odyssey* is another must-see. Built by the team that created *Back to the Future: The Ride* and *Terminator 2: 3-D,* this superb simulator-based attraction plunges the visitor to the bottom of the sea to rescue a trapped submarine from an underwater volcano. Another show not to be missed is *Fiestaventura.* Here is a great display of Universal's creativity and technology that features a dazzling combination of light, water, fire, and music. The Universal Mediterranea Resort, open from March to January, has two themed hotels on-site: Hotel Port Aventura and Hotel El Paso.

Universal Port Aventura is just an hour from the Barcelona airport and fifteen minutes from the Reus airport. To get there by car from Barcelona, plan one hour by the A7 highway (La Jonquera–Valencia). Take the direct exit to the park (exit 35). Likewise, you can take highway N-340 (Barcelona–Valencia), N-420 (Tarragona–Teruel), or N-240 (Tarragona–Lleida). Universal Mediterranea also has its own station on the national Spanish railway network (RENFE).
http://www.universalmediterranea.com

The **Futuroscope** park in Poitiers, France, offers many attractions, stage shows, and movies screened in an amazing array of formats—Showscan, Imax, Omnimax, 3-D, Dynamic Cinema, etc. Accessible by the A10 Autoroute and the N10 national highway, the TGV, and from the Poitiers-Biard Airport, located ten minutes away. The park is open from the beginning of April to the beginning of November.
http://www.futuroscope.com

A trip to Florida must definitely include a visit to the **Orlando/ Orange County Convention Center & Visitors Bureau** Web site. There is information on all the parks and attractions in Florida, as well as on hotels and transportation. Information can also be obtained from its offices at 8723 International Drive, Suite 101, Orlando FL 32819. The center is open seven days a week, from 8 A.M. to 7 P.M. The *Orlando Magicard*, which can be used for discounts at many museums, shows, attractions, and restaurants, is free for the asking. Several different passes can be purchased for using the I-Ride Trolley, which travels the length of International Drive, offering easy access to the other attractions located near the Disney and Universal parks.
http://www.orlandoinfo.com

Warner Bros. Movie World: Characters from the Warner Bros. studios (Batman, Bugs Bunny, et al.) appear in varied and well-conceived attractions. Movie World parks are located in Germany, Belgium, and Spain. In the United States, the parks are called "Six Flags." Information on all the parks can be found on their Web site.
http://www.movieworld.de and http://www.sixflags.com

Terra Mitica: A beautiful Spanish park devoted to mythology. Its fine attractions and rides evoke the Egyptian, Greek, Roman, and Spanish cultures of ancient times.
http://www.terramiticapark.com

Space Park Bremen: This German park is entirely dedicated to the exploration of space and to science fiction. The television series *Star Trek* and *Stargate* have been transformed into attractions. Visitors get to explore a huge set depicting a lunar base station. The park also has a high-tech planetarium and an Imax theater.
http://spacepark.d3.net

Las Vegas Shows and Attractions

The Las Vegas Convention and Visitors Authority offers practical information regarding attractions, shows, and the main hotels in Las Vegas. There are more than 110,000 hotel rooms available in this city of games, but it is always wise to reserve in advance. It's been known to happen that during conventions the main hotels can be 90 percent full. Room prices increase on the weekends and during major trade shows. If you are planning to spend only three or four days in the city, try to visit during the week and avoid the times when conventions are held.
Las Vegas Convention Center, 3150 Paradise Road.
Tel.: +1 (702) 892-7575 or toll-free from the U.S.: (800) 332-5353.
http://www.lasvegas24hours.com

Caesars Palace: Caesars Palace opened in 1966 and cost twenty-five million dollars. It was the first themed hotel in Las Vegas. The new hall dedicated to Atlantis presents a fight between robotic creatures, as well as the *Ride for Atlantis* attraction, a virtual race in Imax 3-D. The vast Coliseum theater, with its forty-one hundred seats, was expressly constructed for Céline Dion's extraordinary show *A New Day,* a Dragone creation being presented from 2003 to 2006. The theater cost ninety-five million dollars, and the equipment for the show thirty million dollars more! Tickets for *A New Day* can be purchased at www.ticketmaster.com or by calling +1 (702) 474-4000. Caesars Palace can be reached at Tel.: +1 (702) 731-7110 and Fax: +1 (702) 731-6636.
http://www.caesars.com

Treasure Island: It is in front of the Treasure Island Hotel, with its facade decorated like a pirate village, that a stunning sea battle takes place six times a day.
Tel.: +1 (702) 894-7111 and Fax: +1 (702) 894-7446.
http://www.treasureislandlasvegas.com

Luxor: The great black pyramid of the Luxor is home to the *Secrets of the Luxor Pyramid* attraction, conceived by Douglas Trumbull, and the excellent stage show *Blue Man Group,* which mixes music, absurd humor, and a series of happenings.
http://www.luxor.com

Circus Circus: This hotel dedicated to the world of circuses has a nice theme park, The Adventuredome, which was built under a giant dome and is air-conditioned.
http://www.circuscircus.com

Special Effects Restaurants

Rainforest Café: In a setting of an equatorial jungle, the robotic gorillas, elephants, and wildcats all play their roles. A tropical storm briefly bursts forth from time to time. Rainforest Cafés can be found in most large American and European cities. In France, the restaurant is located in the Disney Village next to Disneyland Paris.
http://www.rainforestcafe.com

Mars 2112: A very pleasant trip to the planet Mars. The sets and animations are especially popular with young children.
1633 Broadway, New York, NY 10019
Tel.: +1 (212) 582-2112 and Fax: +1 (212) 489-7955.
http://www.mars2112.com

Jekyll and Hyde Club: Animated monsters in a very entertaining ambience. You get the feeling that you're dining in the Addams Family's mansion.
1409 Avenue of the Americas (near Central Park), New York, NY
Tel.: +1 (212) 541-9505
http://www.eerie.com

ACKNOWLEDGMENTS

Chris & Stanley Bielecki (SB International/Universal), Martin Bower, Marc Spess (AnimateClay.com), Roger Chance, Bob Gurr, Alain Carrazé, Roy E. Disney, Steve Kirk, Martina Stuben & Margaret Adamic (Disney), Stan Winston, Robert Schlockoff, Sylvain Chomet, Evgeni Tomow, Elisabeth Meunier (Columbia-TriStar Home Video), Dick Smith, Ed French, Matt Denton, Brian Penikas, Scott Essman, Ray Harryhausen, Bob Hoffmann, Douglas Trumbull, Anne Lara & Alexis Rubinowicz (Columbia France), Marquita Doassans & Carole Choman (Warner France), Patrick Tatopoulos, Oana Bogdan, Pitof, Stephanie Brunnig & Mike McGee (Framestore CFC), Sabine Thellier (Fox Pathé Europa), Karine Mestrejean (Paramount Home Video), Caroline Decriem (UIP), Michèle Abitbol-Lasry, Cécile De Lavénère (Warner Home Video), Siobhan Hall (Nimba Productions), Sora Lee (Tin House), Nikki Penny, Sylvain Despretz, Dan Bateman (Henson Productions), Miles Teves, Micky Bister, Sylvie Désormière & Barbara Sabatier (Minerva), Caroline Raudnitz (Carlton Productions), Volker Engel, Ed French, Mark Coulier, Christopher Tucker, Peter Bailey (4:2:2), Alice Robertson (John Adams Productions / The Future Is Wild), John Lasseter (Pixar), Peter Lord & Nick Park (Aardman Productions), Phil Tippett & Melissa Gauthier (Tippett Studios), Todd Sokolove & Lee Northworthy (Hallmark Productions), Lisa Pistacchio (SGI), Marie de Crozals (BBC), Barb Nicholson (Disneyland), Willy Persello (La Martinière), François Cazenave, Joseph Viskocil (Viskocil Effects), Fumi Kitahara (DreamWorks), Steve Wang, Gene Rizzardi, Nathalie lund, Philippe Degeneffe & Jennifer Dunne (Dragone / A New Day), Jeff Kleiser & Amanda Roth (Kleiser-Walczak), Natalia Kurop (Animal Logic), Terry Curtis, Benjamin Gaessler (Universal Home Video), James Taylor (American Dime Museum), Walt Conti (Edge FX), Ellen Pasternack (ILM), Webster Colcord, Robert Short, Jan Sherman (Sally Corporation), Tom Atkin, Jean-Marie Vivès, Isidoro Raponi, Pierre-Olivier Persin, Alain Nevant, Henri Loevenbruck, David Oghia, francis m., Almudena Mazuelos, Ron Mandelbaum, Susan Richmond, Richard Slovak, Laurel Hirsch, Tina Thompson.

All photographs without credits noted are by Pascal Pinteau.

Front cover: A mechanized replica of Arnold Schwarzenegger's face in *Terminator 3: Rise of the Machines* (2003). Photo courtesy of the Stan Winston Studio. Image reproduced with permission of Photofest, New York

Project Manager, English-language edition: Susan Richmond
Editor, English-language edition: Richard Slovak
Cover design, English-language edition: Michael J. Walsh Jr and Christine Knorr
Design Coordinator, English-language edition: Tina Thompson
Production Coordinator, English-language edition: Kaija Markoe

Library of Congress Cataloging-in-Publication Data
Pinteau, Pascal.
 [Effets spéciaux. English]
 Special effects : an oral history : interviews with 38 masters spanning 100 years / Pascal
Pinteau ; translated from the French by Laurel Hirsch.
   p. cm.
 Includes bibliographical references and index.
 ISBN 0-8109-5591-1 (flexibind)
 1. Cinematography—Special effects. 2. Cinematographers—Interviews. I. Title.

TR858P5613 2004
778.5'345—dc22

2004007699

Printed and bound in China
10 9 8 7 6 5 4 3 2 1

 Harry N. Abrams, Inc.
100 Fifth Avenue
New York, N.Y. 10011
 www.abramsbooks.com

Abrams is a subsidiary of

 LA MARTINIÈRE
G R O U P E